I0802391

Peasenhall Press is truthfull

Also from The Peasenhall Press

Reflexion, by Lynette Fromme

Also by George Stimson

The Cincinnati Crime Book
The Iron Cross 1. Class (with Dietrich Maerz)
The War Merit Cross 1. Class (with Dietrich Maerz)

Goodbye Helter Skelter

Goodbye Helter Skelter

A New Look at the Tate-LaBianca Murders

by George Stimson

Second Edition

The Peasenhall Press – 2019

Goodbye Helter Skelter Copyright © 2014, 2019 George Stimson. All rights reserved. No part of this book may be reproduced or transmitted in any form or by any means, electronic or mechanical, including photocopying, recording, or by any information storage and retrieval system -- except by a reviewer who may quote brief passages in a review to be printed in a newspaper or magazine -- without permission in writing from the publisher. For information contact The Peasenhall Press, P.O. Box 431, Cobb, CA 95426, USA. First Edition 2014. Second Edition 2019.

Second Edition

ISBN 978-0-9913725-4-6

LCCN 2014908886

Excerpts from *Helter Skelter*, by Vincent Bugliosi with Curt Gentry, W. W. Norton publisher, used by permission.

Excerpts from *Outrage, The Five Reasons Why O.J. Simpson Got Away With Murder*, by Vincent Bugliosi, W. W.Norton publisher, used by permission.

Excerpts from *Will You Die For Me?*, by Charles “Tex” Watson as told to Chaplain Ray Hoekstra, Spire, a division of Baker Publishing Group, © 1978, used by permission.

Excerpt from *These Canyons Are Full Of Ghosts*, by Emmett C. Harder, Real Adventure Publishing, used by permission.

Excerpts from *Reflexion*, by Lynette Fromme, The Peasenhall Press, used by permission.

Printed on 30% PCW recycled paper

for my friends

Table of Contents

Author's Note (2014)

The majority of this book was written in 1998 and 1999. It was originally intended to be published around the time of the 30th anniversary of the Tate-LaBianca murders but personal considerations intervened and the project was shelved.

In 2012 the project was revisited and it was determined that the passage of time had rendered previous reservations moot, so the decision was made to go ahead and put the book out.

While I have made a due diligence effort to check more recent sources of information on the case than were available in the late 1990s, I have included little of such information gleaned from those sources here since little of it did other than to reinforce the conclusions already reached fifteen years ago.

What was true in 1999 (and in 1969, for that matter) is still true today.

G. S.

Acknowledgments

Many people helped me on the long journey that led to the completion of this book, and although I haven't had contact with some of these persons for decades I nonetheless owe all of them my thanks for helping me get to where I am today.

I am grateful to the people I met who were involved with the publication of the original edition of *The Manson File*, all of whom always treated me respectfully and as a friend. In addition to forwarding my first introductory letter to Charles Manson, Nikolas and Zeena Schreck welcomed me to stay in their home on several occasions and I still appreciate their openness and hospitality. I visited Nick Bougas many times during his Victory Boulevard days in Los Angeles and also had a memorable trip with him to Goler Wash. Jon Aes-Nihil was and still is the man to go to for Manson-related material. And Adam Parfrey showed me how the book publishing business works. Thanks to all of you.

Jim Mason and Michael Moynihan provided me with contacts and introductions without which this book would not have been possible, and I greatly acknowledge them for that.

It has been a pleasure to know Emmett Harder. I had heard about this gold mining acquaintance of Charles Manson's years before I finally met him in the desert backcountry near Death Valley. Being with Emmett is like going back in time. Thanks for taking me there, Emmett. (Other desert denizens I had the pleasure of meeting included Don Connolly, Wild Bill, Lightfoot Louie, and Matt & Maggie.)

I have appreciated the National Park Service's stewardship of the Death Valley area ever since I lived there in the early 1980s. In decades of contact with these people I never had a negative experience. And I have especially fond memories of the NPS personnel whom I was able to assist with the clean-up of the Barker Ranch after the main buildings there were destroyed in a fire in 2009.

Mike McCloskey critically read portions of the manuscript for this book and also provided valuable input on other aspects of its publication. Thanks, Mike.

Other people who otherwise helped with the preparation of this book were the high school reader who did the initial editing (Thanks for your excellent pointers!) and Kevin and David in Cincinnati, whose enthusiasm and support were a great encouragement.

There were also people who not only shared information with me but shared years of their lives as well. Thomas "T.J." Walleman and his wife Lori had me as a house guest on many occasions when they lived in Trona, California, and we had many adventuresome and fun trips in the desert backcountry together. Cathy "Cappy" Gillies is another well-remembered desert host. And I got to know Country Sue Bartell on camping trips and while driving around northern California in our VW buses. All of these people openly shared their memories of their times with Charles Manson and gave me valuable insights that I would not have been able to get anywhere else.

Finally, to Sandra Good, Lynette Fromme, and Charles Manson -- it has been a real and rare privilege to get to know all of you. It goes without saying that this book would not have been possible without your friendly cooperation. Since none of you has seen this work prior to its publication I hope that I didn't mangle things too terribly. And I also hope that if anything I wrote here is in conflict with any of your points of view you will still accept this work as a whole in the spirit in which it was written.

Thank you all.

G. S.

Preface to the Second Edition

In the five years since this book was first published interest in the Tate-LaBianca murders and the "Manson Family" has not diminished. To the contrary, it has probably gotten greater. The usual steady trickle of public reminders like recurring parole hearings for Manson's co-defendants, rumors of unsolved murders, and even possible nuptials have continued to make it into the news cycles on a regular basis. (At one point, even Manson's most recent mug shot was considered to be news!) But also since 2014 two events occurred which were genuine milestones in the overall story.

On November 19, 2017, Charles Manson died at age eighty-three in a hospital in Bakersfield, California. He had been in ill health for some time, spending the last few years of his life in the medical unit of the high security section at the California State Prison -- Corcoran, where he had been held for almost thirty years. The official cause of death was listed as acute cardiac arrest and respiratory failure brought on by metastatic colon cancer.

Manson's death was cause for more attention than the simple news of his passing, however, as controversies immediately arose over the disposition of his estate -- and of his remains. The latter concern was eventually resolved after several months when a Kern County court decided that Manson's body should be turned over to an individual who was determined to be most eligible to receive it among the several persons who applied. That person in turn arranged for there to be a funeral service that could be attended by some of Manson's friends as well as a scattering of some of his ashes near a river in the western Sierra Nevada Mountains. I was lucky enough to be able to attend both of these events, and I'm very glad that I could be an eyewitness to the final disposition of Charlie's mortal remains. And although there is still much rancor in the (mostly online) Manson "community" regarding these occurrences, I will always be grateful to Jason Freeman for allowing me to be present -- because he did not have to do that. As for the disposition of Manson's estate (not just the personal effects he left behind in his cell at Corcoran but also of the rights to his music, image, and other intellectual property, likely worth millions of dollars) that issue has not been resolved as of this writing and is unlikely to be settled anytime soon.

The second milestone since 2014 was that in August of 2018 Lynette Fromme's long-anticipated memoir *Reflexion* was finally released. *Reflexion* is the best look at what life was like with Charles Manson from someone who was closely associated with him from May of 1967 to August of 1969. Lacking the usual remorse, regret, guilt, apologies, and blame common to other "Manson Family" books, Fromme's work is a refreshingly honest look at part of a life that has not been colored by fifty years of conditioning -- despite the fact that its author spent thirty-four of those years in federal prisons. I'm honored that Fromme trusted The Peasenhall Press to handle the publication of her book.

Along with these two noteworthy events the public's interest in Manson and the case continued unabated. And in August of 2019 the media boil burst with the 50th anniversary of the Tate-LaBianca murders. Television programs proliferated. At least three motion picture productions based on the subject debuted, including one featuring two of the most bankable actors in Hollywood and overseen by one of the industry's pre-eminent directors. Anybody with any connection to Manson or to the case whatsoever published a book about their experiences. Newspapers and magazines put out special editions and issues, and the Internet bloated with articles and social media pages. Indeed, Manson's presence on the Internet seems infinite, with an amazing array of old television programs, uncut interviews, and previously unseen film footage available instantly at the click of a mouse. Other Internet sources, like web sites and blogs, offer a seemingly unlimited amount of material, such as newspaper and magazine archives, trial and parole hearing transcripts, and crime scene and other relevant photographic images -- although unfortunately much of this material is accompanied by the thoughts, insights, and opinions of anyone with access to a computer keyboard.

But one thing that seems to be sinking in throughout all of these new media efforts is the idea that maybe -- just *maybe* -- "Helter Skelter" wasn't the motive for the Tate-Labianca murders after all. What a thought! (Disappointingly, however, whatever alternative motives that researchers might settle on, Charles Manson continues to be almost unanimously regarded as the evil genius behind all of the murderous events of the summer of 1969. Obviously some things are just too ingrained in the mass mind to be open to any other kind of interpretation.)

In 2015, after an estrangement brought on by bad communication, prison intrigues, and government-ordered restrictions, I was finally able to reconnect with Manson after over ten years. Although we were never able to arrange for prison visits again, in scores of telephone conversations we reached the same level of understanding and mutual respect that we had for each other throughout the 1990s. So, as painful as it was to learn that he was gone in November of 2017 it was very gratifying to me that we departed each other's company on good terms.

In August of 2019 I went to Los Angeles to attend the 30th anniversary screening of *Charles Manson, Superstar*, thirty years after I had attended the original premiere screening in 1989. (It has been a long road.) Besides seeing the film I was also able to meet Mike Brunner, the son of Charles Manson and Mary Brunner who was born in the abandonded house on Summit Drive in Topanga Canyon on that amazing April morning over fifty years ago when everything was still good.

Before and after the film was shown director Nikolas Schreck spoke to the audience on the production of the film and about his own current take on the Tate-Labianca murders. Several hundred people attended the standing-room-only showing, which also served as a grand meeting of Manson aficionados from around the world. Clearly Manson's death has had no impact at all on the attractiveness and appeal that he has to others.

So where will things go from here?

I feel that anyone believing that interest in the "Manson phenomenon" will taper off after the 50th anniversary of the murders will be sorely disappointed. This story is just too big to die. In fact, it's not diminishing but rather getting bigger with every passing day. And just as the story will not die, neither will the influence that Charles Manson has had on the consciousness of the United States and of the world. As long-time Manson friend Gray Wolf said while speaking about Manson's death for a documentary on Manson's funeral, "I don't think he passed; I think he changed. He may be more powerful [now] in some ways than he's ever been."

We shall see.

Why Write This Book?

Goodbye Helter Skelter is the result of almost twenty-five years of my personal investigation into Charles Manson and the Tate-LaBianca murder cases. Although there have already been many books written about this subject this book is totally different from any previous works because it presents not only new information but also a new point of view.

Perhaps you, the reader, have already read one or more of the books written about this case. Perhaps you are familiar with -- and possibly accept -- the standard version of the events surrounding what have become known as the "Manson Murders."

But if you are not familiar with the generally presented scenario of those murders -- or if you are familiar with it but question it -- this book will give you a coherent, understandable, and reasonable answer to the question of why nine people died in Los Angeles California in July and August of 1969.

Why write this book? In the last five decades dozens of books, hundreds of newspaper and magazine articles, scores of television news programs, several movies, and countless Internet sites have been created as byproducts of the Tate-LaBianca homicides. More material has been produced about this case than about any other "solved" crime. (Some unsolved crimes, like the Jack the Ripper or Lizzie Borden cases, have likely been written about more than the "Manson Murders.") Therefore, it would seem that all that can be said about the events of the summer of 1969 and their aftermath has already been said. Still, every few months some event occurs -- a parole hearing, a death, an anniversary, or some other tie-in -- that brings the case back to the forefront of the public's attention. And after fifty years the public still eagerly turns its attention to this case. Why?

When the Tate-LaBianca murders occurred in 1969 the United States was a different place than it is today. The phenomenon of mass murder was not common. The murders committed by Charles Whitman, Richard Speck, and Robert Smith three years earlier in 1966 shocked the nation. Before that, though, one had to go back to the 1959 murder spree of Charles Starkweather and Caril Ann Fugate to find a comparable headline-grabbing example of mass murder.

While today mass killing is practically commonplace, in 1969 the brutal murders committed by some of the people connected with Charles Manson were a major shock to the United States. And even though many crimes since have surpassed those killings in brutality or the number of victims, the story of Charles Manson and his murderous "Family" continues to grip the public mind as a singular example of atrocious madness.

Why are people still so interested in this case? One reason is that they are curious as to where the principal characters involved in the crimes are today and what they are doing. In fact, that would seem to be the main reason, because except for status updates of the convicted killers there is rarely anything truly new about the case that comes to light in most update articles and programs. The same story that's been told since the arrests of Manson and his co-defendants continues to be told today.

That basic tale is unchanged: An ex-con named Charles Manson took a group of disaffected young middle-class people and twisted their values, minds, and lives in order to fulfill his own homicidal needs. Using sex, drugs, music, and a kind of hypnosis, he deluded them to such an extent that they enthusiastically committed murder at his command in the furtherance of his mad and racist "Helter Skelter" dream of world conquest. Everybody knows what happened.

Goodbye Helter Skelter

But what if that *wasn't* what happened? What if the popular perception of Charles Manson and his "Family" is incorrect? What if Charles Manson did not "mastermind" the Tate-LaBianca murders in order to achieve Helter Skelter?

The premise of this book is that the motive that Los Angeles Deputy District Attorney Vincent Bugliosi presented at the trial (and ever since in his best-selling book and in countless media appearances) -- "Helter Skelter" -- is a fantasy. And a further premise of this book is that it is possible that Charles Manson had -- and has -- no legal culpability for the Tate-LaBianca murders (or, for that matter, for any other murders for which he was convicted).

And that is the reason to write this book: because it needs to be written.

It would serve no purpose to belabor the well-worn, popularly accepted version of the events of 1969 again in just another remake of the same old story. That task is better left to the people who have a stake in the same old story -- to the prosecutors, book writers, and members of the news and entertainment media who have invested so much in that story and who, in turn, have made so much money and achieved so much recognition from it.

This book is different. In this book you will find new material, new information, and -- most importantly -- new thinking.

It has been almost fifty years since Charles Manson was convicted of ordering the Tate-LaBianca murders. Fifty years before those murders the population of the United States was just over one hundred million people. World War One had just ended. Woodrow Wilson was President of the United States. The stock market was at 107 points and you could buy a new car for $826.

In 1969 the U.S. population was over two hundred million. The Vietnam War was raging in Southeast Asia. Richard Nixon was President. The Dow Jones Industrial Average was at 875 points and a new car cost $3,278. The world in 1969 was not the world of 1919, because time moved on.

Now it is time to acknowledge that time has moved on again. It is time for a realistic and unbiased look at the events that occurred in Southern California in the summer of 1969. It is time for a reappraisal of the motives and circumstances that led to one of the most infamous series of crimes in United States history.

Why Write This Book?

For a long time it has been popular to second-guess most of the famous criminal cases that have occurred in this country in the last century. Sacco and Vanzetti, the Lindbergh kidnapping case, the Rosenbergs, Sam Sheppard, the Boston Strangler, the MacDonald murders, the Atlanta child killings, and, of course, any of the major political assassinations -- all of these cases have been rewritten with conclusions contrary to the official findings. Most of these revisionist works point to perpetrators other than the people who were convicted of the crimes.2

This book is different from those in that it will not claim that the individuals who were convicted of entering the Polanski (Tate) and LaBianca houses and murdering the occupants there were not the persons who actually committed those murders. Charles "Tex" Watson, Susan Atkins, Patricia Krenwinkel, and Leslie Van Houten -- they did it. The point of contention here will be over the popular perception of Charles Manson as the mastermind of those murders, and of the actual motive for those murders.

But even though this book will dispute the general view of Charles Manson as a mass murderer (or as any kind of murderer) and will attempt to present him more as a human being than as a warped caricature, I should make it very clear that it is not my intention to portray him as an innocent lamb. Much to the contrary, I will gladly concede that he could be a very bad guy. After all, he was on the "other side" for just about his entire life, from the moment that he was born out of wedlock. He was institutionalized almost continuously since he was ten years old. He was categorized as a criminal and a convict for almost seventy years. Therefore there is no doubt that he could be bad. And Manson himself never denied this. Indeed, he often stated that the popular presentations of him as a Satanic mass murderer actually made him look better than he really was.

So I'm not going to ask you to like him.

But I will contend that Charles Manson was not *all* bad. He was not evil incarnate. And I will also contend -- and hopefully demonstrate -- that much of the popular view of Charles Manson is incorrect.

It is also not the intention of this book to present a complete interpretation of Charles Manson's philosophy (as such) or of any of his possible intentions and goals. Still, because Manson's alleged philosophies have been a major portion of the case against him, it will be necessary to present some of his beliefs and his own expressions of his values in order to put the events that occurred in Los Angeles in the summer of 1969 into a perspective which can explain those events in a realistically alternative way to the oft-repeated horror story.

Now, if you believe in your heart of hearts that Charles Manson was the Satanic and dictatorial leader of a murderous group of maniacs, and if you believe that he ordered them to commit some of the most brutal murders in the history of American crime in order to start a race war which would ultimately leave him as master of the world, this book is not for you.

However if you have read the official version of the case and found it lacking, and if you want to get a clearer understanding about what really happened in 1969, this book will be a big step in that direction.

In the five years that I was the web master of what was called "Charles Manson's web site" (*Access Manson*, which was located at the URL www.atwa.com from 1996 to 2001) I received hundreds of queries from people from around the world who still had questions about a case which had had more "information" generated about it than almost any other. A typical example:

> I don't know what to think. Charlie seems like an intelligent guy. He is described as being very charismatic. His concern and attention to the environment [are] highly commendable. But I don't understand. All these books [*Garbage People*, *Manson In His Own Words*, *Desert Shadows*] are so concerned with fueling the myth of Charlie as some kind of brainwashing demon, and I don't think that can possibly be a fair or truthful representation. You're in contact with Charlie, Mr. Stimson. There must be more to Charlie than the demon he is painted to be, but I don't think that we will ever get to hear what that is. I want to understand what he must really be like, to inspire all this love and devotion from people like Lynette Fromme and Sandra Good. I want to hear a view that isn't chock-full of ridiculous Beatles theories and the usual "brainwashing guru" image. Help me to understand, Mr. Stimson. I would really appreciate it.

Here is another reason to write this book. I think that people like the writer of this letter deserve an answer to their questions. And this book will go a long way towards answering such honest, heartfelt, and intelligent queries as this one.3

And there is still one other and final reason to write this book. Charles Manson died in 2017 after being locked up in prison for almost fifty years for an exaggerated involvement in certain spectacular crimes that he did not actually commit. In this book I think that I can convincingly demonstrate this contention, and I hope that such a demonstration will go some way towards dispelling the image of Charles Manson as one of the most evil men of all time.

And also undeserving of their reputations for evil are most of the other people convicted of the Hinman-Tate-LaBianca-Shea murders. These individuals have long ago ceased to be mere criminals. Instead, they have been elevated to the level of larger-than-life demons and monsters horrible beyond human comprehension. They have also ceased to be mere inmates, instead becoming figures to be used in the political machinations of the state of California. At one time even the original prosecutors of the cases estimated that most of the principal characters involved would have been released by now. No more. It is now more advantageous to keep Charles Manson and everyone connected with him locked up forever as a permanent sign that the authorities are doing their jobs. Thus, a person who drove a car somewhere forty-five years ago is deemed to be more dangerous than, for example, someone who axed the forearms off of his victim and left her for dead.4 Women of late middle age are now the most dangerous persons in the state.

With a case as famous as this one -- with the multitude of information and misinformation that has been generated about it -- it would be impossible to address every conceivable aspect or to respond to every story or allegation in just one book. I do not attempt to do so here. So if I have not addressed every statement or claim from every available source it is not from any inability to do so. The reason I haven't is simply because it would probably take forty more years and forty more books to respond to every misconception or lie that has ever been presented about this case.

Nevertheless, I still have tried to cover as many of its relevant aspects as I could.

This book is intended as a whole product. Everything in it is here for a reason. The Acknowledgements, the Preface, the Afterword, the Footnotes -- it is all part of the whole. If you read this book, please read it all.

Lastly, I have to make one very important point. *Goodbye Helter Skelter* is an attempt to present a reasonable and more true explanation about the series of crimes which have become known as the "Manson Murders" than that which has generally been accepted. But although over a period of ten years Charles Manson was extremely cooperative with the author, this is not his book. Also, though this book does contain much first-hand information from Manson himself, it does not -- and cannot -- purport to represent his entire point of view. The same should also be said about other persons -- persons such as Lynette Fromme and Sandra Good -- who have also cooperated with the author. This book is not their book and it does not claim to speak for them.

The conclusions reached and expressed in *Goodbye Helter Skelter* are solely mine, based on my own personal investigation and study of this case over a period of over forty years.

Chapter Notes

1 On July 14, 1966 Richard Speck murdered eight student nurses in a Chicago townhouse. Two weeks later Charles Whitman killed sixteen people and wounded another thirty-two in a sniping rampage from the clock tower at the University of Texas in Austin. (He had previously killed his mother and wife.) On November 12 eighteen-year-old Robert Smith killed five persons at a beauty college in Mesa, Arizona because "I wanted to get known -- to get myself a name." Charles Starkweather and his girlfriend Caril Ann Fugate killed ten people in a week-long murder spree in Nebraska and Wyoming in January of 1958.

2 Actually, the "Manson Case" has been rewritten as well, but not like other famous murder cases. No revision of Manson's case has attempted to exonerate him or any of his co-defendants. To the contrary -- and in keeping with the general perception of Charles Manson as the devil incarnate -- when his case has been re-investigated it has only been

to reveal that Manson is actually more evil than the reader previously thought. Thus it is possible to find books alleging that Manson is also responsible for, or involved with -- besides the Tate-LaBianca murders -- the Son of Sam Murders, the Zodiac Murders, and just about every other unsolved homicide that occurred in any place even remotely connected with Manson or any of his acquaintances between 1967 and 1972 or so.

3 Dominique from Salford, England -- thanks for the great letter!

4 This would be Bruce Davis vs. Lawrence Singleton.

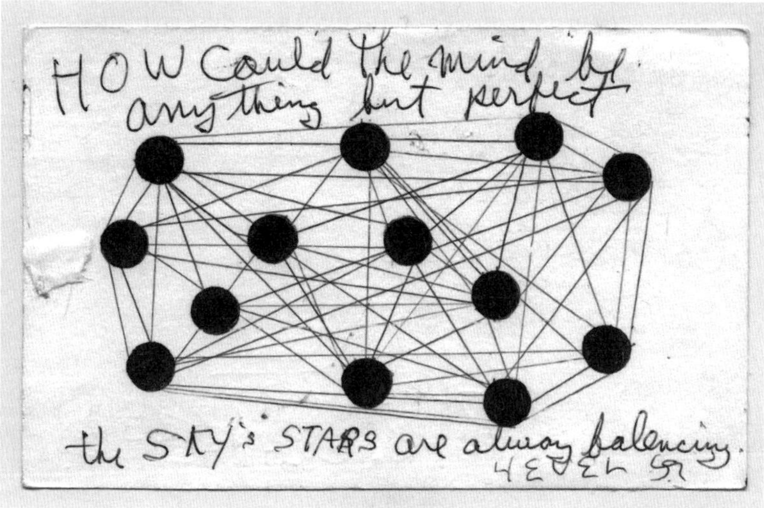
HOW could the mind be anything but perfect
the SKY's STARS are always balancing.

On Sources, Methodology, and Terminology

I consulted many sources during the preparation of this book. No other solved criminal case has had as much material generated about it as this one has. Books, magazine and newspaper articles, videotapes and DVDs of television programs and parole hearings -- anyone interested in collecting information about the Manson case can easily fill a small archive.

Several of the participants in the case have co-authored books. These include *Helter Skelter*, by Vincent Bugliosi and Curt Gentry, *Child of Satan, Child of God*, by Susan Atkins and Bob Slosser, *Will You Die For Me?*, by Charles "Tex" Watson and Chaplain Ray Hoekstra, and *My Life With Charles Manson*, by Paul Watkins and Guillermo Soledad. I used all of these books.

Other books I consulted were *The Family*, by Ed Sanders, *The Manson Women*, by Clara Livsey, *Witness To Evil*, by George Bishop, *Five To Die*, by Jerry LeBlanc and Ivor Davis, *The Killing of Sharon Tate*, by Lawrence Schiller, and *Trial By Your Peers* (later changed to *Blood Family* for the paperback version) by William Zamora. Many other books were consulted which are not listed here. If quoted, these works are credited in the Footnotes.

Some of these books deserve a closer look.

Helter Skelter has long been considered to be the authoritative source for information on Charles Manson and the Tate-LaBianca murders. I have often wondered why this is the case, since it is likely that any book written by the district attorney who prosecuted a case would be a bit one-sided in its presentation of that prosecution (and that prosecutor). *Helter Skelter* is certainly that. Any reader of the work would be forgiven if he thought that but for the extraordinary and single-handed efforts of prosecutor Bugliosi Charles Manson might not have been convicted. Bugliosi's self-aggrandizing tone is so apparent that even serious Mansonphobes have often remarked on it with disdain.

Although *Helter Skelter* has some reliable factual information (Charles Manson himself concedes that Bugliosi "got the names right, and he got the dates right."1), it also contains many innuendoes, exaggerations, and wildly biased misinterpretations. In *Goodbye Helter Skelter* I hope to conclusively demonstrate this.

The Family, by Ed Sanders, would probably be considered to be the second most important chronicle of the Charles Manson saga. But while this book might make for entertaining reading, with its unsubstantiated allegations, unattributed anonymous quotations, and pages of totally irrelevant and unnecessary ancillary material, entire chapters of *The Family* can be dismissed out of hand. (In fact, one chapter *was* dismissed out of hand. The chapter on the Process Church of the Final Judgment, which appeared in the first edition of the book, was so unfounded that the Church initiated legal action which resulted in the chapter being deleted from all future editions.)

Another well-known work, Nuel Emmons' book *Manson In His Own Words*, is one of the great misfortunes of the entire Manson experience. Written in *Emmons'* own words, the book is full of inaccuracies and falsehoods. For example, Emmons has Manson claiming that he went to Cielo Drive after the murders there to check out the scene. (He did not.) Emmons also has Manson recalling the time that he was gang-raped at the Indiana School for Boys at Plainfield, Indiana. (I was present at a visit with Emmons and Manson at the California State Prison at Corcoran when Emmons admitted that he had fabricated the story of the rapes.) Emmons has since said that he never intended the book to be taken as Manson's autobiography and that his own proposed title for the book was *Without Conscience*. He says that his original manuscript was changed by the publisher, Grove Press, in order to improve the book's marketability. But the biggest problem with *Manson In His Own Words* is that it is regarded as Charles Manson's book. It is not, and Manson himself has famously characterized it as "bullshit." 2

In a letter addressing a young correspondent's questions arising from the book, Manson wrote:

> Don't believe that book that they wrote. They only write that for money. That's not my words, That's nothing I said. I didn't say anything like that. Somebody said I said that and then had me locked up so I couldn't do anything about it. So you believe me. I didn't write that book....
>
> You're caught up in what the book is telling you for money. They're selling your fears. They're selling your insecurities, to believe things that make them money -- anything they can buy and sell.
>
> These people that take my life and represent my life to you, and tell you those things they want you to believe -- they're pimping your brain. 3

Unfortunately, *Manson In His Own Words* has often been cited by authors and researchers as a legitimate representation of the viewpoint of Charles Manson. But Manson's concise, one-word review of the book is correct. I didn't use anything from *Words* for this book.

Some of the principals involved in the case (Charles Watson, Susan Atkins, and Paul Watkins) have co-written books about their memories of their time with Charles Manson.

Watson's and Atkins' memoirs (*Will You Die For Me?* and *Child of Satan, Child of God*, respectively) recount their lives and their eventual and eternal conversions to Christianity. Written after all of the trials were over and when the "hippie cult leader" image of Manson was well established (and, more significantly, after the realities of their sentences and resulting situations had sunk in) both of these books attempt to place the overriding blame for everything that went wrong in 1969 on Charles Manson. In these works Charles Watson and Susan Atkins -- the actual main participants in the crimes generally known as the "Manson Murders" -- try to use Manson and his supposed domination of them as an explanation for their crimes and as a mitigation of their own actions.

Paul Watkins' *My Life With Charles Manson* is the third "Manson Family" memoir. In it Watkins recalls his time with Manson as a "summer of love to summer of slash" story. Watkins also places the blame for the murders on Charles Manson and the corrupting influence that he supposedly had on some of the people around him.

In 2018 Lynette Fromme published the book *Reflexion*. A detailed chronicle of her life with Charles Manson from May of 1967 to October of 1969, *Reflexion* is a refreshing change of pace from these earlier autobiographical efforts in that it is not hindered by regrets, apologies, or placing blame. Instead, Fromme recalls the Manson she perceived, and the result is a book that should be required reading for anyone interested in the Manson phenomenon. (I used portions of *Reflexion* in *Goodbye Helter Skelter* to replace similar earlier versions of Fromme's recollections from a previously unpublished manuscript.)

Some books (*Manson In His Own Words*, *Taming The Beast*) have qualified and attempted to justify their admittedly inaccurate quotations of Charles Manson by saying that the conversations quoted were held under the conditions of prison visiting where no tape recorders or note taking were allowed. Therefore, the authors of these works say that the quotes, although substantively correct, are not totally accurate.4 Other books, such as those penned by former "Manson Family members," have reams of quoted conversations presented as accurate even though they were reconstructed without source reference material several years after they allegedly took place. I regard such second-hand hearsay quoting to be questionable, to say the least. I might believe what these people say about themselves, but I do not lend much credence to their quotations that supposedly came from the mouth of Charles Manson. So I have not used any of their alleged Manson utterances in this book.

As for other sources, I also watched videotapes and/or read transcripts of numerous parole hearings for Charles Manson, Charles Watson, Susan Atkins, Patricia Krenwinkel, Leslie Van Houten, Bruce Davis, Steve Grogan, and Bobby Beausoleil.

Besides watching a dozen or so television interviews with Charles Manson (many of which were the uncut versions of the entire interview) I also watched interviews with or programs featuring other main characters related to the case such as Patricia Krenwinkel, Leslie Van Houten, Paul Watkins, Linda Kasabian, Vincent Bugliosi, and Stephen Kay.

Charles Watson's former wife used to run a website on his behalf, and I got some of his current thinking on his past from that source. Other case principals also have (or had) websites, and I consulted them as well.

I had unprecedented cooperation from both Sandra Good and Lynette Fromme. Good allowed me to listen to hundreds of hours of her taped telephone conversations with Charles Manson and gave me unconditional access to boxes full of letters, photographs, news articles, court transcripts, and other documents. Fromme was also very helpful, answering many questions that I had about her and her life with Charles Manson.

Last and certainly not least, I also consulted Charles Manson himself. I was fairly well acquainted with Manson personally for a period of about a dozen years, and I conversed with him hundreds of times, both on the telephone and in person. Most of my telephone conversations with Manson were tape-recorded. I also received several hundred letters and other pieces of correspondence from him. This length and depth of my relationship with Manson allowed me to make certain conclusions regarding what he had to say. After all, when you are around someone for a decade or so you can reach a certain level of familiarity, ease, and trust with that person. And I think that I reached that point with Manson. In my years of interaction with him he earned a great deal of my trust. And he also earned a great deal of my respect, both with regard to him as a person and with regard to what he had to say.

All quotes and statements in this book are from what I consider to be reliable, verifiable sources. Often these sources are friendly to the person quoted, i.e., they are the speakers themselves speaking on their own behalf at parole hearings or in interviews, or are statements taken from their books or other media where they presumably exercised some control over content. There are no anonymous sources in this book. There is nothing from persons who didn't want to be identified for fear of whatever. Here any quotes from Charles Manson or from anyone else are exact, verifiable quotes. (In the prison visiting room environment Manson can and did talk at length in a verbal style that would be almost impossible for anyone to remember completely accurately. But while I had many long conversations with Manson in various visiting rooms I have generally not put any portions of those conversations, or the thoughts or ideas derived from them, in quotation marks here because I could not honestly vouch for their absolute accuracy.)

I was not present at any of the murder trials, nor did I read the complete transcripts of them, but that was not necessary for the purposes of this book. Several books (*Helter Skelter*, *Witness To Evil*, *Blood Family*, *Reflections On The Manson Trial*, and the 20th-anniversary-of-the-murders updated edition of *The Family*) are either completely about the trials or have large portions devoted to them, and it is unlikely that any important evidence or occurrence in the proceedings was omitted by the authors. (In fact, these books often present more "evidence" than was presented in court, because rules of evidence, unfortunately, do not exist for non-fiction books.) So the fact that I did not read 50,000-plus pages of trial transcript does not mean that I missed anything important. Besides, it is fairly common for authors who did not attend trials or read a trial's entire transcript to write authoritative and well-respected books about famous cases. Vincent Bugliosi did just that when he wrote *Outrage, The Five Reasons O. J. Simpson Got Away With Murder*.

One honest question that every reader should ask is whether a researcher/writer can simply choose only those facts or alleged facts that fit the premise of his project. In this case, however, the prosecutors and other book authors have done just that. They have concluded that anything allegedly bad about the defendants and their friends or supporters must be true and that any positive interpretation of a situation or action is to be ignored. Thus, any negative comment made by any of the participants in the case -- no matter how tenuous the source or under what circumstances the statement might have been made -- has been accepted by the prosecutors as the truth. Further, any negative connotation or interpretation with regard to solidly factual evidence also has been accepted as reality.

Thus, for example, when Susan Atkins told her fellow prisoners in the Los Angeles county jail for women that she had tasted the blood of one of her victims, that statement became a "fact" even though Atkins later denied it and said that she only said it because she was afraid in jail and wanted to frighten the other inmates into leaving her alone -- which is a reasonable explanation.5 Thus, when Spahn's Ranch ranch hand Juan Flynn, in a singular remark, recalled that Manson bragged about killing thirty-five people, that number of victims became a reality that prosecutors and some researchers have enthusiastically accepted ever since, even though there is no other evidence whatsoever to support such a claim.6 And thus, when Sandra Good allegedly said that the death of one of the defense attorneys was "the first of the retaliation murders"7 that supposed pronouncement became an accepted "fact" -- and the attorney became a "murder victim"8 -- when in actuality the cause of death was officially listed as "undetermined" (and very likely accidental) and Good denies even making the "retaliation murder" statement in the first place.9

The purveyors of the Helter Skelter myth are relentless in presenting such unsubstantiated material as facts, and they continue to use examples like these to bolster the anti-"Manson Family" case. But what does it say about that case that it has to be supported, in large part, by such misrepresentations and outright lies? I think it says that the presenters of that case do not want people to know the truth.

This book, on the other hand, will not rely on hearsay or other unsubstantiated material to make its case. All quoted material here is always from the speakers themselves, talking about themselves, and it is always from an easily verifiable source.

What about the credibility of the people involved with this case? Besides the literally scores of books written about the case itself or which have chapters about the author's or subject's connection to it, there are many other sources (like interviews or parole hearings) where the case's principal characters have made their positions known. Everybody has his own point of view. Here

I will try to present all of those different points of view and, if relevant, consider the possible motivation that an individual might have for making a certain statement -- especially if that statement contradicts the premise of this book.

A good example of this is when Manson's co-defendants now say that Manson was indeed the mastermind of the murders. Since that is not the premise of this book, what do I do with such statements? I consider them within the greater context of an imprisoned individual who is saying what they think the powers-that-be want to hear so that they (or someone they are trying to help) can get a parole date.

No one who is angling for a release is likely to say that Charles Manson did not order the Tate-LaBianca murders because that is a "fact" accepted by the parole board specifically and by the public generally. Parole boards are not interested in retrying the cases of the inmates appearing before them. The Board of Prison Terms (the California agency which considers granting parole dates to inmates) "accepts as true the Court findings in the case," namely the court's determination that the inmate is indeed guilty of the crime for which he or she is incarcerated.10 And as such it does not want any deviation from those findings.

So, if any of the convicted killers said that Manson didn't order the murders -- a key finding determined by the court -- it would be akin to claiming that they weren't even involved with the crimes. And since admitting guilt is a prerequisite for an inmate's consideration for parole, denying that guilt (or any other of the court's conclusions) would not be a good strategy for gaining a parole date. Therefore, I consider that some of what Manson's co-defendants now say is what they think the parole board wants to hear.

All of the people who were convicted of murder in the various cases involved here (Watson, Krenwinkel, Van Houten, Beausoleil, and Davis) want to get out of prison. Getting caught in any kind of lie or discrepancy is a sure way to torpedo the chances of anyone getting out, perhaps for years to come. Therefore I believe that while Manson's co-defendants might not be telling the whole story (especially when it could add to their own criminal culpability), except for their obligatory agreement with the court's findings they are telling as much of the truth as they can. I believe that what they are saying now is either the truth or what they believe to be the truth.

An example of "what they believe to be the truth" would be some co-defendants' current claims that Manson was indeed the mastermind behind the murders, or that he was at least calling the shots. This is a contention that did not begin to be made until years after the trials. I believe that these persons might now believe this to be true. After decades of being cut off from their former friends and reading and hearing from books and television about how they were brainwashed -- plus possibly trying to find some way to mitigate their own responsibility and guilt -- these people have reflected on their time with Manson and have come to see their willing participation in his world and in the greater world around them as being more a result of his manipulation than of their enthusiastic participation in their own realities.

Any confusion on the part of Manson's co-defendants about what really happened in 1969 was well-articulated by Patricia Krenwinkel at her 1993 parole hearing when she said:

> And on that [Manson's running of things], not everything was always clear and absolutely defined, and especially throughout the years, because *so much has been said by so many. Sometimes I'm not sure who said what and what really happened, because there is so many accounts from everyone.... I don't have absolute recall of twenty-five years ago*.11 (emphasis added)

I also believe that Manson's co-defendants will not admit to anything that they know is not the truth.

For example, because of a rope burn found on one of the victim's cheek, the post-trial prosecutors have frequently maintained that the victim was hanged before her death. 12 But none of the people who were present at the crime recall this happening. At one parole hearing, Charles Watson said, in reply to this hanging accusation:

> I [do] disagree with the fact that Sharon Tate was hung while I was present, while she was still alive. I don't remember that part -- her hang-

ing -- I don't remember that. I do [deny hanging her]. I haven't denied too much at all, because I'm guilty. I haven't denied too much of the crime that has been brought against me. I've confessed to all of it. But there's some areas such as that that I cannot attest to, because I don't remember her being hung. 13

In other words, Charles Watson knows what happened, and he is willing to admit to what happened. But he is not willing to admit to something that he knows didn't happen. And why should he? It would only make a bad case against him even worse.

The same holds true for the motive for the murders on Cielo and Waverly Drives. None of the persons convicted for those murders (except for Leslie Van Houten, whom I will address later) say that the motive for those killings was to start a black-white race war. And they don't say it because they know that it is not true.

What about Charles Manson's credibility? Since much of the material supporting the claims made in this book comes from Manson himself, it is fair to raise the question of his truthfulness.

I have heard Charles Manson called many things, but "liar" is not one of them.14 Nowhere in *Helter Skelter* is Manson called a liar. It is true that Manson sometimes exhibits a seeming evasiveness when answering a question, but he never simply resorts to a lie. Even Vincent Bugliosi has acknowledged Manson's honesty. In *Helter Skelter* Bugliosi noted how Manson would never just deny having been involved with the murders, which, in the District Attorney's mind, would have been a lie. And in a 1997 interview he even conceded that Manson did have "an element of honesty to him."15

In my years of personal experience with Charles Manson I never knew him to lie, either to me or to anyone else. And as I said above, over the years of knowing him I developed a level of trust in him. Therefore, when it came to evaluating his versions of certain incidents I extended to him the same courtesy that I would extend to anyone who is not an obviously blatant liar: Absent any evidence to the contrary or fundamental flaws in what the person is telling me, I believe them. In other words, with regards to anything Manson ever told me about the incidents recounted in this book, I believed him. And I believed him because there was never any rational reason not to.

On terminology, one of the main problems confronting anyone interested in this case are the incorrect terms of reference in relation to it. Many of these terms have been hammered into the public's consciousness for almost five decades.

One purpose of this book is to dispel misconceptions, and a main misconception concerning this case is that there existed from 1967 to 1971 or so a group of people who called themselves "The Family" or "The Manson Family." This is not true. The term "Manson Family" was in fact an invention of the same label-happy news media that have applied catchphrases or nicknames to virtually every phenomenon that has occurred since the invention of the printing press. Nevertheless, there might be times in this book that the terms "Manson Family" or "Family" are used. This is done only because these terms are so universally accepted as referring to a group of people who were closely associated with Charles Manson in the late 1960s and early 1970s that they inevitably arise in any discussion of the subject.

But the occasional use of those terms in *Goodbye Helter Skelter* is in no way meant to imply that any self-styled group going by that name ever existed. These terms, when used in this book, will always be enclosed within the quotation marks that they so richly deserve.

So will "Manson Murders." This book will show that this term is also not accurate. Charles Manson's role in the homicidal episodes of the summer of 1969 (yes, he did have one) was not such that he deserves to have the entire ensuing affair named after him, alliteration notwithstanding. Still, this term, skeptically qualified by quotation marks, may occasionally appear in *Goodbye Helter Skelter*.

Chapter Notes

1 Manson made this concession during a 1985 interview at the California Medical Facility at Vacaville.

2 He wrote this review on the title page of the copy of the book he sent

to Nick Bougas. See *The Manson File*, page 185.
3 Manson in a letter to an unidentified correspondent. Sandra Good Archives.
4 Emmons wrote that aside from rare instances when he was able to tape record Manson for commissioned articles, "I had to make mental notes [of conversations] until I could record them on tape or in writing. I spent many hours in the prison parking lot, writing down names and specific phrases that typified Manson's speech and his ideas." (*Manson In His Own Word*s, page 15.) George said, "The conversations throughout the book, including my conversations with Charles Manson, have been reconstructed from my recollection and, in some instances, from notes made immediately after those conversations." (Author's Note, *Taming The Beast*.)
5 From the Susan Atkins 1993 parole hearing transcript, page 21: "And I used to hear Charlie in my head over and over and over again tell me things like, 'When you're in jail and people pick on you, you be big and you be bad, and you be mean. So much so that everybody will just leave you alone.' I was very frightened. I had nobody -- no support mechanism around me, and I remembered that when people would question me as to why I was in jail, all I knew was that I had to convince people that I was big, I was bad, I was mean, leave me alone, stay away from me -- in order to survive.... and I said things that I, in fact, did not do."
6 Flynn didn't just say that Manson boasted of committing thirty-five murders, he said, "[Manson] admitted -- he boasted of -- thirty-five lives taken *in a period of two days*." (emphasis added, see *Helter Skelter*, page 452). Proponents of the "thirty-five killed" theory, who often try to link Manson and his friends with just about every unsolved homicide that occurred in any location even remotely connected with them (Los Angeles and Mendocino, California, Ashland, Kentucky), don't seem to take seriously the time limitations of Flynn's statement. The first half of the statement is apparently credible while the second half is not. (Sandra Good supposedly verified this number of corpses in her "retaliation murders" statement (*Helter Skelter*, page 652), but since this statement was never actually spoken by her it does not count as corroboration.)
7 This non-existent confession is recalled in *Helter Skelter*, pages 651-652.
8 Hughes is described as a murder victim in *Helter Skelter*, in the caption accompanying his photo, wherein Good's "retaliation murder confession" is again presented.
9 "I never said that, because it wasn't true. Retaliation for what?" Sandra Good to the author, April 29, 2014.

10 As explained to Charles Manson at his 1992 parole hearing, transcript page 5.

11 Patricia Krenwinkel, 1993 parole hearing, transcript page 74.

12 L.A. County Coroner Thomas Noguchi first raised the image of a hanged victim during the original murder trial. He testified that the rope burns found on the victim's cheek were the result of her being hanged "for less than a minute." (See Noguchi's trial testimony, recounted in *Helter Skelter* on page 457.) Why the perpetrators of the crime would choose to hang a victim for some seconds and then let her down is not clear. In fact, it is not really clear that the victim was hanged at all. Noguchi's trial testimony is a misrepresentation of his real findings, recounted in his own book *Coroner*. On pages 130 and 131 of *Coroner* Noguchi presents his real conclusion regarding hanging, an oxymoronic finding that "Tate and Sebring had been only partially suspended by their murders, *with their feet still on the floor*." (emphasis added). In other words, the victims were hanged, but not really. (My conclusion is that the victim got the burn on her cheek while she was struggling with the rope around her neck.)

13 Portions of this parole hearing, date unknown, are presented in the 1987 video *Death Diploma*.

14 Pat Krenwinkel said that Manson was lying in her interview on *A Turning Point*, but she was referring to a difference in perceptions of reality. Catherine "Gypsy" Share called Manson "a liar" in a 1994 episode of *Inside Edition*, but she was not specific and gave no examples.

15 Interview with Vincent Bugliosi in the December 1997 issue of *Playboy* magazine.

Above, the author with Charles Manson and Nuel Emmons
Below, with Manson and Ed *Taming The Beast* George

Who Am I?

"He's the only guy I've trusted enough to open up and give him all the data he wants."

-- Charles Manson, talking to
Sandra Good about the author

Before I get into the matter of this book I feel that I should explain to the reader who I am, how I got to know Charles Manson, and how I developed the ideas, thoughts, and opinions expressed herein.

Like millions of other people around the world I have read about and been fascinated by the so-called "Manson Murders." My interest was initially piqued in September of 1975 when "Manson Family member" Lynette Fromme crossed paths with U.S. President Gerald Ford in Capitol Park in Sacramento, California. Generally regarded as an assassination attempt, this encounter was headline news for weeks. At the time I was a senior in college in upstate New York, and I read all of the news accounts of Fromme's action with great interest. Since so much of that material referred to the Tate-LaBianca Murders (which had occurred only six years previously) I then began to read everything I could about those murders and about Charles Manson and his "Family."

Goodbye Helter Skelter

My first major source of information was former Los Angeles County Deputy District Attorney Vincent Bugliosi's book *Helter Skelter*. The library at my college had a copy of this book and I checked it out and read it several times. I thought that it was well written and fascinating, but there were aspects of it that I didn't think were believable.

In 1976 I watched *Helter Skelter*, the TV-movie based on Bugliosi's bestselling book, as well as Robert Hendrickson and Laurence Merrick's 1974 movie documentary Manson, which had been re-released to cash in on the publicity surrounding Fromme's action and the success of *Helter Skelter*, both movie and book. As time went by I bought every book that came out about the case. Early volumes were Ed Sanders' *The Family* (even less believable to me than *Helter Skelter*), and *Child of Satan, Child of God* and *Will You Die For Me?*, by murder participants Susan Atkins and Charles Watson. (Eventually I collected an entire mini-library of Helter Skelter-related books.) I also obtained videotaped copies of various Manson interviews and other news and media presentations of his case, and heard the so-called *LIE* album of Manson's pre-arrest music and audiotapes of some of his music done in prison after his convictions.

But throughout all of this accumulation of material I always had a sense that I was not getting the full story, that the versions of the murders that were being so routinely peddled were not true. This sense of doubt instilled me with a continued curiosity about Manson and the Tate-LaBianca murders that compelled me to dig further in my search for some satisfactory alternative scenario of the killings of 1969 -- something besides "Helter Skelter" -- that I could find sensible and believable.

As the 1970s turned into the 1980s I traveled to California to visit family and friends, and while I was there I also visited the crime scenes (from the streets) and the locales where Manson and some of his friends had lived in both the Los Angeles and Death Valley areas. These travels led to extended stays in the Golden State, and as circumstances developed I ended up living in Death Valley for three years and Los Angeles for two in the early '80s.

And during all this time my curiosity about the murders and the man supposedly behind them did not diminish. Eventually, like thousands of other people, I wrote to Charles Manson. I wrote two letters to him in the mid 1980s. I did not get a reply, though, so I forgot about corresponding.

Then in the summer of 1988 I walked into a bookstore in Cincinnati, Ohio (my home town, where I was by then again living) and saw the book *The Manson File*. This book was a truly remarkable work, for not only was its tone sympathetic to Charles Manson but it had also obviously been compiled by persons who had a regular contact, through correspondence, with Manson himself. After finishing the book I wrote to its editor and thus began corresponding and speaking by phone with several of the individuals who had put the book together. In the spring of 1989 I traveled to California and met most of the people responsible for the book.1

One of those people was working on a video tentatively titled *Charles Manson, Superstar* that he planned to release in August of 1989, the 20th anniversary of the Tate-LaBianca murders. Since I had a familiarity with the Death Valley area from my years there in the early '80s the video producer asked if I would assist with his filming of some of the "Manson Family's" old haunts in the desert. I said that I would, and he, his film crew, and I spent several days filming in the Goler Wash area of the Panamint Mountains on the western border of Death Valley. (If you have ever seen this video, that's me driving my 1965 Volkswagen bus up to the gate of the Barker Ranch.) I also helped with taping done at the site of the Spahn Movie Ranch in Chatsworth. For these two technical assists and some photos I provided I was given "Contributing Editor" and "Still Photographer" credits in the finished work.

The *Manson File* people asked if I corresponded with Charles Manson and I said that I did not. I explained that I was sure that he was busy enough, that he probably had lots of people writing to him, and that he didn't need somebody else coming to him with their outside problems. But they assured me that this wasn't the case and said that if I wrote him a letter they would enclose it with one of theirs, by way of an introduction. So I wrote a quick note that they enclosed in their next mailing to Manson along with some photos that I had taken in the desert.

Two months later, back in Ohio, I got a reply: an envelope containing a letter to send along to someone named Bill and a postcard to me that read:

> Like photos. Nice. That's an old dream I had once beyond a time. You're not clear in what you want. Any photos is nice. Did you get any of the Lotus gold mine, or Willow Springs or the Stone house? I like to tryp in that part of the world. I just love that desert -- no people. You sent no pictures of you. Pictures a person can believe more than what you say. Send one of George -- Saint George. [signed] Manson.

I immediately wrote back. My reply to his "not clear in what you want" was that I didn't want anything. But since he was asking, I asked him to send me some of his hair. (I had seen locks of Manson's hair, artfully arranged into swirling swastikas, framed with his picture on the walls of some of *The Manson File*'s people's homes in Los Angeles.)

By then the summer of 1989 had arrived and I traveled out to L.A. for the very well received premiere of *Charles Manson, Superstar*. Waiting for me in Ohio upon my return was a second envelope from Manson. Postmarked August 9, 1989, the 20th anniversary of the Tate-LaBianca murders, the envelope was full of hair.

In reply to this hirsute missive I sent more photos and explained that since I had hundreds of them from my years in Death Valley I would begin sending them in sets based on subject matter, like desert roads, abandoned vehicles, mining structures, backcountry graves, etc. I also asked Manson if he would send me one of his famous string scorpions.

He didn't, and I didn't hear from him again. But I kept sending the batches of photos, along with news articles or anything else that I thought he might find interesting.

In April 1990, eight months later, I finally heard from Manson again. On a postcard he wrote:

> As it grows, under mind. I can see what you and people like you never do much 4 yourselves in others. I've paid for every good I've ever done. I began to realize, if you help or do for someone, they think

you're food and want to eat you. If I ever get out I'm gonna beat people whenever I get the chance. I'm gonna help them go to heaven. (signed) Charles Manson.

Despite this somewhat negative message, I wrote back and continued to send photographs and other material. Eventually Manson started to respond. I got perhaps a half dozen replies to my many mailings to him.

In the late summer of 1990 a friend asked me to contact Sandra Good because she wanted good quality videotaped copies of several of Manson's television interviews. The friend knew that I would be able to make such copies.

Good, considered to be an original "member" of the "Manson Family" was then living in Bridport, Vermont while she completed the five-year probationary period of a fifteen-year federal prison sentence that she received in 1976 for conspiracy to mail threatening letters and issuing threatening communications through interstate commerce. Good was still fiercely loyal to Charles Manson and to Lynette Fromme, with whom she had served part of her sentence.

I made the interview copies and sent them to Ms. Good, along with a short cover letter. Even though I had included my telephone number in the letter I was surprised when she called me several days after I mailed her the package. We had a good initial conversation and then spoke several more times over the course of a few months. In one conversation I asked if it would be all right for me to visit her at her residence in Vermont. She said that it would.

In the fall of 1990 I drove from Ohio to Vermont and spent three days visiting Good in the beautiful Lake Champlain area in the northwest corner of the Green Mountain State. While I was there she shared with me her vast accumulation of Manson-related material -- correspondence, legal documents, photographs, news articles, and artwork. We had many agreeable conversations covering a wide variety of subjects. I was amazed to realize that despite my extensive research into Manson and his case I was still misinformed.

Good was an amazing source of information. She was the first person to tell me that Manson and his friends never referred to themselves as "The Family." She also stunned me with the revelation that she and Joel Pugh -- a young man usually presented in Manson lore as Good's husband and a possible murder victim of "The Family" -- were never married and had not even been in touch for a number of years before Pugh's demise in a London hotel room.

Good was aware of my correspondence with Manson and suggested that I try to visit him, so when I returned to Ohio I wrote to him and asked for a visiting application form.

A few weeks later, it arrived. I carefully filled it out and sent it in. The form said that it would take about six weeks for the processing to run its course and that if I was disapproved the prison would inform me of the disapproval and the reasons for it. If I was approved, it was the inmate's (Manson's) responsibility to let me know.

Weeks went by and I heard nothing. The weeks turned into months. Finally, in April of 1991, I called the California State Prison at Corcoran and asked the people in the visiting department if, since I had never received a disapproval notice from them, I had been approved. After some checking they informed me that, yes, I was approved to visit. The first thing I did upon learning that was to make arrangements to travel to Corcoran to visit Manson.

My first visit occurred on May 31, 1991. Having never been in any kind of jail or prison setting I approached the visit with some apprehension. I imagined that someone as evil and dangerous as Charles Manson would have to be held in some kind of bunker deep beneath the institution, a la *The Silence Of The Lambs*, and I was not looking forward to a long trip into the concrete bowels of California State Prison -- Corcoran.

I was also apprehensive about something else. What if, I thought, after all of this time corresponding and imagining, Manson came into the visiting room and it was obvious that my preconceived ideas of him were wrong and that he was plainly a bad person?

What if he was just *oozing* evil?

At CSP -- Corcoran I parked my vehicle and then boarded the prison bus for the ride to the section of the institution (Level IV) where Manson was being held.

At a separate visitor processing center at Level IV I signed in and walked through a metal detector before walking outside of that building and through the two sixteen-foot-high concertina wire-topped perimeter fences of the prison proper. I then crossed an open area perhaps a hundred feet wide and arrived at the visiting room entrance. At the time of this initial visit Manson was being held in the most controlled part of the prison, the Security Housing Unit (SHU). That meant that the one-hour visit would be non-contact over a telephone through thick, chicken wire-reinforced glass.

I walked into the visiting room and handed my visitor's pass and driver's license to the correctional officer who was seated at a raised desk in the center of the room. He took them and then directed me to the visiting cubicle where Manson waited for me.

As I approached the cubicle I could see him through the glass. He was facing the other way, saying something to a correctional officer through the door to the four-by-six foot room he was confined in. He wore a yellow jumpsuit. His hair was very short -- almost skinned out -- and he was clean-shaven. He was short, but certainly not the legendary five-foot-two. (I am six-foot-three.) I sat down and picked up the phone.

Manson became aware of my presence, turned around, and looked at me with a smile on his face.

"Well, it's about time you got here," he said.

He *wasn't* oozing evil.

"Hello," I said. "How are you?"

"Perfect," he replied.

We then began to speak to each other, and I experienced what could be better described as a ride than as a conversation. The logistics of SHU visiting allowed for talking only, so there was none of the long pausing, getting up and moving around, or any other alternate activity that occurs when people outside visit each other under normal circumstances. The visit was pretty much all talking.

I looked at Manson intently, always meeting his eyes. I wanted to see if there was anything really hypnotic about him, if there was some power coming out of his eyes. There wasn't. Although he easily dominated the conversation (I am not the most verbose person you will ever meet) I never felt that I was being overwhelmed, hypnotized, or brainwashed. There was no "pull" there. But that Manson possessed a great amount of charisma and charm was readily apparent.

I visited Manson again over the next several days before I had to return to the real world of employment in Ohio. But throughout the rest of that year I continued to correspond with him and with Sandra Good, who had since moved to the small city of Hanford, California (about twenty miles north of Corcoran) after her federal probationary period ended in December of 1990. And at the same time I also began an intermittent correspondence with Lynette Fromme, who was then incarcerated at the Federal Correctional Institute in Marianna, Florida. By the end of 1991 things had developed to the point where I decided that I would move to California and begin visiting Manson on a regular basis and see where the road would lead.2

Over the course of the next ten years I visited Manson almost two hundred times. All of these visits except one (which took place at Pelican Bay State Prison after his temporary transfer there in 1997 on a questionable -- and later discreetly dismissed -- drug trafficking charge) occurred at CSP -- Corcoran, either in the SHU visiting room or in the Protective Housing Unit (PHU) visiting room.

When Manson was in PHU, visits were "contact." We could sit at tables or walk around the room, share refreshments purchased from vending machines, have photographs taken (sometimes), and play board games, cards, or chess. We talked with the correctional officers on duty and sometimes briefly socialized with other inmates and their visitors. Besides visiting, I also spoke with Manson on the telephone hundreds of times and continued to correspond with him by mail.

During those years I got to know Charles Manson probably better than any other person on the outside at that time, with the exception of Sandra Good. I saw him in many different moods for many different reasons. I saw how he reacted to different situations. I saw his interaction with correctional officers and with other inmates and visitors. We discussed countless subjects and ideas over hundreds and hundreds of hours of conversation. I gained some insight into what his interests were and were not. We genuinely shared many levels of the human experience.

I probably had many more long, in-depth conversations with Charles Manson than many of the people who knew or lived with him in the late 1960s. It's possible that I got to know him better than a lot of those people did. I'm certain that I knew Manson better than anyone who had ever prosecuted him. And I can definitely say that I knew him better than any member of the general public who ever formed an opinion of him based on books, newspaper and magazine articles, television programs, or films.

But I must clarify that while I did know Charles Manson to a certain extent I still only scratched the surface of the man, because my contact with him was always limited to the very restrictive environment of the California Department of Corrections' visiting situation. I only saw him in those prison visiting rooms. I never saw him outside, in society, or beyond. We never drove around together, worked, camped, partied, or faced any particularly dangerous situations. My experience with Manson was only a very small fraction of what that experience could have been. Still, I can draw certain conclusions about him based on my relationship with him.

Because of my relationship with Charles Manson I was transformed as an individual. And by that I don't mean that I experienced any particular epiphany by being in his presence, but I definitely did become something else. I went from reading books about Manson to being *in* books about Manson.3 I was described in media news stories and on the Internet as Manson's "intermediary,"4 his "right-hand man,"5 and, of course, as a "follower."6 I was labeled as a white supremacist and a practicing Satanist even though I was neither. It was implied in print (in books!) that I might have vandalized property and threatened people.7 On the Internet it was worse. There it was suggested that I had committed arson and murder. I had my relationships with my friends distorted and sensationalized. I saw what few statements I made to news media representatives be twisted and taken out of context -- while other things I said were ignored -- in order for the reporter to grind out yet another variation of the same old story. I was insulted and threatened via e-mail by anonymous strangers because I had an opinion -- and likewise via regular mail. I had the house I lived in watched, filmed, and presented on television and the Internet by persons who had no legitimate interest in my private life. (I still do not consider myself to have a public one.) I was interrogated by the United States Secret Service. I was impersonated by individuals who contacted the media and purported to be me and to speak for Manson (something that I would never do). I was approached by phonies and liars of all kinds who wanted to use me to get a piece of Charles Manson, or a piece of some kind of action, or simply to get attention.

As a result of all of this attention to my situation I began to gain a true appreciation for what Manson and many of his former associates from the late 1960s had experienced for almost thirty years. Of course none of the lies about my character and my life, and none of the insults and inconveniences I endured, could even begin to compare to the calumnies that have been heaped upon Charles Manson and his friends, especially those friends who remained loyal to him. I was not kept confined in the worst conditions that the state of California has to offer. I was never given different treatment by a parole board because my case was associated with that of one of the most infamous criminals in the world. And I was not denied any of the equal protection and due process rights that I am supposed to enjoy as a citizen of the United States.

To those persons who might be tempted to suggest that Manson could have brainwashed me into my (or rather, his) way of thinking, or that he conned me, I say this: Such a thought is reasonable, but it also shows the extent to which *you* have been brainwashed. I am not a robot. In fact, I'm very resistant to being told -- or sometimes even just asked -- to do things. And I very much retain my own individuality, character, life experiences, conclusions, and values. I retain them very much.

I never idolized Charles Manson, but I did (and do) respect him to a great extent. I never tried to emulate his personality, nor did I consider him to be God or Jesus Christ. And while I think that Manson and I did have many common beliefs and ideas, there were also times when we disagreed and even argued vigorously and loudly. We were not the same person, not by a long shot.

Manson and I didn't see eye to eye on many things, but if I had always agreed with him then I might have to concur with people who suggest that he is some kind of mind-controlling fiend. But our disagreements were actually part of the genuineness of our relationship, and to me our disputes made more real the observations and perceptions that I put forth as part of the material supporting the arguments presented in this book.

And therein lies the most important thing that I took away from my experience with Charles Manson, namely that it finally allowed me to deduce an answer to my original question of what really happened in Los Angeles in the summer of 1969. And that answer is the basis for this book.

What more should the reader know about me? I was born in 1954 and raised in Cincinnati, Ohio where I was educated in the very fine public school system there. I got a bachelors degree in German from a liberal arts college in upstate New York in 1976. My conventional religious training and experience (such as it was) was in the Episcopal Church. I have pursued an interest in the history of 20th Century Europe since I was about ten years old. I have also delved deeply into the genre of writing called "true-crime," both as a reader and as a writer, for over twenty-five years. The criminal cases that are most interesting to me, after Manson's case, are the Jack the Ripper murders, the murders of Andrew and Abby Borden in Fall River, Massachusetts in 1892, and the Lindbergh Baby kidnap case. I wrote several dozen true-crime articles that were published in the old *True Detective* series of magazines (and in some of their anthology books) and I published my own work, *The Cincinnati Crime Book*, which chronicled thirteen of the most infamous and sensational murder cases that occurred in Ohio's Queen City between 1896 and 1996.

Besides listing my education and writing credentials I should perhaps also point out that I grew up at a time -- the late 1960s and early 1970s -- when the phenomenon known as the "Counterculture" was ascendant. The Vietnam War, the struggles of various civil rights movements, the changing attitudes towards sex, drugs, and long-held values, and the perception of the American government and society as being evil -- these were the big issues when I was in my teens and early twenties. They were a great part of the reality of my life, and I'm certain that they infused in me a certain experience that came in handy when approaching this case.

At that time I was much more conservative than most of the members of my peer group when it came to politics, but socially I was pretty much of a liberal. I never cared about or judged other peoples' lifestyles unless they negatively affected mine. I never cared who people slept with or when (that is to say, before marriage) or whether they used illegal substances.

And as to the latter, I personally started drinking when I was seventeen and then a year or so later began to "experiment" with various other substances besides alcohol. Some of these substances -- like marijuana, LSD and other hallucinogens, speed, and cocaine -- I experimented with enough to know quite a bit about. And I was frequently around people who were into many more things than those. Some of these substance-related experiences also gave me insights that were useful when it came to writing this book.

And I guess that's enough about me for the purposes of this book. I hope that this short autobiography gives the reader some sense of the mindset of the person presenting the points of view expressed here. While I have met many people with unconventional ideas and outlooks, I consider myself to be a common-sense conservative. So I have always tried to look at the case of Charles Manson conservatively and with common sense. And I believe that in doing so I have come up with a scenario of that case which is more understandable, believable, and true than the version that has been peddled to the public for the last fifty years.

Chapter Notes

1 They were Boyd Rice, Nikolas Schreck, Nick Bougas, Adam Parfrey, and Jon Aes-Nihil.

2 Besides getting to know Charles Manson, Lynette Fromme, and Sandra Good, I also eventually met other people who were parties to the events of 1969, people like Thomas "T.J. the Terrible" Walleman (who was present when Manson shot Bernard Crowe), Catherine "Capistrano" Gillies (whose grandmother owned the Myers Ranch), Country Sue Bartell, and others who knew and associated with Manson back then but

who would probably -- even after fifty years -- not want their names or past relationships revealed to the general public.

3 That's me, misspelled and misrepresented on page 692 of the 25th Anniversary edition of *Helter Skelter* (paperback edition). That's me again on pages 199 to 202 of *Taming the Beast* by Ed George and Dery Matera. I'm the "disciple" whose time Jason Moss was wasting on pages 124 & 125 in *The Last Victim*. And was even included in the 2011 updated super-edition of *The Manson File*.

4 *Helter Skelter*, 25th Anniversary Edition, page 692.

5 I have been introduced to people as that.

6 For example here: http://murderpedia.org/male.M/m/manson-charles.htm

7 *Taming the Beast*, page 201.

As It Grows - UNDER
MIND

I CAN SEE what you
+ people LIKE you
never DO MUCH 4 your
selves in others - I've
payed for every good
I've ever done - I've
begun to realize IF you
help or do for someone
they think your food +
want to eat you - IF
I ever git out I'm gona
beet people when ever I
git the chance I'm gona
help them go to heaven

[illegible]

The Mood of the Time

"And a little girl in California, sitting on Indian Mesa, looked up from the campfire.... and I'd say, 'What would you give to stop the war?'

"And she said, 'We would give our *lives* to stop the war.'

"And I said, 'You would?'

"'Yes. We would.'"

-- Charles Manson

One cannot seriously analyze the so-called "Manson Murders" without an examination of the times in which they occurred. The era of the late 1960s and early 1970s was one of the most intense periods in American history. It would be practically impossible for a person who did not live through that time to comprehend and appreciate the mindset of the era, a mindset that was a reality for millions of people in the United States and around the world. Nevertheless, some understanding of that frame of mind -- and the reasons for it -- is necessary here, so this chapter will present a brief synopsis of that time so readers can better realize the whole of the circumstances which contributed to the murders that are the subject of this book.

In the summer of 1969 the United States was a country at war on many fronts. Not only was it involved in an actual armed military conflict in Vietnam in Southeast Asia, it was also seriously divided at home between various factions and groups in the general population.

The war in Vietnam was easily the most controversial and divisive event to affect this country since the Civil War. Indeed, ghosts from the Vietnam War still loom large and influence the American psyche even today, over forty years after the last U.S. military personnel left that country.1

The Vietnam War was such a pervasive and emotional issue for a simple reason: Young American men were dying in it at an increasingly rapid rate. By the spring of 1969 over 33,000 servicemen had been killed in combat in Southeast Asia. These deaths cast a pall over everything else in the late 1960s and early 1970s. The Vietnam War was not just another news story; it was a literal matter of life and death for thousands of American men.

The United States' presence in Vietnam began in the late 1950s after the Vietnamese defeated their former colonial rulers, the French, at the battle of Dien Bien Phu. In 1964 two American warships were allegedly fired upon by North Vietnamese forces in the Gulf of Tonkin off the coast of North Vietnam. President Lyndon Johnson used this questionable incident to persuade Congress to pass the Gulf of Tonkin Resolution, which gave the president unlimited authority to pursue military actions in Southeast Asia without the benefit of a formal declaration of war. Thereafter the conflict in the region continued to escalate and worsen, and by mid-1965 the United States was involved in a full-fledged, if undeclared, war in Indochina.

For several years there was a general public acquiescence of U.S. policy in Vietnam. But by the last year of the 1960s a large segment of public opinion, both in the United States and around the world, had been affected by a combination of factors (the increasing roll calls of the dead, the seeming inability to defeat the enemy, the belief that the regime in South Vietnam was corrupt, and pacifist feelings against war generally, for examples) which caused many people to oppose the conflict. By the late 1960s antiwar marches and rallies with participants numbering in the tens of thousands were common.

But opposition to the War often crossed the line from demonstrating to demolishing, and while the Vietnam experience did bring out a pacifist nature in many people, it was also a case where violence begat violence. Bombings, arson attacks, and other criminal acts committed by some of the more radical anti-war protesters were as commonplace as peaceful demonstrations. And even the peaceful demonstrations often degenerated into riots when protesters encountered overzealous law enforcement officers or counter-demonstrators.

As the anti-war feeling grew, it evolved into an "anti-U.S. government" sentiment. Then it evolved into an even more general "anti-Establishment" or "anti-System" mood, and as people chose sides in this ever-growing split in the national personality an "Us vs. Them" mentality set in.

The largely generational conflict between Us and Them was also fueled by another phenomenon of the decade, the general acceptance and sometimes widespread use by mostly younger people of mood altering substances and drugs, most predominantly marijuana and lysergic acid diethylamide (LSD). In the late 1960s Timothy Leary's mantra of "Turn On, Tune In, Drop Out" was heard as often as "In God We Trust." The perception altering nature of these substances made it very easy for a person to enter and exist in a world separate from that of "the System."2

Another alienating result of illegal substance use, apart from the mood altering effects, was that it automatically transformed the user into a criminal. Any person who took just a single puff off of a marijuana cigarette was, even if unknowingly, entering into the criminal underworld. Thus, thousands of young people were arrested and recorded as criminals simply for smoking pot. With this additional reason to be on the other side of the Establishment (and its police), the chasm between Us and Them became even wider.

And a revolutionary breaking down of sexual taboos added to the mix.

In the 1960s old and conservative attitudes towards sex fell by the wayside as a widespread and out-in-the-open regard for sex as a purely pleasurable activity took hold. For many people sex outside of marriage, previously done discreetly if done at all, became the new norm. Other people experimented with group sex and homosexuality. "If it feels good, do it" and "Free Love" were two popular slogans of this newly liberated hedonism.

The anti-Establishment feeling fueled by the seeming official madness over the government's policy in Southeast Asia, the altered consciousness and lack of respect for the law brought on by the use of drugs, the new looser attitudes towards sex, and other factors such as the eternal and natural rebelliousness of the young -- all of this resulted in a questioning of institutional sacred cows and a disaffection with the stereotypical middle-class lifestyle. And out of this sentiment a new social movement known as the "Counterculture" arose.

The Counterculture represented youth, idealism, and radical change. The Establishment represented the older generation, hostile resistance to new philosophies and ideas, and the maintenance of the status quo.

The Establishment, with the eager and willing cooperation of the news media, was quick to lump all young people into one category, regardless of the actual political or social convictions of those young people as individuals. Thus, any young person who sported the then-revolutionary fashion styles of long hair and unconventional dress was labeled as a "hippie," a "flower child," or a "freak."

The Counterculture responded in kind to this offensive categorizing and stereotyping. "Don't trust anybody over thirty" was the most often voiced expression of how they felt about their elders. They also adopted their own descriptive labels for members of the System. Establishment members were "squares," "straights," or, to the more extreme, "pigs."

But disagreement over the war in Vietnam and generational differences in social attitudes were not the only factors contributing to a fragmented American society. In addition to the anti-war and Counterculture movements there were other groups of people who were organizing and making their impacts on the country.

The racial, or "civil rights," movement was moving forward on various levels to combat the perceived oppression of racial minorities by a supposed white power structure. What had started in the late 1950s with isolated incidents of marching and boycotting was becoming organized into a very real instrument of change. Beyond the mainstream activism of groups like the National Association for the Advancement of Colored People (NAACP) and people like Martin Luther King, Jr. there were groups such as the Nation of Islam and the Black Panther Party, both of which suggested very different tactics for achieving their goals than the marching, boycotting, and other generally pacifistic methods used by the more conventional organizations.

The Nation of Islam (or "Black Muslims") had been founded in the 1930s. Its program was based in part on the belief that blacks were the original race of man and that the white man was a bleached-out race of devils created 6,600 years earlier by a disaffected black scientist named Mr. Jacub in order to wreak havoc on the world.

By the late 1960s the Nation of Islam was a formidable group, attracting many adherents with its demand for a portion of United States territory in which to establish an all-black country, the release of all of its members convicted of federal crimes (and of all blacks convicted of capital crimes on state levels), and its doctrines against drinking, drugs, sloth, and miscegenation.

The Black Panther Party was founded in Oakland, California in 1966. Openly militant and defiant, the party organized paramilitary groups around the country that were assigned to protect black neighborhoods and to implement self-help programs for the residents of those neighborhoods such as free breakfast programs, health clinics, and schools.

In October 1966 the Black Panther Party published its "Platform and Program" which demanded decent housing, full employment for blacks, black exemption from military service, and the release of all blacks held in all U.S. jails and prisons.

In 1968 the infamous *Black Panther Coloring Book* appeared, a book supposedly designed by the Black Panther Party to be distributed to young black children. The book included graphic illustrations of black warriors brutally killing white pig-men. The true origins of this publication have always been murky, but whether it was the genuine article or a government-created forgery it was still indicative of the rapidly worsening relations between the races in the United States at the time.

The racial movement, as much as the anti-war movement, was often characterized by polarization, violence, and death. Confrontations between integrationists and segregationists frequently escalated to warlike proportions. In the southern United States black churches were firebombed and civil rights workers were murdered. In February 1965 Nation of Islam Minister Malcolm X was shot to death at a mosque in New York City (albeit by fellow Black Muslims). Three years later a similar fate befell the well-known preacher-turned-activist Martin Luther King, Jr. in Memphis, Tennessee. There were major race riots in most large American cities during just about every summer in the mid and late 1960s. Members of the Black Panther Party were involved in several deadly firefights with police officers. By the summer of 1969 it sometimes seemed as if there was going to be an all out war between the races.

And if these generational, racial, and social conflicts did not create enough confusion and strife, constantly hovering over everything else was the nagging threat of total worldwide annihilation in an all-out nuclear war.

It might already be hard to remember, but from the late 1940s to the late 1980s the world was divided into two major competing factions: the United States and its allies which adhered to the economic system of capitalism, and those countries which favored Communism. The Communist world was further divided into two sub-factions, between Russia and its satellite countries (the Union of Soviet Socialist Republics, or the U.S.S.R.), and the Peoples' Republic of China ("Red China") and its allies. Thus, for four decades there seemed to be a constant and very real possibility that any military conflict or event involving any combination of these three camps and their allies could instantly escalate into a nuclear conflagration capable of destroying all life on the planet. If World War Three ever came to pass no one would be spared by geographical good fortune such as that which had saved the United States from massive Axis attacks during World War Two. Instead, any incident occurring on the other side of the globe an hour ago could have conceivably (or perceivably) caused the deaths of most of the people in the United States right now. And many members of the post-World War Two generation *expected* this to happen.[3]

Such was the world that the younger generation had been bequeathed by its elders, a world in which all life on Earth could be destroyed in an instant as a result of ideological differences between old men. Justifiably, many young people resented this, and they frequently perceived the conflict between the generations to be a literal battle between the forces of life and death.

Conflict, confrontation, and war: All of these themes were reported daily by the news media for years. To the younger generation, which was nurtured and raised on this diet of news, "Us vs. Them" was a real battle, a thought war perceived by them as being between the new, idealistic proponents of change for a better life and the old purveyors of oppression and death. By the last year of the 1960s, revolution -- a new civil war between the old and new ways of thinking -- seemed to be a real possibility.

And popular culture acknowledged the divides growing out of the many political, sociological, and ideological differences present in day-to-day life. Much of the popular literature of the time was revolutionary or confrontational.

One bestselling book was *Soul On Ice*, by Eldridge Cleaver, a convicted rapist who in 1968 was the Minister of Information for the Black Panther Party. Contemplating a future violent conflict between whites and blacks, Cleaver wrote:

> Blacks are looking [at white America] and asking tactical questions. They are asked to die for the System in Vietnam. In Watts they are killed by it. Now – NOW! – they are asking each other in dead earnest: Why not die right here in Babylon fighting for a better life, like the Viet Cong? If those little cats can do it, what's wrong with big studs like us? A mood sets in, spreads across America, across the face of Babylon, and jells in black hearts everywhere.4

Soul On Ice promoted itself as "the book that has set the imagination of an entire generation on flame."5

(After charges were filed against him in connection with a 1968 shootout between Black Panthers and police officers in Oakland, California Cleaver jumped bail and fled the country, living in Algeria, Cuba, and France. In 1975 he returned to the United States and was placed on probation for assault in the 1968 incident. He then became a born-again Christian and ran for a California state senate seat as a member of the Republican Party. "Everybody changes," he explained. In 1998 Cleaver was again placed on probation, this time for burglary and possession of crack cocaine. He died in Los Angeles that same year, at the age of sixty-two.)

Do it!, by the radical anti-war/Establishment personality Jerry Rubin, was another popular book. In it Rubin concluded:

> The most important political conflict in the United States today is the generational conflict.... We live in a land that has declared war on its own children, on the future. We live in the midst of a dying beast that will kill anything that moves. To be young is a crime. Any crowd of kids automatically constitutes a riot. The Law has become Illegal. Our bravest brothers are beaten and killed in the streets, exiled to strange lands, or thrown into detention camps called jails.... Fuck Amerika.6

(By the mid-1970s Jerry Rubin had sold out his revolution -- and his generation -- and was a successful stockbroker on Wall Street. He then got into "networking" and promoted vitamin sales. In 1975 he wrote *Growing (Up) at 37*, wherein he presumably justified turning his back on the thousands of young people he influenced in the late 1960s. He did very well financially and easily made the transition from subversive to sellout. In 1994 he was struck by a car and killed as he crossed Wilshire Boulevard in Los Angeles.)

Jerry Rubin's *Doppelgänger* in the 1960s was Abbie Hoffman. Hoffman, one of the most visible personalities of the Counterculture movement, wrote *Revolution For The Hell Of It* (under the pseudonym "Free") and *Steal This Book*. *Steal This Book* was a how-to tome on methods of ripping off practically every aspect of American society from pay phones to pizza deliverymen. In *Revolution For The Hell Of It* Hoffman declared:

> This book was written with treason in my heart. It was written with the knowledge that the institutions and values of imperialism, racism, capitalism, and the protestant work ethic do not allow young people to

experience authentic liberation. And finally, make no mistake about it, it was written with the hope of destroying Amerika. Yippie!7

Hoffman's final exclamation here was both an exuberant outburst and a reference to the so-called "Yippie Movement," an outgrowth of the equally so-called "Hippie Movement." Yippies were members of the Youth International Party, a group dedicated mainly to presenting radically shocking media events in order to bring attention to their causes and to themselves.

(In 1973 Hoffman was arrested for selling cocaine. Instead of facing the legal process he jumped bail, dropped out of sight, and went underground for six years before finally turning himself in to authorities in 1980. He served a short prison term on the cocaine charge and then continued with his activist activities, but on a less flamboyant and inflammatory scale than in the old days. He committed suicide by intentionally overdosing on cocaine in 1989.)

Both *Soul On Ice* and *Do It!* were bestsellers and very popular with many of the disaffected young people of the era. I remember both books being present in large numbers at my high school and college. (*Soul On Ice* was required reading for one of the courses that I took at the latter.) Jerry Rubin, in fact, went to the same high school that I attended, and his remembrance of returning there for a visit in 1968 -- which I witnessed -- was recounted in *Do It!*.8

Other books that were popular and reflected or influenced the times included *Slouching Towards Bethlehem*, *On The Road*, *Dharma Bums*, *Catch 22*, the *Little Red Book* of Chinese Communist leader Mao Zedong, and anything by J.R.R. Tolkien, Hermann Hesse, or Carlos Casteneda. And the book literature of the era was supplemented by countless underground newspapers and magazines such as the SDS (Students for a Democratic Society) publication *Fire* and the Hollywood-based *Tuesday's Child*. Almost every major population center had at least one underground newspaper. In Cincinnati we had *The Independent Eye* and *The Queen City Free Press*.

The news and book publishing industries' reflections of the era were conjoined with those of the Hollywood image-making machine. Some of the movies of the period, like *Zabriske Point* and

Easy Rider, focused on the often-violent polarization of the time, while others like *Bonnie and Clyde* and *Butch Cassidy and the Sundance Kid* featured famous American outlaws from the past in a new light as attractive anti-heroes. Some of the other films chronicling, impacting, or otherwise expressing some aspect of the time included *The Graduate*, *Alice's Restaurant*, *Guess Who's Coming To Dinner?*, *Catch 22* (again), *2001: A Space Odyssey*, *M*A*S*H*, *In The Heat of the Night*, *Bob & Carol & Ted & Alice*, and *Woodstock*.

But nowhere were the conflicts of the day better reflected than in popular music. Alienation, hostility, the desire for an alternative style of living -- all of these concepts were presented in the lyrics of much of the music of the time. And of course, this music also served as a real-life soundtrack of those years.

"Protest Music" was not a new phenomenon in the 1960s (see Pete Seegar and Woody Guthrie, for example) but in that decade it actually became a predominant musical form (as well as becoming a huge money making enterprise). The Vietnam War and other perceived injustices gave people plenty to protest against. With regards to the Vietnam War, or war in general, there were Bob Dylan's "Blowing In The Wind," Barry McGuire's "Eve Of Destruction," Country Joe and the Fish's "I Feel Like I'm Fixing To Die Rag," the Doors' "Unknown Soldier," Crosby, Stills, and Nash's "Wooden Ships," Edwin Starr's "War (What Is It Good For?)," and John Lennon's "Give Peace A Chance."

Besides protesting war, the music also capitalized literally on such other themes as teenage alienation and *Angst*, the younger generation's rebellion against its elders (many aspects of which, in fact, were merely a timeless phenomenon that the news media suddenly "discovered" and labeled the "Generation Gap"), the desire to have a good time, and the new liberation of sexual mores.

The music was also frequently about drugs, reflecting the younger generation's widespread acceptance of these previously unknown and forbidden fruits. Songs like Jefferson Airplane's "White Rabbit," Donovan's "Sunshine Superman," and Jimi Hendrix's "Purple Haze" gave substance use an encouraging and exciting legitimacy. (Of course many recording artists, no doubt under orders from the record companies that paid their salaries, denied that their lyrics promoted, endorsed, or even were about illegal drug use.)

The attitudes and lifestyles of the 1960s were not, for many people, just a fad or an exercise in fashion, but rather were realities that had been slowly conditioned into their minds over a period of many years. The Counterculture was a very real way of life for millions of people around the world. In fact, many people dropped out of society to the extent that they joined communities of like-minded people in order to create their own societies and realities in the tradition of such earlier breakaway groups as the Quakers, Mennonites, and Mormons.

Although most written works or news/entertainment programs on the Manson case touch briefly on the mood of the time, it is really not enough to vaguely refer to "Flower Power" or the "Summer of Love" to fully explain the spirit of the late 1960s and early 1970s. That spirit cannot be conveyed into a sound bite, for it was in fact derived from an accumulation of experiences and events that took place and affected peoples' minds (and especially young peoples' minds) on a daily basis for years.

Here is a chronology of just some of the major happenings of the times which helped form the mindsets and realities of many of the people who were alive and growing up in the 1960s, including, of course, many of the persons who are characters in this book. Although the particular events which will eventually concern us here began occurring in the spring of 1967, this chronology starts at the beginning of 1966 so that the reader can see how many of the factors relevant to this case were already in motion long before any of the characters involved in it ever even met each other.

*   *   *

By 1966 the United States' involvement in the Vietnam War was already a predominant issue. Almost 200,000 U.S. troops were stationed in the Southeast Asian country. On January 11 anti-war college students had their draft status changed from 1-H (exempt from service because of college enrollment) to 1-A (the first to be called up for service). Thus, any student could now find himself drafted into front line combat duty in Vietnam at any time. At the end of the month, the United States resumed its bombing North Vietnam after a lull of several months. The top selling record album was the Beatles' *Rubber Soul*. "The Sounds of Silence," a song by Simon and Garfunkel that included a lyric about prophets writing on walls, was the number one single record.

In February, the U.S. government began regulating the drug LSD. (On April 18 it would take over all pharmaceutical distribution of the hallucinogen.) The first of the young men to be put on trial for draft card burning were convicted on February 10. By then Truman Capote's book *In Cold Blood*, the "non-fiction novel"9 about the brutal and senseless mass murder of a Kansas farm family, had reached the top of the bestseller lists and was paving the way for the "true-crime" literary genre.

In March there were worldwide protests against the Vietnam War during the "Antiwar International Days of Protest" (March 25-27). The patriotic pro-soldier song "The Ballad of the Green Berets" (sung by real-life U.S. Army Green Beret Barry Sadler) was at the top of the singles charts. The folk rock group The Mamas and the Papas released its debut album *If You Can Believe Your Eyes And Ears*, which contained the hit single "California Dreamin'."

On April 8 *Time* magazine's cover wondered, "Is God Dead?" By the end of that month 3,047 more U.S. servicemen had been killed in Vietnam.

On May 14 Stokely Carmichael, the black radical who coined the slogan "Black Power," was elected head of the Student Non-Violent Coordinating Committee (SNCC), a civil rights group that encouraged and practiced aggressive civil disobedience. Two weeks later Ray Charles released the single "Let's Go Get Stoned."

Civil rights advocate James Meredith was shot by a sniper while marching in Mississippi on June 6. On June 28 a group of twenty-eight women in Washington DC founded the feminist group the National Organization for Women (NOW). The next day the U.S. stepped up its bombing of targets in North Vietnam, for the first time including its capital city of Hanoi.

On July 2 the musical group the Fugs released its first album, called simply *Fugs*. Band members included a vocalist named Ed

Sanders. Two weeks later Richard Speck murdered eight student nurses in a townhouse in Chicago. Throughout the rest of the month black rioters ran wild in Chicago, Brooklyn, Cleveland, and Baltimore.

August was ushered in by Charles Whitman's sniping spree from the clock tower at the University of Texas in Austin. Whitman killed sixteen people before police finally killed him. On August 4 John Lennon opined that the Beatles had become "more popular than Jesus." (Lennon's group would perform its last live performance in San Francisco at the end of the month.) The Loving Spoonful's "Summer in the City" was the top single record.

In September British singer Donovan Leach's "Sunshine Superman" climbed the charts while former Harvard psychology professor Timothy Leary proclaimed that LSD was a religious sacrament. On September 12 the television program *The Monkees*, Hollywood's answer to the Beatles movie *A Hard Day's Night*, premiered. A week later Beatle George Harrison made his first trip to the Maharishi Mahesh Yogi in India in search of a spiritual fulfillment that his unprecedented material success in the music recording industry did not provide.

By October the Vietnam War was costing the U.S. Government 4.2 billion dollars per month. By mid-month there were more American soldiers fighting for South Vietnam than there were South Vietnamese soldiers fighting for their own country. In Oakland California Bobby Seale and Huey P. Newton co-founded the Black Panther Party. At the end of the month *Rush To Judgment*, Mark Lane's controversial and seminal book critical of the Warren Commission's investigation into the assassination of President Kennedy, was the number one bestseller.

The year closed out with the Beach Boys' single "Good Vibrations" at number one, but for many people in the country the vibrations were anything but good. The number of U.S. troops in Vietnam had more than doubled during the year and the U.S. death toll there had also more than doubled since April, to 6,407 servicemen killed in action.

February 1967 saw the debut of a Buffalo Springfield song that has since become one of the major audio flashes of the era, "For What It's Worth," which was written in reaction to riots involving teenagers and the police on the Sunset Strip in Los Angeles. Also in February the National Organization for Women was formally incorporated, and the Mothers of Invention released their debut album, *Freak Out*.

March brought the first reports of genetic damage allegedly caused by LSD, as well as the release of the albums *Surrealistic Pillow* by the Jefferson Airplane and the Doors' debut effort *The Doors*. On March 13 Senator Eugene McCarthy introduced the Equal Rights [for women] Amendment to the United States Constitution to the U.S. Senate.

In April the first tourist buses started taking people to the Haight-Ashbury neighborhood in San Francisco to show off the growing "hippie" population there. On April 15, Income Tax Day in the United States, 100,000 demonstrators in New York City protested the Vietnam War. Four days later Kathy Switzer became the first woman to run in the Boston Marathon. (She had to register for the race as simply "K. Switzer" in order to conceal her gender from race organizers.) On April 28 the professional boxer Muhammad Ali (formerly Cassius Clay) was stripped of his heavyweight boxing title for refusing to be inducted into the U.S. Army.

In May North Vietnamese leader Ho Chi Minh's book *Ho Chi Minh on Revolution* was published in the United States. On May 11 a black student at Jackson (Mississippi) State College was shot to death during rioting there. The Grateful Dead and Cream both put out their debut albums, and the Young Rascals' "Groovin'" was the number one single record.

The major news story in June was the Six-Day War (June 5–10) between Israel and several of its Arab neighbors. Aretha Franklin sang about "Respect." One of the defining musical entertainment events of the decade, the Monterey Pop Festival, opened at the Monterey, California fairgrounds on the sixteenth. Three days later Beatle Paul McCartney admitted that he had tried LSD. From June 23 to 25 President Johnson met with Russian Premiere Alexi Kosygin at a summit in Glassboro, New Jersey where they agreed not to allow any international crisis to escalate into a Third World War. On June 28 Rolling Stones band members Mick Jagger and Keith Richards were held overnight on drug-related charges.

(Both were later convicted but their convictions were eventually reversed on appeal.)

In one way the summer of 1967 was a repeat of the summer of 1966: In July twenty-six persons were killed in race rioting in Newark, New Jersey. More than 1,500 people were injured and 1,000 were arrested. Forty-three persons were dead after similar disturbances in Detroit, Michigan, where 2,000 people were injured and over 5,000 left homeless because of arson fires. In both of these instances federal troops had to be called in to restore order. Against this backdrop of violence the Beatles' *Sergeant Peppers Lonely Hearts Club Band* LP soared to the top of the album charts while the Door's "Light My Fire" achieved the number one single position.

In August rock guitarist Jimi Hendrix debuted on the international level with a heavily drug-influenced album that asked its listeners, "*Are You Experienced?*"

The next month United States troop strength in Southeast Asia reached 464,000. President Johnson approved a $20 billion bill that would pay for U.S. involvement in the war through 1968.

By October, 13,643 American servicemen had lost their lives in Vietnam while another 756 were listed as missing in action. On October 21 and 22 protestors reacted to this news by storming the Pentagon building in Washington DC during demonstrations there.

November 9, 1967 was the publication date for the first issue of a new quasi-underground, music-oriented magazine called *Rolling Stone*. As the United States' population reached a record 200 million at the end of the month, *The Confessions of Nat Turner*, a novel by William Styron based on the true story of an African slave who tried to instigate a race war by entering the homes of several wealthy, white, slave-owning families and slaughtering the inhabitants, was the number one bestselling book.

In December Black Panther leader Bobby Seale offered this bleak observation on the worsening relations between the races and classes in America:

> If we worry about what's going to happen to us, we couldn't accomplish anything. Justice is going to come when the mass of people rise up and

see justice done. The more they [the Establishment] try to come down on us, the more we'll expose them for what they are -- pigs.10

January 1968 brought the debuts of the Beatles album *Magical Mystery Tour* and the Rolling Stones' *Their Satanic Majesties Request*. On January 21 North Korean military forces seized the United States Navy ship *USS Pueblo* and its crew of eighty-three men in the Sea of Japan. Since the North Koreans were allied with China and not Russia the Glassboro agreement between President Johnson and Premier Kosygin to prevent such an event from leading to all-out war did not apply. For months thereafter there was fear that the seizure of the *Pueblo* might lead to a nuclear confrontation between the United States and Red China. On January 30 North Vietnamese troops and the Viet Cong (guerilla soldiers for the communist cause made up of South Vietnamese volunteers) began a military offensive on their New Years holiday, Tet. Although the Tet Offensive was eventually repulsed by regular South Vietnamese and American troops, because of its size and scope it was widely considered to be a victory for the communists as well as a sign that the war would not be easily and favorably concluded anytime in the near future.

On February 8 Alabama governor and ultra-segregationist George Wallace announced his third-party candidacy for President of the United States. Police on the campus of South Carolina State College in Orangeburg opened fire on black student protestors, killing three and wounding thirty. Eight days later the Selective Service System cancelled the deferments of most college students, thus making them all eligible to be drafted into combat duty in the ever-escalating war in Southeast Asia.

In March, while a Gallup poll revealed that forty-nine percent of the people polled believed that the United States' involvement in Vietnam was a mistake, the country's combat deaths reached 19,670. *CBS News* anchorman Walter Cronkite publicly voiced his opposition to the war during a television news broadcast on March 6. On the last day of the month President Johnson stunned the country by announcing that he would not run for re-election for president in November. (He also announced a reduction in the bombing of North Vietnam.)

By the middle of April race rioting had erupted in practically every major American city after Martin Luther King, Jr. was shot to death in Memphis on April 4. In Oakland California seventeen-year-old Black Panther Bobby Hutton was killed by police in a shootout that also wounded Eldridge Cleaver. Chicago's mayor, Richard Daly, responded to riots in his town by ordering police to "shoot to kill arsonists." On April 23 radical students took over Columbia University in New York City. (One thousand police officers ended the takeover a week later.) Four days later, tens of thousands of antiwar protestors demonstrated in seventeen U.S. cities.

In May worldwide disaffection with U.S. involvement in Vietnam became apparent as rioters in France effectively paralyzed that country for almost three weeks. On May 17 antiwar protestors (and Catholic priests) Daniel and Philip Berrigan burned draft files in Catonsville, Maryland and eventually went on trial as part of the "Catonsville Nine."

On June 6 New York Senator Robert Kennedy was fatally shot (he died the next day) at the Ambassador Hotel in Los Angeles after winning the California Democratic primary. The same day Steve Miller released his album *Children of the Future*. A week later a controversial film about devil worshipping -- *Rosemary's Baby*, directed by Polish immigrant Roman Polanski -- made its debut. Benjamin Spock, the pediatrician who wrote a bestselling series of child rearing books in the 1950s, was convicted later in the month for conspiracy for his activities in various antiwar protests.

On July 29 Pope Paul VI flew in the face of the ongoing sexual revolution by issuing his encyclical *Humane Vitae* that forbade for Catholics voluntary sterilization and artificial birth control methods.

By the beginning of August there were well over half a million U.S. troops in South Vietnam. On August 8 protestors in Miami, Florida rioted after Richard Nixon and Spiro Agnew were nominated in that city as the Republican Party's presidential ticket. International affairs continued on their dark path as troops from the Soviet Union invaded Czechoslovakia on the 20th, crushing the so-called "Prague Spring" of minor democratic reforms. A week later the FBI reported that marijuana-related arrests were up one hundred percent from the same period in 1966. On August 28 violent demonstrations accompanied with unprecedented instances of police brutality erupted in Chicago during the Democratic National Convention there that nominated Hubert Humphrey and Edmund Muskie as the party's presidential and vice-presidential candidates. Demonstrators outside the convention hall took a break from the rioting long enough to nominate their own candidate for president, a swine named "Pigasus."

On October 12 the San Francisco rock group Big Brother and the Holding Company, featuring Janis Joplin on vocals, released the album *Cheap Thrills*. Three days later U.S. Olympians Tommie Smith and John Carlos were thrown out of the Olympic games in Mexico City after they gave the clenched-fist black power salute during their medal awarding ceremony. On the last day of the month the United States stopped all bombing of North Vietnam.

On November 1 the U.S. government announced that it had dropped more bombs on North Vietnam than it had on all of the Axis Powers during the whole of World War Two. Four days later the Nixon-Agnew ticket narrowly defeated Humphrey-Muskie in the presidential election. In that same election Shirley Chisholm became the first black woman to be elected to the U.S. House of Representatives. On November 13 the animated Beatles film *Yellow Submarine* premiered.

The last month of 1968 saw San Francisco State University President S.I. Hayakawa sending police onto his campus to end a student strike there. On December 11 the Vietnam peace talks, which had been convening in Paris France for all of one day, broke down after arguments arose about the proposed shape of the negotiating table. Eleven days later North Korea released the surviving eighty-two crew members of the *USS Pueblo*. At the end of the year the number one album was the latest effort by the Beatles -- a double long-playing record set with a blank white cover, which quickly became known as *The White Album*.

1969 got off to a somewhat twisted start when, in the middle of what many hoped would be the beginning of a new epoch of human evolution, Richard Milhous Nixon was inaugurated as the 37th President of the United States on January 20.

In February, while Sly and the Family Stone sang about "Everyday People" the National Guard had to occupy the campus of the University of Wisconsin after a protest there over black studies turned into a riot.

On March 6 a Viet Cong offensive threatened Saigon, the capital city of South Vietnam. On March 20 John Lennon married Yoko Ono.

By April 3 the combat death toll for U.S. servicemen in Vietnam was 33,641. (The U.S. military presence there peaked in April at 543,400 personnel.) On April 11 students at Harvard went on strike in opposition to the university's Reserve Officer Training Corps (ROTC) program and in support of black studies. On April 19 black students at Cornell University in Ithaca, New York shocked the nation by openly carrying pistols, rifles, and shotguns on the campus. The musical group The Fifth Dimension sang about the dawning of the "Age of Aquarius."

On June 21 the ultra-radical Weatherman faction broke off from its parent group, the Students for a Democratic Society (SDS). The Weathermen advocated using violence in order to achieve their goals. (The group was later linked to several fatal bombing incidents.) On June 28 rioting broke out in New York City after police there entered the Stonewall Inn to harass gay patrons of the establishment. This encounter became an impetus for a gay and lesbian rights movement.

In July the seemingly impossible finally began happening as the Nixon Administration started decreasing the number of U.S. troops in Southeast Asia. On July 18 a young woman named Mary Jo Kopechne was drowned after United States Senator Ted Kennedy drove the car they were both riding in off a bridge and into a tidal basin at Chappaquidick Island in Massachusetts. Two days later a truly historic event occurred as man first set foot on the surface of Earth's moon.

On August 8 President Nixon signed an executive order requiring "Affirmative Action" programs in federal employment. The next day the nation was shocked after five people were found brutally murdered at the Los Angeles home of film director Roman Polanski. A week after that almost a half a million people gathered at the Woodstock Music Festival in upstate New York. One of the most remarked-upon aspects of this three-day musical event was that it did not degenerate into a riot.

In September North Vietnamese leader Ho Chi Minh died. On September 24 the trial of the so-called "Chicago Eight" (eight defendants including Jerry Rubin, Abbie Hoffman, and Bobby Seale) charged with inciting riots at the previous year's Democratic National Convention in Chicago, began. The movie *Butch Cassidy and the Sundance Kid* premiered the same day. The rock album *Blind Faith* was at the top of the music charts.

From October 8 to 11 the Weathermen staged their "Days of Rage" protests against the Vietnam War in particular and American society in general. A few days later thousands of demonstrators marched past the White House in a candlelight parade calling for a moratorium on the war. In the last weeks of the month people amused themselves by searching the lyrics of Beatles songs for hidden clues supporting the rumor that band member Paul McCartney was dead. By the end of the month the United States had lost over six thousand aircraft over North Vietnam.

On November 15, 250,000 people marched in Washington DC against the Vietnam War. Another 200,000 demonstrated in Golden Gate Park in San Francisco on the same day. The next day the massacre of over one hundred Vietnamese civilians in the village of My Lai was revealed. On November 20 radical American Indians seized the former federal prison on Alcatraz Island in San Francisco Bay. The Beatles' album *Abbey Road* was number one.

In December a lottery system was introduced in an effort to instill some sense of fairness into the Selective Service (draft) system that inducted young men into the U.S. military. On December 4 Chicago police raided an apartment occupied by members of the Black Panther Party and killed party members Fred Hampton and Mark Clark. Two days later members of the Hell's Angels motorcycle club guarding the stage at a Rolling Stones concert at the Altamont Speedway near Livermore, California beat members of the crowd with pool cues and stabbed one concertgoer to death. *The Selling of the President*, a cynical look at the 1968 presidential election process, was the number one non-fiction bestseller. The British musical group The Hollies released the single record "He Ain't Heavy, He's My Brother" a cover of an old Everly Brothers song based on a quotation from a statue at Father Flanagan's Boys Town in Omaha, Nebraska. The song eventually reached number seven on the charts. The Rolling Stones closed out the year with the release of their album *Let It Bleed.*

And here we close out this summary of the years leading up to the events that concern us in this book. While all periods of history are unique unto themselves, the history of the United States in the last years of the 1960s was unprecedented in terms of the divisions and strife which predominated in a society which could have instead still been reveling in the continued growth and prosperity that followed World War Two. But instead of experiencing a comfortable and conservative existence, the U.S. was rife with conflict, hate, revolutionary rhetoric, violence, and death. And such was the mood of the time in America in the summer of 1969.

Chapter Notes

1 Ghosts still loom large from the Civil War as well.
2 Of course this is still true today. But in the 1960s the drug experience was still a new phenomenon, and it was easy to think that drug use was part of a real, revolutionary, and positive evolution on the part of the younger generation, especially if you were high.
3 One of the earliest memories of my educational career is of the whole school being led into the basement of the school building and kneeling against the wall, heads covered, during a practice drill in anticipation of a nuclear attack. And even though these drills stopped after a year or so, the signs designating the school basement as a Civil Defense bomb shelter remained in place for at least as long as I attended that school. Similar signs were also posted in the basement of my high school.
4 *Soul On Ice*, by Eldridge Cleaver, Dell Publishing Co., Inc.; New York; 1968; page 129.
5 From the promotional blurb on the back cover of the paperback edition.
6 From *Do It!*, by Jerry Rubin; Simon and Schuster; New York; 1970; pages 14, 242, and 250.
7 *Revolution For The Hell Of It*, by Free (Abbie Hoffman); Dial Press; New York; 1968; pages 5 6.

8 *Do It!*, page 216.
9 Capote's term.
10 This famous quote of Seale's was reproduced, among other places, on posters published by Berkeley Graphic Arts, Berkeley, CA.

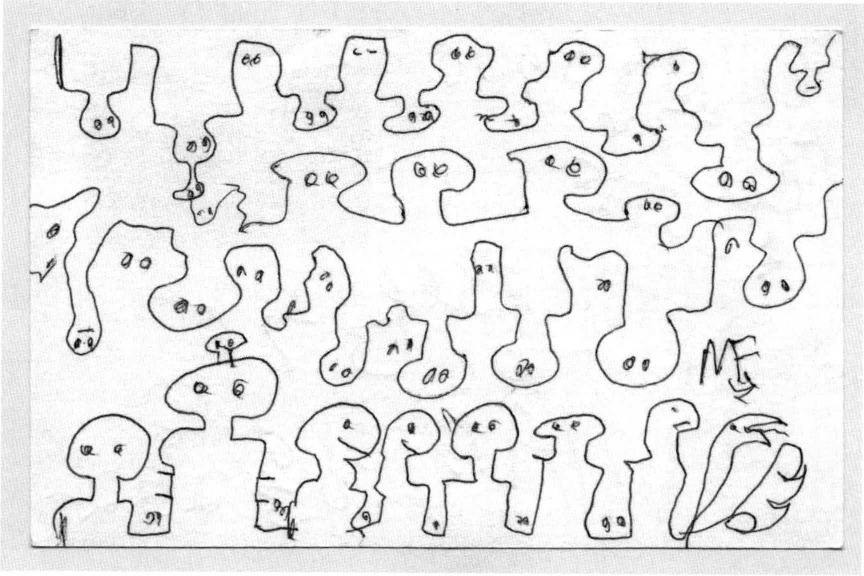

Spring 1967 to Summer 1969

"My love is that ranch. My love is those horses. My love is all the beauty that I was shown by all those angels that I met.... I met a whole bunch of angels in the City of Angels. They fell out of the sky. They were beautiful to me."

-- Charles Manson

The previous chapter presented some of the major historical and sociological events in the United States and the world from the beginning of 1966 to the end of 1969. One news item left out of that chronology, however, was that on December 1, 1969 law enforcement officials in Los Angeles California announced that they had solved the mystery of who committed the murders at Roman Polanski's house in Bel Air the previous August. That announcement was the beginning of the public's experience with Charles Manson and his so-called "Family."

Always simultaneous to the headline-making events of news and history are the important occurrences in the lives of everyday individuals. And like everyone else, Charles Manson and the people around him had their own history. This chapter will present some of the major events in the lives of Charles Manson and those people during the time they were together in order to establish a framework of the characters, dynamics, and circumstances that later contributed to the various murders connected with Charles Manson.

Although the chronology in the last chapter began at January, 1966 this chronology will begin with the date that Charles Manson was released from the Terminal Island (TI) Federal Prison at San Pedro, California: March 21, 1967.

It has often been stated that Manson "begged" not to be released from prison in 1967, with the implication being that if only he had been listened to dozens of people might still be alive today. This contention, though, like much else in the Manson story, is not exactly true.

Manson did sometimes express reluctance about being outside of prison, as when he explained that he was uncomfortable about being let out of jail:

> [be]cause I had never been outside. I've been in jail all my life. I understand inside. I never understood outside, see. Outside scared me, man. I was a hobo. I lived in garbage cans, man. I didn't know any outside. I never rented a car, or [wrote] a check, you know.1

But Manson's seeming apprehension did not mean that he did opposed release simply because he felt that he couldn't make it on the outside. I once asked him about his "begging not to be released" and he said that he had another reason for why he did not want to be paroled in 1967 other than that he couldn't deal with the outside world:

> What it was, was, I was working in the kitchen. And I'd been working in the kitchen for so many years I just got fed up with it. Washing pots and pans, mopping floors, slaving -- kitchen's a slave job. And I said, "You know what? I'm not working in the kitchen no more."
>
> And the captain says, "You'll work in the kitchen."
>
> And I said, "Fuck you."
>
> So he put me in the hole. And he says he's gonna keep me in the hole until I work in the kitchen. And I said, "I'm not gonna work in the kitchen."
>
> And he said, "Well, I'll take your good time [time off of an inmate's sentence earned for good behavior or for working]."

I said, "Go ahead and take it."
He said, "You don't want out?"
I said, "Out of what?"
He said, "Prison."
I said, "What prison? Are you in prison?"
And he said, "No. You're in prison."
And I said, "No, *you're* in prison. I'm just *here*."

So I was just doing that to be contrary. And then they said, "Well, we're gonna take your good time."

And I said, "Take it."

So then they wouldn't take it. They didn't take it. Then they said, "Well, sign for your parole release."

And I said, "I'm not signing. I'm not gonna work in the kitchen and I'm not signing for no parole."

Then I seen where they *wanted* to let me out, more than I wanted to get out. So I played that, and I told them, "You know what, man, like [if you let me out] I'm not gonna report on parole. Just keep me in until [all of] my time's up and let me go. Because all my life you've had me on some kind of Goddamn fucking string."2

In other words, Manson didn't express a reluctance to be released because he was afraid that he couldn't make it on the outside, but rather because he did not want to submit to parole supervision. According to Manson, he did not beg not to be released -- he *refused* to be released. But regardless of his wish he was let out of TI on Tuesday, March 21, 1967.

Shortly after this release Manson traveled north to the San Francisco area. Across the bay from San Francisco at the campus of the University of California at Berkeley he met Mary Brunner, a twenty-three-year-old woman who worked at the university library. In Manson Brunner saw an alternative to her lifestyle, which she regarded as repetitive and mundane. She later said of Manson, and his effect on her:

He's so hard for me to talk about because he's so many things to me. Like, he opened me up. I was living with my dog in an apartment and having just a real – go to work, go home, go shopping, go to work, go home, go to the movies, go to bed, go shopping -- you know, it was so routine that it was really a drag, and it was getting to me. And then he came in and I just dropped it -- whatever was happening -- and took off.3

Soon after their meeting Manson moved in with Brunner and she stopped working at the library. Mary Brunner was the first of the people Manson came into contact with on the outside who would later become known as "members" of the "Manson Family."

Not long after meeting Brunner, Manson went to Los Angeles to check on some contacts he'd been given by a friend in prison. Failing to hook up with these persons, he decided to visit Venice Beach, the colorful oceanfront community south of Santa Monica. There, he saw eighteen-year-old Lynette Fromme sitting on a bench by the beach. In her 2018 memoir *Reflexion*, Fromme later remembered that night:

> One night my father and I clashed over something silly -- a word or a definition. Suddenly enraged, he pointed to the door and yelled, "You get out of this house and never come back!" I cried, stuffing a big purse full of books and make-up and miscellaneous junk. I called my college boyfriend to pick me up, but he said he was too drunk to drive and suggested I hitchhike. It was nearly 9 p.m. when I trudged to the nearest freeway on-ramp and stuck out my thumb -- but I wasn't going to see my boyfriend.

Instead, Fromme went to a place that she and her friends had explored before, Venice Beach, which was then a rundown neighborhood:

> Venice Beach was dark, damp, and utterly deserted, all familiar landmarks gone. A light far down the strand turned out to be from a new bookstore/gallery whose proprietor and customers seemed too cool to notice me searching for a face I could trust. The man behind the counter began to close out the cash register, but I could not bring myself to speak.
>
> Outside, I moved for cover beneath a gazebo, facing a gloomy sea. The store's light behind me was doused from the sidewalk, its glass doors locked, and as footsteps and car engines faded, I was left in the dark, completely alone, and at a standstill.
>
> My dilemma was broken by a blur -- a man in a smuggler's cap, flight jacket, and jeans hopped the half-wall in front of me and leaned against it. Animated, smiling, he was old -- or young -- I couldn't tell. He had a

two-day beard and reminded me of a fancy bum, elegant -- but my fear was up.

"Name's Charlie," he said, looking directly in my eyes. "In San Francisco they call me 'The Gardener.'" Sensing my alarm, he said simply, "It's alright," and I felt, within the tone of his voice, that it was. He moved with smooth confidence. He appeared both big and small. I was enchanted, yet flustered and mentally hiding -- and then he wasn't there at all -- until I sought him back in earnest, and he was seated on the wall. I gathered in the pieces of my mind.

"So, your father kicked you out," he said with certainty, and once again my mind went with the wind. But before I could ask how he knew, I began to tell him about a life I imagined living, and the so-called reality in which I felt trapped. He said, "The way out of that room is not through the door." I puzzled and considered trying windows.

"Don't want out," he said, "and you're free. The want ties you up. Be where you are. You got to start some place." He had a cleft chin and a Southern country accent I would later recognize as typically West Virginian, more a strum than a twang. He said that what I wanted OUT of was "thought" rather than "place." Instead of sounding cockeyed, this reminded me of a poem I'd written one sleepless night in a dead-end depression after staring at my grey-and-red-checkered pajamas. Just as children imagine being small enough to walk around the designs in curtains and blankets, I'd found myself on the grey and red checkerboard, trapped in one grey square; I could not cross its borders. Around and round its edges I'd paced like a caged animal, collapsing in one corner "to gnaw the bare bones of despair." But when I'd looked up, within this fantasy, my square had become a diamond; changing my perspective had changed my world.

Within Charlie's laugh, I felt understood. It seemed ironic that it would take a stranger for me to know this comfort.

I was most arrested by his eyes. They knew me. He was a present and active intelligence. I didn't understand it. I didn't know what made his face a comfortable place to rest my eyes. He was an older man, I was sure now, with loose brown curls showing beneath his cap, and a jaw line that could've been used in shaving commercials. He, in fact, had recently shaved, leaving only the stubble of a full mustache to run down the sides of his mouth and connect with the shadow of a goatee. It was not attractive to me, this sandpapery facial hair. It was too bum-like, too much like neglect, but beneath it were decent features; he was neat, and appeared clean.

He knew something about being trapped, he said, because he'd only recently been released after seven and a half years in prison. Then he revealed to me a glimpse of a life spent in and out of confinement, of the hurt, the anger, and the peace he said finally came with knowing and accepting himself. He was going north to see his mother, he told me, and I could come with him if I wished. I thought about my boyfriend, far from that moment, but this man was a complete stranger.

He glanced down the walk; apparently, someone was waiting for him. I struggled with the decision. Finally, he said, "I can't make up your mind for you." He smiled sympathetically and was on his way. I watched him go half a block before grabbing up my bag of books and running to catch up with him.4

Manson, Brunner, and Fromme spent much of the remainder of the spring and summer of 1967 traveling around northern California before eventually arriving in San Francisco's Haight-Ashbury neighborhood where they stayed for a while at a house at 636 Cole Street. Haight-Ashbury, of course, was one of the Meccas of the Counterculture movement.

The Counterculture was already in full flower when Charles Manson was released from prison in late March of 1967. Haight-Ashbury was as different from the world he had left behind when he entered prison almost eight years earlier than a psychedelic-painted Volkswagen bus was to a 1958 De Soto station wagon. Manson later remembered an encounter with a young street person who opened his eyes to the lifestyle being chosen by many of the disaffected young people of the day:

There was this kid, a sixteen-year-old kid. I said, "Where do you sleep?"

He says, "Wherever I lay down."

I said, "Well, don't you have an apartment?"

He said, "No, I sleep in the park."

I said, "How do you do that?"

He said, "Sleeping bag."

I said, "That right? What do you eat?"

He said, "Food."

I said, "Man, where do you get it?"

He said, "Wherever I can."

I said, "Don't you have a job?"

He said, "No, [I get food] down at the Diggers."

So I went and I looked around and I said, "Hey, this is love here. This is love here."5

That summer in San Francisco was the famous "Summer of Love," a cultural and media event resulting from a massive influx of alternatively-minded young people to the city. This influx was caused, in part, by news coverage of such events as the previous year's "Trips Festival," the January 1967 "Be In" at Golden Gate Park, and the Monterey Pop music festival that had been held just down the coast in June. Many people regard the Summer of Love as the apogee of the so-called "hippie" movement. Unfortunately, not long after reaching this lofty peak of experience the petals began to wilt on flower power. And Charles Manson could see it:

> The [love] was happening. But you gotta realize, I came in on the *end* of that. I only went *through* that. I never got stuck up in that, because I seen the pitfalls, I seen the speed freaks. I seen the falling of it.6
>
> When I heard Timothy Leary say, "Tune in and drop out" I knew where [young people] were dropping out *to*, because I had been under that, on the under road, on the backside of what's happening. In other words, in darkness.7

In July of 1967 Manson met a man named Dean Moorehouse by that often-serendipitous practice of hitchhiking. Back in those days people not only picked up hitchhikers but they also sometimes invited them into their homes. Moorehouse brought Manson to his, where Manson met another fellow who gave him a piano. Manson then sold the instrument to a music store. The $1,000 sales proceeds went towards the purchase of a Volkswagen camper van, and before the end of the summer Manson, Brunner, and Fromme climbed into it and drove away from San Francisco.

In September the trio traveled south to Los Angeles. At an apartment in Manhattan Beach, Manson met a young woman named Patricia Krenwinkel. Later, at her trial for murder, Krenwinkel recalled this meeting:

> I was residing in Manhattan Beach with my sister. I was working for an insurance company as a file clerk. I was working like everyone else. I had my apartment, paid my bills, etc.
>
> I had a friend, and one evening I went to his apartment where I saw this man sitting on the floor playing a guitar and singing. He played the

guitar well and he sung beautifully. I sat down and watched him. His name was Charlie. I loved what I saw and I was very happy.

I fell in love with him. Charlie showed me how to love because I had been held in so long. I had been afraid of loving. It was the first time I started to feel free.8

Manson, Brunner, and Fromme returned to San Francisco a few days after their arrival in Los Angeles. Eighteen-year-old Patricia Krenwinkel went with them.

By then the "Summer of Love" was over. On October 6, 1967, barely two weeks after the calendar end of that season, residents of Haight-Ashbury held the "Funeral of Hippie, Son of Mass Media" in Golden Gate Park.

Also by then the Volkswagen camper had become too small for four people to live in, so Manson and the girls got rid of it and bought an old school bus that they converted into a home on wheels. Painted black, the bus had sleeping accommodations, a Coleman-type gas stove, and a sink fed from a water tank in a box on top of it. With this more sufficient rig the group continued its nomadic wanderings.

Back in San Francisco in November of 1967, Manson met Susan Atkins, a twenty-year-old girl who had spent the previous few years adventuring in the Counterculture and in the criminal underworld.

In her book *Child of Satan, Child of God*, Atkins recalled meeting Manson after she ducked into a house while ditching a police tail: "Seated on a couch in front of a bay window was Charles Manson, playing a beat-up old guitar remarkably well and singing in a clear, but soft, voice."

It didn't take Atkins long to make a decision: "After listening to Charlie sing and talk, after dancing with him and making love, after sensing and seeing the power of his mind, I knew I would go with him if he asked me."9

When the black bus left to go back to Los Angeles a few days later, Susan Atkins was on it.

At a 1993 parole hearing, Atkins elaborated on her frame of mind at the time she met Manson, as well as on the circumstances that led up to the meeting. She also explained the reason why she joined him:

I had, though my own actions, been involved in drug abuse for approximately a year to two years prior to my having met Charles Manson. I got involved with drug use and drug abuse, I think, as a product of being just young with no direction.

I had left home at eighteen.... I came from a very dysfunctional family. Again, it's not an excuse, they are just statements of fact. I came from a dysfunctional family of two alcoholic parents. I suffered sexual molestation as a young child from a family member and from people surrounding my family.

When I left home at eighteen I was extremely angry, extremely vulnerable, directionless. And couple that with my own involvement in drug abuse and my own need to be loved and accepted from almost at any cost at that point in time [*sic*], I had become very susceptible to the times.

When I met Charles Manson he was an extremely charismatic individual. He was attractive to me in that all of my experiences up to that point led me to believe that there was absolutely nothing left for me to do. And there was this person who seemed to offer me some hope in a somewhat hopeless situation. And I know [that it] might sound very strange to you, that somebody like Charles Manson would present hope, but he did, to me, at that time.10

Susan Atkin's background was not unique or even uncommon. Many of the people who ended up associating with Charles Manson had experienced trouble in their parents' homes and had previously used alcohol and/or drugs. But now, after meeting Manson, they felt that they could consign these negative experiences to the past. There was a clear realization by Manson and the people around him that it was possible to begin new lives in a new world of their own making. Manson saw this metamorphosis even in himself. As he later said to an acquaintance from that time:

Before I met you, I didn't give a fuck about nobody. I burglarized everybody's pad. I'd do anything I wanted to. I was a terrible person, man. But I paid for all that and I started over.

That's what we were doing. We were a rebirth movement, trying to establish trust, friendship, love, honor, truth -- all the things that we'd lost.

We didn't lose them; our *parents* lost them. So we had to start all over.11

In those early months there was a certain carefree spirit that resulted not only from the new physical freedom that Manson was experiencing after so many years in prison but also from the natural restlessness and adventuresome spirits of the younger people around him. The real story of Charles Manson and his friends is an odyssey, a story of people trying to get out of what they regarded as a hostile and dying way of thought, and away from conventional society. That odyssey would involve many places, characters, and events that gelled into the shared experience of the group. They traveled extensively throughout California, north into Oregon and Washington, and to Arizona, New Mexico, and Texas. Later, as more people attached themselves to the group and easy travel became less practical, there would be more serious considerations and concerns. But for now, people were just coming and going with the flow. Manson:

> I used all the girls that was in the bus, to think. Because I didn't *know*. I'd just got out of prison. I didn't know what the fuck was going on outside. I'd never been outside but a couple of days, two or three times. So, I started using everybody else's head to think. And I wasn't really involved in it.
>
> What we did was, we had a school bus and we left the pink slip in the glove compartment and we let the bus belong to itself, and anybody could come and leave if they wanted to come and leave.12

Manson had learned to play the guitar during his time in prison. Besides playing, he also composed his own songs. In November 1967 he followed up on a contact he had been given at Universal Studios in Los Angeles, and for a while it looked like he might have some kind of future with the show business industry.

Manson actually had several different brushes with the entertainment industry, and "Manson and Hollywood" has become one of the major sub-themes of his saga. One of his early experiences involved a project at Universal where a producer named Gary Stromberg was working on a movie based on the premise that Jesus Christ had returned to Earth as a black man. In a 1970 article in *Rolling Stone* magazine, Stromberg remembered the project and why he wanted Manson's help with it:

> Charlie is very Christ-like and has a Christ-like philosophy. And he was technical advisor to what Christ's position would have been relative to certain things.... [Manson] has a very sophisticated knowledge of Biblical things. He doesn't read, but he seemed well-read. And we would bounce things off Charlie in developing the story.
>
> [But] the movie was never made. Universal hated it, despised it.13

In addition to consulting with Stromberg on the black Jesus film, Manson also made some recordings of his music at Universal. But like the movie deal these never panned out. Manson later said:

> They wouldn't accept my music in Hollywood because they wanted me to feed on the black people.
>
> I thought movies were for entertainment; I never realized it was brainwash. When I wouldn't go for the deal that they offered me, they called me a racist.
>
> They wanted me to use the black people. I said, "I don't use people. Because if I use black people, then black people can use me. I don't use them, therefore I'm not in the will of God to be used back by them. I'm not in that karma. I don't have no bad coming there. *You're* the people that fucked over those people. I haven't fucked over anyone. I don't have that coming."
>
> So they kept playing all kinds of little games with me, trying to get me to do the music the way they wanted me to and when I wouldn't, then they blackballed me from the music. That's when I ended up over there with the Beach Boys.14
>
> So, then when I seen that [working in show business] was a bigger prison than the one I just got out of, I just threw up my hands and said, "Hey, I don't want nothing to do with that." And I think that everybody that was close to me in that time knew that I wasn't trying to get over in that. I had *already* got over in it. I got over and looked at it and said, "Hey, this is not what I want."
>
> I could have did anything I wanted in that studio. I had Universal Studios. I had it. I could have stood up there and took the whole thing, but I didn't have no reason to, then.
>
> They offered it to me and I said, "No, no."
>
> They said, "We can do this and make you so and so."
>
> And I said, "No, no." I was sleeping in Cary Grant's bed, thinking about, "No, this is a bigger prison than the one I got out of." And it *is*.

> You know, it's like, you gotta do more in that perspective [the show business industry] than you do in this perspective [being in prison]. Over here I don't have to do half as much as I do out there. When I'm out there, I gotta work for ten business managers. In here I've gotta work for a couple of cops. So it's a hell of a difference.15

Because they did not have a permanent residence to stay at in Los Angeles the travelers in the black bus frequently parked the vehicle near the intersection of Topanga Canyon Boulevard and the Pacific Coast Highway beside a house that, because it had a circular stairway, was known as the Spiral Staircase House. Here Manson continued to meet people.

One of the people he met was twenty-year-old Robert "Bobby" Beausoleil. Beausoleil was handsome, self-assured, outgoing, flamboyant, and very talented artistically and musically. He was sometimes known as "Cupid," a nickname he acquired as a teenager. Because of their common interest in music, Manson and Beausoleil hit it off very well. Beausoleil later recalled:

> I met Manson shortly after he got out of prison. I think he had been out ten months or so, living in Topanga Canyon.
>
> I joined a band called "The Milky Way" that Charlie was in. That's how I met him. He was a very talented songwriter, good musician, lyrically just excellent. He was somebody with an incredibly intense, vivid, expanded imagination because of all the [prison] time he's done.16

Manson remembered Beausoleil as well. Almost three decades after he met Beausoleil, he still held him in high regard. "Bobby's very good. He's a young genius. I was really impressed by that youngster. He could really get down. He's one of the most magic human beings that I ever met."17

Another person who came into contact with Manson and his group during their stay at the Spiral Staircase House was a thirty-year-old music teacher named Gary Hinman. Hinman lived nearby in a small, two-story house on Old Topanga Canyon Road. Hinman sometimes allowed people to stay at his place. Bobby Beausoleil lived there for a short time.

Still another person Manson met at the Spiral Staircase House was a fourteen-year-old girl name Dianne Lake.

Dianne Lake had already been around before she got to Topanga Canyon. The daughter of "hippie" parents, she was a true child of the decade, having lived in communes, used drugs such as LSD, and participated in group sex when she was barely a teenager. Diane Lake was nicknamed "Snake."

While many people came and went at the Spiral Staircase House, some people came and stayed. One of these latter was seventeen-year-old Nancy Pittman, who was more frequently known as Brenda McCann. Pittman, a pretty, intelligent, and competent girl, later told a jury:

> I first met Charlie on a dirt road. I was walking with a girl, the daughter of [film actress] Angela Lansbury. I think her name was Didi. We approached the bus. They were singing, so I listened, and then I began to talk to Pat. [Susan Atkins] was there, and the others. I felt like they were my sisters. They asked me to stay -- so I stayed forever.18

Soon the group got better living arrangements than a bus parked near a house; they moved into an abandoned residence discovered by Bobby Beausoleil up in Topanga Canyon on Horseshoe Drive. Located in seclusion at the end of the road, this house had a burned-out second floor but still had a kitchen, a couple of bedrooms, a bathroom, and a living room with a fireplace. The house was perfectly adequate for the expanding clan.

Susan Atkins was transformed by her stay at the house on Horseshoe Drive. During a brainstorming session to think up names to use on phony identification cards, the group came up with an alias for her that would later become as well known as her given name. From that moment on she would also be known as "Sadie Mae Glutz."

The group also lived in another house in Topanga Canyon, on Summit Drive. Lyn Fromme later said:

> The other one was a condemned house. It didn't have working plumbing. The landlady didn't have the money to put into it. She had been renting it out, and then she was told by somebody that she couldn't

rent it without the plumbing. The law got on her. And we just moved in. We were squatters.19

Joining these squatters in the spring of 1968 was a carefree, twenty-five-year-old, part-time construction worker from Tennessee named Bruce Davis. In 1993 Davis recalled the chance encounter that would change his life:

> I went with a friend who had borrowed a saw -- or he was borrowing a saw, I don't remember which it was -- so he said, "Hey, I've got to go up on the hill here" -- we were in Topanga – "and get, do some business."…. And he said, "Why don't you come with me?" He said, "This guy up here is really crazy. He's got all these pretty girls around him and all they do is get loaded all day."
>
> Well, that got my attention, and I said, "Oh, yeah! Sure!"
>
> And so that's how I met [Manson].20

In March 1968 a young man named Paul Watkins went to the house on Summit Drive looking for a friend who used to live there. The friend was gone, but inside the house were Charles Manson and about a dozen other people. In a 1989 television appearance Watkins remembered:

> I was a young, seventeen-year-old hippie. I was just out wandering the country, acting out my antisocial tendencies that I had at the time. And I just met some young people up in Topanga and was fascinated by them. There was this little guy that was in charge. He was fascinating, and I became addicted to him.
>
> I was also interested in the music. [Charles Manson] was very talented and animated, and seemed shamelessly uninhibited. He was a trip, as we'd say.21

Watkins stayed one night at the house, then he left to follow an impulse to go north to Big Sur, where he spent the next three months.

A few days after Paul Watkins' overnight visit to the Topanga Canyon house a twenty-four-year-old college student from San Francisco named Sandra Good also showed up and met the group. Good later told an interviewer:

A friend had an airplane that he borrowed from a friend. He was going to L.A. to sell paintings. He asked if I wanted to come along. He spoke incessantly about Manson, [but] all I cared about was going surfing.

I went with the fellow. I met some people with Manson, and Manson -- and I never left. We stayed that evening at the house that Manson and various people were living [in], and I never left that group of people.

What did Good find so appealing about Charles Manson?

He was unlike any person I ever met before. He -- I hate to use the term "blew my mind," but he did. He didn't compute. He was nothing that I could assess with words and put into any kind of category. He sang that evening. His music was different from any music I ever heard. It was almost like he was singing what was inside of my mind that I didn't want exposed, and it put me quite a bit on the point. It made me uncomfortable, to tell you the truth.

I was impressed by the peacefulness of the environment. It was an old, condemned house that they were living in. I was impressed by the harmony and peace in the environment, and by his smile. His eyes, his warmth, and his motions, and his music, I'd say, were the first things that impressed me.22

Almost immediately after Good's arrival on the scene a truly monumental event occurred in the lives of the residents of the Summit Drive house. On April 5, 1968 Mary Brunner gave birth to Charles Manson's child. The delivery, which occurred in the condemned house without the assistance of any medical personnel, had a profound effect on the people who were present to witness it. This shared experience was not only intense because of the spectacle of the birth itself, but also because it added a representative of the next generation to the group. In this child, a boy called variously Sunstone Hawk or Pooh Bear, Manson and the others could see the literal embodiment of the possibilities of their futures.

And the birth had still another effect on the persons who witnessed it: It changed their relationships to each other, bonding and elevating them to a greater level of seriousness and commitment to each other beyond that of just being friends. With the arrival of this child the group became more like a family.

By May of 1968 the people staying in the condemned house were forced to move because the landlady decided to make the repairs necessary to be able to rent it out again. One day Susan Atkins was hitching a ride back to the house from a nearby store. When she mentioned her and her friends' predicament about a place to live the person giving her the ride suggested a place in Chatsworth, a neighborhood in the San Fernando Valley north of Los Angeles, where they might be able to stay. The place was a rundown horse riding ranch and sometime western movie set called Spahn's Movie Ranch. Atkins told her people about the ranch and they decided to check it out. After doing so and getting the okay from the owner, an eighty-year-old blind man named George Spahn, they determined that they could stay there.

Today, Chatsworth has been dramatically developed. Anyone who has not been there since the late 1960s would be dumbstruck by the number of apartment buildings, gas stations, fast food restaurants, and miscellaneous small businesses that have sprung up along Topanga Canyon Boulevard. But even today, the site of Spahn's Ranch (the ranch's buildings burned down in 1970) is an isolated and fairly undisturbed location. As you turn west onto the Old Santa Susana Pass Road (which was the old route to the ranch; Topanga Canyon Boulevard was modified in the early 1990s to direct traffic west at a traffic light farther north up the hill), the scenery quickly changes from ugly urban sprawl to a more open and natural country sparsely settled with small ranches. Although new structures (most notably a church and a housing development) are encroaching on the Spahn's Ranch site, it is still a beautiful, natural, and somewhat isolated area. Manson and the others first arrived there in the mid-spring of 1968.

Manson and his fellow journeyers got more than a place to stay at Spahn's Ranch. They also met people who would join them in their experiences of the next few years. One of these was a fifteen-year-old youth named Steve Grogan. Grogan's family lived nearby in the San Fernando Valley, but he spent most of his time hanging out at the ranch. At a 1981 parole hearing, Grogan later recalled the circumstances that caused him to drop out of mainstream American life:

> What was happening with me was that there was a point in my life where I was being real romantic about the meaning of life. You know, where I was [a] real philosopher, philosophized a lot about life and its meaning, deep meanings in life, my purpose in life, you know, what I imagine every teenager goes through that same period in his life. I took it to the extreme to the extent that I went to different monasteries, various Buddhist monasteries and meditation groups….
>
> Through the use of psychedelics and marijuana I started experiencing or started delving into my mind. The effects the drugs cause, the states of unconsciousness, what that did, when I viewed my parents, I viewed it as a regular boring life, drab everyday run of the mill and I saw no meaning in it. I thought it was plastic. It was just go to work, you die and you're buried and that was it.
>
> I didn't want to -- at that point I thought there was more to life than that. So I was consequently searching and so consequently I would leave the house. I'd visit these different monasteries, encounter groups, communes. I'd learn what they had to say. I was constantly programming myself to different teachings and things like that. Basic format of all those teachings is that you have to unlearn all that you have been programmed in the past so you become in contact with your true self.
>
> So that was my quest and over time it just got more intense. I'd leave for a day or two and I'd leave for a weekend, week at a time, then a month. So it gradually built up so until I finally severed ties and left on my own. I was around fifteen when I left….
>
> It's strange because it was in the period where it seemed like the whole stream of society was in a constant flux, the '60s, you know. All those -- all those different events seemed like [the] string of society's fiber was coming loose or they were being twisted.... Everything was just really unstable. I think the whole country felt like that. At least I felt like that, lot of parents, most people I've talked to.23

Eventually, Grogan's wanderings led him to Spahn's Ranch:

> I was there when I was about fifteen years old and lived in the back. They had a back ranch house that I lived in and I worked odd jobs, guiding tours for riders and cleaning up the ranch and stuff. They'd give me food and clothing. The rent was free. It wasn't really nothing to pay for

rent. It was just an old shack. It had no electricity or hot water or anything. Just a place to rest.24

Another person who was staying at Spahn's when Manson arrived was a twenty-five-year-old army veteran and societal dropout named Thomas J. "T.J." Walleman.

While it has sometimes been alleged that Manson and the other people who ended up living at Spahn's Ranch did so by imposing some sort of duress on George Spahn, this is not true. To make no mistake about it, Spahn's Ranch was run by George Spahn. Charles Manson recognized this reality and willingly accorded the octogenarian ranch owner his due respect:

> George was always, like, he was always the focal point. That's because I've always had a judge over me. I've always had my father there, and procedures that were over me. There's always been someone over me. So when I was out there, I always put George in that spot.25

People continued to come and go. One of the people who came and stayed at this time was an acquaintance of Bobby Beausoleil's named Catherine Share. Share was born in Paris during World War Two, the daughter of members of the French resistance to the German occupation forces. Nicknamed "Gypsy," the twenty-seven-year-old woman was one of the oldest persons in the group. She was intelligent, articulate, and musically talented as a singer and violinist.

It was also at this time that Manson would develop another connection with the entertainment industry besides the ones he had been given earlier at Universal Studios by his prison friend. That spring Patricia Krenwinkel and another young woman, Ella Bailey, were picked up while hitchhiking by a member of one of the most famous pop music bands of the time -- Dennis Wilson, the drummer for the Beach Boys. After Krenwinkel and Bailey told Wilson about their friends, in the spirit of the times he invited them all over to stay at his house. And some of the Spahn's ranch people, also in the spirit of the times, took him up on the offer, arriving and settling in to one of the houses on his property when Wilson was not home.

The story of the association between "the Manson Family" and the Beach Boys has been covered in many works on the case, usually with the theme of Manson and his crowd being evil parasites leeching off the junior member of America's favorite band. But that characterization is a misrepresentation of reality. In her memoirs, Lyn Fromme recalled Wilson as a willing and amiable host:

> [That first night] the master of the house soon returned and was frightened. He did a quavering dance, mocking himself, as he did not even remember Patty and Ella at first. Then he smiled widely in firelight, inviting us to follow him through the patio into the main quarters....
>
> We talked back and forth, sang a little, and after the evening's exchange, Dennis outright invited us to stay. We told him about the black bus, and the many more of us, and he said to "bring them." Whoever claimed later that we had moved into Dennis' house uninvited was either untruthful or uninformed....
>
> He had been living in the house alone, paying thousands of dollars rent per month, and he was rarely ever at home. We filled it up, playing all of his records, the grand piano, and the antique harpsichord, swimming in the pool, and between the satin sheets....
>
> He was likable and funny without trying to be, loose, whimsical, and with few reservations, but his body was reserved under contract to the music group made up partly of his blood brothers. He said that he wanted to break those ties to go with us on the road or into the wilderness, so we waited between the bus and the house, exploring the short woods between fences....
>
> We were there, yet not there. And it was nice.26

Dennis Wilson extended his hospitality to others than the folks in the black bus. Another house guest who would later associate off and on with Manson was a young man from Texas named Brooks Poston.

And then, still in the spring of 1968, yet another Texan chanced upon Wilson's Sunset Boulevard estate. This refugee from the Lone Star State was a twenty-two-year-old part-time wig salesman and marijuana dealer named Charles Watson. Watson had picked up Dennis Wilson as the latter was hitchhiking home one day on Sunset Boulevard. At the house, Wilson invited Watson inside and introduced him to one of his current house guests, Dean

Moorehouse. As Watson later wrote in his book *Will You Die For Me?*:

> Almost as soon as I came in [Moorehouse] said there was somebody I should meet in the living room. I followed him. There he was surrounded by five or six girls -- on the floor next to the huge coffee table with a guitar in his hands. He looked up, and the first thing I felt was a sort of gentleness, an embracing kind of acceptance and love.
>
> "This is Charlie," Dean said. "Charles Manson."27

After this introduction, Watson settled in for the evening. He smoked hashish, ate food, and listened as Manson played his guitar and sang. Watson liked the whole scene:

> Here I was, accepted in a world I'd never even dreamed about, mellow and at my ease. Charlie murmured in the background, something about love, finding love, letting yourself love. I suddenly realized that this was what I was looking for; love.... the kind of love that didn't ask you to do anything, didn't judge what you were, didn't set up any rules or regulations -- the kind of love that just accepted you, let you be yourself, do your thing whatever it was.... It occurred to me that all the love in the room was coming from him, from his music.
>
> We all lay back and listened to Charlie sing to us about love -- make love to us and for us with his music. I'd never known such peace.
>
> Charlie Manson was the first person I'd met who really knew what love was all about.28

Not all of Manson's friends stayed at Dennis Wilson's house, however. In June of 1968 Mary Brunner, Susan Atkins, Patricia Krenwinkel, and Sunstone Hawk drove the black bus to Mendocino County, almost five hundred miles north of Los Angeles. Part of the reason for going there was to find a possible home for the ever-growing group. (Brunner was familiar with the area, having spent some time there in 1967 with Manson and Lynette Fromme.) Soon, word of the quartet's adventures got back to the people who were still staying at Dennis Wilson's house. But the word wasn't good.

Apparently, someone in the group had dispensed some LSD to a local youth who got so high that the police were called. Once the cops became aware of the source of the LSD they visited the house where Brunner, et. al. were residing and took everyone there into custody. The "Witches of Mendocino," as Brunner, Atkins, and Krenwinkel soon became known, were booked into jail on charges of possession of marijuana and LSD and for distributing a dangerous drug. Sunstone Hawk was turned over to Manson's parole officer and his wife, and the girls settled in for the summer as guests of the Mendocino County Sheriff's Department.

Manson asked Dennis Wilson for funds to bail the girls out, but Wilson explained that his money was tied up in investments and couldn't be used for such a purpose. Manson and the others didn't press him for the money, and the girls remained in jail awaiting the outcome of their cases.

Besides the rest of the Beach Boys band, Manson met other show business people during his time at Wilson's house. In addition to meeting performers, he also met people who worked in the background of the industry, people like talent scout Gregg Jakobson and television and music producer Terry Melcher, who was the son of Doris Day. When Manson met Melcher the latter was living in Bel Air at 10050 Cielo Drive, a property that would later be rented by Roman Polanski and his wife Sharon Tate.

Jakobson spent much time with Manson and found him to be a fascinating individual. He later recalled Manson as "intellectually stimulating.... It was rare to find a man who believed his convictions as strongly as Charlie did -- who couldn't be swayed."29

Jakobson was convinced that Manson and his lifestyle were a marketable commodity. He put quite a bit of effort into trying to interest someone in the show business industry with the whole Charles Manson "package," but he had little success.

Manson did not find a niche in the entertainment industry for several reasons, but a main reason was that show business people were clearly not cut from the same cloth as Charles Manson and his associates. As Manson later put it:

> In the music world, in Hollywood, in L.A., you have people out front. I don't playact, like the *Playboy* magazine type, you dig? We live over in the mountains. We don't playact.
>
> When we play music we take all our clothes off and we all set big fires and we all love each other. We all dance. We dance all night. And

we party all night. We live in tipis. We live by campfires. We live like nomads. We live out in the mountains and we play music so powerful that all these other people from Hollywood, they just run in fear because their ears just break. They want to go crazy because, like, the music we play, we're not playing for the market. The market plays for little girls. We're not playing that kind of music.

We're playing music to change the world. We're playing to God. We're playing the same kind of music that they're playing in the prayer temples at Mecca, only we got it in English.

But we have to hide [our songs] because they're considered criminal. We gotta go out in the mountains and play music in the darkness. We gotta get out into Death Valley and play in the desert, because if they see us they want to call us devils and they want to call us Satan worshippers and all that kind of crazy shit.30

Even though Charles Manson had little interest in exploiting his talents for money, music was still ingrained in him, and while he was moving in the show business circles around Dennis Wilson he sometimes played with people who were in the entertainment industry. The Beach Boys took one of Manson's songs called "Cease to Exist" and transformed it into their own "Cease to Resist." The group not only changed the title of the song, but they also changed some of the words, greatly altering the meaning and soul of Manson's original composition. Although "Cease to Resist" was eventually released as a B side to the single "The Bluebirds Flew Over the Mountain" and on the album *20/20*, Manson never received any royalties for his music and lyrics or even a song writing credit on the released work. These omissions of even the most basic business practices and courtesies, as well as the Beach Boys' mangling of the music, served to further alienate Manson and some of the people around him from those in the entertainment industry.

Manson learned a lot from his experiences with Universal Studios and his exposure to the people around the Beach Boys. And the main thing that he learned was that he wanted no part of their world. As he later recalled:

That's what Brian Wilson asked me one day. He says, "How come you would rather shovel shit than play music with the Beach Boys?" He said, "Man, we're offering you five thousand dollars to come and play music with us, and you would rather shovel shit."

And I said, "Well, that's just about where my mind is. I'd rather live behind that horse's ass, and shovel his shit, than I would put up with that other bullshit."31

As the weeks went by, it became apparent that the living arrangements at Dennis Wilson's house could not go on forever. Lyn Fromme later wrote:

> Increasingly we were perceived by Dennis' managers and advisors as a threat to them. Dennis said he told them he wanted time away from the business to camp and be inspired, and they pulled harder on him.
>
> Dennis and Charlie walked the grounds, comrades of many moods. Charlie asked Dennis if he wanted us to leave, and Dennis insisted not, but each time he declared he was going to take a vacation to travel with us, he only got wound up tighter, and, in turning, looped himself into even more commitments....
>
> Twice Dennis told us he would be home for dinner, and the rest of us waited, and he didn't come, so the next day we left the estate and went back to the valley, where the land is flat and wide, to the foothills above the smog line, to The Ranch.32

After weeks of experiencing "the good life" of show business personalities, the group was glad to get back to the more natural way of living at Spahn's Ranch. Lynette Fromme:

> As we became, and have always become what is around us, The Ranch gave us texture. The sharp rocks and smooth stones, the sticks and grasses beneath our bare feet, the hoot of an owl, even the distant scent of a skunk all added dimension to our experience. The sun heated the mountain boulders above us by mid-morning, and rattlesnakes lay between them. In the deep, cooler places along the creek beneath thick-trunked oaks were shade and dark, moist dirt that felt and smelled good, but also insects, spiders, and poison oak to keep us aware. The medicinal scent of eucalyptus trees cut through the summer humidity, and their rattling signaled a welcome breeze to otherwise sweltering afternoons.33

This last paragraph of Fromme's demonstrates more than just her good attention to detail. It also shows an appreciation and awareness of the natural world that was also apparent to Manson and many of his companions.

Although there was some environmental awareness by the late 1960s, it was not such an issue of urgency that it took precedence in the minds of many people who were already overloaded with the other issues of the day, such as the war in Vietnam or the various social movements.

But the Spahn's Ranch people were an exception to this. They already had an acute awareness of the destruction of the natural world. For them, living on the fringes of society also meant living on the fringes of society's development, and from that vantage point they could see not only the beauty and perfection of the natural world but also the seemingly insane way in which society appeared to be willing to sacrifice that world in order to make money and perpetuate its own over-indulgent and wasteful lifestyle.

Los Angeles was already greatly polluted before the late 1960s. Cars were everywhere, and smog was an unpleasant reality that most people seemed willing to accept as a necessary part of their way of life. Already large areas of the San Fernando Valley around Chatsworth were falling prey to developers. There was even a housing subdivision being built perilously close to Spahn's Ranch.

In such a context, the way of life of most people in society appeared to be more of a way of death to many of the people at Spahn's Ranch, and they thus had one more important reason to recoil from the ugly excesses of American culture, a culture that they viewed as growing rich and fat off of industries that polluted and destroyed life. Because of their own experience, Manson and the people around him knew that there was a way for people to live on the planet without destroying it. Having lived on the road, in the woods, in abandoned buildings, and in the rustic conditions of Spahn's Ranch, they knew that it was possible to live in healthy harmony with their natural surroundings without exploiting and wrecking it. This realization eventually became one of the major foundations of their shared philosophy, and it also became one of the main reasons for their estrangement from mainstream society.

And still another thing that set Manson and his friends apart from the mainstream of American thought was their attitude towards race.

Race consciousness became a predominant aspect of life for many people in the latter half of the 1960s, and especially so for minorities like blacks and American Indians. For the first time these people started to realize and react to the crimes that had been committed against them by the white man, such as the uprooting and enslavement of the Africans and the campaigns of land theft and genocide against Native Americans.

Manson and his circle were aware of these counts against their kind, and they also believed in a karmic balance wherein the white man could eventually fall from the top and pay for his past transgressions. But by turning their backs on the way of life that had caused those past atrocities they felt that they could begin to turn that karma back to a positive direction.

Many whites of the time regarded their own race as emotionally and spiritually stiff, and in comparison to other races they felt soulless. They also yearned for the earthiness and togetherness that blacks, Hispanics, and other minorities demonstrated. The Spahn's Ranch people, however, realized that they already had soul within themselves, and as they discovered the beauty and perfection in themselves they began to bond together as a tribe of evolved and transcendent white people who were in touch with the Earth and with each other.

By July 1968 Paul Watkins was back on the scene. His situation at Big Sur had deteriorated, so he decided to leave and return to Los Angeles. One day while he was hitchhiking near Topanga Canyon he was picked up by Nancy Pittman and Diane Lake. Recognizing Watkins, the girls invited him to visit them at Spahn's Ranch. Watkins did, and he eventually moved onto the property.

On August 16 the Witches of Mendocino were finally released from custody. Some of the charges against them were dropped and others were reduced to such an extent that the punishment meted out by the court was time already served in the county jail. Deciding that Mendocino County might not be such a good place to relocate after all, they immediately headed south and joined the other people at Spahn's Movie Ranch.

Not long after this, Susan Atkins gave birth to a son, and another child was added to the growing colony. Like the birth of

Sunstone Hawk, Atkins' delivery was a communal affair that had an intense and unifying effect on the people who witnessed it.

Also at about this time another person showed up at the ranch -- Charles Watson.

While Charles Watson has frequently been described as one of the core members of "the Family" and even as Charles Manson's "chief lieutenant," in reality he was a somewhat marginal figure at Spahn's Ranch, a part-time resident who frequently came and went between there and Los Angeles, where he had another full and complex life.

Charles Watson first arrived in Los Angeles in August of 1967. Settling in in Hollywood, he supported himself by selling wigs in a salon in Beverly Hills and by dealing marijuana. By the spring of 1968 he had moved to Malibu. Driving there from Hollywood one night he picked up Dennis Wilson, who invited him to his house on Sunset Boulevard. There, Watson met Charles Manson and some of his associates. A few weeks after this meeting, Watson moved into Wilson's house.

He stayed there until August 1968, when Wilson himself moved out of the house. With nowhere else to go, Watson went to the movie ranch in Chatsworth. When he was introduced to George Spahn the ranch owner recognized his Texas accent and gave him the nickname "Tex."

For his first several weeks at Spahn's Watson lived apart from the others in a tent down the hill behind the main ranch buildings. But after a while he moved closer to Manson and the others. He stayed with them for a few months, even going with them to the desert at the end of October 1968. But he left by late November when he had to report for his selective service exam in Los Angeles.

Watson failed the exam and was spared a military experience, but he remained in L.A. He also met and moved in with a woman who soon fell in love with him. Eventually the couple even became engaged. They supported themselves mostly by selling LSD and pot.

This situation lasted for several months, after which time Watson grew tired of his fiancée's possessiveness. He yearned for the carefree life he remembered from his time at Spahn's Ranch. In March 1969 he returned to the ranch but did not become a full-time resident. He continued to move back and forth between Chatsworth and Hollywood well into the summer.

In late August 1968 Bobby Beausoleil also again crossed paths with Manson and some others while they were on a road trip in the black bus. At the time Beausoleil was living in an apartment in Hollywood with his partner Gail and an eighteen-year-old girl named Leslie Van Houten. Van Houten would later remember that encounter on the road:

> Bobby, Gail, and I went to San Jose. There we met a man working in a tattoo shop, who had mistaken Gail and I as two other girls whom he had just left and who had been stranded on a broken school bus. Charlie was there. I was attracted to the group because of the great freedom and happiness, so we stayed [with them] in a prune orchard in San Jose. Eventually, we all moved to the Spahn Ranch.34

Van Houten recalled that when she met Manson, "He just walked up and smiled real nice, you know, and I smiled back. And he wasn't any different than all the others. But I could feel much strength in meeting him. I felt very good feelings towards him."35

In early September 1968 Paul Watkins was picked up hitchhiking by a young woman named Juanita Wildebush. Wildebush was on her way to Mexico with a new camper van and several thousand dollars from an inheritance. Watkins convinced her to stay overnight at Spahn's Ranch. She ended up staying for months, donating both her van and her inheritance money to the common kitty of the group.

Wildebush's beneficence was not unusual. Many times during their time together the Spahn's Ranch people received resources and funding from individuals who wanted to help them or who were simply generous. Very often these gifts were in turn redistributed or given away almost as soon as they were acquired.

Of course, Charles Manson came into contact with many, many people during his wanderings. Some he knew only briefly.

Others stayed with him much longer. Why did some of the people who entered Manson's orbit choose to stay? What were some of the reasons that kept many of these people together? Besides a common disenchantment with society and similar philosophies regarding the environment and race, a bond also formed between many of them because of their shared experiences.

Susan Atkins later said that she stayed because:

> There was an image of communal love and companionship and camaraderie. And the image was born out of love -- free love and loving one another. In the -- if you remember back in the late '60s there were a lot of communes, all over the country. Particularly out here in the West Coast. And we were nothing more than a commune, to begin with.
>
> And again, if you remember I said there were a lot of undercurrent things that were happening, but I think in our hearts each person that was there just wanted to feel like they belonged somewhere. That all we had -- everybody that was at Spahn's Ranch didn't start out at Spahn's Ranch, but everybody that had culminated and come together -- I think we each wanted just to feel loved and to feel a part of a family environment, because we had all come from broken homes or dysfunctional homes.36

Bruce Davis later told a California parole board:

> I was looking for acceptance, to be part of this family. As I think about it, you know, in retrospect, I think being part of this group of people was what I was looking for, a family I never had.
>
> At first when I met Manson and the rest of the people, the agenda was entirely [different] than it had become later on.... It was like just sort of free love, drugs, and -- you know -- living on the fringes of society. But there was no crime, no murder, no violence involved.
>
> I adopted Manson in a sense, because when I first met him I was treated as an equal person. I was treated with some degree of respect that I'd never gotten from my father.37

Leslie Van Houten remembered her life at the ranch:

> It was like having my very own country house, my own home place. It was a good feeling, just existing.

I loved the ranch life in contrast to the city life. I felt the city was a big monster -- noise, car horns, people rushing, etc., in contrast to the peaceful life where only the sniffing of horses or roosters in the morning can be heard. The same when I went to the desert, where only the humming of the wind is what one can hear. I only went to the city to get food. At the ranch I would stay and bake bread, wash diapers. I hardly went out.

It was a very down home place where you had to pump water in the morning so you would have water in the evening, and it was a good feeling. It was a good feeling of just existing, being with your brothers and sisters is what it was. Nothing was hard labor. Even when we had to dig a hole and put a big water pipe in, it was still fun to do it. Everything was.38

In many ways, life at Spahn's Ranch *was* fun. Charles Watson later wrote:

We were children at play, living the fantasies we made. It was, as the Beatles sang, a "Magical Mystery Tour," and Charlie was our guide.... We'd change our roles constantly. One day we'd dress up like cowboys, the next night we might be Leslie's mountain folk, the day after that we were cool Hollywood types in soft shirts and sunglasses.39

Charles Manson also remembered the "Magical Mystery Tour":

I have to explain to you what the MMT [Magical Mystery Tour] means. The Magical Mystery Tour is an album that the Beatles came out with. And everybody was listening to their music as we were moving along in our bus, doing what we were doing. (Sings) "Eight days a week, we love you." You know. And like, all of those children were growing up again.

The MMT was a fantasy that we would play at the ranch. Like we would play cowboys sometimes. We'd dress up like cowboys. And we would playact like we were in that era, in that time, like little children. Then we would dress up and get some motorcycles and ride around and drink beer and talk trash, you know.

So, I was playing Hollywood Business one day, and then I'd go over and play rancher and put on a Gabby Hayes and walk around. I had a pistol and everybody knew I'd shoot 'em if they got in my way or started fucking with me or disrespecting me in any way.

So, we would play like Indians, and we had a little Indian set with wickiups and tipis. Then I had three bathtubs from Brazil in the [creek] bed, that I'd flown over the mountain, for laying around, smoking them nice cigars. And having a good day.

So, nobody was anybody in particular. We was all playacting. It's an MMT. It's a joke. It's like, somebody makes a move and everybody turns into cowboys. And then somebody else makes a move and everybody goes back and puts their motorcycle guy on.

It was a game up until where Tex brought reality into play, with money. We wasn't dealing in money. We wasn't even bothering with it. It was a drag. You had to slow down for it, you know? The garbage was better. I had the Rolls Royce, and I had the money, and I thought, "No, that's a worse MMT than the other MMT."

In other words, I had that surfboard. I had that Hollywood. But I said, "This is no survival. This is total destruction." I said, "We're never gonna get back to the land playing 1943 detectives."

That was the MMT. It was a fantasy dream. It was a Helter Skelter nightclub, that we played with.40

Some people stayed at Spahn's Ranch, but people left as often as they stayed. And not only did casual acquaintances come and go, but practically all of the people who would later become known as hard-core "Manson Family members" -- people like Charles Watson, Susan Atkins, Patricia Krenwinkel, Leslie Van Houten, Mary Brunner, Bruce Davis, Bobby Beausoleil, Sandra Good, Cathy Gillies, and even Charles Manson himself -- all of these people left the circle at various times in 1968 and 1969.

Manson put few conditions on anyone, including himself:

I never committed myself to anyone. I've never said, "I want you to be mine, I'm yours." I never said, "Let's do this...."
I never committed myself to anyone and I never asked anyone to commit themselves to me.

I go out in the desert and sit down. Squeaky [Lyn Fromme] comes out and she says, "Hi."

I says, "Hi."

She says, "Do you want me to come with you?"

I says, "I don't care what you do."

She said, "I'll come with you if you want me to."

I said, "Well, if you want to, come on."

I never went around and asked anyone to come with me. I may have -- maybe one or two people I may have asked to come with me. But I never asked people to go out of their way to do *anything* that they don't want to do. I never ordered people to do a damn thing. I never even told the dog to do nothing.

I never held onto anyone. I never even as much as asked anyone, "Do you want to go with me?" When I'd get up to go somewhere I'd get up and monkey around and let everybody know I was going, and I'd go. If anybody was there, they'd be there. I'd put my bus hat on, walk back and forth a few times. If you wanted to go, you'd be in the bus. If not, then I'll see you later.

I never held anyone against their will for a second about anything. Everybody on that ranch was totally free to be and go and do anything they wanted to do. It was none of my business. I never tried to make you into anything.

Maybe I should have.41

Manson disputed the notion that he was the leader of this group of friends, or that he was consciously directing them in any of their activities:

The ranch was not centered on me. I was just a finger on the ranch hand. I was a reflection of everyone else. All I was doing was reflecting.

You know where my mind was? On a motorcycle, with a sleeping bag, and I was not thinking about having no group of people. I was not incorporating any gang of anyone. I didn't have a "Family." It was just a bunch of people that just followed the music around....

It was a circle of thoughts. And everybody had their own perspective of it. Then no one can put it off on me and say I was the leader or something like that....

All I [offered at] the ranch was another hand. I wasn't the brains behind anything, no more than anyone else. I offered my opinion, like everyone else did. And we correlated those opinions and made moves on everything that needed to be done. I didn't make a conspiracy to clean the barn out. The horses done that, when they shit all over the floor.

Does that ring in your mind as being true? If you look back on what happened, did I appear like I was directing traffic in some direction for some abstract reason, other than just being real for the day?

I just live in the day and I tell you what you tell me back. You're honest with me, and you tell me, "One, two, three," and somebody else tells me, "Six, seven, eight," and somebody else tells me, "Nine, ten." And then I put it all together and say, "One, two, three, four, five, six, seven, eight, nine, ten." Is that me saying it? Or am I just reflecting the minds of everyone around me?42

Manson later explained to a friend from that time how he viewed his life at Spahn's Ranch and his position in it:

> When you go through all of the all [of prison], and you get out on the dark side of the hobo, and you're walking down the dark side of the line, and you meet a bunch of kids that were throwed away, you dig? And all these throwed away kids, nobody wants 'em. So you say, "Well, okay, I'll walk with you, you know. I'll help you."
>
> And then they give you their worlds and then you try to put their worlds together and help 'em with their worlds, you dig? And then you say, "Well, I've already got my world on the ground. I don't need anything society's got [in order for me] to survive, I can survive out here on the edge of nowhere doing nothing," you know? I just set around and feed on fucking flies, if nothing else. I can eat cockroaches, or *anything*. In other words, I'm just another bug.
>
> So then I come and help you all, and then you guys give me, "Well, we don't want the war, we don't want nuclear power, we don't want, we don't want all the way down the line," so all I'm doing is trying to balance each and every world that was on that ranch.
>
> All you people had me in tow. I didn't have you in tow. I wasn't making nobody do nothing. You were all making me do it with being decent to me. You seen things in me that I didn't see in myself.
>
> You guys were my brothers. You were like brothers to me. You weren't my girlfriend or my wife. You were more like my brother, my road dog, my partners. You weren't over me or under me, you were *with* me. I wasn't trying to misuse any of you. I was trying to do the best for all of you.
>
> You know my trip; I didn't *have* any trip. I was off on *you guys'* trip. I was just doing whatever you guys were doing, you know. I was just there. I'm dumber than all you guys. I don't know why you try to make me into some kind of leader. I wasn't leading nobody doing anything. Not really.
>
> The first world that was on that ranch was the horses. The second world was George. The horses and George. Next was the walking stick. And then I come down for the dogs, and then I come down for the cats and the birds and the bugs and the chickens. And then I come down from the chickens, and the last chicken in line, and then I come from

[Sunstone Hawk]. And then I go to Mary and I go to Leslie and Patty and Susie and Brucie and then Tex and Rex.

My priority was at the bottom first. I've always lived upside-down. And I always think backwards.

All I was, was, I was a child without a mother. I was a child without no parents. I was a child left over the edge. I was just, uh, the same thing as Jesus. I was a street kid. I was nothing. I was a garbage dump.

So, when you guys met me, you seen good guy in me, and I said, "Oh, I'm a good guy?"

And you said, "Yeah."

And I said, "Okay, I'll be good guy for *you*. You *know* I'll be. You said I'm love? Okay, I'll be love for *you*, but that's not really what I am."

There ain't nobody but your*self* in love. 'Cause love gives but itself, takes not but *from* itself, possesses not, and nor will it be possessed, because it's sufficient *to* itself. Love is one. And I'm the one with that love on that ranch, with those marks and those dogs and those horses and my Lord George. Period.

When we were in now at the ranch, we were now. We lived in now. And now is eternal. We live right now. There is no time in my mind. I live right now. I've been right now ever since 1934. And I'm still right now. And I don't really have all those considerations that you have. Those considerations that you have is what you got from your mother.

You and I, and the people at the ranch, we've had a place that we could give our loyalty to. We've had a center, a circle of each other, to where we had somebody that was holding their loyalty to us, so we held our loyalty to them.

We were supposed to be, and represent, a rebirth movement. We were reborn -- not into the same old graveyard, not into the same old death trap. We started a rebirth movement. That rebirth movement was *ours*. It came from our mind. It is ours. It's our God. It's our church. It's our wedding ring. It's our life. It's our world. And *anyone* that obstructs that, is fucking with our justice. And our justice is the same justice that Thomas Jefferson and Alexander Hamilton and all them guys laid out in the Constitution of the United States of America. "The land of the free and the home of the brave" and all that.

Outside the ranch, I don't know about that. That's somebody else's dream. As long as they don't come up fucking with me and mine and my shit, whatever they do is none of my business. As long as they don't splash over on me, I ain't gonna bother nobody. If they come fucking with me, I'll do the same thing I always did. I'll do whatever I have to do to protect me and mine and my own.

Here's the bottom line on this whole thing. We got peace on earth at that ranch. We had it. We didn't have to go off of there. It wasn't my problems that took us down the road. I'm still at the ranch. I'm still there, and the horses are still there. And old man George is still there, and I got his cane.

It's right now. It's the same now that was then. That now is right now.43

Manson remembered the horses at Spahn's Ranch with a special fondness:

I never paid that much attention to the broads, man. I was more into the horses and the animals than I was the girls.

I used to be setting on the haystack, and all the horses would be over on the side, and I'd just be setting there, and all of a sudden I'd look up and there's a horse would have come over and stuck their head over the fence, right next to me, maybe about three inches from me, just right next to my head.

And I used to trip, and I used to think, "Man, I wonder why them horses are always doing that to me?"

And when I got on Death Row I set back and I looked at a picture of a horse and said, "They must have gave me some approval. There must be a sign of "You're okay, man, like we'll put our heads over in your thought." And they put their head over next to me....

I lived in the horses' heads. I got eighty-three horses there. And I lived in their heads. As much as I lived in *your* heads, I lived in the horses' heads. And as much as I lived in the horses' heads I lived in the goats' heads. I lived in the mules' heads. I lived in the hawks' heads and the birds' heads. I lived in everyone's heads, because I truly don't have a head of my own. I was raised up running from head to head, looking for my father, my mother, my sister, my brother, my family.

Yeah, I liked the horses. There's a circle of horses with Xs on their foreheads....44

Manson learned lessons from the horses that he applied to his relationships with people:

Remember that Roadrunner I used to have? Whenever I would have any problem with anyone, like Danny or them motorcycle guys want to start some shit, I'd just get 'em in the car and I'd drive over the pass, over to that store on the other side of Santa Susana Pass Road, and I'd get a pack of cigarettes and drive back, you dig?

But when I would drive over there, I would drive so fast, and so close to the edge of those cliffs, that when I got there the guy would generally -- if they didn't puke all over himself -- he would just freeze. He would be frozen dead in fear. I'd have to shake him to bring him back. And then generally they wouldn't get in the car with me to come back.

So then I knew, I would *use* fear.

Like Major? The horse Major? Major taught me that. What I would do was, I would get on Major and Major would get up on the road next to those cars, and them trucks and cars would be coming down the road and Major would be running as fast as he could right down next to those trucks and cars, and then he'd look back at me with one eye. As he was running he'd look back at me, and he'd act like he was gonna buck me off right in front of those trucks, you dig? And he'd look at me like saying, "You stay off my fucking back, motherfucker."

So whenever I would ride back with Major, I would put him back in the barn, and I wouldn't ride that horse again unless I felt real dangerous. Because Major not only was a mean, tough horse, Major was a maniac horse. He was a mean horse. I never met a horse as bad as Major.

So, that's what I would do. I'd get in that Roadrunner, you dig, and I'd put somebody in that Roadrunner and I'd take 'em for a ride right next to death. And when I got there, those people would be trembling, and they'd leave me alone.

That's what that horse showed me.45

Besides taking possible troublemakers on rides next to death, Manson had other methods of dealing with potentially dangerous situations and persons. His habit of handing a gun to someone and offering to let them shoot him has been recounted many times. But there was a practical, down to earth aspect to this "kill me -- kill you" routine:

When I used to give them guys that gun -- when I'd hand 'em the gun and tell them, "Go ahead and shoot me" -- there'd be four empty chambers. They'd have to pull the trigger four times. And by the time they did that, I'd have 'em in the mud, man.46

These last two reminiscences on Manson's part, however, point to some of the problems that began to plague the ranch dwellers' hoped-for idyll, for even with its relative isolation and security Spahn's Ranch could be a disharmonic place. There was simply too much interaction with other humans. People from outside the ranch showed up and caused trouble, and sometimes people at the ranch brought trouble on themselves. Manson remembered Susan Atkins as a particular problem:

> Susie would go to the store, and suck somebody's dick on the way to the store, and then come back and suck somebody's dick on the way back, and then there'd be four or five guys hanging around the parking lot, you know?
>
> And then she'd steal somebody's hash. She stole five hundred dollars worth of hash and come and give me a hundred dollars worth. And then three bikers like to tore my head off:
>
> "Where'd you get that hash at?"
>
> I said, "I got it from wherever I got it. My connection. Why? You want some of it? Sit down."
>
> "Well, that's ours."
>
> "What do you mean 'ours'?"
>
> "That girl called Susie stole our hash. You know the girl called Susie?"
>
> "Well, there's a lot of girls around here. I don't know...."
>
> In other words, she did that shit to see if I was gonna tell on her, you know. [But I didn't run her off the ranch] because I didn't have enough sense to do that. I didn't say "no." I just let everybody be themselves. I didn't -- I never said come or go. I said, "You know, if you tell the truth, hang around. If you lie, get up on that road."47

Besides these problems there was also attention from the police, who were suspicious of the large number of free-living people at the ranch. Law enforcement authorities, usually in the form of the Los Angeles County Sheriffs Office, frequently hassled Manson and the others, either pulling them over on the roads around the ranch or going onto the property itself on one pretext or another.

So while Manson and his friends generally enjoyed their lives at Spahn's, after several months it became impractical and uncomfortable to remain there. They needed another place to stay.

One member of the group, Catherine "Capistrano" Gillies, knew of a vacation ranch owned by her grandmother, Barbara Myers. This ranch was located about 150 miles northeast of Los

Angeles, high up in isolated Goler Wash in the Panamint Mountains west of Death Valley.48

The Myers Ranch sounded like a good alternative to the increasingly hectic, confusing, and dangerous life in L.A., so the group decided to check it out. They left Spahn's Ranch and drove in the bus to Death Valley in the last days of October, 1968.49

Goler Wash was (and is) a steep, narrow canyon that made its way through the Panamint Mountains for about six miles, from Mengel Pass at the crest of the mountain range down to an alluvial fan which spread out onto the Panamint Valley floor. The lower few miles of the wash wound around sharply down through an increasingly steep and narrow area that was frequently devastated by flash floods. Although mining operations sometimes kept the road fairly easy to travel on, in 1968-69 it was practically impassable unless a person was driving a well-equipped four-wheel-drive vehicle and had experience in backcountry driving.

There was no way that a school bus could make it up Goler Wash, so the group parked it on the alluvial fan at the mouth of the wash and began to hike the five miles up to Myers Ranch. While the road might have been too much for most vehicles, it was not a particularly difficult walk. But even so the travelers stopped and spent their first night at the Newman Cabin, a one-room wood plank structure located on a prospector's claim not quite halfway up the canyon. The next day they proceeded to their final destination.

Myers ranch was a collection of a few cabins and outbuildings and a small trailer that sat under cover of Tamarisk and Cottonwood trees watered by ample springs on the property. It was a true oasis, a green gem of life in the midst of some of the most forbidding and desolate country on the planet. About a half mile away, under a similar cover of spring-fed trees, was the Barker Ranch, a smaller and more run-down settlement that was generally abandoned unless a prospector or other desert visitor chose to encamp there. These two ranches, virtually inaccessible and surrounded by miles of uninhabited desert, seemed to be the perfect new residence for Charles Manson and his friends.

Much has been written and said about Charles Manson and the desert. His final arrest at the Barker Ranch has been covered in detail in numerous books and has been the subject of several television programs and video documentaries. Even today the area is still frequently visited by curious people who want to see the scene of that arrest.50

A Los Angeles Deputy District Attorney later claimed that Manson chose Goler Wash as "the Family's" hideout after the Tate/LaBianca murders. But actually Manson and his group had already spent much time in the area many months before those murders and had selected the Barker Ranch as a possible place to settle long before any violence occurred in L.A.51

Today, one thing that immediately strikes any visitor to the Goler Wash area is just how remote a place it actually is. It is really out there. The nearest paved road is twenty-five miles away and the first town is twenty-five miles beyond that. (That town isn't big enough to have a traffic light.) Goler Wash is an extremely remote place. The area suited Charles Manson perfectly:

> When I went out in the desert and I looked up in the sky, man, I spent twenty-two years in solitary confinement since I was ten years old. And when I went out in the desert and I looked up in the sky, my mind took off. I was no longer in darkness, man. All them stars became my mind.52

The desert was a Garden of Eden for Manson and his fellow travelers, and they spent the next several months in the area, exploring and enjoying. Perhaps inevitably, the desert also became the setting for several supposed Manson "miracles" which have become part of the folklore of his case. Several people have recalled Manson's friendly familiarity with rattlesnakes. In *Will You Die For Me?* Charles Watson wrote, "I once saw [Manson] walk through a gully of rattlesnakes, gliding among them and touching them gently on the tails. None of them struck."53

But Manson had an explanation other than divine protection or magical ability that could account for his easy affinity with poisonous reptiles:

> The coyote don't know that you're scared of the snake. So you take a pillow to the desert, right? Let the snake bite the pillow. When the snake

bites the pillow, he ain't got no poison left. Then you can pick him up and do whatever you want to do with him. Then you don't have to be afraid. Yeah. And then when you find out that you really don't have to be afraid of him, and you get over the fear of him, then you don't even need the pillow.54

Another miracle, supposedly, was how Manson later drove the large school bus to Barker Ranch in Goler Wash. If it had been driven in up the wash it might have been a miracle, but Manson brought the bus in a back way via Warm Springs Canyon and Mengel Pass. While this latter route was still very rough, it would not have been a miraculous feat for a determined driver to beat a bus in over the twisting, rocky route -- and Manson did just that.

The newcomers got along fine with the other people who also inhabited the sparsely populated area. One of those other people, gold miner Emmett Harder, was impressed with the cleanliness and strong work ethic of the group. "I found Charlie Manson to be a dedicated person, dedicated to taking care of the people camping with him," Harder later recalled to a grand jury.55 In his 2001 memoirs of his desert life, Harder especially recalled one encounter with some of the females who were with Manson:

One day, later, when I happened to stop by the Barker camp on the way to town I found one of the women there, who was dressed in a pink, frilly outfit, swinging in an old weathered tire that was hanging by a faded rope from the front yard cottonwood tree. The picture reminded me of a scene from the movie *God's Little Acre*. I believe the character was *Darling Jill*. "Hi, Emmett, I am so glad to see you." She unwound herself from her pendulum, coming to the Jeep, she beckoned me to get out and follow her. "Come see our new 'washing machine.'" I did not believe that they had a generator and I wondered what kind of a machine she was talking about. As we came around the side of the main building, I could hear a great deal of laughter.

There in the shallow water tank were four girls. Two brunettes, a redhead, and a blond, quite naked, not models cloned for *Playboy* but real people, different sizes and shapes, frolicking as if they were preparing for a Roman festival. They were having a wonderful time treading their clothes as if the were stomping grapes. It was without a doubt the fanciest washing machine in Death Valley!56

But such an idyllic existence was not destined to last forever. A few months after their arrival in Goler Wash winter descended on the area. The group was not ready for it.

That the desert can be a deceptive place is especially apparent in wintertime. Although the days are usually pleasant, they are also very short. The sun sets quickly and the nights are long and cold. As time went by and it got colder it became impractical for a large number of people to try to stay at Barker Ranch. In January 1969 most of the people moved back to the Los Angeles area to a house on Gresham Street in Canoga Park, about eight miles away from Spahn's Ranch. Only Paul Watkins, Brooks Poston, and Juanita Wildebush remained at Barker's, to keep an eye on the place.

Why didn't the group return to the Spahn's Movie Ranch from Death Valley? They were deferring to the wishes of George Spahn. Lynette Fromme later said:

> The reason that we had to go Gresham in the first place was that George and I had an argument. He had been getting upset because of the beards [on the young men at the ranch], and people had been saying things to him. His [new, would-be business associates] were after him, and they made comments about a bunch of hippies hanging around, and it was affecting the way that he was treating us, and the way that he was behaving.
>
> And I got mad at him. I told him, "You know, this is not a way to treat friends."
>
> And then he explained to me that he wanted to leave his children something and that he felt a failure -- which was normal for men of his generation -- and I understood it.
>
> But I felt kind of desperate. I felt he was going to give up the ranch so that they could bulldoze it. And we had so much fun there and loved the ranch so much that I really didn't want to see him do it. So I had an argument with him, and I said, "Well, do you want us to leave?"
>
> And he said, "Yes."
>
> And so I went and told everyone. And Charlie said, "Okay."
>
> Everybody agreed. Everybody said, "Okay." So we left.

But after about a month or so of Gresham Street, most of the people returned to Spahn's. "We called George on the phone," Fromme recalled. "He wanted us to come back."57

Goodbye Helter Skelter

Back at Spahn's Ranch, the cast of characters continued to grow.

One new person on the scene was a motorcycle club member named Danny De Carlo. DeCarlo met Manson in March of 1969 when he went to Spahn's Ranch to work on some motorcycles. He liked the atmosphere there, and he stayed. "I had a ball," he later told police. A big drinker, DeCarlo later estimated that while at the ranch, from March until August, he was drunk "probably 90 percent of the time."58

Most accounts portray DeCarlo as an outlaw biker, but Charles Manson remembered him as a henpecked husband who was trying to get away from his wife:

> Danny wanted to come up to the ranch, and his wife come and says, "Where's my husband?"
>
> I said, "Uh, out by the barn."
>
> And she would go out and say, "Come on home."
>
> And he would say, "No, I want to stay here with Charlie."
>
> Then she would come and say, "What are you trying to take my husband for?"
>
> I'd tell her, "Hey, witch, I don't want your husband. What the hell am I gonna do with your husband?" You know?
>
> She'd say, "You want my husband for your sleazy fucking women up here that you're running with."
>
> I said, "Man, I ain't go no *idea* about your husband!"59

Manson later remembered, "DeCarlo rode a motorcycle and he was scared to death going fast on it. He had a woman that he couldn't control. He was trying to hide behind us. And then he ended up telling on everybody. So what is *that*?"59

Spahn's Ranch was better than Gresham Street, but the problems and intrigues which had caused everybody to leave the previous fall were still present, so people made a concerted effort to return to the desert with a view toward staying there for quite a while, maybe even permanently. Thus there was much activity in the summer of 1969 as people worked at accumulating the material and knowledge that would be necessary in order to establish a long-term residence in the harsh country around Death Valley.

One moneymaking idea was the so-called "Helter Skelter" nightclub. Lynette Fromme later recalled:

> We needed some money. There were a lot of us. George had started getting on us about being so many. He had a lot of people approaching him who wanted something, and we were just *there*. But these people were not happy that we were there.
>
> We were thinking in terms of just having a little club where it was normal for us to be gathered. Like a nightclub. But of course, you need licenses for all that.
>
> It was kind of like an *Our Gang* movie because we had this whole set and we spray-painted certain areas of it black. We hung up a parachute overhead. We decorated it fully to look like kind of an outer space scene. Then we had sodas and popcorn, and we had a lot of people come and dance. We had a little band. It was a lot of fun, really. And then the police started coming up.
>
> We intended to pay George, you know, give him some of the profits, and make ourselves more enterprising people. We were living very well, but we just had to look better to George, and we thought we would give him a little bit of extra money.60

It didn't work out that way. While the club attracted much local attention it also attracted the attention of law enforcement officials. Because the club was being operated with none of the business licenses necessary for such an enterprise, the police closed the place down.

The "Helter Skelter" nightclub might have been a mistake as far as business ventures went, but it was very far from the worst of the revenue-generating endeavors of the summer of 1969. And it was those worst endeavors that would bring Charles Manson and his associates out of the obscurity of the dusty fringes of Los Angeles and into the front and center of the American consciousness. Those endeavors involved ill-conceived underworld mis-dealings that would soon get out of control and escalate into literal matters of life and death. And those matters of life and death would in turn eventually evolve into one of the most spectacular and infamous episodes of mass murder in the annals of American crime.

Chapter Notes

1 From a tape-recorded telephone conversation in the Sandra Good Archives.
2 From a tape-recorded telephone conversation with the author.
3 Mary Brunner's recollection is from the 1974 documentary *Manson.*
4 From *Reflexion*, by Lynette Fromme, pages 11-13.
5 From Manson's 1986 interview with Charlie Rose on *Nightline*. The San Francisco Diggers were a loose organization of Utopians who served the needs of many people in San Francisco's counterculture by distributing free food and other goods and services in the Haight/Ashbury neighborhood and in Golden Gate Park.
6 Rose interview
7 From the Manson interview in the May, 1985 *California* magazine.
8 From Patricia Krenwinkel's trial testimony, as recounted in *Blood Family*, page 442.
9 *Child of Satan, Child of God*, pages 80 - 81.
10 Susan Atkins 1993 parole hearing transcript, pages 11-12.
11 From a tape-recorded telephone conversation in the Sandra Good Archives.
12 Ibid.
13 *Rolling Stone* magazine, June 25, 1970, page 39.
14 Tape-recorded telephone conversation, Sandra Good Archives.
15 Ibid.
16 Bobby Beausoleil quoted from an undated interview in *Oui* magazine, Sandra Good Archives.
17 Charles Manson interview with Bill Scanlon-Murphy, 1993, transcript pages 12-13.
18 From Pittman's trial testimony, recalled in *Blood Family*, pages 422 - 423.
19 From a telephone conversation with the author, November, 1999.
20 Bruce Davis 1993 parole hearing transcript, page 59.
21 Paul Watkins recalled this to guest host Maureen Reagan on CNN's *Larry King Live* in 1989.
22 Sandra Good's recollection of meeting Manson and his friends is from her 1995 interview for the television program *Rivals: Bugliosi vs. Manson*.
23 Steve Grogan 1981 parole hearing transcript, pages 33-35.
24 Steve Grogan 1978 parole hearing transcript, page 17.
25 From a tape-recorded telephone conversation between Charles Manson and Sandra Good, 1996. Courtesy Sandra Good Archives.

26 *Reflexion*, pages 242-244.
27 *Will You Die For Me?*, page 50.
28 Ibid., pages 50-51.
29 *Helter Skelter*, pages 299 -300.
30 Charles Manson interview with Bill Scanlon-Murphy, 1993, transcript pages 12-13.
31 Tape-recorded telephone conversation between Charles Manson and Sandra Good. Sandra Good Archives.
32 *Reflexion*, pages 251-252.
33 Ibid., page 253.
34 From Leslie Van Houten's trial testimony as recounted in *Blood Family*, page 450.
35 *Alone With The Devil*, page 211.
36 Susan Atkins1993 parole hearing, transcript pages 66-67.
37 Bruce Davis 1992 parole hearing, transcript pages 23-24.
38 These recollections of Van Houten are compiled from *Alone With The Devil*, pages 211 and 213 and *Blood Family*, page 450.
39 *Will You Die For Me?*, page 68.
40 Charles Manson in a tape-recorded telephone conversation with the author, 1998.
41 From a tape-recorded telephone conversation with Sandra Good. Sandra Good Archives.
42 Ibid.
43 This quotation is a compilation taken from several tape-recorded telephone conversations with Sandra Good. Sandra Good Archives.
44 From a tape-recorded telephone conversation with Sandra Good. Sandra Good Archives.
45 Ibid..
46 Ibid.
47 Ibid.
48 Until it was destroyed by a fire in June of 1999.
49 This was the group's second school bus. The first had been disposed of shortly before this first trip to the desert. Lyn Fromme recalled, "It was very early, 1968, the end of summer. There were people living there [at Spahn's Ranch] who wanted to go to Oregon. They were hippies. They lived there before we did.... Charlie gave them the bus. And then with the [money from Sandra Good] we got another one. They were very cheap at the time, something like $600." (Lyn Fromme in a telephone conversation with the author.)
50 The Barker Ranch buildings were destroyed by a fire in May of 2009.
51 As for the idea of Barker Ranch being any kind of hideout, anyone

who spends any time in the desert soon realizes that the isolation becomes more illusory the longer you stay in one area, and especially if you have a large group of people. In 1968-69 there were several well established and inhabited mining claims within five miles of the Barker and Myers Ranches. And five miles in the desert -- where there is generally only one road running between locations -- is the same as next door in the city. While it might be possible for a small band of three or four people to elude law enforcement officials (and even be beyond the awareness of other local residences) indefinitely, it would be (and was) impossible for a larger group with all of its support equipment to do so.

When the group returned to the desert after the murders they did not begin hiding until they started getting obvious attention from law enforcement after the burning of an earth-moving machine on September 19, 1969. Up until that time, Manson and his associates interacted freely, openly, and readily with other desert residents and travelers.

52 Tape-recorded telephone conversation, Sandra Good Archives.

53 *Will You Die For Me?*, page 74.

54 From a telephone conversation with the author.

55 From an undated clipping from an unknown L.A. newspaper in the Sandra Good Archives.

56 *These Canyons Are Full Of Ghosts*, by Emmett C. Harder, page 86.

57 Lyn Fromme's recollections are from a tape-recorded telephone conversation with the author.

58 From an undated newspaper article from an unknown L.A. newspaper in the author's collection.

59 Manson's recollections of Danny DeCarlo are from tape-recorded telephone conversations with Sandra Good. Sandra Good Archives.

60 From a telephone conversation with the author.

Goler Wash

The Shooting of Bernard Crowe

"Tex got me involved in his problems. He's got me down there shooting people for him. I could have handled that situation without shooting someone. He was the one that got all trapped up with that money and that broad. So that's what got me in trouble. So I had to lend him my pants, and let him wear my pants, and carry him. But who *was* he? Who *was* Tex? [He was] his mother."

-- Charles Manson

The shooting of Bernard Crowe by Charles Manson is mentioned in most of the books about the Tate-LaBianca murders, but most often so as simply just another example of the supposed bloodthirstiness of Charles Manson. But this incident has never been carefully examined and placed into a proper perspective in any book about the case. That lack of examination is a fundamental omission, however, because the shooting of Bernard Crowe was actually one of the two main catalysts that ultimately led to the murders on Cielo and Waverly Drives. Therefore it is necessary to examine it in a more thorough and detailed light than it has ever been seen in before.

In the summer of 1969 the people who lived at Spahn's Ranch were actively working towards escaping the increasing confusion of the city and moving to the desert near Death Valley. In preparation for this move they were aggressively accumulating whatever material and resources might be necessary. In late June, in a stupid effort to acquire some cash, Charles "Tex" Watson came up with an idea that would eventually not only lead to the shooting of Bernard Crowe and intensify pressure on Charles Manson and everyone else to get out of the city, but would also create a lethal debt and an underworld favor owed.

Watson's idea was to convince a former girlfriend to get some money together for a marijuana transaction. (This was the same girlfriend who had fallen in love with Watson and with whom he was living before his final move to Spahn's Ranch.) According to the plan the girlfriend would give Watson the money and he would then take it to a dealer in order to buy marijuana. The part of the plan that the girl was not told about was that Watson really intended to take the money and disappear out the back door of the apartment building that the dealer supposedly worked out of, leaving Watson with the money and the girl with nothing.

The girlfriend made a few phone calls and was eventually able to get the money, a few thousand dollars, from a small-time drug entrepreneur named Bernard Crowe. Crowe was black and weighed several hundred pounds. His size was reflected in his nickname, "Lotsapoppa."

On July 1, 1969, the deal went down. Watson got a ride from Spahn's Ranch to Hollywood and met up with Crowe and some of his associates, including the former girlfriend.

The party then drove to the "dealer's" apartment. While Crowe, his associates, and the girlfriend waited in the car, Watson went into the building, ostensibly to score the marijuana. Instead, he went out the back door of the building, got into a car driven by Spahn's Ranch hanger-on T.J. Walleman, and returned to the ranch.1

Then, as Watson tells it, as he was back at the ranch showing off his newly acquired wealth, the telephone rang. It was Bernard Crowe, and he was mad about being cheated. And he was mad enough that he was not only holding Watson's ex-girlfriend hostage but he was also threatening to come up to Spahn's Ranch, burn the place down, and kill everybody there.2

Watson later claimed that it had been previously “agreed” that Charles Manson would “handle” this part of the enterprise. According to Watson, Manson initially tried to handle the situation by telling Crowe that he didn’t know where Watson was. But Crowe didn’t believe this and repeated his threat to come out to Chatsworth and visit much violence on the ranch and its inhabitants. Manson (still according to Watson) responded to this threat by sending Watson and Susan Atkins up into the hills to camp out away from the ranch while he went to settle the problem with the irate Crowe.

In most accounts of this story the responsibility for the eventual shooting of Bernard Crowe is ultimately Charles Manson’s, since he allegedly participated in setting up the drug burn that led to it. But is this version of events credible?

Something has always struck me as odd about this drug burn scenario ever since I first read about it, specifically its audacity. Sure, strong-arm crime is feasible enough if its perpetrator has enforcement muscle, but it never struck me that such a situation existed at Spahn’s Ranch. Further, I think that it would be out of character for Charles Manson to initiate or agree to a provocative and potentially violent criminal scheme wherein he would act as enforcer.

While Charles Manson has been called many things, “criminally naive” is not one of them. By 1969 he had already spent most of his life in prison, immersed in the underworld and very aware of its codes. As such he was well aware of the laws and penalties of criminal society. He would have known that any such rip-off scheme would only result in serious consequences that could very possibly include violence and death. This being the case, is it very likely that Manson would have agreed to participate in any such crude and stupid plan to cheat Bernard Crowe?

Charles Watson, on the other hand, could not be called criminally sophisticated, but by the summer of 1969 he had already established a reputation as a thief. Susan Atkins later said that when she heard about the Crowe incident she thought, “I frankly assumed that Tex had ripped off the dope.”3 And just a few days after the affair with Crowe Watson talked Spahn’s Ranch newcomer

Linda Kasabian into stealing $5,000 from her husband's friend. But while Watson could steal, he could not always do it well. His style was usually to simply take what he wanted with little regard for any consequences.

I think that it is much likelier that Charles Watson, thinking and acting mostly alone (T.J. Walleman did some driving), planned and perpetrated the rip-off of Bernard Crowe. And Watson inadvertently reveals his responsibility for the burn when he writes in *Will You Die For Me?* that after being prodded by Manson to do something to raise some money, "I thought awhile and came up with an idea."4 A little later in the book, Watson refers to the money obtained from the dealer as "what *I'd* stolen from Crowe."5 And later still, Watson calls the Crowe affair "*my* mess."6 (all emphasis added)

All accounts agree that after Crowe's threatening phone calls to Spahn's Ranch Charles Manson and T.J. Walleman went to the apartment where Crowe was located and that Manson eventually settled the dispute by shooting him. But if, as I believe, it is not likely that Manson was really part of the enforcing end of a preconceived drug burn, why did he go to the apartment and shoot Crowe? Why didn't he just write if off as Watson's problem and forget about it?

Two people who were present at the shooting of Bernard Crowe -- T.J. Walleman and Charles Manson -- have each remembered the event, the circumstances leading up to it, and their motivation for going to see Crowe differently from the standard "Manson as enforcer" scenario. Both Walleman and Manson tell of getting caught up in a problem of Charles Watson's singular making, a problem involving serious threats of violence and a terrified young woman.

T.J. Walleman later recalled:

> [Crowe] called up and said he's gonna cut the girl's head off.... because Tex stole money.
>
> And then Tex turns back up with this money and leaves his fiancée there to get her head cut off and says, "I'm going camping."
>
> And we didn't know [that Watson had ripped off Crowe] until the phone call came and asked me for "Charlie."

We [he and Manson] went there [to the apartment] because there was a screaming, crying girl there, that said they were gonna kill her, this girl. And we heard it on the phone, 'cause there was two phones [extensions at Spahn's Ranch]. She asked for "Charlie." So I got the other Charlie [Manson] because I didn't know [Watson] as "Charlie," I knew him as "Tex."

When we got there, they had her tied up on the bed. And we got her out of there. And the only reason anybody got shot -- after Charlie got down on his knees and put the gun into his hands and handed it to the guy and said, "If you gotta take a life, take mine."

The guy laughed and said, "It has to be the girl."

.... Sure, [Manson] shot him once in the chest. What would you do? Leave her there to get her head cut off?7

Here is Charles Manson's recollection of that event:

Here's the story. I'll tell you how it came. I'm setting there, and Tex comes up and says that he wants to get his money back, that broad beat him for his money, should he go get it?

I said, "I don't know. Should you?"

He said, "Well, I think I should."

I said, "Well then go ahead and do whatever you think you should do, man."

So he went over and told the broad, "Yeah, I can make a drug deal with you." He didn't tell me *how* he was gonna get his money back, he just said he was gonna get his money back. He said this woman beat him for his money, when he first came to L.A., and he was gonna go get the money back.

So I said, "All right, whatever," you know....

He told her he could score some drugs for her. She got five thousand dollars gathered up from two or three different drug dealers -- little, petty-ass drug dealers -- and she took him in her car to this hotel and he went in the front door with the money and jumped out the back door and came back to the ranch.

They went back and called me -- Lotsapoppa and that broad went back and called me and said, "Is Tex over there?"

I said, "I haven't seen him."

They said, "Well, he took our money."

I said, "Well, that's not my problem."

And then this guy intervened, this big daddy intervened, and said, "Well, I'm Big Daddy down here and I run this town, you dig, and you don't burn my friends and get away with it. I'm coming up there and burn that fucking ranch down, and rape them kids, and kill them people," and all that shit.

And I said, "Man, don't tell me no shit like that." I said, "Give me a little time. Can I -- can you give me some time?"

He said, "All right."

So I ran over and told Tex, "Man, go back down there and take that money back to them people, man. You done beat some motherfucking *gangster*," you know?

And he said, "Oh, I can't! They'll kill me!" So he got [Susan Atkins] and they ran, 'cause they had already spent the money on the dune buggy.

So then, they kept on mouthing back and forwards, and I said, "Well, where you at?" The guy called back again, talking about he's gonna burn the ranch down and kill everybody on the ranch, and I said, "Where you at?"

And he said, "I'm over at so-and-so's."

I go to Bobby, I said, "Bobby, I'm gonna have some trouble in the yard. You gonna help me?"

And Bobby said, "Well look, man, I gotta go to the hospital. Uh, the doctor told me not to stress. I got a bad heart," you dig?

So I go to Bruce and I say, "Bruce, you gonna help me?"

"No, no I can't."

So I got no backup. If I got no backup, I can't do nothing. If I ain't got two I can't be one. Because it takes two to make one. The only one that would help me at that ranch, when it really came down, I was carrying Tex, I was carrying Bobby, I was carrying Bruce, I was carrying everybody but one person: T.J. T.J. had military training. Bruce didn't have no military training. Bobby didn't. Bobby was mama's boy in Frisco, running around playing Cupid....

Tex ran. He took [Susan] and ran and left me holding the bag. So, Bruce wouldn't back me up, Bobby wouldn't back me up.... no one would back me up but T.J.

T.J. and I went over there, and T.J. got to the door and I had the gun in the back of my belt, and I told T.J., "When we go in, you have first move on the gun. These guys have got guns. There's about seven of them in there." I said, "You make sure you get the gun first, if they make a move."

He didn't. He froze. He just got stiffer than a board. He wouldn't move. He peed all over himself.

So I'm standing there facing this guy. So I had to face the shit down for Tex. And I told [Crowe], "I'm standing in my brother's place." I said,

"You leave that woman alone. Don't be coming over here bothering me, you dig. Don't be doing this shit."

And he's telling me, "Fuck you, punk," and all that shit.

And I said, "Look, I'm not a policeman. I'm not gonna play with you, mister." I said, "Let me get under you here."

He said, "No, there ain't no getting under me, ain't no getting around me," you know.

I said, "Is the chickenshit money worth a life?"

And he said, "Yeah."

So I gave him the gun, and I told him, "Take mine. But leave these people alone. Leave my ranch alone, leave my friends alone, don't be fucking with my woman, don't be fucking with me -- period. You dig?"

He said, "Naw, naw. Fuck that shit. I want all you motherfuckers."

I said, "There ain't no 'all you motherfuckers' to it. There's only one guy here and there's one life here. You either take this life or you leave it alone. If you don't leave it alone, then I'm gonna take you to another step."

He slid the gun across the table at me. He says, "I want everybody involved in this."

And then I says, "I asked you, and I pleaded with you, begged you, and you wouldn't heed my tale. Now I'm gonna tell you. You. I'm telling you. I'm *telling* you. You stay off of me and you stay off of mine."

He says, "You pull a gun on me, use it."

I said, "Very well. That's your order, sir."

Manson pulled the trigger, but the gun just clicked. Crowe was amused at the small man threatening him with an unloaded gun. He got up and started advancing towards Manson. Manson pulled the trigger again:

And I shot him. Actually, he shot himself. I just stood there with him.

And then I seen his partner there. And I thought, "Is this guy gonna come up to the ranch?" And I looked at the dude and I said, "Are we even here?"

And he said, "Yeah."

I said, "You got something to say about this?"

He said, "No."

Then I put the gun down. I put the gun on the empty chambers, and I laid it down, and I says, "Why don't you give me that shirt, man? Can I have that shirt?"

And he says, "Sure."

And he took the shirt off and give it to me. Now I stood back and I looked at the gun and I said, "If you're gonna make a move, make it now. If not, this is dead."

And he said, "It's dead, soul. I ain't gonna fuck with you."

And I said, "All right. Later."

So I went back over to the ranch. And I thought, "Man, I done *killed* somebody!"

Now when you kill somebody, the person you kill is yourself. If you take somebody's life, you owe a life. If I take somebody's life, I've lost my life, man.

And I thought, "Goddamn! I've had to take a motherfucking life! That fucking asshole [Watson] has cost me my fucking life. He cost me my motherfucking life with his stupid, asinine, juvenile, fucking, bullshit, drug dealing, snake-ass, fucking, punk shit." You dig?

At the ranch, Manson found Watson and laid into him for creating a problem that he had to take care of. Manson was especially furious that he had to shoot Crowe -- fatally, he thought -- to put an end to the dispute:

I thought [Crowe was dead], and I got all with Tex and I said, "You, you caused me to *kill* somebody, man."…. So I said, "You *owe* me, mister, and when it comes time to pay this circle, this covenant, this family, this ranch, you'll pay your debt to all these people that feed you, that look out for you, that clothe you, that take care of you, that are honest with you, and that serve the same God that you serve…."

Here's my sin. I told Tex, "Come here. You *owe* me one."[8]

The next day there was a news report that the body of a member of the Black Panther Party had been found in Griffith Park, not far from where the shooting of Bernard Crowe had occurred.[9] When Manson and the other people at Spahn's Ranch heard this, they reached the mistaken conclusion that the slain Panther and the black drug dealer were the same person.

Although this conclusion was a mistake, its consequences would greatly affect many of the people at Spahn's Ranch in the following weeks. The belief that Charles Manson had killed a Black Panther is one of the most important and yet most overlooked occurrences in that summer in terms of understanding the murders that followed it. That belief was a much greater contributing factor to the Tate-LaBianca murders than any supposed grandiose, world-conquering delusions of Charles Manson.

The shooting of Bernard Crowe set a standard. Charles Manson and the people in his circle believed that he had committed murder for the benefit -- for the *survival* -- of the group. Crowe had been shot because he was threatening to mount an assault on Spahn's Ranch. Manson would not allow this to happen and had, so everyone believed, committed the ultimate crime of murder in order to protect his friends and his "brother" Charles Watson. Manson had taken the challenge and the risk and had gone into underworld combat to save the people at Spahn's Ranch. He had demonstrated the extent of his commitment and his love for them.

And the people at the ranch knew it.

And as for Charles Watson, he now owed Charles Manson -- big time.

That Watson owed a debt to Charles Manson is confirmed by him in *Will You Die For Me?* when he writes that on the night of the murders at the Polanski residence Manson "brought up the 'killing' of Bernard Crowe, saying how he had taken care of that for me when it was really *my* mess."10 (emphasis added)

But if the generally accepted scenario of the shooting is true -- that Charles Manson was really just fulfilling his agreed upon role as the enforcer in the drug burn -- it wouldn't follow that there was any debt. If two persons come up with a plan and they each carry out their part of it, as it is frequently claimed happened in this incident (i.e., Watson ripped a guy off and when the guy complained Manson took care of it), where would there be a debt? If Charles Manson was merely fulfilling his part of an agreement when he shot Bernard Crowe, then the incident would be over, the deal would be done, and nobody would owe anybody anything. If Manson had really been merely "taking care of his end of it" when he shot Crowe, Watson's proper reaction to his claim of taking care of "my mess" would have been, "What do you mean, *my* mess? We had a deal. I took care of my end of it and you took care of your end of it. Where do you get any kind of debt out of that?"

But Watson did *not* make this protestation. And the reason he didn't is because he knew that there was no prearrangement with Charles Manson to burn Bernard Crowe. Watson knew that he had ripped off Crowe on his own initiative, that Manson was forced by circumstances to take care of the resulting "mess," and that he, Watson, did indeed owe Manson one.

Again, it must be emphasized how important this incident was to the events which followed it. Manson and everyone else at Spahn's Ranch believed that Crowe was dead and that Manson had killed him. Manson had -- so everyone thought -- committed the ultimate crime, murder (albeit in self-defense), to protect the group.

And besides the establishment of a murderous example, there was another very important result arising from this incident. Because Manson and his friends believed that Bernard Crowe was a Black Panther, their reaction to his "death" was different than if they had instead believed that he was just an underworld drug dealer.

In 1969 the Black Panthers were a highly visible organization that was often in the news spouting violent "off the pig" rhetoric and brandishing firearms. The image of the Panthers as a well-organized paramilitary outfit with the capability for great violence was well known, and they were not a group that anyone would want to have mad at them. In believing that they had incurred the wrath of the militant, confrontational, and heavily armed Panthers, Manson and his people developed an overactive paranoia about blacks. Any black people who showed up at the ranch after the shooting of Crowe were regarded as possible spies or scouts for a Panther raiding party. Thus, even more pressure began to mount on everyone (but especially on Manson, as the shooter) to get away from the Los Angeles area, and the need to get out of the city and to the desert became even more urgent.

But Bernard Crowe hadn't really died, and his reaction to being shot was typically underworld. His friends took him to a hospital, where he told authorities that he didn't know who shot him or why. When his connection to Manson later became known he refused to cooperate with police who wanted to extract the bullet from his body to compare it with bullets taken from the bodies of the victims at the Polanski residence to see if they were fired from the same weapon. (Although the comparison was never made, the same gun was used in both incidents.)

Crowe was later philosophical about being shot. He told Sandra Good that if his role had been reversed with Manson's he would have done the same thing.11 He even expressed gratitude to T.J. Walleman, explaining that getting shot had gotten him off the hook with the people who were demanding their money back from the drug deal fiasco.12

Again, to most of the chroniclers of the Manson saga the Crowe incident is important only because it supposedly demonstrated that Manson was capable of committing murder himself (as opposed to the Tate-LaBianca murders, where the standard story says that he had others do his killing for him). But the real significance of this affair is quite different.

First of all, far from being a cold-blooded act committed to "take care of" Charles Manson's alleged end of a dope burn, the shooting of Bernard Crowe by Manson was actually an act of self-defense committed during an unfortunate and out-of-control underworld business transaction.

Secondly -- and much more importantly -- the shooting demonstrated to Manson's friends just how far he was willing to go for their sakes. Charles Manson had taken up his brother's (Charles Watson's) problem and dealt with it to the extent -- so everyone believed -- of committing murder. To the people at Spahn's Ranch, Manson had demonstrated his love for and commitment to them -- and his love for and commitment to his brother -- by the supreme gesture of killing.

And thus was a murderous standard set. After the shooting of Bernard Crowe there truly was nothing that some members of the Spahn's Ranch group would not do for each other. And so, when the time came for Charles Watson and others to show their love for another brother, they would rise to the example of Charles Manson's level of love and commitment and also be capable of killing.

Chapter Notes

1 This version of events is disputed by no one and is recalled in *Helter Skelter* on page 141, *Will You Die For Me?*, pages 127-129, *Child of Satan, Child of God*, page 116, and in recollections related by T.J. Walleman both publicly and to the author.
2 See *Will You Die For Me?*, pages 127-129.
3 *Child of Satan, Child of God*, page 116.
4 *Will You Die For Me?*, page 127.
5 Ibid., page 131.
6 Ibid., page 136.
7 T.J. Walleman recalled the encounter at Crowe's on the *Geraldo* show's "The Manson Family Reunion" episode in 1991.
8 These recollections of the Crowe shooting are from Charles Manson in a tape-recorded telephone conversation with the author and from interviews with Ron Reagan, Jr. and Bill Scanlon-Murphy.
9 Some sources have the body being found near UCLA. The author, though, has never seen any original documentation, such as a newspaper article, stating that a body of a Black Panther was found anywhere in the Los Angeles area during the relevant time frame.
10 *Will You Die For Me?*, page 136.
11 Good spoke with Crowe during the Tate-LaBianca murder trial. "Crowe told me he would have done the same thing" she recalled him telling her (interview with author, 1998).
12 T.J. Walleman recalled this in a conversation with the author. (Walleman was killed in a car crash in June of 1995 before he could be interviewed on tape for this book.)

The author with Thomas "T.J." Walleman
and some of his children at Barker Ranch in 1994

The Murder of Gary Hinman

"Gary sold some dope to some bad people.... He was playing all kinds of treacherous games that he shouldn't have been playing.

"You see, when you're in the underworld, you've got to be truthful. If you lie and you're faking and you're snitching and it catches up with you, it bites you. You do it to yourself."

-- Charles Manson

The murder of Gary Hinman was the first in the series of killings that have since become known as the "Manson Murders." Like the shooting of Bernard Crowe, the death of Gary Hinman is generally underappreciated as to its importance. And also like the shooting of Bernard Crowe, it was a much greater contributing factor leading to the Tate-LaBianca murders than any personal motive on the part of Charles Manson.

On July 31, 1969 Los Angeles County Sheriffs deputies arrived at the residence of Gary Hinman, which was located at 964 Old Topanga Canyon Road in the Topanga Canyon section of Los Angeles County north of Malibu. The deputies had been called to the home because friends of Hinman had been unable to contact him for several days. Upon their arrival at the house, a brown, wood-shingled structure located up on a hill on the east side of the road, they discovered a grisly scene.

Hinman lay dead on the floor of the living room. It was obvious from the decomposition of the body that he had been deceased for at least several days. It was also obvious that he had met his death violently. Stabbing and cutting wounds were readily apparent on the body. Blood had been smeared on a wall, spelling out the words "Political Piggy" and forming the image of an animal's paw print.

There were no clues at the scene that would immediately point towards any specific suspect, but the dead man's friends told the deputies that Hinman's two cars were missing. Assuming that the killer or killers might have taken them, the officers entered the vehicles, a Fiat and a Volkswagen bus, into their database of missing or stolen cars.

On August 6 a California Highway Patrolman noticed a Fiat parked on the shoulder of Highway 101 near San Luis Obispo and stopped to investigate. Inside the car, Bobby Beausoleil was asleep. A quick check showed that the car was registered to Gary Hinman, a murder victim from Topanga Canyon near Los Angeles. More patrolmen were called to the scene. As the officers searched the car they found a bloody knife in the trunk. Beausoleil was taken into custody and was soon charged with Hinman's murder.

What are the circumstances that led to the death of Gary Hinman? In many accounts (*Helter Skelter*,1 *The Family*,2 *Will You Die For Me?*,3 and *Child of Satan, Child of God*4) his murder supposedly arose out of another one of Charles Manson's strong-arm robbery endeavors, similar to his alleged plan to rip off Bernard Crowe. According to these accounts, Manson believed that Hinman had just received an inheritance and commanded his "followers" to get it from him (and, in some versions, to also get him to "join the family"5). When Hinman refused to turn over the money, so this version of the story goes, he was killed on Manson's orders.

But is this what really happened? While prosecutors and some people peripherally involved in the incident, like Susan Atkins, tend to support the "rob him and kill him" motive, others do not.

Two of the persons later convicted of murdering Gary Hinman -- Bobby Beausoleil and Charles Manson -- say that the real reason for the murder was something other than a previously planned robbery/homicide. According to Beausoleil and Manson, the real cause of the murder was that a drug deal went bad and led to a series of unplanned and unfortunate events that culminated in Hinman's death.

Although many accounts portray Gary Hinman as a simple and innocent musician and music teacher who unfortunately happened to befriend the "Manson Family,"6 it has long been known that he was in fact also a small-time drug dealer who manufactured and sold hallucinogens.7 Bobby Beausoleil later recalled to a California parole board the circumstances leading up to his eventual fatal confrontation with Hinman:

> Well, it was a couple of days before Gary was killed.... [The Straight Satans Motorcycle Club], I was looking up to these guys. I kind of -- I was kind of romanticized that their lifestyle was something that I liked. I kind of thought they were cool. I was young, and these guys were ten -- fifteen years older than me. And I wanted to impress them, and they were going to have a party at Venice Beach. I wanted them to invite me. I wanted to go along on the party. They said that they wanted to -- it was like a ten-year anniversary party for the, you know, for their ten-year motorcycle club anniversary, or something like that. And they wanted to score something different, some psychedelics for their party. And I thought that I might be able to impress them to, you know, to kind of get in with them if I were to set up a deal for them. I knew someone in Topanga Canyon who made mescaline out of peyote cactus buds. That was Gary Hinman. I'd known Gary for a couple of years, and I saw an opportunity to sort of ingratiate myself in these -- with these people. So I set up a deal. It was 1,000 tabs or capsules of homemade mescaline for 1,000 dollars. [But] the next day [after the mescaline was delivered to the club], [they] came back to the Spahn Ranch and essentially [they] kind of beat me up. You know. They hit me in the stomach and, you know, pushed me around and held a knife up to my throat and said they wanted the money back because I had sold them bunk. They said that they had gotten sick on the drugs, and they wanted their money back. So I told them I would do everything I could to get the money back.8

Of course the business of making and selling illegal drugs falls within the realm and under the rules of the underworld. People who use or deal drugs are in a criminal reality whether they like it -- or even realize it -- or not. In this reality, outside the mainstream of civilized, structured society, the ultimate rules and laws are those of the street -- rules of muscle, might, and fear. A person in the underworld is solely responsible for dealing with any problems that might arise from any illegal business transaction in which he is involved. He can't report malfeasances or disputes to the Better Business Bureau, the Chamber of Commerce, or the police. And often when something goes wrong and problems arise in the underworld the choices of remedial action available to the injured party are not good. Sometimes those choices are only that a person can either be big enough to settle the problem or he can get hurt very badly. Such was the case here. And in this instance, when something went wrong with his mescaline deal with Gary Hinman, Bobby Beausoleil decided to be big enough to take care of the problem. And his attempt to do so eventually led to murder.

Some of the precise details of this version of the story vary with who is telling it (and when), but it is generally agreed that on July 25 Bobby Beausoleil went with Mary Brunner and Susan Atkins from Spahn's Ranch to Gary Hinman's house in an attempt to straighten out the situation. The trio was driven to the house by Bruce Davis, who also loaned Beausoleil a tool of persuasion, a 9-millimeter semi-automatic pistol.

After Beausoleil and the women arrived at Hinman's residence and began to explain the situation a problem arose immediately because the motorcycle club members had not given Beausoleil any of the mescaline back so that it could be checked as to its quality. Hinman, who was preparing for a trip abroad, was not interested in settling something that he thought might be a scam.

But Bobby Beausoleil was on the spot. The Straight Satans were acting very upset about the mescaline, and they wanted their money back now or else Beausoleil could expect to be on the receiving end of more violence.

Hinman remained skeptical. He said that he was sure about the quality of his product. The whole problem sounded like a con to him, and he wasn't going to give Beausoleil any money.

The situation then went from bad to worse. Beausoleil produced the gun (he had also brought a knife) and told Hinman to make good on the deal. Hinman refused, so Beausoleil struck him several times with the weapon.

As Bobby Beausoleil recalled at his 1992 parole hearing:

> I went there for the purpose of collecting $1,000 that I had been put in the middle on -- or at least in my view, I had been put in the middle on -- and I did not tell Mary Brunner or Susan Atkins what I was going there for. I mean, if they're saying that they had no knowledge of my going there to collect money on a drug deal, then that would be the reason why. (This explanation for any vagueness on the parts of Brunner and Atkins also explains why Bruce Davis too claims that he did not know exactly why Beausoleil was going to Hinman's house: because Beausoleil didn't tell him. See Footnote 15.)

Beausoleil continued:

> I wasn't going to the residence of Gary Hinman for the purpose of killing him. And when these two girls -- and they were girls at the time -- asked to go along, they knew Gary. In fact, everyone in the area knew Gary. And when they asked to go along, I didn't have any problem with them coming along. They weren't coming along for the purpose of being partners to a crime. They were simply going along for the ride.

The parole commissioner at the hearing expressed skepticism that Atkins and Brunner did not know the reason for the trip to Hinman's house. "You see," he said, "I would think that somewhere during the time, they would have heard you say to the man, the victim, 'I want that $1,000.'"

Beausoleil responded:

> They did. This did occur when we arrived at the residence. But at the time that they asked to go along, they had no knowledge of what I was going there for. When we arrived at the residence, and I think I may have mentioned something along the way, as we were going over there, that yes they eventually did become aware of what was happening.

The commissioner asked, "Did Manson order you to kill the victim?"

"No sir."

"At any time?"

"No sir."

"Did you call -- during the phone call to Manson, did he order you to, [or] one of the other crime partners, to harm the victim?"

Beausoleil answered:

I never spoke with Manson on the phone. In fact, until he came to the residence, I didn't know that a phone call had been made to him. In fact, I still don't know that a phone call had been made to him. I do know that a phone call had been made to the ranch. To the Spahn Ranch. And I assume that some message had been given to him. Maybe. I don't know. It would only be conjecture on my part.

(These statements by Beausoleil contradict those of other persons involved in this incident. Susan Atkins and Bruce Davis have both contended that Beausoleil himself did call Manson.9 Manson, too, is adamant that Beausoleil called him at Spahn's Ranch, asking for his help.)

Beausoleil continued his version of the story:

I would like to clear something up here maybe. [It] may make it a little easier for you. First of all, I want to make -- you mentioned something about torture. And I don't understand where that's coming from. There's never been any evidence at any point, presented that I tortured the victim....

I never meant to harm Gary Hinman at any point, you know, I take responsibility for the choices that I made that put me in that position. Because I did, in fact, put myself in that position. But I didn't go there with the intention of killing Gary Hinman. And I acted irrationally....

As I stated, I never made a call to Manson myself. A call, apparently, had been made to Spahn Ranch. I'm not sure who the individual was who made the call. I'm sure it was one of the two girls. And I don't know who that person spoke to, but apparently -- now this is conjecture on my part, because I was not part of the conversation directly -- but the conjecture is that Manson got the message that his girls were in trouble, because at the time that the phone call was made I was struggling with the victim over the gun. He had taken possession of the gun.... And I was struggling with him. At that time, there was, I guess one of the girls that was there panicked and called Spahn Ranch, and apparently, I presume, based on what had occurred, that Manson got the message that one of his -- his girls were in trouble.

Manson, in response to the phone call, was driven to Gary Hinman's house by Bruce Davis. The distance from Spahn's Ranch to Hinman's was about fifteen miles, a half-hour or forty-five minute drive. Beausoleil continued his narrative of events:

> Subsequent to [Manson's arrival], Gary Hinman and I had worked out our difficulties. He had signed over two pink slips to two -- they were old cars, they were pretty much wrecks, but they were worth enough that I could take them to the bike club and give it to them in lieu of the $1,000 that they wanted back. There was a beat-up VW van that I felt they could use to cart their motorcycles around in or something. And that they would accept this. It was the best that I could do. But this -- we had worked out our difficulties. Gary and I had worked out our difficulties. He was no longer being held by the point of the gun. He was no longer being held by his will. I was ready to leave the residence.

(Susan Atkins contradicts this order of events, saying that the signing of the pink slips took place on July 27, two days after Charles Manson came and went.10 In *The Family*, author Ed Sanders claims that the signed slips were dated July 26, 1969.11 Manson says that the slips were signed some time after he arrived at Hinman's residence. See below.)

> At this point Manson showed up at the door. I had no idea what he was there for. Gary was free to walk around the house. And he answered the door. He was glad to see Charlie. He opened the door and said, "Hi Charlie."
>
> And the next thing that happens is, Charlie Manson slashes him across the face with a knife. Walks in the room, says something like he's showing me how to be a man. And I'm just, I'm dumbfounded. First of all, I had never seen a violent act like that against another human being. The man is bleeding from his face profusely. And it was totally uncalled for. There was no reason for Manson to have attacked him. Manson puts out his chest, like he had done something really profound, and tells me that he was showing me how to be a man and how to protect his girls, or something to that effect. And [then he] leaves the residence.

And here I am -- all of a sudden -- I mean, where I had resolved the differences with the victim Gary Hinman, I was suddenly left with this incredible mess.

If you ask me if I would protect Charles Manson, or imply that I was protecting Charles Manson, I mean there is no love lost between me and that individual. I have no desire to protect that individual. Considering the problem that he left me with -- I had no prior experience of any sort of criminal activity, never committed a violent act against anyone, and here all of a sudden I'm left with this bleeding person on my hands, who is scared for his own health. He's talking about how he wants to go to the hospital. He wants to turn me in to the police. We both understand that this would be part of the process of him going to seek medical treatment. I tried everything conceivable to....

The parole board commissioner interrupted to ask if Hinman was killed because he was a witness. Beausoleil answered, "I killed him because he had threatened to go to the police, yes.... I panicked at the thought of finding myself in the jaws of the judicial system, so to speak."12

So, according to Bobby Beausoleil, Gary Hinman was killed to keep him from going to the police and turning Beausoleil in for the assault that arose out of the disagreement over the drug transaction.

What is Charles Manson's version of this story? I asked him about it once and this is what he told me:

Bobby hit on me in the camp fires about did I know anything about the brotherhood, and could he be a brother? And I told him, "Well, pretty much the brotherhood is, you have to do what brother says as much as brother does what you say. And you're in the same will, and you can't ever lie to each other. And like, pretty much that's it. There's no complication to it. You've got your life and brother's got his. Just don't lie to each other. And if you give your word for something, you keep it."

So then when he asked me what should he do about his money [that he had lost in the deal with Hinman] I said, "Well, if you're big enough, go get it. If you're not, sit down and be quiet."

He said, "What would you do?"

I said, "Forget it, it's only sixty-four dollars."

So he said it was a matter of principle and he wanted to go get it.

So I told him, "Well, that's on you."
So when he went over there, he told me, "Well, Gary got a gun."

Since at his parole hearing Beausoleil denied making any phone call, I specifically asked Manson if Beausoleil himself called on the phone and told him about Hinman having a gun:

Yeah. And then Bobby tells me, "He's got a gun, he's got a gun."
I said, "Well, if he's got a gun he must be afraid of something. Most people that got guns are scared of something." So I said, "Take it away from him."
He said, "How do I do that?"
I said, "Well, don't reach for the gun. He'll put his mind on the gun and he'll shoot you." I said, "Smack him in the mouth first. And then he'll put his mind on his mouth and then you grab the gun out of his hand."
He said, "Well, you're crazy! I'm not gonna do that!"
I said, "Oh wow, man. I told you if you was big enough to do it. You said you was. Now why you gonna invoke me? You got me back in the penitentiary with this shit."
He said, "Well, you're my brother. Come and help me. You said you was brother. Help me."
Then I had to go over there and face his problems for him because he can't stand up for himself, you dig?
So then I cut the guy's ear off, and when he's thinking about his ear, then I snatched the gun out of his hand. He shoots the side of the wall, you know, then I throw the gun over on the bed, and I say [to Beausoleil], "There. That's how you do it. If you was afraid -- I told you not to come over here if you was scared...."

Having seriously cut Hinman, Manson was now confronted with the possibility of him going to the police about it:

Then I'm thinking, "I got to scare this character." So I am what they call in the underworld a "bad actor." I say, "All right, now I got to kill you, Hinman. I got to dust your ass, man."
And he said, "Oh man! Don't kill me!"
I said, "I got to. It's a better chance I got to survive and not go back to prison if you're dead, because if you're alive and you tell my parole officer, I'm back in jail for the rest of my life."

He said, "I won't tell! I give you my word, I won't tell!"

I said, "Why don't you be a man about what you're doing and pay your debts? Pay your debts. Because if you owe my brother, you owe me." I said, "You've got to pay, you got to pay the bill, man. You made the bill, now pay it. Be a man about yourself," you dig?

So then he said, "All right." So he paid, and I think that's when he signed the slips. I don't know whether he signed them when I was there or when I was gone, but right in that area is -- he didn't sign no slips until after I got there.

So I says, "Are we paid?"

And he said, "We're paid."

And I said, "Okay. I'm out of here."

And then, three days went by, they were in his house. We got some scotch tape and put his ear back on. He was all right. He swore that it was over, and he apologized for being stupid and not doing what he was supposed to do.

And actually, all it was, was, court was in session. I went there as the judge to preside over the situation. So I didn't actually break any laws. I just tried to put it in order and make it right.

So Hinman got well.... He got the gun and he said, "I'm gonna go kill [Manson]."

Bobby said, "No, I can't let you do that. You gave your word."

[Hinman] said, "That don't mean nothing to me. He cut my ear, I'm gonna go [get him]."

And Bobby said, "No, I can't let you do that because he was standing up for me...."

Hinman pushed by Bobby and Bobby handed him the knife.... And he says, "I'll not let you harm him, because he was standing in my place and he's my brother...." He gave the knife to Hinman and told him, "Kill me."

Hinman says, "I don't want you."

Bobby said, "You gave your word as your bond and your bond as your life. If you make one more move towards it, I'm taking you away."

And [Hinman] made the move. And Bobby took him. And he died.

I'm three days down the road. I don't have any idea what the hell's going on there....

Hinman killed Hinman. That's what it comes down to. I didn't have nothing to do with that. The only thing I did, on the telephone, is I said the same thing I would say to anybody. "You know what to do. You got a mind and a brain of your own, man. I'm not your father or your mother. You ran away from home trying to get away from that shit. I don't tell you what to do. I tell you what you *can* do, I give you a point of view, [but] what you do is up to you. You got your own mind and your own soul and your own will. You got your own mark on your own head. Use it. Don't ask me what to do because I don't know any better or any more than anybody. I'm not nobody's leader. I don't want to be nobody's leader."

I asked Manson why Beausoleil denied making the telephone call to him:

His point of view, he's giving it to the people that want to hear that shit so he can get transferred out of state. In other words, he had an ulterior motive to adjust his point of view towards that. And he's probably convinced himself pretty much that that's the way it came down.

I mean, that's Bobby, man. That's *his* move. That wasn't my move. My move was, I stood there on the ear, on the earring. In other words, like, I had no thought in that. I was standing up in my brother's place.

I was trying to show that boy how to stand up towards his own problem, you dig?

And when he seen me stand up, then all he did was he stood back up to where I stood up. Because wherever you're at when you stand up -- when you stand up in the *man* -- there's only one person there.

There's only one person in the field of honor. The field of honor holds one human being in that field. And that's God. That's the battlefield. That's the graveyard. That's the Iron Cross. That's our father, who art in heaven. That's the priest every Sunday, when he stands up and does the mass, and serves the cups and all that stuff. In other words, we've always stood up in that high fear level situation, where a man of God gives his *life*.

When you give your life and you're totally into giving your life for your honor, then that sets you on the bench as a judge. That puts you in a high office, like being the president....

It really has nothing to do with me as a person, as a personality. Because personally, I would have ran. I told him to forget it. But he said it was a point of honor. Well the point of honor was not *my* point of honor, it was *his* point of honor. I just stood up and told him how to hold it. I said, "Here's how you hold it, boy. You stand up here with it like this." You dig?

And I told Gary, I said, "Give me that gun."

And he said, "Rah rah rah, I'll shoot you."

I said, "You're not gonna shoot nobody. Give me the gun." And he wouldn't give me the gun, so Whack! I whacked him real quick. And while he's settin' there -- "Wow!" -- then I grabbed the gun out of his hand and I threw it. If I'd have reached for the gun first, his attention would have been on the gun and he would have shot me.

There's only one mind and there's only one person in that mind. When you get up on that high fear level, you don't have a choice. You move on the moves that are being made. Like I told you about the guy that showed me the big knife? I had no choice. I had no choice at all.13

Some things don't make sense in most of these versions of the Gary Hinman murder. In the prosecution's (and Susan Atkins') variation there are several problems.

First of all, according to the prosecutors, Bobby Beausoleil and the others went to Gary Hinman's house in order to strong-arm him out of an inheritance that they thought he had. Part of this version, though, is the contention that Hinman *didn't* have an inheritance, and since he would not and could not give up something that he didn't have, the killers started beating him and cutting him and ended up hurting him so much that he had to be killed (on Charles Manson's orders) to keep him from going to the police.

But since Hinman had no inheritance, it is a mystery why Manson and the others supposedly thought that he did. Of course, people do dumb and criminal things based on faulty or incorrect information all the time (see *In Cold Blood*), so it's possible that some sort of misinformation about an inheritance was floating around Spahn's Ranch. Still, where did Manson or anyone else get the idea of this supposed inheritance? There is no real answer to this question.

Another question arising out of this version is just when such violence-oriented behavior supposedly became the norm for the people at Spahn's Ranch? From whence sprang the strategy of taking other persons' possessions by force, even to the extent of murder? Was this to be a continuing revenue-generating enterprise that could be applied to numerous other acquaintances and/or relatives of any of the persons living at Spahn's Ranch?

Again, while much is in the realm of possibility, this version of the motive for the murder of Gary Hinman doesn't provide much in the realm of probability. But it does provide something very important to the prosecution, namely a scenario wherein Charles Manson ordered a premeditated crime to be committed which resulted in murder. In other words, it provides a motive for Charles Manson to have committed murder. And this is a very important point, as will become apparent later in this book.

The district attorney's version of the events motivating the eventual murder of Gary Hinman is convenient from a prosecutorial point of view, but it lacks any evidentiary foundation. It is also inconsistent with the previous behavior of the persons involved. But if one finds that explanation lacking, there is another more complete, logical, reasonable, and likely explanation for the murder. And that is the explanation given by both Bobby Beausoleil and Charles Manson, specifically that a dispute over a drug deal escalated into homicide.

But even so, there are some things about Bobby Beausoleil's account of this murder that also don't make sense.

For one thing, at his parole hearings Beausoleil has never offered a credible explanation as to how he went from demanding money and struggling with Hinman for a gun to a point where he had worked out his differences with him. At his 2003 parole hearing he claimed:

> After we had struggled with the gun for a minute or two, the gun went off, and, you know, no one was hit, but it was loud, and we were both sort of stunned by the sound, and it caused us to kind of freeze for a moment because, you know, both of us thought we were shot. I managed to, in that moment, to get the gun back from Gary. And after that -- you know, after we kind of both calmed down, and Gary and I were both trying to -- you know, we were both ashamed at that point of what had happened. And we just [thought it was a] ridiculous thing to have been involved in. And Gary offered to sign over his -- he had a couple of old cars, and he offered to sign these over to -- as something that I could take to the bike club that might be worth 1,000 dollars.14

But even if the gun did go off and startle everyone, why would Hinman suddenly forget Beausoleil's earlier threats and violent behavior and just offer to sign over his vehicles in order to appease the bike club?

Beausoleil also says that Manson showed up at the house and immediately sliced the side of Hinman's face with no provocation and for no apparent reason.

Bruce Davis, however, who drove Manson to the Hinman house and went inside with him, remembered an argument preceding the cutting. At his 1994 parole hearing, Davis recalled:

> This pistol that I owned, had been fired in the house. Nobody got shot with it, but it had been fired in the house. I [previously] left the pistol off with Bobby.
>
> And I was getting ready to leave and Charlie and -- Charlie Manson and Gary had a confrontation and Charlie had a knife and he made Gary stay there... They were having an argument.... just sort of back and forth.... [Manson cut Hinman and] he just grabbed his face.... I don't remember what he said. But I'm sure like he screamed or something. I mean, I'm not really good on that. I -- I didn't really remember.15

Is it likely that Charles Manson cut Gary Hinman's face for no reason whatsoever? Manson is not a violently assaultive person, so why would he slice a person's face and invite all of the trouble that would inevitably arise out of such an action for no reason at all? I don't believe that he would. Bobby Beausoleil's version of Manson's sudden and totally unprovoked cutting of Gary Hinman does not make sense and it does not ring true.

Beausoleil further claims that before the cutting he had "never even seen a violent act like that against another human being" and "never committed a violent act against anyone" even though he claimed he was violently assaulted a few days previously by members of the Straight Satans Motorcycle Club and admitted to having been in a violent struggle with Hinman over the gun. In *Child of Satan, Child of God*, Susan Atkins recalled a brutal struggle between Beausoleil and Hinman.16

At some point during the incident with Hinman the 9-millimeter pistol was discharged, sending a bullet into the wall under the kitchen sink. When did the gun go off, and under what circumstances? Beausoleil has said that the gun went off while he was struggling with Gary Hinman over it. Susan Atkins also says that the gun went off during a struggle between Beausoleil and Hinman early in the days-long event. Bruce Davis recalled that the gun "had been fired in the house." Charles Manson, as we have seen, says that the gun went off at the moment he cut Gary Hinman on the side of his face.

So although both of these versions of the ear cutting might seem credible, only Manson's presents an explanation for the slicing that doesn't depend on him being a violently assaultive person, something that he is not.

In a final analysis then, Bobby Beausoleil's version of what happened to Gary Hinman is much more credible than the prosecution's version, but there are still some areas where it has holes or does not quite make sense.

Charles Manson's version of the circumstances that led to Gary Hinman's murder, on the other hand, makes complete sense. Read it again. There is no hesitation or vagueness, and no hazy or false motivating factors. There are no holes or unexplained aspects to the story, It is complete, it is understandable, and it is reasonable. It could also be the truth.

Prosecutors have long contended that Gary Hinman's murder was a process that took almost three days to transpire, complete with beatings and torture. This claim is an attempt to make a series of acts into one long act so that Manson's cutting of Hinman's ear becomes just another part of the murder process rather than being a separate violent incident which occurred days before Hinman was finally killed.

But when Charles Manson left the house on Old Topanga Canyon Road there was no thought of killing Gary Hinman. Hinman had assured Manson that he had no beef over his cut face. Those who stayed behind after Manson left fed Hinman and administered first aid to his wound. (People who intend to murder someone usually do not administer first aid to their victim before killing them.) The killing only occurred after Hinman went back on his word not to go to the authorities over his slashed ear.

Bobby Beausoleil told his parole board that he killed Gary Hinman to keep him from turning him (Beausoleil) in to the police. But why would Gary Hinman threaten to turn Bobby Beausoleil in for something done by Charles Manson? If, as Beausoleil claims, he and Hinman had "settled our differences" before Manson showed up at the house, why would Hinman be threatening to turn Beausoleil in to the authorities over his cut ear, an assaultive incident supposedly totally separate from the settled disagreement over the bad mescaline? Hinman's issue would have been solely with Manson. And this conclusion lends further credence to Manson's version of the event, namely that Beausoleil killed Hinman in order to keep him from turning Manson in to the police.

Thus, it is entirely possible that when Bobby Beausoleil killed Gary Hinman he killed him to keep him from telling on Charles Manson and sending him back to prison.

In other words, it is entirely possible that Bobby Beausoleil killed Gary Hinman for his brother.

Chapter Notes

1 *Helter Skelter*, page 102.
2 *The Family*, page 245. Sanders goes for this version only in the first edition of his book. By the time of his 1989 updated edition he has dropped mention of an inheritance in favor of the "drug deal gone bad" theory.
3 *Will You Die For Me?*, page 126.
4 *Child of Satan, Child of God*, page 120.
5 As claimed, for example, by Los Angeles County Deputy District Attorney. Stephen Kay at Charles Manson's 1992 parole hearing, transcript page 72.
6 Bugliosi in *Helter Skelter* (in the photo gallery), for one.
7 I have often wondered if sheriff's deputies found drug manufacturing and dealing paraphernalia in Hinman's house while investigating his murder there.
8 Bobby Beausoleil 2003 parole hearing, transcript pages 23-25.
9 In *Child of Satan, Child of God* Atkins recalls Beausoleil exclaiming, "I'm going to call Charlie." (page 126)
10 *Child of Satan*, Child of God, page 128.
11 *The Family*, updated 1989 edition, page 210.
12 This version of Gary Hinman's murder is from Bobby Beausoleil's 1992 parole hearing, pages 60 to 67.
13 Manson's recollections are from a 1998 telephone conversation with the author.
14 Bobby Beausolei, 2003 parole hearing, transcript page 27.

15 Bruce Davis at his 1994 parole hearing, transcript pages 15 and 18. Although Davis recalls an argument between Manson and Hinman before the ear slashing, he is not sure about the "get Hinman's inheritance and force him to join the Family" theme. In 1992 he said, "I recall that kind of idea associated with Bobby and Mary and Susan going there try to persuade him about it.... [But] I was not in a general discussion about what about Gary, what to do, or what not to do about Gary. I knew about the discussion from *kind of second hand.* I wasn't there. I mean, I didn't sit down -- we didn't sit down and say this, that, and the other. I was asked to drive them over to Gary's house. I drove over there. I left. I left them off and I left." (emphasis added) As to the alternate possibility that a drug deal gone bad led to the murder, Davis is not sure but he doesn't rule it out: "There was no drug deal, there was no prior debt, *to my knowledge*. It was just Gary had some money, they thought they could get it from him.... *I have no knowledge* of a drug deal with -- in regard to him." (emphasis added) Bruce Davis obviously had no precise or firsthand knowledge of the reason why Bobby Beausoleil was going to Gary Hinman's house.
16 *Child of Satan, Child of God*, page 125.

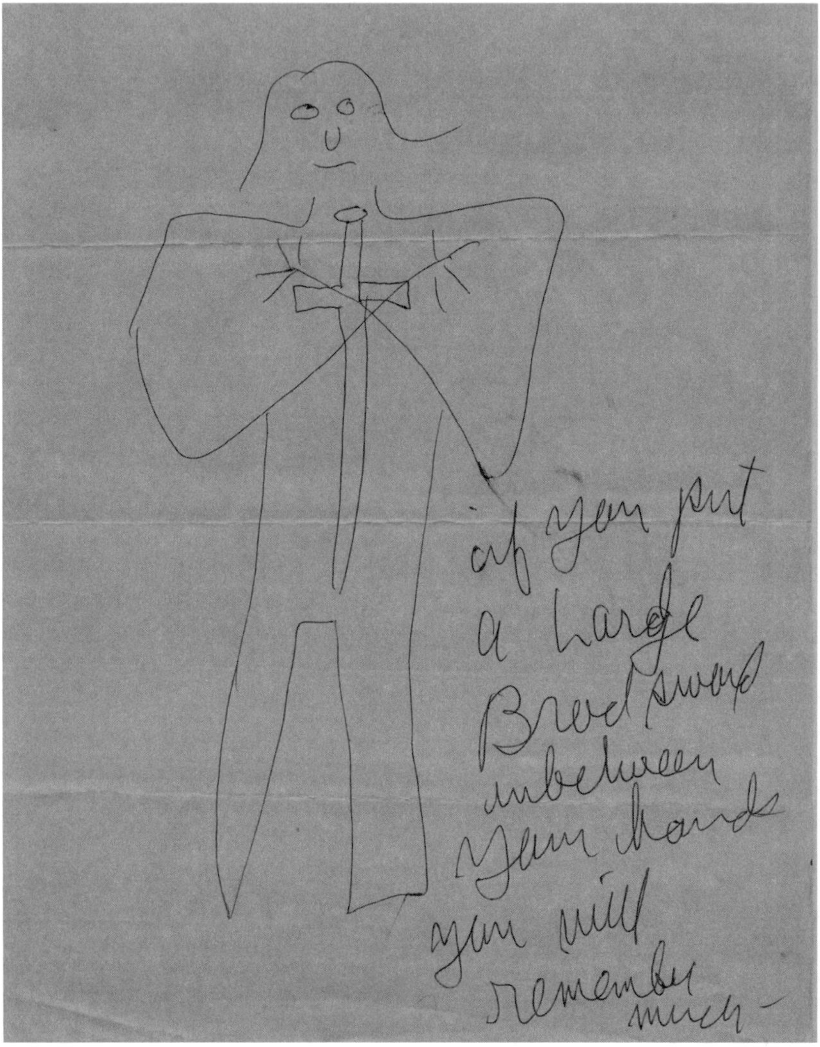
if you put
a large
Brodsword
inbetween
your hands
you will
remember
much –

Introduction to the Tate-LaBianca Murders

The notoriety of the murders which occurred in the Bel Air and Los Feliz neighborhoods of Los Angeles on August 8 and 9, 1969 resulted in those two spectacular instances of homicide dominating the entire string of killings (and presumed killings) that Charles Manson and some of his associates were involved in during the summer of 1969. Thus, Charles Manson is forever linked in the popular mind with the "Tate-LaBianca Murders."

But this exclusive linkage between Charles Manson and the Tate-LaBianca murders distorts the full reality of the events of that summer. The killings which occurred at the Tate (Polanski) and LaBianca homes were regarded by the legal system of the state of California (and by much of popular opinion) as a separate and isolated (and yet conjoined) pair of crimes. But in reality they were actually part of a longer series of real and assumed killings that not only included the persons killed at those residences but also Bernard Crowe, Gary Hinman, and Donald "Shorty" Shea.

When the murders at the Polanski and LaBianca residences are placed in the full and correct context of all of the events of the summer of 1969, they can finally be seen in their correct perspective -- not as isolated, primary acts committed as an attempted catalyst for a race war and eventual world conquest (as they are generally and officially presented and assumed to be), but rather as secondary actions committed during a longer series of events arising out of illegal drug transactions gone awry, underworld favors owed, and an ill-conceived plan to divert police attention from a previous murderous occurrence.

FIRST HOMICIDE INVESTIGATION PROGRESS REPORT

DR 69-059 593

DECEASED:	FOLGER, Abigail Anne, CC No. 69-8794 FRYKOWSKI, Wojiciech, CC No. 69-8793 PARENT, Steven Earl, CC No. 69-8792 POLANSKI, Sharon Marie, CC No. 69-8796 SEBRING, Thomas John CC No. 69-8795
DATE AND TIME OCCURRED:	August 9, 1969, 2400-0415 hours
LOCATION OF OCCURRENCE:	10050 Cielo Drive
DIVISION OF OCCURRENCE:	West Los Angeles Division

TO: Lt. R. J. Helder, Supervisor of Investigations, Robbery-Homicide Divn.

Sir:

RESUME OF THE CRIME

On the evening of August 8, 1969, Sharon Polanski called friends she had previously invited for the evening and stated that she was not feeling well and was going to remain home with Abigail Folger and Wojiciech Frykowski, two friends that had been living in her home since March, 1969. She also stated that Jay Sebring, her one-time fiance, would probably drop over later in the evening. She cancelled the above invitation.

Sharon Polanski had been with her husband, film producer-director, Roman Polanski, in London, England from March 1969, until approximately July 21, 1969, when she returned home to the property they leased at 10050 Cielo Drive. Her husband was to remain in Europe and return to California on August 12, 1969.

In addition to the house that the Polanskis leased, which is located at the center of the Cielo property (Addendum 1), the owner of the property, Rudy Autabelli, had his home at the very southernmost portion of the grounds (Addendum 1 and 1B). Autabelli had left his house (Addendum 1 and 1C) and several dogs in the care of William Garretson, his houseboy. Garretson's only duties were to care for the dogs and keep Autabelli's home (Addendum 1C) in good order. The main house leased by the Polanskis was their own responsibility as to maintenance and domestic help. Garretson was at home at the time of the murders and was visited by Steven Parent from 2345 on 8-8-69, until 0015 hours, 8-9-69.

Sometime after midnight, August 9, 1969, an unknown suspect or suspects entered the Cielo property via the front gate which is operated by an electronic push button that can be operated from outside the gate. From this point there are three possible theories which have been reached after analyzing the physical evidence.

The Murders on Cielo Drive

"Well, it's hard to explain. It was just a thought, and the thought came to be."

-- Patricia Krenwinkel, on the murders

The murders that occurred at the Roman Polanski residence at 10050 Cielo Drive in the Bel Air section of Los Angeles during the night of August 8, 1969 were one of the landmark events of the 1960s. Five persons were brutally killed by shooting, beating, and stabbing.1 Their bodies were scattered throughout the property. The word "PIG" was written on the front door of the residence in the blood of one of the victims. It was one of the most shocking mass murders ever to have occurred in the United States.

The bodies were discovered on the morning of Saturday, August 9. The number of victims and the brutality of their murders instantly made the story front-page news. But beyond that, the fact that one of the victims -- Sharon Tate -- was a television and movie actress married to a famous film director gave the homicides literal star quality and guaranteed that they would be the subject of much more publicity than if the victims had not included such a celebrity.

The basic circumstances of these murders (which are really disputed by no one) are that on the evening of August 8 four persons at Spahn's Movie Ranch -- Charles Watson, Linda Kasabian, Susan Atkins, and Patricia Krenwinkel -- assembled, got into a car, drove to 10050 Cielo Drive, and killed five people there.

All four of these participants have admitted to what they did at Cielo Drive. But since this book is about Charles Manson's possible involvement in various murders, and because everyone agrees that Manson was not present at Roman Polanski's house when the people were killed there, the specific details of what Watson, Kasabian, Atkins, and Krenwinkel did at that residence need not be recounted here.

But what, if anything, did Charles Manson have to do with these five murders? He is generally believed to have "masterminded" them. Did he?

Manson has never denied that he was involved in these murders. "I had everything to do with it," he told an interviewer in 1993. "I was on the edge of everything that happened. And I affected everything that happened. But *unknowingly*. I didn't realize the effect I was having on people."2

Beyond this and similar admissions, though, Manson has repeatedly denied having any legal responsibility for the so-called "Tate Murders" (or, for that matter, for any murders). Can he be correct?

Let's look at the early evening of August 8, 1969, before Charles Watson, Linda Kasabian, Susan Atkins, and Patricia Krenwinkel left Spahn's Ranch, from the points of view of those four persons (three of whom were later convicted of the murders). Also, we will see what Charles Manson says about that night.

Charles Watson remembers Charles Manson coming up to him and saying:

> I've got a favor I want you to do for me tonight.... But it'll take a lot of nerve to do it....
>
> I want you to go to that house where [Terry] Melcher used to live -- I want you to take a couple of the girls I'll send with you and go down there.... and totally destroy everyone in that house, as gruesome as you can. Make it a real nice murder, just as bad as you've ever seen. And get all their money.

Watson recalls Manson giving him detailed instructions on how to commit the murders. After receiving these instructions, Watson says, he met Kasabian, Atkins, and Krenwinkel in the parking lot of the ranch. After the quartet got into the car and started to leave, Manson caught up with them, leaned into the car window, and said, "Remember to leave a sign. Something witchy."3

Linda Kasabian remembers that Charles Manson told her to get a change of clothing, a knife, and her driver's license and to "go with Tex [Watson] and do whatever Tex tells you to do." She also recalls Manson approaching the car as they left the ranch and saying, "Leave a sign. You girls know what to write. Something witchy."4

Susan Atkins remembers, "Charlie walked up and called four of us aside.... He spoke to each of us, together, yet separately: "Get a change of clothes and your knife and go with Tex. Do whatever he says to do."5

Patricia Krenwinkel has a similar recollection. "[Manson] came in and got me out and he told me to go and do whatever Tex said.... just follow whatever Tex said."6

Charles Manson remembers telling the three girls to get knives and changes of clothing and to go with Charles Watson and do whatever he said to do. He once explained these instructions, which at first glance might appear to be incriminating. Manson:

> Yeah, that was an automatic thing. Let me explain something so you'll understand the whole thing.
>
> That wasn't unusual. It's like, when you go on a garbage run, what they'd do is they get a change of clothes, and they get something sharp, and they roll the change of clothes up, and they go down in the big garbage bins, and they get in the garbage bins, with all the apples or pineapples or whatever's in there, they cut out the bad parts and put the good parts in a basket, right? Then they leave the bin and go to the filling station, change clothes -- take the dirty clothes off, go across the street and put a quarter in the washing machine, throw the clothes in the washing machine and wash the clothes, and then come back with the vegetables and stuff.
>
> So, when I said, "Hey man, why don't you get a change of clothes and go with Tex and let him show you what he's doing," that's a mere garbage run. It didn't have nothing to do with going and doing all that other stuff they said.7

Manson also remembered telling the departing foursome, "If you're gonna do something, leave something witchy.... If you're gonna do something, do it well. And leave something witchy. Leave a sign to let the world know that you were there."8 Finally, Manson remembered giving the people in the car an old pair of glasses to leave wherever they went, in order to create confusion. "When they was leaving to do what they did.... I told 'em, 'Here, take and drop these glasses.'"9

Because there isn't too much discrepancy between these five stories it's fair to assume that what these people are collectively saying is essentially true, with one substantial exception: I think that Charles Watson is either lying or mistaken about what he claims Charles Manson told him to do that night.

But *why* did Watson, Kasabian, Atkins, and Krenwinkel go to Cielo Drive? What was the reason for such incredibly savage killings? What was the motive? And who formulated and possessed that motive? The motive for the murders on Cielo Drive is not only the crux of this entire case, but it is also the least understood, most carelessly explained, and the most misrepresented aspect of this entire case.

The previous chapters of this book on the shooting of Bernard Crowe and the murder of Gary Hinman presented those events based on the recollections of the persons involved, along with the possible motivations of those persons, and concluded with crime scenarios that not only fit all of the known facts of the crimes but also make complete sense. The only thing possibly wrong with those scenarios is that they contradict the popular conception that Charles Manson was responsible for either the Crowe shooting or the Hinman murder.

The same analytical technique can also be applied the murders committed at 10050 Cielo Drive. By carefully reviewing the known facts of that crime, the memories of the various people involved, and -- most importantly -- by seriously examining the variety of motives that have been suggested by different people over the years, a reasonable conclusion can be reached as to why those five people died that night. And as with the cases of Bernard Crowe and Gary Hinman, there is a sensible explanation for those murders that does not include a guilty Charles Manson.

That explanation will be forthcoming in this book. But before we get to a closer examination of the murders on Cielo Drive and the evidence regarding the motive for them that was eventually presented at Charles Manson's murder trial, there is still more history to be covered, including the stories of several more murders.

Chapter Notes

1 They were Sharon Tate Polanski, Jay Sebring, Voytek Frykowski, Abigail Folger, and Steve Parent. One other person on the property, caretaker William Garretson, who was staying in a guesthouse away from the main residence, was not killed.
2 From a 1993 Manson interview with Bill Scanlon-Murphy for BBC television.
3 *Will You Die For Me?*, page 136.
4 *Helter Skelter*, pages 349 - 350.
5 *Child of Satan, Child of God*, page 136.
6 Patricia Krenwinkel at her 1993 parole hearing, transcript page 19.
7 Charles Manson in a telephone conversation with the author.
8 From a Manson interview with Diane Sawyer for ABC Television's *A Turning Point*, first broadcast in1994.
9 From a Charles Manson telephone conversation with Sandra Good, 1996. Sandra Good Archives.

The gate at 10050 Cielo Drive in 1984

The Murders on Waverly Drive

"If I walk with somebody that's breaking the law, I'm not obligated by law to tell on that person. And I'm not obligated by law to make them do anything. So if Tex decides that he's gonna go in and kill everybody in that house, I mean, that's up to him."

-- Charles Manson

On the night of August 9, 1969, one day after the homicides on Cielo Drive, Leno and Rosemary LaBianca were killed in their home at 3301 Waverly Drive in the Los Feliz neighborhood of Los Angeles, about eight miles from the Polanski residence. Like the homicides the previous night at the Polanski house, the murders of the LaBiancas were committed with incredible savagery. Both victims had been bound and were stabbed multiple times. Leno LaBianca had the word "WAR" carved into his stomach. A knife was imbedded in his neck and a carving fork had been stuck into his abdomen. The words "Rise," "Death to pigs," and the cryptic "Healter Skelter" had been written on the walls and the refrigerator in the blood of the victims. It was a horrific scene.

What are the circumstances that led to the murders of the LaBiancas? Continuing with the methodology used throughout this book, let's look at the events of the night of August 9 -- events which ultimately culminated in those murders -- as later presented by the prosecution and as recalled by the people who were involved.

According to the prosecution's version of things, the previous night, after the murders at the Polanski residence, Charles Manson had received a full report of what went on there, and he didn't like what he heard. Those murders, Manson allegedly said, were "too messy," and there was too much confusion. This night he was going to lead the murder party himself and show everyone "how to do it right."

Sometime after dark on that Saturday night, Charles Manson drove a car away from Spahn's Ranch. With him were Charles Watson, Linda Kasabian, Susan Atkins, Patricia Krenwinkel, Leslie Van Houten, and Steve Grogan. This group drove around for several hours over a wide area of greater Los Angeles. Sometimes Manson drove, and sometimes Linda Kasabian drove. They made several stops throughout the evening, supposedly looking for people to kill.

At the first stop, possibly in Pasadena, Manson got out and scouted a house for a potential murder. He ruled the place out, however, saying that he had seen pictures of children on the walls inside and that he didn't want to start killing children -- yet.

They looked at another house in Pasadena, but Manson apparently decided that it wouldn't do because it was located too close to neighboring houses to commit a noisy mass murder.

They stopped at a church, where Manson said he would go inside and murder the minister and hang him on the cross over the altar (or, variously, upside-down on the cross). He went to the rear of the building but soon returned to the car saying that the place was locked up tight.

At a traffic light on Sunset Boulevard Manson announced that he was going to kill the driver of a nearby sports car. But just as he jumped out of the car to effect this murder the driver sped away.[1]

So far it appears that at least four murder attempts had been foiled only by the benevolent hand of fate. (Charles Watson remembers another one. See below.) At the later trial of Manson and his co-defendants, Deputy District Attorney Vincent Bugliosi ended his description of these alleged murder attempts with the observation that on August 9, 1969 no one in the greater Los Angeles area was safe from the murderous marauding of Charles Manson and his cohorts. And yet, scary talk aside, none of these supposed incidents had actually resulted in any real criminal activity or in any harm being done to anyone.

Finally, however, after the unsuccessful attempted murder of the motorist on Sunset Boulevard, Manson directed Linda Kasabian very specifically to drive to a house on Waverly Drive in the Los Feliz section of Los Angeles near Griffith Park. Manson and the others in the car were familiar with this neighborhood. The house that they drove to, at 3267 Waverly, had previously been occupied by a friend named Harold True. Most of the people in the car, including Manson, had visited True at his residence several times in the past.

At the time that everybody had earlier been at True's house the house next door to the west, number 3301, had been vacant. This night, however, it was occupied by Leno and Rosemary LaBianca.

It was probably about 2 o'clock in the morning on August 10, 1969.2 The LaBiancas had just returned from a long round-trip drive to Lake Isabella, a large, man-made recreational lake located about 130 miles north of Los Angeles. They had gone there to retrieve their motorboat, which a son had borrowed for a few days.

Upon their return home the LaBiancas left their car with the boat still on its trailer parked on Waverly Drive in front of the property on the west side of their lot. They then walked up the long driveway to their house. Once inside, Leno LaBianca let the family dog out into the fenced side yard on the east side of the house and began to read the Sunday newspaper while his wife got ready for bed in the bedroom in the home's southwest corner.

Outside, the car bearing Charles Manson, Linda Kasabian, Charles Watson, Susan Atkins, Patricia Krenwinkel, Leslie Van Houten, and Steve Grogan pulled over to the curb in front of the house and parked. What happened next?

In *Will You Die For Me?* Charles Watson devotes an entire chapter to the night of August 9-10. He recalls the pre-trip discussion at Spahn's Ranch, the citywide murder search, and the arrival at Waverly Drive. (Watson says that the LaBiancas' car and boat were parked in the driveway; they weren't.)

At Waverly Drive, according to Watson, Charles Manson went up to the LaBianca house alone, then came back to the car and got him. The two of them then walked up to the house and entered it. (Watson also says that Manson had a gun.) Inside, they found Leno LaBianca dozing on the couch in the living room. After Manson and Watson woke LaBianca up, Watson tied his hands behind his back. Manson asked if anyone else was in the house and LaBianca responded that his wife was in the bedroom.

According to Watson, Manson went and got Rosemary LaBianca and brought her into the living room. They then asked the couple if they had any money. Rosemary LaBianca volunteered that she had some cash in her wallet in the bedroom, which Manson sent Watson to get. After this, Manson and Watson decided to separate the couple, so they took Rosemary LaBianca back to the bedroom. Watson says that he then gagged the couple by placing pillowcases over their heads and securing them with lamp cords.

Then -- still according to Watson -- Manson left the house with the gun and Rosemary LaBianca's wallet, but not before telling him, "Make sure the girls get to do some of it, both of them."3

Although Watson maintains that he stayed in the house, he nevertheless claims that Manson then went down to the car and told Patricia Krenwinkel and Leslie Van Houten to go into the house and to do whatever he (Watson) told them to do. They did. Manson then got into the car and drove away.

According to Susan Atkins, Manson left the car for a short period of time and went up the driveway to 3301 Waverly. In her grand jury testimony (as reincarnated in the book *The Killing Of Sharon Tate*) Atkins says that Manson told her that he had a gun.4

Then Manson returned to the car and spoke with Watson for a few moments before saying, "Tex, Katie [Patricia Krenwinkel], Leslie, go into the house. I have the people tied up. They are very calm." And, "Now, the last time [at the Polanski residence] you blew it. You panicked the people. Don't panic the people this time. Let them think it's going to be okay -- so at least they'll go in peace."5

After Watson, Krenwinkel, and Van Houten got out of the car and started walking up towards the house, the rest of the people drove off.

At her 1993 parole hearing, Patricia Krenwinkel remembered, "And then Manson started talking again.... He was going to go out looking for someone else to kill...."

The parole board commissioner asked, "Did Mr. Manson tell you why he wanted to go out and kill somebody else?"

"That night, no," Krenwinkel answered. "It was difficult to say exactly why Manson decides to do anything, because it always changed...."

At 3301 Waverly, "I'm not sure how he got in, to be honest.... I know he went inside."

Where was she?

"In the car."

With everyone else?

"Yes, everyone else was in the car.... He eventually came out and got Tex. Tex and he were in for a while, then he came back out and told Leslie and myself to go in."6

Leslie Van Houten recalls a similar story, but is unsure of many of the details. At her 1993 parole hearing she said:

> I remember late evening, I think I was on the boardwalk [at Spahn's Ranch] when Charles, again, I -- I'm telling you how I remember this part twenty-five years later. Parts of the crime are very clear to me, that will never leave me; *other parts*, I'm not -- I'm not trying to be evasive. *They just aren't that clear....* (emphasis added)
>
> But that evening, I *believe* that Tex and the others were getting close, and Charlie came up to me and asked me, did I believe enough that I could go with them and that I could kill. Was I crazy enough to believe in him? And I said, "Yes." (emphasis added)
>
> Everything in my personality, you know, body language -- I made it very clear that I wanted to go....

Van Houten only vaguely recalled the city-wide search for murder victims. "Most of the time I was sleeping," she said. But "finally, we pulled up in front of the LaBianca home....

"We pulled up to the house. I'm, *I'm not clear on some of the things* up until I go in the house. I know that Manson went in the house and *I'm not sure if Watson went in the house, also. I'm confused on that.*" (emphasis added)

A parole commissioner tried to resolve the confusion by pointing out that if the LaBiancas were already tied up when Van Houten entered the house, as she claimed, it was not likely that only Manson had been in the house before she got there.

"Right," she replied.

The commissioner asked about Manson remarking that he "wanted to show you how to do it right." Van Houten answered:

> *I'm not sure if I heard that personally or if I've overheard it and read it myself....* I hope you understand, I'm trying to go as much on what I absolutely remember and not [on speculation].... Lots of information that, you know, like these days there's lots of speculation on why this house, why that -- and *I'm trying not to [confuse] my memory with those things.*
>
> So then Manson came back out and he selected Pat and I to go in the house. And at some point I remember him telling Watson that all of us were to do something and not to frighten the people like he had the night before. That's why I don't under[stand] -- *I'm not sure Watson was [still] in the house or not*, because *I seem to remember* [Manson] talking to Watson.7 (all emphasis added)

(In a 1989 interview Van Houten was even less sure about what happened at this point. "Manson came back [to the car] and I believe Tex did too.... He looked at the car and he pointed to Pat and I and told us to get out and to do what Tex said.... And *I don't remember if he said this in front of me, or I heard it later or something*, but he said to Tex to make sure that everybody did something...."8 {emphasis added})

Thus we have the versions of the events of August 9-10 from all of the people who were present except Steve Grogan. What are Charles Manson's recollections? In a telephone conversation with Manson in 1998 I asked him what he remembered about that night, after the carload of people arrived at Waverly Drive. He said:

> And I went to see Harold [True]. Harold wasn't there, and I looked over and I seen a light over on the other side, and I walked over and there

was a little dog there. So I patted the dog on the head and I opened the door and there was a dude sitting on the couch.

And when I walked in, I said, "Oh, hey. Hi."

He said, "Hi."

I said, "I didn't know anybody lived here."

He said, "Oh yeah, we moved in here last week," or something like that. Da da da.

I asked Manson if Leno LaBianca was upset over the fact that he had just walked uninvited into his house very late at night:

No. No. There was no fear involved. It's just like -- that's what I say. I move in a level -- I move beyond all that fear.

Tex was -- he come in behind me. And me and the guy got into a conversation, "Wah-wah-wah, roo-roo-roo," and I said, "Well, you know, I gotta go."

And then Tex moved in and started talking to him. And I walked on out.

It didn't have a fucking thing to do with me.

I asked Manson if he used a leather thong to tie Leno LaBianca up.

"No.... Leather thongs is what I always kept around my neck. That's called a outlaw handcuffs. You know, I've always kept that around.... for emergency. But I never had any thought [about tying LaBianca up]."

Did he tell the girls to go into the house with Charles Watson?

"No."

When he went back to the car, did they just get out of the car on their own?

"I don't remember. I'm not sure. I think they were coming up.... And he [Watson] may have come back out of the house. I don't even remember that. Because I was pretty loaded, actually."9

(Manson does remember telling the people going up to the house not to let the LaBiancas know if they were going to be killed. "If you're going to war," he explained, "and you're fighting your enemy, and you kill him when he's afraid, it's a bad omen. It's bad."10)

"I don't think," Manson elaborated during his telephone conversation with me. "I don't think that much. I quit thinking. People don't realize this:

> Here's the thing. When you clear your mind, and there's no thought in your mind, there can be no malice aforethought. In other words, like, all monks and all holy men, or holy people -- they don't think. When you spend ten or fifteen years in solitary, you either quit thinking or you'll die. Because you know that your thinking doesn't really mean anything. It's just your own talking to yourself.
>
> So I wasn't thinking about nothing. I was just moving on what I was moving on, and doing what I was doing.... You have to realize. I'm a soldier. And I'm a soldier in my own right and my own way, doing my own battle in my own perspective. That's called "doing your own time" in prison.
>
> That's what we were doing at the ranch. Everybody was in one thought, like on the mainline [in prison]. Everybody was looking out for everybody else's welfare. And when one guy fell in trouble, the rest of us fell in trouble with him....
>
> It was everybody's mind in one. It wasn't just *my* mind. There's no one person [that] can be the one. But one person can hold the *thought* of the one....
>
> When you're in a mainline and someone says something's coming down, and you're walking right next to it, it doesn't affect you. So, you just learn to kind of close your mind to things around you. I mean, not that you're not aware of what's going on -- it's just none of your affair.11

By all accounts Charles Manson departed Waverly Drive shortly after he and his carload of companions arrived there. "I left because I left. I didn't know [people were going to be killed]. I didn't *not* know," he later recalled in a television interview.12

After leaving Los Feliz, the car drove around for quite a while before Manson pulled over into a gas station in Sylmar, almost twenty miles from the LaBianca residence. Then, according to Linda Kasabian (and, later, the prosecution), Manson instructed Kasabian to leave Rosemary Labianca's wallet in the women's restroom. Manson supposedly thought that a black person would find the wallet, use the credit cards in it, get caught, and thus put suspicion for the murders on black people. (Sylmar was not a black neighborhood, but Manson allegedly thought that it was.) Kasabian disposed of the wallet well, placing inside the tank of the toilet.13

Manson remembered the wallet episode somewhat differently. I asked him if he told Linda Kasabian to get rid of the wallet. He said that he did, but only after he became aware of the wallet's presence in the car and because he assumed that it was "hot." I asked him if he told her to put the wallet actually inside of the toilet tank in the restroom. Again, he said that he did. When I asked him why, he said, "Because in prison everything goes into the toilet."14

As for Manson mistakenly thinking that the neighborhood was populated by blacks, he told me that he knew that it was not. (Sylmar is located very far out in the San Fernando Valley, farther north even than Spahn's Movie Ranch. It is many miles -- and a mountain range -- away from any of the generally known black areas in Los Angeles, and it is hardly likely that anyone would mistakenly conclude that it was a black neighborhood. Indeed, it was not.15)

According to Linda Kasabian they drove on, eventually reaching the ocean somewhere south of Venice Beach. Kasabian and Manson took a short walk on the beach, where she claimed they were stopped and questioned briefly by two police officers. (These officers could never be located later to corroborate this part of Kasabian's narrative.) They then rejoined Susan Atkins and Steve Grogan in the car.

Then, still according to Kasabian, Manson suggested that they kill an actor who lived in the area who had given her and Sandra Good a ride a week or so earlier. (Susan Atkins remembers that Kasabian suggested killing the actor, and that she did so while they were still in Sylmar.16)

Kasabian said that she took Manson to the man's apartment building but pointed out the wrong apartment. Because they were unable to make contact with the actor this murder attempt, like the others earlier in the evening, was scrapped. Manson then left Kasabian, Atkins, and Grogan on the beach near Venice and drove alone back to Spahn's Ranch. The trio hitchhiked back to the ranch later.

So did the people who had been left at Waverly Drive, but not until after they had killed Leno and Rosemary LaBianca.

Much of the accepted information about this night of murder comes from Linda Kasabian. Her character, credibility, and possible motivations for saying what she says will be examined in a later chapter. For now, however, let's look at some of the variances in the different stories of that night (besides those previously discussed) and try to come up with some sensible conclusions.

With regard to the alleged city-wide murder search, the various accounts of this hunting expedition are all confusing and contradictory. None of the persons who recall the particulars of the victim quest recall them occurring in the same order. Some people remember more "murder attempts" than others do.17

I asked Manson about the supposed city-wide search for victims which preceded everyone's arrival at Waverly Drive. He would not go into the specifics of the various alleged murder attempts, but he suggested that there was not enough time for the people in the car to have left Spahn's Ranch after dark and do all of that driving and stalking around greater Los Angeles before arriving at the LaBiancas' house in Los Feliz at around 2 a.m.

Of the other persons in the car (excluding Patricia Krenwinkel and Steve Grogan, neither of whom have, to my knowledge, commented on this part of the evening), all of them remember the lookover of the house with the pictures of children. But Susan Atkins doesn't remember Manson talking about not killing children; she says that Manson didn't want to harm children by killing their parents. Also, while all other accounts say that Manson scouted this house alone, Charles Watson says that he accompanied Manson to look in the window.

As for the incident at the church, while all participants (again excepting Krenwinkel and Grogan) have remembered this, both Linda Kasabian and Leslie Van Houten have no specific recall of Manson's possible intentions. Kasabian "believed, but *wasn't absolutely sure*, that [Manson] told them that he was going to 'get' the minister or priest."18 (emphasis added) At her 1993 parole hearing, Leslie Van Houten said:

"[Manson] said he wanted to do something to the minister, *or something.... I think* he wanted to put the minister up on the cross."19 (emphasis added)

As for the house that was too close to the neighbors for a murder, only Charles Watson and Linda Kasabian have recalled this. Watson remembers the house as a "mansion." If so, it must have been a mansion on a small lot to have been so close to the other homes on the street that a murder committed therein would have aroused the attention of the neighbors. (Linda Kasabian later pointed out a house she claimed was this one to Vincent Bugliosi when he took her around the city looking for sites related to the case while preparing for the murder trial. None of the other passengers in the car have confirmed that the house Kasabian showed Bugliosi was *the* house, however. In any case, Kasabian could have pointed out any house that fit her vague description of one that was too close to the adjacent homes.)

(Watson also has a memory of a "couple pulling into their driveway" that Manson supposedly considered killing. None of the other passengers in the car have voiced any memory of this.20)

The alleged incident with the driver of the sports car is puzzling. According to Linda Kasabian and Charles Watson, earlier in the evening Charles Manson had aborted one murder attempt because the target house was too close to the neighbors. A short while later, however, he is apparently ready to gun down a motorist at an intersection on Sunset Boulevard presumably in front of any witnesses who might have been present on a Saturday night. (It is only Linda Kasabian and Charles Watson who recall this alleged incident.)

Is it believable that Charles Manson, who was earlier supposedly too concerned with noise and attention to kill people inside a house, would now be so carefree and careless that he would jump out of a car at an intersection on busy Sunset Boulevard on a summertime Saturday night and kill someone by firing off an extremely loud .45 caliber pistol? (See Charles Watson's identification of the gun as a .45, below.) If he had done this, there would have been a great risk of him being heard and seen by other drivers and/or pedestrians. And why would Manson attract even further attention to himself by getting out of the car? If Linda Kasabian was driving and Manson pointed out the sports car and told her to "pull up beside it" on the generally four-lane (two going in each direction) Sunset Boulevard, that would put Manson directly to the sports car driver's left, just a few feet away. At that distance the driver would have been an easy target. Why would Manson get out of the car? Having to get back in the car after any shooting would only have added to the getaway time and would have afforded more chances for witnesses to see him and the vehicle he was riding in.

Is it believable that Charles Manson, a man who had supposedly exercised such caution everywhere else during the evening would suddenly become so careless in this instance? The reader can come to his own conclusion, but I don't think that it is. I think that the story is likelier an apocryphal embellishment of Linda Kasabian's narrative that was later repeated by Charles Watson in his book.

There is confusion as to whether a gun was along for the ride. Charles Watson says that Charles Manson had a gun, a .45 caliber pistol. Susan Atkins remembered that Manson *told* her he had a gun. Linda Kasabian says that she saw a gun at different times during the evening but did not recall Manson taking it with him when he left the car at Waverly Drive. Nor could she describe the weapon.

Neither Patricia Krenwinkel or Leslie Van Houten mention a gun.

Charles Manson said that he had no gun.

So the only persons who talk with any specificity about a gun are Charles Watson and Linda Kasabian. Watson's claim that the gun was a .45 caliber automatic is from his book; it's not part of any testimony given at Charles Manson's trial. (Watson did not testify at the trial of Manson and his co-defendants.) Kasabian's recollection is so vague that she could not even describe whether the weapon, which she nevertheless claimed to have seen several times, was a revolver or a pistol. If Charles Watson is correct about the gun being an automatic pistol, it strains credibility that Kasabian could not even describe it generally, especially if she had seen it several times, since most .45 automatics are very simply and distinctively designed. Her hazy non-remembrance of the gun's appearance is not very convincing proof of the weapon's existence.

I think it is unlikely that Manson had a gun. Such a weapon has never been accounted for, either before or after that night. Where did it come from, and where did it go? In *Helter Skelter* Vincent Bugliosi postulated that Steve Grogan got rid of it, possibly by burying it, at the beach in Venice.21 Since Grogan was never charged in connection with any of the events of August 9 he has never answered any questions about those events, so we don't know what he might be able to say about it. But why would people who were actively and purposely trying to accumulate survival supplies for an extended stay in the desert get rid of a perfectly good firearm, especially when it had not been used in any crime?

Another question is which house on Waverly Drive did Charles Manson initially go up to? Charles Watson and Susan Atkins say that he went up to the LaBianca house.22 But both Charles Manson and Linda Kasabian say that he went up Harold True's driveway, to 3267 Waverly. Vincent Bugliosi, following Kasabian's lead, accepts Manson's route up the hill as being towards True's house.23 This being the case there is no real reason to believe that he did not first go to True's house, just as he says he did.

There is also some confusion as to the order that people went into the LaBianca house. Charles Watson says that Manson went up to 3301 Waverly but didn't go inside. Then he came back to the car and got him and they both went up to and into the house together.24

Linda Kasabian says that Manson went up to the house, subdued the LaBiancas by tying them up, then came back down and got Watson, Krenwinkel, and Van Houten and sent them into the house.25

Susan Atkins has a recollection similar to Kasabian's.26

Leslie Van Houten is not sure.27

Patricia Krenwinkel says that Manson went up to and into the house, came out and got Charles Watson, went back to the house, and then came back to the car for Leslie Van Houten and herself.28

But Kasabian, Atkins, and Krenwinkel are undoubtedly wrong when they say that Manson went into the house alone first and subdued the LaBiancas, for even though Charles Watson says that Manson first reconnoitered 3301 Waverly without entering and then came back to the car for him, both Manson and Watson say that they initially entered the house more or less together, and there is no reason to disbelieve them. Certainly if Manson had really gone into the house alone first and bound and gagged the LaBiancas Watson would be more than happy to say so.

It is more reasonable to conclude that what really happened was that Charles Manson and Charles Watson went to the LaBianca house together and that Manson (and possibly Watson) returned to the car -- just as Manson says it happened.

Another discrepancy involves the amount of time that Manson was away from the car.

Susan Atkins said, "He was gone for a considerable time -- although none of us was keeping track of the time."29

Patricia Krenwinkel and Leslie Van Houten are vague and unsure.

Charles Watson says that he and Manson went into the house (after Charles Manson first went to the house alone), got the drop on Leno LaBianca, reassured him, tied him up, and asked about other people in the house. Manson then "disappeared for a minute or two" before bringing Rosemary LaBianca into the living room. Manson and Watson then conversed with the LaBiancas. Then Manson waited with the couple while Watson looked around the house for money. After this search, they took Rosemary LaBianca back into the bedroom, then returned to the living room and bound, gagged, and put a pillowcase over the head of Leno LaBianca. Then they went back to the bedroom again and did the same with his wife. Finally, after all of this activity, Manson left the house.30

Charles Manson said that he was only in the house briefly, for a few minutes at the most. I asked him about Rosemary LaBianca and he said that he never even saw her, that she was in "the back bedroom." (To someone coming into the LaBianca house from the direction of Harold True's former residence, the master bedroom in the southwest corner of the LaBianca house would be in the "back" of the house, relatively.)

So how long was Manson away from the car doing whatever he was doing at 3267 and 3301 Waverly Drive?

Linda Kasabian, star witness for the prosecution, testified at the murder trial that, "he got out of the car. He disappeared up the walkway, up the driveway leading towards Harold's house, and I could not follow him any longer, he just disappeared."

Prosecutor Bugliosi asked, "How long after he left the car did he return to the car?"

Kasabian answered, "I remember we all lit up cigarettes, and we smoked about three-quarters of a Pall Mall cigarette, however long that takes."31

Three-quarters of a Pall Mall cigarette.

Smoking three-quarters of a non-filtered Pall Mall cigarette (the preferred brand of many of the people at Spahn's Ranch) would probably take about three or four minutes. And that is certainly not enough time for Manson to have done all of the things that either Charles Watson or Linda Kasabian said that he did inside the LaBianca residence.

But it does allow Manson enough time to do what he said he did.

Cigarettes are pretty good timers. If Linda Kasabian is correct in her memory of this cigarette smoking (and why wouldn't she be?), then Manson was only away from the car for a few minutes -- just long enough to walk up Harold True's driveway, determine that no one was there, notice the light on in the house next door, hop the fence and walk to 3301 Waverly, go inside, talk briefly with Leno LaBianca, and then return to the car -- in other words, just enough time to do exactly what he said he did.

As for discrepancies about what happened after the carload left Waverly Drive, I have already discussed the "wallet in the toilet" episode and the unlikelihood that the wallet would be planted in a non-black neighborhood so that a black person would find it, use the credit cards, get caught, and thus put suspicion for the LaBianca murders on blacks. I have also noted the unlikely circumstances surrounding the supposed presence and disappearance of the vapory .45. As for the incident with the actor in the apartment building in Venice, here again what happened to Charles Manson's supposed earlier concern about not committing murders where the neighbors were too close by? And did Kasabian really point to a wrong door? She says that she did, knocked, and a sleepy man eventually answered.32 (Susan Atkins says that no one answered.33) But if another person answered at another door, why weren't they murdered? Did it have to be the actor? (Like the police officers who Kasabian claimed confronted Manson and her on the beach, this lucky "wrong apartment" dweller could never be located to corroborate whether this part of Kasabian's story ever really happened.)

When it comes to the differences in the recollections of the people convicted of murdering Leno and Rosemary LaBianca, we are left with a hodge-podge of inconsistent and contradictory stories about what happened on the night of August 9-10, 1969. But there is no discrepancy or question that cannot, by a careful and fair consideration of all of the evidence, be explained and resolved to fit the version of events as given by Charles Manson, a version in which he committed no crime.

Chapter Notes

1 This account of the evening of August 9-10 is taken from several sources, including Linda Kasabian's re-enactment of that night as she drove around the city with Vincent Bugliosi, as recounted on pages 361-363 of *Helter Skelter*, Charles Watson in his book *Will You Die For Me?*, pages 146-147, Susan Atkins in *Child of Satan, Child of God*, pages 145-146 (and in her later recanted grand jury testimony as presented in the book *The Killing of Sharon Tate*, pages 111-112), and by Leslie Van Houten at her 1993 parole hearing, transcript pages 15-16.

2 Here accepting the time as given by the prosecution at the murder trial, based on the recollection of the newsstand vendor who sold the LaBiancas a newspaper at about 1:30 a. m.

3 *Will You Die For Me?*, page 148.

4 *The Killing Of Sharon Tate*, page 112.

5 Ibid., page 113.

6 From Patricia Krenwinkel's 1993 parole hearing transcript, pages 20 & 26.

7 From Leslie Van Houten's 1993 parole hearing, transcript pages 14-19.

8 Leslie Van Houten on *Larry King Live*, 1989.

9 From a tape-recorded telephone conversation with the author.

10 Manson remembered this to Diane Sawyer on ABC Television's *A Turning Point*.
11 Charles Manson telephone conversation with the author.
12 Manson to Diane Sawyer, *A Turning Point*.
13 As recounted in *Helter Skelter*, page 365.
14 We had this conversation about the wallet during a visit at the California State Prison at Corcoran.
15 There was a black neighborhood in the San Fernando Valley, Pacoima, that was on the likely route that the Spahn's Ranch riders took from the LaBianca house to Sylmar, but it was four miles south of Sylmar, and even if Manson was aware of it existence there is no explanation for why the wallet was not ditched in this actual black neighborhood instead of a white one several miles farther up the road.
16 *Child of Satan, Child of God*, page 147.
17 Charles Watson remembers (in this order) the house with children, the houses too close together, the church, a couple in a driveway, and the sports car. Linda Kasabian recalled the house with the children, the too close houses, she is not sure about the church, and is sure about the sports car. Susan Atkins remembers (in order) only the church and the house with the pictures of the children. Leslie Van Houten remembers the house with the children and, vaguely, the incident at the church (See Footnote # 1.).
18 *Helter Skelter*, page 362.
19 Leslie Van Houten 1993 parole hearing, transcript page 16.
20 *Will You Die For Me?*, page 146.
21 *Helter Skelter*, page 369.
22 Watson in *Will You Die For Me?*, page 147 and Atkins in *The Killing Of Sharon Tate*, page 112 and *Child of Satan, Child of God*, page146.
23 *Helter Skelter*, page 363.
24 *Will You Die For Me?*, page 147.
25 *Helter Skelter*, page 364.
26 *Child Of Satan, Child Of God*, page 146.
27 Leslie Van Houten 1993 parole hearing, transcript page 17.
28 From Patricia Krenwinkel's 1993 parole hearing transcript, page 25.
29 *Child Of Satan, Child Of God*, page 146.
30 *Will You Die For Me?*, pages 147-148.
31 This testimony is recalled on page 165 of *Witness To Evil*, by George Bishop, and also by trial juror William Zamora in *Blood Family*, page 108.
32 *Helter Skelter*, page 367.
33 *Child of Satan, Child of God*, page 147.

3301 Waverly Drive in 2013

The Murder of Donald "Shorty" Shea

"You just can't come up and take Shorty away because you don't like the way Shorty lives. You got to have *earned* Shorty. When you've earned the right to take Shorty, you reach over and take Shorty's hat off and put it on his foot and lay him down and cover him up with dirt if you want to. Because you've earned that. Because you walk with God. And when you walk with God, you can run with the devil."

-- Charles Manson

The last of the so-called "Manson murders" was that of Donald Jerome "Shorty" Shea, a hired hand at Spahn's Movie Ranch.

In 1969 Donald Shea had worked at Spahn's sporadically for over a decade. Besides being a ranch hand he also was an aspiring actor. Occasionally he left his job at the ranch for brief stints of work in television or movies, frequently as a stunt man. At the end of August 1969, Shea left Spahn's Ranch for good.

By late August life at the ranch was edgy for a lot of reasons. Besides the pressures and paranoia brought on by the string of violent events of that summer there were also other factors which created conflicts and tensions between various people on the property.

George Spahn's family was pressuring him to sell the ranch. A would-be entrepreneur, Frank Retz, wanted to buy it. The presence of Charles Manson and others was seen by some people as an unnecessary and troublesome impediment to the future financial possibilities of the property. Thus there were efforts by some of the people who had pecuniary interests in the ranch to have Manson and the people with him thrown off of it.

One such effort involved poisoning the mind of George Spahn. Donald Shea was one person who said bad things about Manson's crowd to the ranch owner. Lynette Fromme, who spent much of her time caring for the eighty-two-year-old Spahn, heard Shea's aspersions against her friends and told Manson about them. As the people at Spahn's Ranch drifted into separate factions with concerns over the future of the property, Donald Shea was clearly on the side that wanted Manson and his associates out -- and they knew it. So to them he was perceived as an enemy.

But George Spahn showed little inclination to evict anyone, so other means were employed to bring pressure upon unwanted people to leave. One of these means was to call the police down on them at every possible opportunity.

Law enforcement attention had been focused on the ranch for some time. Of course the police pay attention to any place within their jurisdiction, but they especially did so to Spahn's Ranch, where there seemed to be a great amount of unregulated activity. Also, it was known that persons with criminal records resided there.

The ranch was raided by Sheriff's deputies numerous times in the spring and summer of 1969. On one of these raids the authorities shut down the "Helter Skelter" nightclub. On other occasions they invaded the place on the pretext of looking for stolen vehicles or other property, or just to count heads.

On August 16 a very big raid occurred, a pre-dawn affair involving over one hundred law enforcement officers. It netted twenty-six suspects, most of whom were charged with grand theft auto. All of them were released a few days later when it was discovered that their arrest warrant had been misdated.

On August 24 Charles Manson was in one of the "Outlaw Shacks" near the back ranch house (these structures were located away from the barn and main movie-set buildings of the ranch, down a roadway that the ranch denizens called "Lover's Lane") with a girl named Stephanie Schramm when two Sheriff's deputies kicked in the door and took them both into custody. Schramm was soon released, but because an apparent marijuana cigarette was found on or near Manson's clothing he was booked on a possession charge and kept in jail.

While Manson was in jail, the bad blood between him, some of his associates, and Donald Shea continued to boil. As Kitty Lutesinger, a girlfriend of Bobby Beausoleil, later recalled, "While he [Manson] was in jail, Shorty was doing a lot of nasty talking about Charlie."1

After a few days Manson was released when the "marijuana" turned out not to be pot. He returned to the ranch where, naturally, his most recent arrest was discussed. In discussing this arrest and other law enforcement invasions of the property it seemed apparent to some people that many of the recent busts were based in part on specific information provided to the police by an informant. In other words, the ranch had a snitch.

In the underworld -- and especially in prison -- no one is regarded with more derision than a snitch. And there is a good reason for this: The frequently exaggerated (or flat-out untrue) and generally self-serving statements given to authorities by such informants can often cause the subject of those statements to lose years of their lives -- or even the life itself -- for the mistake of misplacing a trust. Many people feel that snitching strikes at the core of mutual respect and honor among men, and history is replete with examples of infamous and loathed tellers, from Judas Iscariot to Edward Snowden.

On a world level, the punishment meted out to a person who sells out his friends -- that is, his country -- is severe. Depending on the circumstances, such as whether or not a country is at war, the penalty can even be death.

In the underworld the penalties for telling are also high.

When Donald Shea decided to inform on the people around him, he did not realize how dangerous the world he was playing in was. He was not aware of the full dynamics involved with the people with whom he was dealing. He did not know how far their level of devotion and commitment to each other had evolved. Nor did he have any idea of what some of them had already done to demonstrate that devotion and commitment.

Donald Shea did not know that they were at war.

Shortly after Manson's release after his arrest on the phony marijuana charge, Donald Shea vanished.

Shea's disappearance from Spahn's Ranch was soon noted. Ruby Pearl, a fifty-ish former horse wrangler who worked for George Spahn as a ranch manager, later told a reporter, "We're very concerned about him because he hasn't showed up. And if he were in this area he would show up, because he left his things here." When the reporter asked for a description of Shea, Pearl responded, "Heavy-set, husky build, and strong."2

"Shorty" Shea was, in fact, a large man.

After Shea's disappearance about all that was known about the missing ranch hand was that he was missing. But many people heard stories about what happened to him.

Killing a snitch serves two purposes. Besides removing the direct threat created by the person going to authorities, it also sends a powerful message to other people who might also be thinking about talking. That message is: Don't. Thus the killing of Donald Shea was referred to with some frequency and candor by some of the people at the ranch. The story was also exaggerated and embellished with each telling. It became "common knowledge," for instance, that Shea was beheaded and cut up into nine pieces.

For years the missing decapitated and dismembered corpse of Donald Shea was one of the most sinister and eerie images connected with the "Manson Murders." But this image was really just a macabre mirage. In 1977 Steve Grogan agreed to tell authorities where Shea's body had been buried near Spahn's Ranch. When Shea was exhumed he was certainly dead, but he was otherwise intact. (Grogan was quietly paroled in 1985.)

Eventually, Charles Manson, Bruce Davis, and Steve Grogan were convicted of Donald Shea's murder. All three men received life sentences. At least four other persons who were known to have participated in the murder and its immediate aftermath (i.e., the disposal of Shea's body and possessions) were never prosecuted.

Of all of the murders connected to Charles Manson there is less information and material available on the Donald Shea homicide than on any other. One reason for this is that the Hinman-Shea murder trial was largely eclipsed by the higher profile Tate-La-Bianca trial that preceded it. After the conclusion of the earlier proceeding, the media and the public had less interest in the less spectacular Hinman-Shea trial. But the main reason for the lack of information is that there simply isn't any. There was no physical evidence or direct eyewitness testimony that necessarily connected

any of the persons eventually convicted of the murder to it. For a long time, even after the convictions were obtained, there was still some doubt as to whether there had even been a murder, because Shea's body was not recovered for over eight years.

But some details of the Shea murder have come to light in the appearances before California's Board of Prison Terms by two of the persons later convicted of that killing. In 1979 Steve Grogan recalled to the board the circumstances that led to the murder:

> Well, it was like a growing hostility. They didn't like him. Charlie didn't like him because he was -- he was always drinking and he thought he was a slob. He was, you know -- he was always talking about messing with the girls that were there. And it was like, you know -- it was kind of subtle at first, the way, you know, [Manson] voiced his dislike and disapproval of the man. Like he would bring it up in conversation at dinner when we all sat around and ate. Over a period of time it grew worse until -- and then we were raided by the police where everything we had was taken, that we had bought legitimately. And plus the children were taken, too. Everybody was arrested on the ranch. In fact the only person left was George Spahn, and he was blind.... Mr. Shea had told the police that we had a stolen car ring. Okay? Well, we spent three nights in jail, and we were released, and we didn't get back none of our property -- to four or five dune buggies that we couldn't get back from them; the children put into foster homes. And what it really did is made everybody really upset at this guy, because I was led to believe that he was doing it to get us evicted off the ranch, to get us thrown off the ranch. And that was the only place we had to stay at the time. And it was through his actions that he caused us this trouble.... There was, you know, a feeling of almost hatred toward the guy because of what he made us go through, the children and stuff. Like we held the children in almost the highest position. They were home-delivered and breast-fed. It was like -- our feeling for the children was really the highest thing we felt. This was mostly the whole

reason we were all together, to put the children in a good environment, free from social indoctrinations and stuff, try to raise them as natural as we could. And then to have someone come along and form a false story and have them put in foster homes, it was really a blow to the women and men that were at the place at the time.

I was convinced that because of his actions, that caused the harm to come to everything we had and the children. That was -- it was like kind of everybody's feeling at the ranch towards him.... I used to work with him before earlier, when I used to stay there earlier, when he used to come for maybe a month at a time. He'd work for a month for room and board, maybe a few bucks. Then he would leave. He was kind of like a drifter. He would come back for maybe seasonal work. And at one point in time we did talk to him and befriended him and was nice to him. And as we started suspecting him as being an influence that was trying to hurt us, threaten our position at the ranch, you know, we generally cut him off, and no one would talk to him. And I guess the belief that he wasn't any good just kept increasing in intensity. I was thoroughly convinced that he was out to get us evicted, kicked off the ranch.3

As for the actual murder of Shea, Grogan remembered:

Well, that morning I was awakened by Charles Manson and still, you know, half asleep, [and he] told me to get to the car and handed me like a pipe wrench. Told me to hit Shorty in the back of the head as soon as Tex gave me the go ahead or gave me the signal.

At that point Tex and I entered the back seat behind the driver, which was Jerome Shea; and Tex was on his right hand side. We proceeded down Santa Susana Pass toward San Fernando Valley. And about a quarter mile down from the ranch there was like a turnoff where cars, you know, like a rest area. And Tex mentioned that he had some parts over there that he had to get, pick up before he went to the store.

I still haven't got over, you know, the emotional part. You know, so sometimes it's kind of hard to, you know, overcome the atrocity that I did....

Then we pulled off the road. Tex got out. The car was still in gear. I think he just had his foot on the brake, and they got out and they looked around the bushes like he was looking for some parts.

In the meantime, I was supposed to hit this guy in the back of the head. And like I never, you know, hit anybody or hurt anybody like that before, and it was hard, you know. I kept on hesitating in my mind, you know, looking at the cars on the highway hoping maybe because of the traffic I wouldn't have to hit him because it was just ten feet off the lane.

And Tex was urging me, you know, come on hit this guy. I kept hesitating. He pulled out a knife he had. I guess that's what finally, you know, put me over the edge. I just hit the guy. I wasn't really -- there was no accurate shot or nothing like that….

Well, the blow stunned him but it didn't knock him out. And he jumped to the passenger side of the seat. That was, the car door was already open and exited through there….

The blow knocked him forward so he hit the steering wheel and surprised him and he jumped out the side and I had to reach over the seat and get in the driver's seat to stop the car, because the way it was parked there was an embankment, you know, like cul-de-sac ditch. And the car ran -- drove into the ditch. So, meantime, I'm jumping over the seat trying to put the brake on, put the car in gear, stop the motor, he had already been stabbed….

I imagine Tex did [it]. I didn't actually see him stab him. My head was turned, you know. The car had left. My peripheral vision, I didn't catch what was going on. [I] came out of the car and he was laying on the ground in a semi-conscious state. He was already going or something. At that point Manson arrived on the scene with another person….

And I was handed a knife and told to stab him. I stabbed him twice in the chest. And some others were told the same….

[Manson] might have slashed him. I don't recall if he stabbed him….

Well, at that point, couple minutes after he was dead I was told to take him, drag him into some bushes that were further from the highway, cover him up till night, come back at night and bury him. And the others left so I came back at night and buried him.4

Bruce Davis has also often been quizzed about the murder. In 1993 he told a parole board:

And then the thing with Shorty went down. I just -- I just stood there. And we were at the ranch early in the morning. Manson came down [and] said, "We're going to kill Shorty."

I said, "What for?"

"Well, he's a snitch."

Charlie is there. [Name deleted] is there. He says, "You guys take him -- ask him to take you down the hill to get some car parts and -- and kill him on the way down the hill."

And you know, the part that made me sick all the way through the whole thing was that I didn't have enough guts to say, "I'm not going."

I just went along. When the attack on Shorty initially started I didn't do a thing. I couldn't even believe what I was -- I don't know, I was sort of in a different world.

I was *there*.

And so, we got in the car. Steve [*sic*] drove; we got in the back. I was in the back, and Charlie Manson -- [no, it was] Charlie Watson. Charlie Manson was not in the car. Manson was behind us in another car with one of the girls.

We started down the hill of the ranch, down towards the valley, and, and somebody -- probably, probably Watson – tells Shorty to pull over.

And Shorty said, "What for?"

At this point, Watson stabbed Shorty Shea in his eye. I couldn't -- I mean, I was in the back and I couldn't see, but that's -- I'm sure that's what happened. And [he] pulled the car over.

And Steve -- Steve hit Shorty with, with a pipe wrench. They got him out of the car. Or actually, Charlie Watson got Shorty out of the car. I -- we were headed down the hill. They drug him out of the passenger side of the car. And I thought, I -- I don't know....

Then later when I went down to where this -- where they had actually killed him -- when I showed up, you know -- he was incapacitated. I don't know. You asked me if he was unconscious? I don't know. He may or may not have been. He didn't seem conscious. He wasn't moving or saying anything.

And it started off, Manson handed me a machete as if I was supposed to -- I mean, I know what he wanted. But, you know, I just couldn't do that. And I -- in fact, I did touch Shorty Shea with a machete on the back of his neck. I didn't break the skin. I mean, I just couldn't do it.

And then I threw the knife -- and then he handed me the bayonet, and it -- I just reached over and -- I don't know which side it was on, but I did cut him right about here on the shoulder, just with the tip of the blade. Sort of like saying, "Are you satisfied, Charlie?"

And I turned around and walked away. And I -- I was sick for about two or three days.5

Later in the same hearing, Davis elaborated a bit more:

Well, I'll tell you about my attitude toward Shorty. I was not personally mad at him. I thought the thing about him being a snitch was superfluous. I mean, everything we were doing was right out in the open anyway. So, I mean, it doesn't take a wise guy to tell what was going [on]. So the thing about Shorty being a snitch, he wasn't saying anything that a million other people couldn't have said at that point.

So I was not -- I was not angry at Shorty. I had talked to Shorty before, out there. We didn't have a great relationship, you know. We talked together and he told me about being a stunt man and his -- what he was doing, and this and that.

When Charlie said they want -- we was going to kill Shorty because he was a snitch, it, it was -- I couldn't believe it.

I don't remember if -- I don't remember much conversation at all about it.... That got worked out between Charlie and -- and Grogan. Between Watson and Grogan.

A parole board member asked Davis why he went along and participated in the murder. Davis answered:

"I think part of it was everybody standing in close proximity. I was standing there with Watson, Grogan, [name deleted], me. Manson walked up and said, 'This is going to happen.'

"I'm not going to say, 'No, it was not.'"6

A year later at a different parole hearing, a parole board commissioner
asked, "Was everybody given an assignment on the day of Shorty Shea's murder?" Davis replied:

I don't know. I didn't hear them get an assignment. From the way it played out, it looked like they very well did. I, I wasn't -- I was told to go along. So that was my assignment. But the way it came down, you could look at it and say, well, everybody knew what they were going to do.7

One night Charles Manson called me and I asked him about the murder of Donald Shea. He told me:

The ranch was like the [prison] mainline. We were walking on the mainline, drinking coffee and smoking cigarettes. In other words, the guard is not shaking the gate; the guard was up on the highway. It's just a different level of prison. I never got out of prison. We were all in prison at the ranch. The guard was just up on the [highway], and when he came to shake down, it's the same thing when they come and shake your cell down in here.

I wasn't thinking about anything. I was just thinking about what all everybody else was thinking about. I was reflecting everybody else back at themselves.

And I got involved with Bobby's troubles with Hinman, I got involved with Shorty's [*sic*] troubles with Shorty, and our conflict with him, and, like, I dealt with it the way they deal with it in prison. And that's not the same way you deal with it when you're outside.

Shorty snitched on us. And he was trying to kick us off the ranch. And he was selling us out to somebody who was paying him to do something, and I'm not exactly sure. I don't remember exactly what it was. But two or three people got mad at him, and somebody else got mad at him. And he had tried to fuck one of us.

You know, when you're bound together in a spiritual circle -- you know, like you got ten people setting in a circle, and you're meditating and you're together -- it's like, if you're bothering one of us you're bothering us all. [Shea] tried to get over on somebody for something. I'm not sure whether it was one of the girls, or what it was, [if] he tried to play some homosexual thing with one of the dudes -- the guy was, he was really twisted.

First he come up with a Negro woman and he said that his woman was the number one woman and that she was the best whore in town. I told him, "That's bullshit. My mama's always been the best whore in town." So, we got into an argument about that.

I asked Manson why they got into an argument about that. He said:

The way I was raised up, I was raised that you don't do that, that you don't cross that racial line. So, it was my thought to fuck him up.

And then somebody else caught up on that, and then two or three other people caught up on it, and then someone else said, "Let me do it."

And it was an episode that was psychotic.

And it was running in the minds of four or five people. Somebody else picked it up that I don't want to mention, [because] they didn't get arrested for it. And right there is a little area of my thought -- that I can't tell on other people.

There was a circle there, and the influence of that circle, I influenced it with my thought about not crossing racial lines. Especially if you're Irish. Or Scot. Because that's the thought that I was raised in.

[Shea's snitching] wasn't just my concern. It was [Lynette Fromme's] concern. She heard him talking to George. And she told us what he said. It was [name deleted]'s thought, because he had some thought in it. I don't think Steve really had any thought in it. He was just going along with everybody else. And Bruce was pretty much carrying around the same thought I was carrying.

So, it went on to where there was kind of like a fight. And Bruce was mealy-mouthed about it. I told him, "Man, ain't you ever been in a fight in your life?" I said, "When you have to do something, you pick it up and do it."

I moved on Shea. I discombobulated him. In other words, like, he had everybody buffaloed. He was big, and he had everybody frozen in fear. They were all frozen in fear. Like, the same thing happened with Lotsapoppa.

What I didn't understand was that people outside [prison] don't live in those fear levels. They can't even move in those fear levels. But I didn't realize that because I didn't even know outside. I was only -- what? -- a year and a half old? I was only a year, maybe a year and a half, in that thought. I was about two years old in that thought.

We all drove down there in a car, and the fight started in the car. And then the fight got out on the edge of the road. When the fight got out on the edge of the road, [Shea] had everybody buffaloed. And there was about five or six guys around. So, I took it in hand, I took the procedure. I took the thought. I took what I was looking at in hand. Do you know what I'm saying by that?

So, I showed Bruce, and, uh, I don't even know who was there. I don't know whether Tex was there or not. I know some of the people that were there. But it was a group thing. And then somebody else got mad at him, and they kicked him, or something.

[I did cut him], but I didn't cut him mortally. I cut him to bring him down, to take control of the picture.

What I'm looking at is me. And anything that I get into -- if I can make it me -- then I can deal with it. But I have to go up over the fears that are in the minds of all the people that are in that circle.

So when I went up over the fears of all of that, and I put that in hand, and I said, "Here." Then I handed the weapon back to Bruce. And I said, "Look, man. I don't want to break the law, and you've got me in here fighting people."

In other words, I had a thought, and I used to hold my finger up [for] this: "I'm never gonna break the law, and then I don't have to go back to prison. What you guys do is your affair." I never broke will in that thought except for a couple times. And that was one of the times that I broke will.

I did [force Bruce Davis to cut Shea]. I did.

But even if I broke will, I was still in the will of my circle. Once I entered into that circle and I committed myself to that circle, I know that you don't break a covenant with the universe. If you break a covenant with the universe, you're calling the wrath of God down on you. And I don't do that. I wouldn't be that stupid. I wouldn't have survived this far had I been breaking God's law. I stay in God's law. If I commit myself to a situation, I stay with that situation for eternity, because I know that when you enter into an agreement to be with that in eternity, and you break that, then you've lost your soul forever.

I weighed 120 pounds at that particular time, and I'm dealing with a guy that weighs 250 pounds, and he's no slouch. The guy could break me in half with one hand, you know. I can't play. I can't be half-stepping on a situation like that. So I moved in and took control of the situation. And then I gave it to Bruce. Because I felt that he was my brother in that thought.

See, if you've got a brother you've got one up on the world. Well, I'm brother. You got to *be* brother first to *have* a brother. You have to have honor in order to be honored.

So then, I got up on the road, man, and I said, "You know what, man? I done broke the law here." And I said, "You guys have got me back in trouble again."

And I walked down the road and I stuck my thumb out and I was maybe twenty-five or thirty feet, and there was some bushes in the area, and then I got in a car, and I drove down the road, and I looked back, and they were all fighting.

So what happened was, all the chickens jumped on Shorty. It's a pecking order. And that's what happened, man. It didn't basically -- there was no malice aforethought. There was no plot. There was no plan. Nobody was headed out to destroy anyone. It was an episode, man. It got out of hand. And when I tried to put it *in* hand, it didn't work out.

Because what I should have did was went ahead and put him in a car and took him to the hospital, you know, and been a humanitarian. [But] I'm not really a humanitarian. I'm not one of those do-good guys that my heart bleeds all over the place. I survive. And that's all I've ever learned, see.

You could blame me, and the world could blame me for my ways, but my ways have been set by the prison. And I survive. If there's eight or ten dudes out there in the yard with knives, I'm not gonna go out there and tell nobody what to do.

But if I have to, then I'll do whatever it takes to do whatever it takes. And if you're with me, and somebody fucks with you, and I don't stand up for you, then when it comes my turn I have nobody standing with me.

Well, I'm not that guy that won't stand up with you. If it comes to push to shove, and somebody's gonna get off on you, I'm gonna be there, and I'm gonna do all I can to put your situation into where you can deal with it. I'm gonna help you, in other words. I'm giving you my hand.

My hand was in that circle. But my heart and mind was not in that circle. It was in the circle that I got off on Shorty something terrible about him telling me that he had the woman. I told him, "That's bullshit." I said, "You might as well go to the zoo and marry somebody." But when he brought that into my world, I told him, "Hey get that shit out of here. Get away from me with that."

[People] don't come to me with that shit [race mixing] because I'll kill 'em. That's where my mind is and that's where my soul and my heart and my thought and my kin and my uncles and my fathers who art in heaven, hallowed be thy name, thy kingdom come, and all the angels that exist there within. I stand strong with that and true with that and I'll die with it.

I'm a rotten son-of-a-bitch and I ride a motorcycle and I've got a big, long pig sticker and I know how to use it. It's that simple. And Shorty transgressed against that and he got whatever he had coming, man. He got the mirror off the wall.

It came out of all kinds of different minds, and the people were willing to take the responsibility for that. They were willing to take the witness stand and tell everybody what happened, but they wouldn't let that happen. Red [Lynette Fromme] wanted to explain what happened there. That was partly George Spahn, That was partly his son. It was hooked up with a tent that I got from Mary Brunner from Wisconsin. I had a big, twenty-man tent, and he wanted to trade me the tent for a buffalo robe. And I traded, and the buffalo robe had holes in it. And Shorty had lied about that.

And everybody at the ranch knew that we didn't lie. And he started lying and playing other double-dealing games, and I told him, "You're lying around here, everybody's in the coop, and you're gonna get tangled up in your own bullshit."

I asked Manson if he said to Bruce Davis, "We're going to kill Shorty." He answered:

No, not directly. I said, "You know, we have to do whatever it takes to do whatever we have to do." You know, there's no need to enter into a conspiracy. And I had spent twenty-two years in school learning about conspiracy. You don't break in line on the mainline and get in a conspiracy with somebody else's life, because you get tangled up in that and it'll get you. I always stay loose from all that.

The first thing I learned in Sociology in 1948 is that you can't tell nobody else what to do. You can help them, but you can't make them do anything. You show them the way, and whatever they do is up to them.

All I did was, I held to the truth. I just held it as well as I could to honor and the truth and what I was raised up to believe in. I didn't have anything particularly I was grinding up, or biting off on somebody for anything. If other people are doing wrong, and selling bad things, and lying, and cheating, I mean that catches up with them. It's got nothing to do with me personally.

You know, like, I helped Bruce do whatever he wanted to do. I stood up with him whenever he asked me. Whenever he invoked me to be brother, I was there. But when it came time for him to deal with his death or his life -- you can only do that by yourself. I can't do it for him. I just can't do it. It's not in the soul to do that. You know how that works.

You have to learn to stand on your own two feet. Somebody that can't stand on their two feet, I can't walk with them. If they can't stand on their two feet -- that's what I told Bruce: "Don't hesitate if you have to do something. Do what you have to do when you have to do it. [But] if you have fear, then go somewhere and sit down and shut the fuck up."

I don't think it was just Bruce. It was a whole collage of being misused by somebody that was lying on us, that was cheating us, that was doing us bad and was doing us harm, and it just happened through the minds of many people. It happened through the mind of George, it happened through the minds of everybody there. No one in particular was dividing or conquering or trying to move anything or do anything in particular.

They was just having a good day, man. It was all a good day until all that negative came around and overwhelmed us. We got so involved in it, and all I did was, I just tried to hold it up for everybody as well as I could -- just like I've done all the way down the line.8

Chapter Notes

1 *The Family*, updated 1989 edition, page 314.
2 Ruby Pearl interviewed by KNXT-TV (now KCBS-TV).
3 Steve Grogan 1979 parole hearing transcript, pages 18-20 and 23-24.
4 Steve Grogan 1981 parole hearing transcript, pages 17-20.
5 Bruce Davis 1993 parole hearing transcript, pages 23-24.

6 Ibid., pages 74-76.
7 Bruce Davis 1994 parole hearing transcript, pages 74-75.
8 From a tape-recorded telephone conversation between Charles Manson and the author, 2001.

KA
RE
WE
ASTROBEE

Back to the Desert

"The desert is not a place. The desert is my mind. I have landed my mind on the earth."

-- Charles Manson

Life could be hectic at Spahn's Ranch in the summer of 1969. Lyn Fromme later wrote about one of the police raids from that time:

It was late at The Ranch when four Sheriff's cars jammed into the yard, flashing. Most of the girls and kids were at the back farmhouse. Somebody stepped in the cafe and called them on the field phone. I was asleep in the stuffed chair in George's house. When I sensed the light and commotion, I leapt up to warn Sherri. Danny could've been jailed if caught sleeping with her. Sherri had already gone for the woods. Ruth and I sat on the porch and shivered, watching the sheriffs roust out all the men at gunpoint. Tension was high. Every ranch vehicle was being sequentially lit up and examined. A flashing squad car came bumping up Lovers Lane from the farmhouse to rejoin others in the yard.

"We found the field phone," a hefty deputy growled. "No," he continued, "Nobody there."

The cops in the yard were questioning Bruce, Danny, Tex, Charlie, and Bobby. They were looking for stolen cars. Danny looked groggy-eyed but smirking as the conversation turned funny. Finally everything checked out to their satisfaction. They had no intention of pursuing the rest of us in the hills, but they did flood the woods with lights, providing a hair-raising, perfectly frozen moment for half a dozen teenagers. They left and we all went back to sleep.

Next morning in George's kitchen, before going out the door with a pan of hot cinnamon rolls, one of the girls told me that Gary Hinman was "floatin' in the cosmos."1

As the need to flee the city became even greater, all efforts focused on realizing that goal.

One such effort was when Charles Manson went to the office of the business manager for the Beach Boys to see if they intended to pay him any royalties for their use of his song "Cease To Exist." He did not have much success. As he later recalled:

> I went into the Beach Boys' office and I said, "You owe me money, man. What are you doing with my music? You're changing the words to my songs. You can't change the words to my motherfucking music. What are you doing? Are you gonna pay me?"
>
> [The guy said], "No, we're not paying you. We're not giving you nothing. We're not putting your name on the songs and we're changing the name of your songs," you dig?
>
> [I said], "Well, who in the fuck are *you*?"
>
> And he says, "My name is Buginatti, and I can call New York [and have a contract put out on Manson]."
>
> So I'm thinking, "How in the fuck can they do this? How can they keep doing this? They don't have no power to do this. They don't have no authority to do this."
>
> The only reason they're doing this, is because we're *lettin'* 'em do it.2

There was little that Manson could really do about the situation, however, and by the first week in September he and the other people who wanted to had left Los Angeles and made their way back to Goler Wash. By now the group included Sandra Good's newborn child, a healthy and robust baby boy called Cho.

But things in the desert had changed. During the time that Paul Watkins, Brooks Poston, and Juanita Wildebush had stayed at Barker Ranch to keep an eye on the place the area had been invaded by gold prospectors. Some of these prospectors presented alternative viewpoints to those to which Watson, Poston, and Wildebush had been accustomed, and eventually the trio was affected by this. Wildebush fell in love with a miner and left the area. Watkins and Poston began to see one of the prospectors, forty-six-year-old Paul Crockett, as a mentor. These changes altered the dynamic in Goler Wash and caused some disharmony in the desert after Manson and the others returned there.

In *Helter Skelter*, Vincent Bugliosi mentions at least three occasions when Manson or some of his companions "creepy-crawled" the bunkhouse at Barker Ranch while Crockett, Watkins, Poston, and Juan Flynn (a Spahn's Ranch hand who occasionally associated with Manson and his friends) were inside. Bugliosi implies that these attempted invasions would have culminated in the murders of the four bunkhouse occupants but that three times they heard something that aborted the supposed murder plan.3

But these frightening claims of the District Attorney are not likely true. First of all, why would hearing something abort any plan? Barker Ranch was miles and miles beyond the outermost fringes of any human establishment. Manson had at his disposal -- supposedly -- the unquestioning services of Charles Watson, Steve Grogan, Bruce Davis, Susan Atkins, and several other tested-by-fire killers who were on the premises. So why didn't they simply kick in the bunkhouse door and take over the situation? If Manson had really had at his disposal twenty or so brainwashed slaves it should not have taken them long to do so. So why weren't Crockett, Watkins, Poston, and Flynn killed? The likely answer to this question is that no one was ever trying to kill them.

Paul Crockett admitted as much in a television interview shortly after the news of Manson's possible involvement in the Tate-LaBianca murders broke. A reporter asked Crockett whether he had been frightened by "the Family" when he was with them at Barker Ranch. "No," the miner replied. When the newsman asked if any murders were ever discussed in his presence, Crockett would only say, "I heard interesting things." Recalling the young people who arrived at Barker Ranch with Manson, he said:

Some of them were what you consider actual hippies, and others, I think, were using the veilance [*sic*] of hippies. It would be hard to say what their motives were, and yet it was evident that they were using other people to their own ends. And yet, if you look at it another way, and it could mean something else.

Crockett said that he never saw any drugs being used and that there was no ritualistic activity, such as people wearing hoods or being hanged. When asked if he had seen Manson and the group participate in any kind of ritual, he replied:

They would sit in a circle around a big bonfire, and one of the men would play guitar, and they would sing songs. All of the songs that they would sing were their own songs, that they wrote themselves. And I don't mind saying so, some of them were pretty nice.4

Charles Manson and the people around him might have been disappointed that they couldn't have Barker Ranch all to themselves, but the situation was by no means dire. The desert around Death Valley was immense, and there were many places to go and things to do. Not being able to settle at Barker's was not a big problem; everybody simply went somewhere else.

On September 19, during a ride from the Saline Valley hot springs to Jail Canyon in the Panamint Mountains, Charles Manson, Charles Watson, and some other individuals stopped to set fire to a Park Service earth-moving machine that had been parked overnight at the top of the Lippencott Road in the Racetrack area of Death Valley National Monument.

Park Service soon discovered this act of ecotage (the earth mover was still smoldering when the first rangers arrived on the scene), and they were especially infuriated because the machine, a Michigan brand articulating loader, had just recently been purchased.

After setting fire to the Michigan loader the arsonists got away, but only temporarily. The ensuing persistent law enforcement investigation into the burning of the machine finally resulted in the capture of most of the members of the group at Barker Ranch, where they were arrested on various charges on October 10 and 12, 1969. After their arrests they were taken to the Inyo County Jail in Independence, 120 miles away. Many of them, including Charles Manson, were still in custody several weeks later when police in Los Angeles discovered that some of them were involved in the Tate-LaBianca murders.

Ironically, it was the desire of Manson and his circle to stay together that ultimately led to the loss of everything that they had spent the last two years evolving towards. If they had simply left the desert area and returned to the city and separate lives as soon as they became aware that law enforcement was after them for burning the earth mover (which was soon), the arrests at Barker Ranch would never have occurred and the story of Charles Manson and "the Family" would have been very different -- if it would have existed at all. But the desire of those people to remain together in the desert as a group was so strong that it blinded them to such a simple solution to their problem of being wanted by the local law. Thus, they were apprehended as a group. And thus, also as a group, they unwittingly played into future legends.

Chapter Notes

1 *Reflexion*, pages 443-444.
2 From a tape-recorded telephone conversation with Sandra Good. Sandra Good Archives.
3 *Helter Skelter*, page 314.
4 Paul Crockett in an interview with KNXT-TV, Los Angeles.

The Barker and Myers Ranches in Death Valley

Introduction to the Motive

"This trial in Los Angeles wasn't a *who*dunit;
this was a *why*dunit."

-- Krenwinkel Defense Attorney Paul Fitzgerald

There are three essential elements that tie a particular person to a particular crime: means, motive, and opportunity. This formula is almost like a mathematical equation. If one of these elements is absent from an individual's relationship with a crime, the equation falls apart and it is impossible for that person to be guilty of that crime. In the case at hand, motive is the most important of these three elements.

Motive is the catalyst for crime because man is a reasoning creature. He plans and performs certain acts because he expects some kind of positive result. This holds true in all aspects of man's being, including the commission of crimes. If a person has no specific motivation to do something, he won't do it. If an individual has no motive to commit a crime -- no personal motive -- he won't commit it.

Thus, there is no such thing as a motiveless crime. The motive might be obscure, inscrutable, or even insane, but there is always some kind of motive, some reason why a particular person commits a particular crime.

Introduction to the Motive

In his book *Helter Skelter* Vincent Bugliosi points out that while it is not the duty of a prosecutor to introduce evidence of motive in a criminal trial it is usually to his advantage to do so because the presence of a motive is very strong circumstantial evidence of a person's guilt. And this is true. But, as Bugliosi also says, it is conversely and equally true that the lack of a motive is very strong circumstantial evidence of a person's innocence.1

Much of *Helter Skelter* (over sixty pages of the standard paperback edition) is a recounting of the Los Angeles County District Attorney's office's frantic efforts to establish a motive for the murders on Cielo and Waverly Drives -- a motive for Charles Manson, that is. This effort, however, was grounded in an unshakable conclusion that Charles Manson was actually responsible for those murders.

Pre-trial publicity about the Tate-LaBianca murders universally assumed Manson's guilt. From the instant that Charles Manson appeared on the world scene as a suspect in the murders, his fate was sealed. (Any researcher can examine all of the pre-trial media attention to this case and not find even one article that entertained the possibility of Manson's innocence.) In the mind of the public his conviction was an absolute necessity. Thus, Deputy DA Bugliosi had to prove that Charles Manson was guilty, and he knew that if he could not establish a personal motive for Manson in connection with the murders he would have an extremely difficult time in obtaining a conviction. So Bugliosi searched and searched and searched, and interviewed and interviewed and interviewed, until he finally found what he considered to be a true and suitable motive for Charles Manson to have ordered the homicides at the Polanski and LaBianca residences: Manson wanted to provoke a race war called "Helter Skelter" which would eventually result in him becoming the leader of the world.

Although motive is a fundamental element of any crime, a prosecutor is not required by law to demonstrate it in court in order to obtain a guilty verdict. But in this case it was necessary to show a motive because there was literally no other evidence tying Manson to these murders. In fact, so important was this motive of "Helter Skelter" to selling the whole package of Manson's guilt that Bugliosi later used the term as the title of his bestselling book about the case.

Goodbye Helter Skelter

But if "Helter Skelter" was not the motive for the Tate-LaBianca murders, then that would change not only the popular perception of those murders and why they were committed, but it could also change -- or even remove -- any legal culpability for those murders on the part of Charles Manson. Because if Charles Manson had no personal motive for the Tate-LaBianca murders, then he could not -- because of the means, motive, opportunity equation -- be responsible for, or guilty of, those murders.

The next chapter of this book will examine prosecutor Vincent Bugliosi's explanation of the motive for the Tate-LaBianca murders: Helter Skelter.

The chapter after that will examine the real motive.

Chapter Notes

1 *Helter Skelter*, page 291.

TATE CASE MURDERS

'Bizarre' Motive Claimed in Deaths

By LINDA DEUTSCH

LOS ANGELES (AP) — The state says it knows why beautiful actress Sharon Tate and six others were slain last August, and "the motive is even more bizarre than the killings themselves."

That motive, Deputy Dist. Atty. Vincent Bugliosi said yesterday, won't be disclosed until opening arguments and testimony begin Friday in the trial of four persons charged with murder-conspiracy.

The prosecution will put 40 to 50 persons on the stand. But the spotlight will be on pretty, petite Linda Kasabian, 21, who reportedly has promised to tell details of the killings in exchange for her freedom.

Mrs. Kasabian, sandy-haired mother of two infants, is expected to be granted immunity from prosecution after she testifies.

Bugliosi said she would take the stand Monday and was expected to testify for "three, four or five days." He added, "It will be key testimony."

Mrs. Kasabian also is charged with murder-conspiracy but has been granted a separate trial. She was a member of the nomadic, hippie-style "family" led by a shaggy-haired, bearded ex-convict, Charles Manson, accused of planning the killings.

Manson, 35, is on trial with three shapely women followers, Susan Atkins, 21, Leslie Van Houten, 20, and Patricia Krenwinkel, 22.

Mrs. Kasabian, who has been under heavy guard in jail since it became known she would testify for the state, is expected to tell how she went with other members of the Manson group to the two homes where the killings occurred.

She is said to have waited outside Miss Tate's rented tomato red house while the pregnant actress and four visitors were stabbed and shot. The next night, Mrs. Kasabian also reportedly waited outside the home of market owner Leon LaBianca while he and his wife Rosemary were slain.

Chief prosecutor Aaron Stovitz said he also hoped to call film director Roman Polanski, Miss Tate's husband, but said there was some doubt whether he would appear. Polanski, who was in London when the killings occurred, lives in Europe.

Paul Fitzgerald, head of a defense team of four lawyers, said they would call about 20 witnesses, many of them members of Manson's "family."

"In addition to rebutting the prosecution's claims of guilt, we may have to rebut them on the defendants' life style," Fitzgerald said. "We'll get into drugs and LSD."

Court was recessed for two days after six alternate jurors were sworn in yesterday. The alternates, four men and two women, along with the regular jury panel of seven men and five women, will be locked up in the Ambassador Hotel each night for the trial's duration — estimated at three to six months.

The Helter Skelter Motive

"Lincoln said, 'You can fool all of the people some of the time, and some of the people all of the time, but you can't fool all of the people all of the time.' But there should be an addendum to that: 'You can fool most of the people most of the time.'"

-- Vincent Bugliosi

The murders that took place on Cielo and Waverly Drives were brutal and seemingly bizarre. There were multiple victims killed by multiple means (beating, stabbing, and shooting). One victim had the word "WAR" carved into his abdomen. Cryptic words were written in the victims' blood on the walls at the crime scenes. For months there was no apparent solution to the crimes. Fear was rampant in the Los Angeles area and shock was nation-wide.

Rumors of weirdness abounded. The press reported that the victims had been hooded. Some sources claimed that the bodies had been sexually mutilated. "Ritual Murder" was an early (and inaccurate) description of the manner of the deaths. Because of the strangeness of the killings (as reported in the media, that is) all sorts of far out theories were advanced in attempts to explain them. And out of this concept of a bizarreness of the murders the idea began to grow that the motive for them might also be bizarre.

The thought that the motive for the murders might be out of the ordinary was reinforced for the authorities investigating the slayings by Roman Polanski's remarks during his polygraph examination after the murders at his house wherein he offered his opinion that, "If I'm looking for a motive, I'd look for something that doesn't fit your habitual standard, with which you use to work as police -- something much more far out...."1

Los Angeles County Deputy District Attorney Vincent Bugliosi apparently agreed. "From the moment I was assigned to the case," he later wrote, "I'd felt that for murders as bizarre as these the motive itself would have to be almost equally strange, not something you'd find within the pages of a textbook on police science."2

At the time of Charles Manson's indictment for the murders (almost four months after those murders occurred), and even up until the time of the trial itself, authorities still had little idea about what the motive for the killings was. There were theories of drug deals gone bad, of orgy killings, of homicidal LSD freak outs, of Mafia hits, and of robbery cover-ups, revenge killings, and class warfare. But there was nothing solid.

After the identification of Charles Manson, Charles Watson, Linda Kasabian, Susan Atkins, Patricia Krenwinkel, and Leslie Van Houten as suspects in the homicides, police discovered some evidence, such as fingerprints and suspect statements, which indicated that at least some of these persons were indeed involved with the murders. The problem confronting authorities, however, was that there was no evidence -- besides a few witness statements -- that linked Charles Manson to the crimes. And linking Charles Manson to the crimes was an absolute necessity.

It is important to recall the press coverage after the announcement that arrests had been made in the Tate and LaBianca murder cases. Again, these killings had gone unsolved for several months, during which time the entire Los Angeles area was in a nearly constant state of panic. The announcement that the cases had been "solved" was very big news. Unfortunately, this news was accompanied by journalism of the most sensational and irresponsible kind.

The now iconic photograph of Charles Manson on the cover of *Life* magazine on December 19, 1969 is one of the best known examples of the prejudicial press coverage of Manson and his supposed role in the Tate-LaBianca murders. This photo, the most publicized picture ever taken of Manson, was a mug shot. In the picture he arches his left eyebrow and glares in an apparently evil fashion. *Life*'s cover labeled Manson and the people arrested with him as "The Love and Terror Cult" and declared Manson to be the "cult leader." Inside the magazine his associates were called "the Family."

Life was not the only publication guilty of this type of extremely misleading and prejudicial reporting. *Time* and *Newsweek* magazines both had extensive coverage of the arrests. *Time* called Manson "The Demon of Death Valley" and led its article on his arrest with a totally fabricated quote of the supposed orders he had given to his "slaves" on the murder night.3 Newsweek referred to "The Case of the Hypnotic Hippie" and used a photo of a buckskin-clad and manacled Manson, with a disoriented and spacy expression on his face, being led to a court appearance in Independence, California.

And these were the *national* news magazines. In the Los Angeles area, where the crimes naturally received much more publicity than anywhere else, the press went even further in its coverage of the "pseudo-religious cult known as 'The Family' whose leader was known as 'Jesus'."4

All of this grossly inaccurate and highly prejudicial news coverage identified Charles Manson in the public consciousness as the leader of a killer cult from the minute the news of his arrest was announced. Further, his responsibility (and guilt) for any killings that the cult might have committed was also very much assumed.

Between the announcement of the indictments in early December 1969 and the beginning of the trial four months later there was a constant drumbeat of the theme that many people still accept today: Charles Manson was the hypnotic leader of a group of followers whom he sent out to commit murder at his command.

And why not? It was a great story, and one that the public would eagerly pay to hear and read about. It was a story that would "scare the hell out of you."5

Because of this massive amount of negative publicity, the idea that Manson might actually be innocent (and perhaps even acquitted) was unthinkable. Manson himself could read the signals as early as December 17. "The news media has already executed and buried me," he said in a Los Angeles courtroom. "The people are hypnotized by the lies being told to them."6

As the Crime of the Century evolved into the Trial of the Century, the Los Angeles County District Attorney's office knew that anything less than a guilty verdict for Charles Manson was out of the question. But the only thing wrong with this foregone conclusion of Manson's guilt was that there was no apparent personal motive for him to have committed or ordered the murders. And without a motive there could be no conclusion of guilt, because motive is one of the three basic and essential factors necessary for the demonstration of a person's culpability for a crime. Deputy DA Vincent Bugliosi knew this. Therefore, even though he was not required to do so by law, he knew that he had to come up with a motive that would prove Manson's guilt.

This was no small task. Bugliosi remembers his colleagues referring to his assignment to the case as a "bummer."7 His own reaction to that assignment was "a low whistle."8 The lack of motive for Manson resulted in "desperation," and the DA and his staff were forced to go to "unlikely lengths in trying to ascertain why Manson had ordered these murders."9

None of the standard motives for murder -- things like robbery, revenge, greed, jealousy, or passion -- fit the crimes. But Bugliosi still needed a personal motive for Charles Manson. And if he could come up with a far out motive to fit the seemingly far out circumstances of the crimes, so much the better.

Then Bugliosi discovered that there was something in the peripheries of the consciousness of some of the people at Spahn's Ranch that could be called "Helter Skelter." And once he took "Helter Skelter" and fleshed it out, he believed that he had perfectly overcome his main obstacle in his prosecution of Manson. He believed that he had established both a personal and far out motive for Charles Manson to have ordered the Tate-LaBianca murders.

The Helter Skelter motive has many components. In fact, it is probably the most complicated and fantastic motive ever offered up by a prosecuting attorney. Basically, it goes like this:

Goodbye Helter Skelter

Charles Manson was a megalomaniacal racist who dreamed of ruling the world. In order to make this dream a reality, he hoped to capitalize on a social catastrophe. Manson thought that fairly soon there would be a race war between whites and blacks. Manson referred to this war as "Helter Skelter," supposedly deriving the term from the Beatles' song of the same name on the group's *White Album*. (This song contained lyrics that referred to a person on the bottom coming back to the top, a reference, Manson supposedly believed, to a black victory over whites.) Manson also allegedly believed that it could be possible for him and his "Family" to benefit from such a war. In Manson's supposed theory of this conflict, blacks would fight whites and would win after killing most of the white race. While this carnage was ensuing, Manson and his people would be hiding out in the desert, far from the racial battlefields.

Once the war was over, however, the black man would soon realize that he lacked the intelligence and experience to effectively run his newly acquired world. Needing a bright mind to run things, he would then turn to the only group of white people who were left -- Charles Manson and his "Family" -- and hand over the reigns of power to them (him).

But Manson had a problem: The war wasn't starting soon enough to suit him. So, in order to trigger the conflict, Manson ordered his "followers" to commit a series of atrocious murders of white people that would be blamed on blacks. In the ensuing outrage over these murders, Manson supposedly believed, whites would attack blacks and the race war Helter Skelter would begin. And once this jump-started war was over and the black man's follow-up society collapsed, Charles Manson would rule the world.10

This is the essence of the Helter Skelter motive.

Far out.

But the Helter Skelter motive didn't stop there. Beyond the unusual nature of the core scenario, there were many literally fantastic details that supposedly supported it. For example, while Manson and his companions were hiding out in the desert and waiting out the race war they would be living in an underground city located in the "bottomless pit," a subterranean paradise where food grew and rivers ran. (According to some later accounts, like that of Deputy District Attorney Stephen Kay at Patricia Krenwinkel's parole hearing in 1993, the "Family" would be in "miniaturized form" when they did this. See below.)

Even more fantastic were the supposed influences that allegedly made Manson come to the conclusion that he was destined to preside over a post-Helter Skelter world. According the prosecution, Manson was deriving his philosophy (and his game plan) from both the Book of Revelations in the New Testament of the Bible and from the lyrics of songs on the Beatles' *White Album*.

The Biblical references that Charles Manson and "the Family" supposedly used to reinforce the concept of Helter Skelter (and Manson's roll in it) come mostly from the last book of the New Testament, the Book of Revelation, and specifically Chapter 9 of that book. And as is often the case with the Bible, some of these references in Revelation 9 do seem to make some kind of sense and have some kind of application -- especially if a person is determined to believe it.

Revelation 9 contains images that were claimed to have been of special interest to Manson because they supposedly referred to the Beatles and thus combined the musical group and its music with the apocalyptic prophecies of the Bible. For example, the "four angels" mentioned in the book were supposed to be the four member of the Beatles.

Besides the Beatles/angels, there was:

> another angel ascending from the east, having the seal of the living God; and he cried with a loud voice for the four angels, to whom it was given to hurt the earth and the sea, saying Hurt not the earth, neither the sea, nor the trees, till we have sealed the servants of our God in their foreheads.

This fifth angel, supposedly, was Charles Manson. (Or, alternatively, the fifth angel could have been the "fifth Beatle," original group member Stuart Sutcliffe, who died in 1962.)

More from Revelation 9:

> And the fifth angel sounded, and I saw a star fall from heaven unto the earth: and to him was given the key of the bottomless pit. And he

opened the bottomless pit: and there arose a smoke out of the pit.... and there came out of the pit locusts upon the earth; and unto them was given power, as scorpions of the earth have power....

The locusts, too, were supposed to be the Beatles (locusts = beetles = Beatles).

Getting back to the angels, they were described as "their faces were as the faces of men. And they had hair as the hair of women...." This again was a clear reference to the bearded and long-haired British singing group. The angels also had "breast-plates of fire, of jacinth, and brimstone." This was a description of the Beatles' electric guitars.

"And they had a king over them, *which* is the angel of the bottomless
pit, whose name in the Hebrew tongue is Abaddon, but in the Greek tongue *hath* his name Apollyon."

The references in the book of Revelation to the bottomless pit seemed to coincide with a supposed obsession that Manson had with a bottomless pit in Death Valley.

Even one of the translations of the name of this fifth angel seemed to fit the prosecution's version of a death-oriented Helter Skelter scenario. In one edition of the Bible (the Catholic Douay version) the translation of this fifth angel's (i.e., Charles Manson's) name is "Exterminans."

Besides the Bible, the other supposed major contributor to the Helter Skelter philosophy was the music of the Beatles.

Of course, no one could deny the importance and influence of the Beatles' music (and that of other popular musical groups) on the minds of millions of people around the world in the late 1960s, including those persons involved in the killings that took place on Cielo and Waverly Drives. Music was influential in the lives of young people of the time, as it generally is to young people of any time. (It is worth noting, however, that much of the musical soundtrack of the summer of 1969 and the years preceding it contained lyrics having to do with conflict, revolution, and violent death, which were new themes in popular music.)

But the importance of the Beatles' music to Charles Manson has been overemphasized. He was, after all, not raised within the experiences of the 1960s generation. He was born in 1934, during the Great Depression, and grew up and was formed in the 1930s, '40s, and '50s. The music of that time -- the music that Manson says *did* influence him -- was music in the then popular style of Frank Sinatra and Bing Crosby -- not that of the Beatles. When the Beatles started getting very well known and popular in late 1963 and 1964, Charles Manson was almost 30 years old.

But according to district attorneys past and present, the supposed influence of the Beatles on Charles Manson went far beyond him simply appreciating their music (something that he has never denied). Los Angeles Deputy District Attorney Stephen Kay said, for example, that "[Manson] thought that the Beatles were the five prophets talked about in the Book of Revelations."11

Vincent Bugliosi claimed that Manson was obsessed with the Beatles and was particularly affected by the songs on the group's *White Album*, especially "Revolution One," Revolution Nine," "Piggies," "Blackbird," and "Helter Skelter." These songs supposedly contained hidden messages that Manson thought were aimed specifically at him. Other songs from the double-album with allegedly relevant and meaningful significance to the "Manson Family" included "Sexy Sadie," "Happiness is a Warm Gun," "Honey Pie," and "Rocky Raccoon."12

But so what if they did? In the late 1960s it was not unusual for people to look for all sorts of hidden meanings in music, and especially in the music of the Beatles. The best known example of this phenomenon is that for over a year prior to the summer of 1969 (and even after) rumors spread that the group's bassist Paul McCartney had died some time before and that clues to his death were present in the Beatles' lyrics and album cover art.13

Almost everyone gets some kind of meaning or message from music. Even Vincent Bugliosi and his *Helter Skelter* co-author Curt Gentry could not resist the temptation to find hidden significance in the Beatles' music when they noted supposed similarities between the lyrics of "Cry Baby, Cry" from *The White Album* and the events which transpired at the Tate and LaBianca residences on the nights of August 8 and 9, 1969.14

Manson himself said, in 1993, "The music gives everybody messages. That's what music does. I mean, how do I have to appear like I'm some kind of maniac because I can hear something that the music says?"15

As noted earlier, the main task facing Vincent Bugliosi in his prosecution of this case was finding a personal motive for Charles Manson to have ordered the Tate-LaBianca murders. And again, this was no small task. Bugliosi spends over sixty pages of his book presenting his version of the motive to the reader. Sixty pages is a lot of selling, but since Bugliosi's objective was to obtain a conviction of Charles Manson at all costs no amount of convoluted reasoning or fantastic speculation would be overlooked or unused in the pursuit of that objective. After all, Manson was obviously guilty.

And with "Helter Skelter," Bugliosi had his far out motive for a far out crime committed by the far out Charles Manson and his "Family."

But in fact this motive is absurd. And to get an impression of just how unrealistic it really is all one has to do is listen to a recounting of it by Assistant DA Stephen Kay at Patricia Krenwinkel's 1993 parole hearing. Kay's account starts during a description of the wounds inflicted upon Leno LaBianca:

> [Krenwinkel] stabbed Mr. LaBianca seven times with a carving fork.... a two-tine carving fork. She stabbed him seven times so there were fourteen puncture wounds in him from the carving fork. He had twelve stab wounds in addition to that. And she left the carving fork imbedded in his abdomen and there were these angry red welts where she carved the letters W - A - R.
>
> And then the words she wrote in his blood. RISE over the inside -- above the inside part of the front door, DEATH TO PIGS on the living room wall, and HEALTER SKELTER on the refrigerator. These all had -- had great significance to Ms. Krenwinkel and to the revolution. These came from the Beatles' *White Album.*
>
> And what the Family members would do is they would sit around on LSD -- and this wasn't just Manson, this was all the Family members speeding -- and well, "What do you hear in the song?", and they came up with the Beatles were the prophets talked about in Revelations Nine and Ten in the Bible.
>
> And the Beatles were prophecizing [sic] the message to the blacks, that the blacks should rise up and, and kill the whites. The word RISE

comes from a song in the Beatles' *White Album* called "Black Birds," and I'm not going to sing it, so don't worry. But "Black birds singing in the dead of night, take these broken wings and learn to fly, all your life, you've been waiting for this moment to arise." Well, that's where RISE came from and the Family thought that the black birds that the Beatles were singing about were the black men. And "singing in the dead of night," both of the murders, both at the Tate house and the LaBianca house were committed in the dead of night because they, they had to blend in with what the prophets were telling them.

Now, Revelations Nine and Ten talks about five prophets, men with heroic women. Well, they could justify that because originally there were five Beatles and then one, one died. The DEATH TO PIGS had significance. Pigs were not police officers. Remember, PIG was written in Sharon Tate's blood on the front door of the Tate residence. DEATH TO PIGS in Mr. LaBianca's blood. PIGS were, basically white people who had nine-to-five jobs.

And there was a song in the Beatles album called "Piggies" and it talked about the piggies going out to eat with your piggy wives, clutching your forks and knives. Well, the fork, of course, was in the abdomen of Leno LaBianca. And when we got to the coroner's office and took off the pillowcase, we found a knife embedded in his neck with the knife handle sticking out one end and the blade traversing his neck, severing a carotid artery, and part of the blade sticking out at the other side of his neck.

And of course, last but not least, on the refrigerator in Mr. LaBianca's blood was HEALTER SKELTER, which was the name of the Beatles song on *The White Album* and which the Family had -- with Manson certainly as the leader -- had given the name of the revolution.

And, and [Krenwinkel] talked about, well, they were amassing dune buggies. Yes, they did. They had dune buggies with machine guns mounted on 'em, they had a gun room out there, they were preparing for war, the war that she carved in Mr. LaBianca's abdomen.

And what this war was going to be, was the black/white race war that was going to be ignited by these murders, blaming the murders on, on blacks and the Family and Manson felt that the blacks were going to win this race war and they were going to kill all of the whites except, of course, for the Family.

And the Family was going to go live in the bottomless pit, she told you today about, they were going to look for a hole in the desert. Well, the hole that they were looking for was the bottomless pit, talked about in Revelations Nine and Ten of the Bible. And they were going to live in miniaturized form for fifty to a hundred years in this bottomless pit and then they would grow to the size of the twelve tribes of Israel, 144,000.

And at the end of this fifty-to one-hundred-year period, since they were racists, they felt that the blacks would be too stupid to maintain power and so they would, the Family would come out of the bottomless pit and immediately, the blacks would run up to them and turn over all power. Now, it wasn't clear whether or not they were going to rule the world or just the United States -- at least it was going to be the United States.

This is absolute craziness, but these people believed in this motive enough to kill seven innocent people.16

The first part of Kay's concluding sentence is correct; the second half is not.

Not only does Kay's recitation sound somewhat loopy, but there are several instances where his claims conflict with the evidence in the case, or where he simply fabricates "facts."

For example, Charles Watson says that he, and not Patricia Krenwinkel, carved the word WAR into Leno LaBianca's stomach.

Kay's contention that the victims at Cielo and Waverly Drives were killed at night so as to jibe with the lyrics of the song "Blackbird" is a stretch, to put it charitably.

"They had dune buggies with machine guns mounted on them." This is a fabricated claim. One dune buggy had a "gun mount" affixed to its back, but there was apparently no gun on the mount (this according to *Life* magazine). But even if such a mount existed, it is just a mount. It could just as easily have been a mount for, say, a telescope (like the one that Charles Manson took from Terry Melcher's Malibu house17).

None of the "Manson Family's" vehicles were mounted with machine guns. In fact, "the Family" did not possess, or even have access to, any machine guns. Danny DeCarlo did have a World War Two-vintage German Smeisser MP-40 (which would more accurately be described as a "sub-machine gun"), but it was broken and only capable of firing one round at a time.18 (This gun of DeCarlo's was the infamous "submachine gun in its violin case" pictured in *Helter Skelter*.)

"The Family" was going to live in the bottomless pit "in miniaturized form"? This specific detail about size-shifting was not presented during the murder trial of Manson and his co-defendants, or at least it was not recalled anywhere in the 600-plus pages of *Helter Skelter*, or in any of the other books about the trial. (Perhaps it is testimony from one of the retrials of Leslie Van Houten?) But wherever this notion of a miniaturized "Family" comes from, it is literally incredible.

"At the end of this fifty-to one-hundred-year period.... the Family would come out of the bottomless pit...." It is hard to understand how effective a world (or even just a United States) leader Charles Manson would be if he were between eighty-five and 135 years old.

These instances, and the rest of Kay's version of the motive, are fantasy.

In her book *The Manson Women* Clara Livsey wrote that if anyone were a true adherent of such a fantastic story as the Helter Skelter offering they would have to be mentally ill. Calling the acceptance of Helter Skelter as a motive by Bugliosi "absurd," Livsey wrote "If one were to accept that they truly believed the helter-skelter fantasy and that it really motivated these murders, one would have to conclude that they were psychotic.... But they were not psychotic, clinically or legally."19

This is a very good point. And it also illustrates just one of the odd contradictions that plague the prosecution's version of this case: How can people crazy enough to embrace the various aspects of this alleged motive not be too crazy to stand trial? Of course, a person can be psychotic and not legally insane, but such a warped and fantastic motive as Helter Skelter would surely be indicative of someone with a serious detachment from reality, a detachment perhaps serious enough to rule out the application of the death penalty.

But while all of these claims about the Biblical and Beatle sources of the supposed motive for the murders on Cielo and Waverly Drives might make for interesting reading, a sensible reader could very well wonder if any of it should be taken seriously. Was the triggering of Helter Skelter really such a strong consideration of the people around Charles Manson in 1969 that it motivated them to commit mass murder? Perhaps the best way to answer that question is to hear what the persons who committed those murders say about why they left Spahn's Ranch on those August nights in 1969.

Charles Watson, the main killer at the Polanski and LaBianca houses, said in his book *Will You Die For Me?* that there were three main reasons for the killings: to ignite Helter Skelter, to get money for the move to the desert, and to get Bobby Beausoleil out of jail by committing murders similar to the one that he was charged with (the "copycat" motive).20

Watson's book was published in 1978, seven years after the Tate-LaBianca trial and four years after the publication of *Helter Skelter*. By then the "race war" theme was well known and accepted. Is it possible that Watson is lying or mistaken when he briefly mentions Helter Skelter as part of the motive?

Watson testified that he went to the Polanski house on the night of August 8 simply because Manson asked him to after dinner one night. At his own trial for the murders he expressed no real knowledge of any motive, saying instead, "I wasn't real clear on what was to be wrote on the walls, *or clear about the whole thing, really*."21 (emphasis added)

At his 1990 parole hearing, Watson, even though he had by then had plenty of time to learn the accepted (that is, the Helter Skelter) version of his own crime, and even though he had already said in his book that Helter Skelter was part of the motive, still does not seem to think that his actions were committed in order to bring down the Establishment. To the contrary, the remarks at the hearing fit the premise that the society was falling anyway and that Watson, along with Manson and the others, just wanted to get away from that fall. "I had come to the conclusion at the time [August 1969] that the end of the world was coming and that everyone was going to die," Watson told the parole board. But when asked by a parole board member to clarify the cause of the end of the world, Watson said that the end would "not [be] based on my crime."22

So despite a very brief reference to it in his book, Charles Watson does not appear to believe that the murders on Cielo and Waverly Drives were committed to start a race war called Helter

Skelter that would eventually bring about the fall of society. But why, then, does Watson even mention Helter Skelter as part of the motive at all? Well, as he said, he "wasn't clear about the whole thing," so he may, in retrospect, have assumed that it was part of the motive. Or it also could be that he knows the real reason for the murders, and that a large part of that reason is him, and he wants to deflect attention and responsibility away from himself and onto something and someone else.

In *Child of Satan, Child of God* Susan Atkins also discounts Helter Skelter as a motive. "It is entirely possible that some in our group -- perhaps including Charlie himself -- had in our satanic state slipped into such ideas. But to the best of my knowledge [Helter Skelter was not the motive for] the Tate-LaBianca murders."23

At her 1993 parole hearing, Patricia Krenwinkel's explanation of her belief as to why she and her friends were going out on the evening of August 8 was not that they were going to commit murders to spark a race war, but rather that she didn't even know what they were going to do, much less why.

The parole board commissioner asked Krenwinkel, "So when you pulled up [at the Polanski residence], is that the first time you knew what you were going to do?"

"No," Krenwinkel replied. "Not until we were already across the fence."

"Okay. What did you think you were climbing over that wall for, or that fence?"

"Probably to rob, 'cause that had been -- recently there had been this push to try to get money so that we could go out into the desert, so there had been dune buggies stolen and there had been people, you know, like, stealing money."

Later in the same hearing the commissioner asked again, "Then when you went there [to the Polanski house], and Mr. Watson was cutting the telephone wires, you -- you were pretty well aware of what you were going into the residence for, weren't you?"

Krenwinkel replied, "I wasn't sure what we were going to do until [Watson] said what we were going to do. I had no idea because at that point in time, like I said, we had been going and doing robberies basically and stealing things. I had no idea that

that's what the intention was [to kill people] at all.... That had never been expressed."

"Did you think that you were going to kill anyone?"

"Absolutely not.... I had no idea what we were going to do when we went to that residence, when all the madness took place.... All I was doing was carrying through a macabre dance."

In discussing the LaBianca murders a few minutes later, a parole board member asked, "Were these murders intended to instigate the revolution [Helter Skelter}?"

"*That was not my intent*," Krenwinkel answered, "'cause I had no idea why we were doing it. *Later on that has become something that Manson has used and said, yes*."24 (emphasis added)

Leslie Van Houten has recalled the Helter Skelter motive. In 1993 she told a California parole board, "About two weeks before the Tate murders, Manson started changing his talking about surviving the Helter Skelter war and that perhaps we would have to do something to instigate it, because it wasn't coming along as quickly as he had anticipated."

"Nobody ever questioned [this decision]?" a board member asked.

"No one ever spoke out.... After we were all arrested, lots of people said they didn't believe in [Helter Skelter]. But they didn't indicate that at the time."25

At the time of the murder trial, however, Van Houten did not subscribe to the Helter Skelter motive theory and instead offered up another motive. (We will look at Van Houten's change of mind and that other motive in the next chapter.)

In 1992 Bobby Beausoleil was asked by his parole board, "Had you heard Manson, or any of the family members talk about Helter Skelter and war between the blacks and whites? Had you heard that before?"

Beausoleil replied, "No I had not heard that *until in the media*. I never heard that. I did hear, there was a song called "Helter Skelter" by the Beatles. And I had heard the song, of course."26 (emphasis added)

At his 1993 parole hearing Bruce Davis offered his opinion of the Helter Skelter motive. "I don't believe the part about the race war," he said. "I mean, it was fantasy. I don't think anybody really believed that as that's what's going to happen."27

Not even the prosecution's star witness, Linda Kasabian, says that the reason she and the other people went to the Polanski residence to commit murders was in order to instigate a race war. At the trial she testified that she thought the group was simply going out on a "creepy-crawly" mission.28

So, aside from Leslie Van Houten, none of the actual participants in the Tate-LaBianca murders have said that the motive for the murders that they committed was to start a race war called "Helter Skelter."

But if Helter Skelter was not the motive for the murders, what was it? Where did it come from? Who thought up this idea of a racial conflagration named after a rock song?

The idea of a race war in connection with the killings was put forth very soon after the announcement that arrests had been made. The December 7, 1969 issue of the *Los Angeles Times* featured an article titled "Manson Wanted Race War, Friends Say." Despite this headline, however, the article conceded that "*Manson never discussed his entire plan for fomenting a black-white race war* with any [of the story's sources]. But each [source] had heard part of the plan, and together *they pieced it together*."29 (emphasis added)

The December 12, 1969 issue of *Time* magazine also mentioned a planned race war. This was the same article with a fabricated quote from Charles Manson.

The famous December 19, 1969 issue of *Life* magazine mentioned a race-war motive, and even has some details of the war's supposed inspiration from the Bible. But this was the same issue of *Life* featuring machine gun mounts and a "love and terror cult" called "The Family."

None of these early mentions of a race war called it Helter Skelter or made any mention of a connection to the Beatles' music.

Charles Manson refutes the idea that Helter Skelter was the motive for the murders. But he doesn't refute Helter Skelter itself.

Goodbye Helter Skelter

In a telephone conversation with me, Manson said, "We had a Helter Skelter thing going. We had the proposition of the thoughts that we talk about now."

I told him that I would not be surprised if he and his friends had talked about some sort of Helter Skelter scenario, even with all of the weird details.

"Yeah," he replied. "It was in the social consciousness. The Beatles were singing 'Why don't we do it in the road?'"30

In a 1993 television interview Manson said, "Helter Skelter was [the Beatles'] song. They wrote it. [It] didn't have no particular meaning to me. The District Attorney picked up on that and made it into his trip.

"'Helter Skelter' just means 'confusion.'"31

And "helter skelter" is, in fact, a phrase meaning "turmoil," or "a disorderly confusion." The term is also used as a descriptive of something that is "in headlong disorder."32 "Confusion" is also what the phrase connotes to Charles Manson, and he and some of the people around him have been known to use the phrase in reference to the apparent direction that society was heading in 1969.

At his trial Manson testified:

> [Helter Skelter] means confusion, literally. It doesn't mean any war with anyone. It doesn't mean that some people are going to kill other people.... Helter Skelter is confusion. Confusion is coming down around you fast. If you can't see the confusion coming down around you fast, you can call it what you wish.33

Disagreement that Helter Skelter was the motive is not confined to the participants in the murders and their friends. At Bruce Davis' 1993 parole hearing, the representative of the Los Angeles County District Attorney's office, Deputy District Attorney Jeffry Jonas told the board:

> And I'm convinced that Helter Skelter was used as a means to convict Manson.... I've read a lot of the things that [Bobby] Beausoleil said and I'm not really satisfied in my mind that Helter Skelter was the overriding thing as to why they went out and did what they did with all these other people. I think a lot of it had to do with the violence and the original act

of Gary Hinman and what -- the drugs, and all.... and the '60s and all of that. And I don't think that it was a specific motive, Helter Skelter, that caused that.

"You mean the revolution, Helter Skelter?" a board member asked.

"Yeah," Jonas replied. "And Mr. Bugliosi did an excellent job with that -- and I'm sure that was part of it and he was able to sell that to the jury...."34

Yet another person who has always had doubts about the Helter Skelter motive is Vincent Bugliosi himself.

In *Helter Skelter* Bugliosi recalled his reservations about the Helter Skelter motive at the time that he was preparing for the trial. "I felt we had a [personal motive for Manson]. It was just that it was almost unbelievably bizarre." "[Helter Skelter] was "far out.... admittedly bizarre,"35 Bugliosi conceded, and he "told [a co-prosecutor] it wouldn't take me two seconds to dump the whole Helter Skelter theory if he could find another motive in the evidence."36

In a 1976 interview in *Penthouse* magazine Bugliosi elaborated on his belief that Helter Skelter was not a personal motive for Manson:

> I cannot conceive of his believing some of the things he preached about, such as the bottomless pit, the Family growing to 144,000 people, and himself becoming leader of the world. Oh, he was a megalomaniac and would've loved to become leader of the world, but I find it difficult to think he believed those mass murders would actually start a worldwide race war between blacks and whites. My guess is that he used Helter Skelter as a vehicle to work his followers into such a lather that they were willing to kill for him. *Whether he believed it, I have to guess no.*37 (emphasis added)

Therefore, not only do most of the convicted killers refute the Helter Skelter motive, but even the senior Deputy District Attorney who actually prosecuted the case and other lawyers in the DA's office don't believe that Helter Skelter was the motive for the Tate-LaBianca murders.

Goodbye Helter Skelter

Why don't the convicted and admitted participants in the murders at the Polanski and LaBianca houses come right out and say that the motive for these crimes was to ignite the race war Helter Skelter? After all, most of these people harbor some hope of being released from prison some day, and they know that in order for this to happen they have to agree to the criminal justice system's way of looking at their crimes.

In order for them to have any chance for parole, inmates must admit their guilt. And in the case of Charles Manson's co-defendants it is useless for them not to, because their participation in the killings has long been established. Inmates must also admit to anything else that the parole board accepts as true. In California the Board of Prison Terms (the "parole board" that can grant an inmate a release date) accepts as true the court's record of an inmate's case, including whatever motive for the inmate's crime was presented at their trial. So, Watson and the three female defendants generally parrot the records from their trials and rarely disagree with the parole board's perception of what is true.

But despite coming around to the prosecution's point of view on practically every aspect of the case and Charles Manson's role in it, none of Manson's co-defendants in the Tate-LaBianca murder trial (except Leslie Van Houten) has said that the motive for the murders was the motive advanced by the prosecution -- the only motive that indicates specific and personal guilt for Charles Manson -- namely that the murders were committed to start a revolution which would culminate with Manson being the ruler of the world.

But why don't the convicted Tate-LaBianca killers claim this, especially when they know that it might be to their advantage to do so? They don't claim it because they know it is not true.

The Helter Skelter motive is incredible for many reasons. But the main puzzlement about it is (and should be) why so many people who were actually involved in the murders disavow it as the reason for those murders.

Chapter Notes

1 *Helter Skelter*, page 84.
2 Ibid., page 293.
3 "That man has wronged me. Society has wronged me. We'll kill whatever pigs are in that house. Go in there and get them." *Time* magazine, December 12, 1969, page 22.
4 *San Fernando Valley Times*, December 2, 1969, page 1.
5 As paperback editions of *Helter Skelter* promise the reader on the very first page.
6 *Helter Skelter*, page 270.
7 Ibid., page 257.
8 Ibid., page 159.
9 Ibid., page 257.
10 The version of the Helter Skelter motive in this chapter is distilled from the version presented in *Helter Skelter*, "Part Four -- The Search For A Motive," pages 281-344.
11 Stephen Kay quoted from the online *New York Cybertimes* web page, October 21, 1997.
12 Bugliosi decided that supposed hidden meanings in other Beatles songs, like "Blue Jay Way," were just too incredible to present to a jury. *Helter Skelter*, page 325.
13 For examples, the flowers on the *Sergeant Pepper's Lonely Hearts Club Band* album cover are over a grave and form the word "Paul." The hand over McCartney's head on the same cover is an esoteric symbol of death. The "OPD" armband he wears stands for "Officially Pronounced Dead." The walrus from *Magical Mystery Tour* is another symbol of death. In the song "Glass Onion" on the *White Album* John Lennon disclosed that "the walrus was Paul." Paul wears a lone black flower in the musical number pictures included with the *Magical Mystery Tour* album; at the end of "Strawberry Fields Forever" a voice seems to declare, "I buried Paul" (or "cranberry sauce"?). Paul is out of step and dressed like a corpse on the *Abbey Road* cover. George, Ringo, and John are the gravedigger, undertaker, and minister, respectively.)
14 See the title page for the section "Part Two -- The Killers" in *Helter Skelter*.
15 Manson interview with Bill Scanlon-Murphy, transcript page 21.
16 Patricia Krenwinkel 1993 parole hearing transcript pages 90-93.
17 Which Manson admitted to me during a prison visit that he did "just to fuck with him."
18 Manson recalled the MP-40 at his 1992 parole hearing (page 84), "The machine gun was a World War Two relic. It would only shoot one

bullet at a time. It wouldn't even go 'pop, pop, pop' because it was all worn out, it was so old."
19 *The Manson Women*, by Clara Livsey, Richard Marek Publishers; New York; 1980, pages 47-48.
20 *Will You Die For Me?*, page 135.
21 This quote is taken from Watson's trial transcript.
22 Watson said this at his 1990 parole hearing. I do not have a transcript of this hearing, but Watson's remarks are clear on the videotape of the proceeding.
23 *Child Of Satan, Child Of God*, page 134.
24 Patricia Krenwinkel 1993 parole hearing transcript, pages 19-20, 62-63, 65, 68-69, 72.
25 Leslie Van Houten 1993 parole hearing transcript, pages 9-11.
26 Bobby Beausoleil 1992 parole hearing transcript, pages 56-57.
27 Bruce Davis 1993 parole hearing transcript, page 65.
28 *Helter Skelter*, page 351.
29 *Los Angeles Times*, December 7, 1969, bylined Eric Malner.
30 Charles Manson in a tape-recorded telephone conversation with the author.
31 The last paragraph of Manson's analysis of Helter Skelter come from a 1993 interview with Bill Scanlon-Murphy of BBC Television, transcript pages 20-21.
32 These definitions are from *The Merriam-Webster Dictionary* and *Webster's New Collegiate Dictionary*.
33 *Helter Skelter*, page 528.
34 Bruce Davis 1993 parole hearing, transcript page 84.
35 *Helter Skelter*, page 292.
36 Ibid., page 293.
37 *Penthouse* magazine interview, unknown month 1976, page 101.
38 Patricia Krenwinkel 1993 parole hearing, transcript page 93.

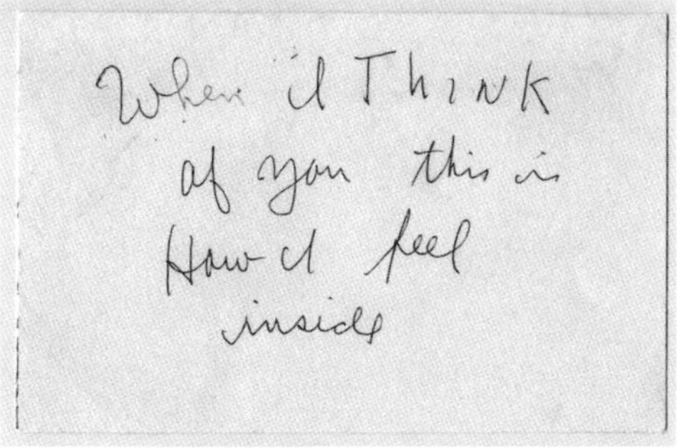
When I THINK
of you this is
How I feel
inside

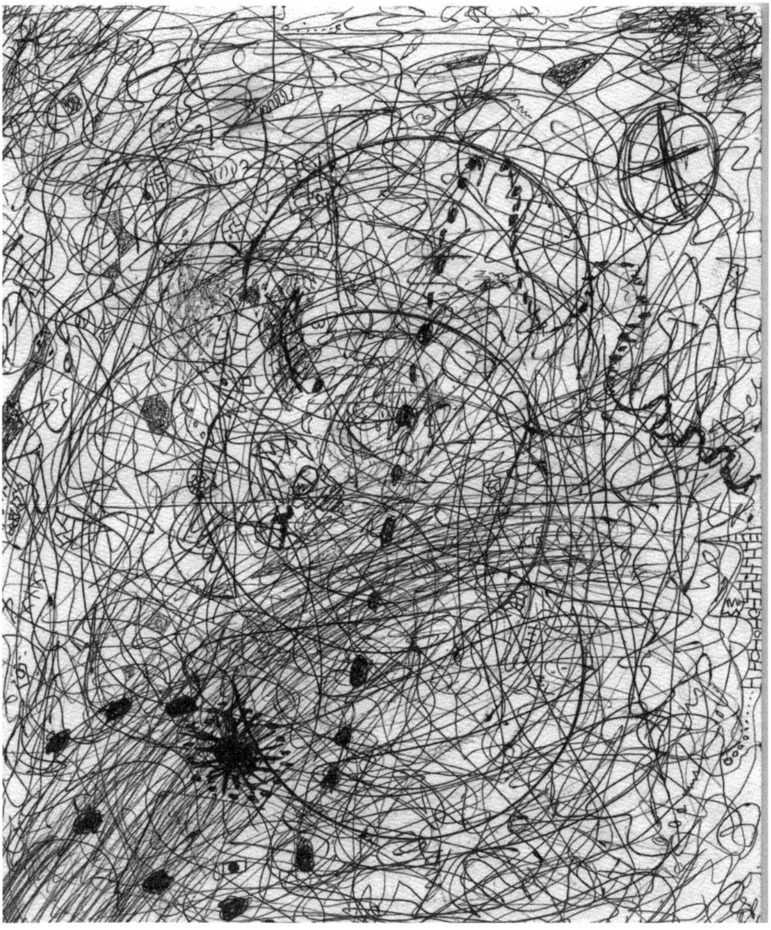

The Real Motive

"There's all kinds of motives that they play with. But did you ever think he didn't do it? You're always looking for the motive before you find out whether he really did it!"

-- Charles Manson

Proponents of the Helter Skelter motive have often pointed out that the bizarreness of the Tate-LaBianca murders was indicative of a bizarre motive and, of course, of a bizarre person behind that motive -- Charles Manson. However the notion that the motive for the murders had to be bizarre because the murders were bizarre was fundamentally flawed, because the murders, in fact, were not bizarre.

Many of the things initially reported about the slayings in the news media (and thus imprinted into the public's mind) -- things like devil worshipping, sadomasochistic sex, and ritual murder -- were unusual, but none of these widely purported and reported aspects of the case was factual. The homicides at the Polanski and LaBianca residences were brutal and savage, and they included many victims, but they weren't particularly bizarre. In fact, with regard to the Polanski residence the number of victims (and, to a lesser extent, the "celebrity" of some of those victims) was about the only thing unusual about the murders there.

People are shot, stabbed, and bludgeoned to death all the time. Mutilation, such as cutting or carving a word into a body, is also fairly common. Even the writing on the walls was not particularly unusual. A Los Angeles police spokesman at the time commented, "This [writing on walls] is a rather common type of thing in homicides. We've had many cases before where a suspect has written in blood, or lipstick, or various things of that nature."1

The understanding that the murders on Cielo and Waverly Drives were not really bizarre is significant, for if a bizarreness of the murders was not indicated or supported by the factual information and physical evidence of the crimes, maybe the motive also was not bizarre and was not something as fantastic and freaky as Helter Skelter.

What was the real motive for the Tate-LaBianca murders? If Helter Skelter was not the driving force behind the killings that occurred on Cielo and Waverly Drives, what other reason could there have been for their commission?

When the prosecutors themselves sense the unbelievability of Helter Skelter as a motive (they know that it is weak) they have often offered alternate, secondary personal motives for Charles Manson to have ordered the murders.

One alternate motive has Charles Manson lashing out at the show business establishment in general, and Terry Melcher in particular, because Melcher did not do enough to help Manson become a successful recording artist.

To some extent, Terry Melcher's lack of help in getting some sort of beneficial arrangement for Manson was a factor in the minds of the people who went to his former residence on Cielo Drive on August 8, because that perceived lack of assistance put Melcher and his reality (like his old house) into their thoughts. As Charles Manson later explained it:

> It was Terry Melcher's house because, the people were -- at that ranch -- was mad at Terry Melcher because he didn't do what he said, number one. Number two, he sent somebody over there [to the ranch] to fight. He caused some trouble, he almost got some other people killed, [and] some people put their life on the line because of Terry Melcher. [But] Terry Melcher didn't even know about [these conflicts].... No one ever told him about it.2

In other words, the perception that Terry Melcher had done Charles Manson wrong was in the minds of some of the people at Spahn's Ranch, and it might even have been a subconscious factor in Charles Watson's decision to pick that particular house on August 8. But there is no evidence that it was in the mind of Charles Manson, or that it was any primary motive for the murders. (And it certainly couldn't be a motive for the murders on Waverly Drive.) The main reason that the house on Cielo Drive was chosen was because, as Charles Manson has said, "Tex had a familiarity of the surroundings."3

Deputy DA Stephen Kay has claimed that Manson wanted to send a message to Melcher that, "there but for the grace of God go you."4 But if killing people in his old house was supposed to send Terry Melcher some kind of message he probably didn't get much meaning out of it, because until the arrest of Manson and the others he had no idea who had sent it. As Vincent Bugliosi later wrote, "though Terry and [10050 Cielo Drive owner] Rudi [Altobelli] had spent many hours discussing the murders, and possible suspects, Manson's name was never mentioned."5

It is hard to believe that anyone would order five vicious murders (and risk the tremendous amount of law enforcement heat arising therefrom) to send someone a vague, anonymous message. This purported alternate motive is just not credible.

The second alternate motive for the Tate-LaBianca (and Hinman-Shea) murders is that Charles Manson is supposed to have an uncontrollable lust for violence and death. Vincent Bugliosi laid this motive out in a 1976 interview in *Penthouse* magazine in which he explained:

> The third motive [after Helter Skelter and the "message to Melcher" motives] was [Manson's] preoccupation with death. He was always lecturing the family about death and how beautiful it was. In fact, most of the songs he wrote contained constant references to death. And where did he lead the family after the murders? Death Valley. Paul Watkins, who left Manson before the murders, said it best: "Death was Charlie's trip."6

But this assertion also does not stand up to scrutiny.

First of all, Charles Manson is not -- and was not -- preoccupied with death. In my many personal conversations with him he seldom talked about it. (In fact, I'm only writing "seldom" out of fairness, because I cannot actually recall any specific conversations about death that I ever had with Manson. But the subject must have come up at least a few times during the hundreds of visits and phone calls that I had with him.)

As for "most of the songs he wrote contained constant references to death," this is simply not true, as anyone who has listened to any (or even every) piece of Manson's music can confirm.

Bugliosi's inference that Manson took his "followers" to Death Valley after the murders because, in effect, it was named Death Valley is absurd. Manson and many of the people he knew had already spent much time in the area and planned to go back there long before there was any literal death in their lives.

For someone who is supposedly obsessed with violent death Charles Manson shows a marked disinclination to violently kill anyone, as his apparent lack of success in doing so on the night that the LaBiancas were killed attests. The "obsession with death" motive is not convincing. It is vague and ultimately unsupportable for the simple fact that it has little -- if any -- foundation in reality.

Besides these two shaky prosecutorial efforts there has been another motive given for the murders on Cielo Drive, namely that they were committed in retaliation for a drug burn perpetrated by one of the house guests at the residence. In this scenario the guest ripped off some of the people at Spahn's Ranch, who retaliated by going to the Cielo Drive house and killing all the people there.

This motive arose out of the drug use and rumored dealing by some of the people at the Polanski residence and was fueled by rumors and tips provided to police by underworld informants. But although this avenue of investigation was avidly pursued by law enforcement it eventually led nowhere (including Spahn's Ranch), and for good reason; a drug burn had nothing to do with the murders. (And this motive, too, like the "message to Melcher" motive, would not have been applicable to the LaBiancas.)

Alternate motives have also been given by the persons who actually participated in the murders.

Charles Watson has listed three motives: one, to ignite Helter Skelter; two, to acquire money so "the Family" could complete its move to the desert, and; three, to get Bobby Beausoleil out of jail by committing copycat murders that would convince the police that the real murderer of Gary Hinman was still at large.7

Susan Atkins apparently initially said that the reason for the murders was to instill fear into the Establishment and to show the black man how to make war on the white man. These motives are advanced in the book *The Killing of Sharon Tate*, which was based on Atkins' tape-recorded confessions to the murders. But it has long been known that this book, as well as Atkins' "confession" as it was printed in Los Angeles newspapers and around the world, was in fact a reworked version of her story that was compiled by two reporters for the *Los Angeles Times*, so the accuracy of this information should be viewed with the same skepticism due to the reporters of other inaccurate (if sensational and marketable) information about the case, such as devil worship and sexually mutilated and hooded corpses.

In any event, Atkins soon recanted that testimony and ever since -- at the murder trial, in her book, and at parole hearings -- has disavowed the "race war" motive and said that the reason for the murders was to commit a copycat crime that would cause the police to release Bobby Beausoleil.

In court during her trial, when she was asked why the victims on Cielo and Waverly Drives were killed, Atkins replied, "Because I believed it was right to get my brother out of jail. And I still believe it was right."8

"We didn't know how to get Bobby out of jail, so someone mentioned that we should do something equal as to make it appear like someone [else] had done it and not Bobby, who wouldn't be present."9

In her book *Child of Satan, Child of God* Atkins wrote, "To the best of my understanding, the copycat plan was the primary motive behind the.... Tate-LaBianca murders."10

At a 1993 parole hearing Atkins was questioned about the murder of Gary Hinman and how that killing led to the deaths of the people at the Polanski and LaBianca residences. A parole board member asked:

"You understood that you were going there [to Gary Hinman's house] to get money?"

"Yes."

"Okay. And then when [Beausoleil] murdered the victim there, then it was decided to commit these other crimes to help him, because he was at that time in jail."

"Yes."

"So that they would think, well the crime patterns are continuing, so...."

"Right."

".... it must have been done by somebody else."11

Linda Kasabian seems to have no understanding about any motive for the murders. She testified at the trial that on the first night she thought they were only going out to "creepy-crawl" a house.

Patricia Krenwinkel testified at the trial that the copycat motive was the real motive for the murders:

> About August 4, 1969 Bobby Beausoleil got arrested for the murder of Gary Hinman.... Then one day [Susan Atkins, Leslie Van Houten, and I] were speaking about it, and Linda was present. We thought about how to free Bobby. We put a lot of thought into it and one [thought] stayed in our minds. We thought of doing some killing like sidetracking the police to make them believe that someone else did it.
>
> Some people just think -- but we did it right away. We all got in the car and did it.12
>
> It's hard to explain. It was just a thought, and the thought came to be.13

Krenwinkel has changed her recollection of the night of August 8, 1969 since the trial. At her 1993 parole hearing she said she thought she was going out to commit a robbery that night. (I have never heard her explain what she thought was motivating people on the second night of murder.)

Leslie Van Houten has also vacillated in her recall of the motive for the murders. In statements made in the late 1990s she said that the motive was to instigate the race war Helter Skelter. But at the murder trial, and even after, she testified that the motive was to get a brother, Bobby Beausoleil, out of jail. At her 1977 retrial Van Houten was still talking about killing for brother. Even as late as 1996 she downplayed Helter Skelter, explaining that she committed the crimes:

> for Manson and his approval. To let him know that I was a good soldier and that I was willing to lay my life on the line for him.... I see my motive of the crime as more of one of trying to please Manson than putting together the idea of Helter Skelter.14

But why would Van Houten go back and forth between the Helter Skelter and the "get brother out of jail" motives? For one thing, she was at one time the likeliest of the Tate-LaBianca defendants to be released on parole, and it was thus in her interest to go along with the prosecution's version of her crime. Another reason was her relationship with Bobby Beausoleil. Van Houten described herself as "Bobby Beausoleil's woman" while she lived at Spahn's Ranch. As such, she might have had a greater role in planning a series of copycat murders designed to get him out of jail than she would care to admit to. Would Leslie Van Houten lie? In 1977 she told a psychiatrist, "I don't lie, and I don't con others *unless when it's to make something more comfortable for myself.*"15 (emphasis added)

Spahn's Ranch resident Catherine "Gypsy" Share testified during the penalty phase of the murder trial that Linda Kasabian thought up the idea that the girls should commit murders similar to that of Gary Hinman in hopes that the police would believe that the real killer of Hinman was still at large, thereby setting Bobby Beausoleil free.16

Catherine "Capistrano" Gillies testified, "You know, I am willing to kill for a brother. We all are.... To get a brother out of jail I would kill. I would have killed that night [August 8] except I did not go."17

Sandra Good told a documentary filmmaker:

> The motive for the murders was love of brother, because we knew we would do anything to get Bobby out of jail. It was simply that Bobby had been arrested for the murder of Hinman, and the girls, to get him out of jail, decided to commit copycat killings, with the writing on the walls

and the whole thing -- you know, multiple stab wounds -- therefore leading the police to believe that the killer was still at large....

We knew Charlie would give his life for a brother [because of the incident with Bernard Crowe].... and the girls loved Bobby enough to do this. They were willing to die. As they took these people's lives they were willing to give their own lives, which they're doing right now. They're on Death Row.18

In 1972, while he was still on California's Death Row at San Quentin Prison, Bobby Beausoleil recalled his relationship with Charles Manson and its consequences:

I don't have to ask him anything. He already knows what to do. Charles Manson is one of my brothers, you know, and I'll follow my brother through all time, through all the hells and fire and back again. And I have -- for no better reason than because I love him.

He has shown me a number of times that he is willing to do anything for me. And many others have shown me by their words and by the things they have done, that they will do the same for me. For anyone willing to look, that's easy enough to see -- let the actions of my lovely, but deadly, family testify to that truth....

When the police put me in chains -- put me in jail and threatened to kill me -- eight or nine people were killed in an attempt to free me. That's a strong love. That's the allegiance we have with each other.19

In a later interview with *Oui* magazine, a more moderate Beausoleil said:

I do believe there was something to that ["get brother out of jail" motive], yes.... I don't think that whoever's idea it was to commit these [Tate-LaBianca] murders would have been able to get the participation of those involved unless there had been this noble concept.... Perhaps they interpreted the thing [him killing Hinman] that I had defended them from him.... You've got to understand that these people were not totally without some kind of scruples.... I think [Hinman's death] led to a situation in which Charlie and the others, who had made similar commitments to each other, were forced into a situation of acting on their commitments.20

Charles Manson said of his co-defendants at the trial, "These children, everything they done, they done for the love of their brother."21

In fact, Charles Manson has always maintained that the main reason for what happened at the Polanski and LaBianca residences was to get Bobby Beausoleil out of jail. Here Manson tells how he remembered the circumstances and motivations that led to the murders on Cielo and Waverly Drives:

I agreed with everybody, I got along with everybody, and I did everything that everybody asked me. Up to a point. And that point was when I cut Hinman's ear off. And then I started to pulling back, saying, "Whoa, man. This is all going into insanity." And I told everybody there, "You're all putting me back in the penitentiary. I'm getting out of here."

And everybody said, "Oh, don't leave! If we have any trouble we'll deal with it."

So I said, "All right," you know. And I hung around....

And then everybody comes around and says, "Bobby's in jail."

I said, "I'm not gonna let my brother in jail." In other words, I'm very strong on the brotherhood. And I don't let my brother down.... I *am* my brother. If I don't help me, I'm not -- there *is* no brother.

So they say, "What do we do?"

I say, "I don't know what you do. Get him out of jail."

They say, "How do we get him out of jail?"

[I said] "I'm not educated. I don't go to school, man. I don't know how you do it, you know. That's what you went to school for. You do it. You do it."

"Well, how do we do it?"

I said, "How do I know what you do? I don't have no idea what you do. [But] I know you owe me your life, tramp. You owe me your life. Pay me, or get the hell away from me. You know. It's that simple. I stand up for you. I've marched to hell with you. I go through all the things it takes to save your life and then you come back to me.... You got a brother over here. Get him out of jail."

They say, "Well, we'll get a lawyer."

Someone said, "When you get a lawyer, lawyer's just gonna take your money and lie." Somebody else said something else, somebody else said something else. I got in a truck. I went to Big Sur. I was gone for two or three days. I came back....

When Manson got back from his trip to Big Sur the people at the ranch were still talking about Bobby Beausoleil:

[I said], "Well, what are you willing to do?"

And they said, "We're willing to do anything."

I said, "You're willing to give your life?"

And they said, "Yeah."

I said, "You're willing to go into combat conditions and take a life?"

They said, "Yeah."

I said, "Well, then, pick up your banner, go on and do whatever you have to do to do whatever you want to do. If you really believe in your God and your country, He'll be with you. Have faith in that and go about your business. Go on and think that, and it'll happen."

[See], I thought [that I had killed Bernard Crowe]. And I got all with Tex and I said, "You caused me to kill somebody, man. You owe me. You owe me. Susie, you owe me. I fought three guys for you that wanted to rape you. I kept you up out of it, man. You owe me, you owe me, and you owe me. You got me fighting all over this town for you, man, 'cause you won't stand up for yourself. I'm not the policeman, man. Go to the cops and get them to do your fighting."

Every time it's someone's turn to die, come and get Charlie, put him on the line, let him die. Put me out front and let me face it. Let me face everything that no one wants to understand or no one wants to look at. Let me take the gun and go off into hell with it.

So I said, "You owe me, mister, and when it comes time to pay this circle, this covenant, this family, this ranch, you'll pay your debt to all these people that feed you, and that serve the same God that you serve....

Here's my sin. I told Tex, "Come here. You *owe* me one."

So then, I come back to Watson, I say, "You pay [Beausoleil] what you owe me."

He said, "How do I pay it?"

I said, "[I] don't know. I'm not your father. Do what you're told. Pay your debt, or get off my road."

So he pays what he has to pay. And he does what he has to do. I didn't direct him to do anything. I told him to be a man, stand up for himself. I didn't tell him what he should do or how he should do whatever he had to do....

I never directed traffic on no street corner about anything. Man, I haven't got time for that.22

Let's take a closer look at the copycat or "get brother out of jail" motive.

To begin with, it must be conceded that the copycat plan was not a good idea. If the purpose of the killings subsequent to Gary Hinman's was to make the police think that the people responsible for Hinman's death were still at large it is unclear why a series of copycat crimes would necessarily make them think that Bobby Beausoleil was not involved in the murder. They already had a very good case against him. His fingerprints had been found at Hinman's residence and he had been arrested in the dead man's car with the murder weapon still inside the vehicle. If similar killings were committed, why would the police think that Beausoleil was innocent? Wouldn't they likelier think that he must have had accomplices in the Hinman murder who were still at large (which in fact was the case)?

But despite this fundamental flaw, the ill-conceived and executed copycat motive *was* the main reason for the Tate-LaBianca murders. The arrest and imprisonment of Bobby Beausoleil for the murder of Gary Hinman was the catalyst for the murders that were committed on Cielo and Waverly Drives -- not some fantastic vision of race war born out of the megalomaniacal mind of Charles Manson.

Before examining the specific dynamics and circumstances that led to "get brother out of jail" as being the motive for the Tate-LaBianca murders, it is important to realize that in addition to the base motivation of getting a brother out of jail there were several other factors which contributed to the mindset that led to the murders. One very important factor was the historical time in which those murders occurred. The mood of that time produced a consciousness and frequent acceptance of violence as a solution to problems in the mass mind -- and especially in the *young* mass mind. That revolutionary spirit, imbued in impressionable young people over a period of years by the events of those years, is one of the greatest underrated contributing factors to the Tate-LaBianca murders, for despite all of the talk at the time about "giving peace a chance" as a cure to the world's ills there was also a strong feeling among many people that violent action was the only way to deal with an Establishment that was warring on young people -- and on life itself -- through the Vietnam War, oppression of various classes, and by ravaging the environment with over-development and pollution. And the killers themselves have frequently acknowledged the impact that the time had on them.

In 1993 Susan Atkins told her parole board, "[In 1969] the country seemed to be split into two factions. You had the very patriotic group of people, and you had very, very rebellious young people who were dealing with what they regarded -- myself included -- to be hypocrisy."23

Pat Krenwinkel said at her third parole hearing:

> I was a child of the '60s, and there's something to be said for the '60s. It was an incredible time. I grew up in the '60s. It was the beginning of the marches and the movements. There was dissatisfaction everywhere. The young men I met were burning their draft cards. I couldn't seem to find any bearing in my world.24

Charles Watson remembered, "At the time in 1969 there was a very revolutionary-type atmosphere. I was very rebellious to society."25

And besides the revolutionary and action-oriented spirit of many of the young people of the time there was another factor in the lives of some of the individuals involved in this case that should also be taken into consideration. That factor could not really be called a reason or motive for the murders, but it could be called a motivating component. That component was the use of speed -- methamphetamine -- by at least two of the major participants in the killings.

The acceptance of drugs as an aid to dropping out of society was a common circumstance in the late 1960s. Marijuana and LSD are perhaps the best known, but speed was another mind and body-altering concoction that also gained a fairly broad acceptance.

Both Charles Watson and Susan Atkins have said that they used speed rather often while they lived at Spahn's Ranch in the summer of 1969. These admissions are important for a couple of reasons.

First, these claims are important because Charles Manson is fairly well on record as being anti-speed (and indeed for being anti any drug that can become addictive). His thinking in this regard is well established. ("Charlie, for all his use of acid, was absolutely against speed,"26 writes Watson.) So the fact that Watson and Atkins were using speed gives lie to their (and other persons') claims that Manson directed every aspect of their lives. To the contrary, it shows that they did pretty much whatever they wanted to do.

Charles Watson seems to have been particularly partial to the drug. *In Will You Die For Me?* he writes of his surreptitious speed use and concludes that he loved it so much that "I was willing to kill for Manson, but I wasn't willing to give up my speed."27 Even decades later, when recalling his late 1960s drug experiences, Watson seems to remember speed with a special fondness, although his descriptions of solid objects becoming fluid and music "rolling over you like breakers"28 while being under the influence of speed sounds more like an acid trip than the experience of being wired on methamphetamine.

Watson's and Atkins' choice of drugs is also important because if they were doing speed it might explain some of the aspects of the crimes they committed.

One doesn't have to look far on the Internet to find information on speed (Susan Atkins specified what she used as "methedrine"29) and to see its possible contribution to the events of the nights of August 8 and 9, 1969.

One informational source states, "Psychological effects [of prolonged amphetamine use] include agitation, panic, aggression, and suicidal or homicidal tendencies. Paranoia, sometimes accompanied by both auditory and visual hallucinations, may also occur."

More: "Chronic abuse produces a psychosis that resembles schizophrenia and is characterized by paranoia, picking at the skin, preoccupation with one's own thoughts, and auditory and visual hallucinations. Violent and erratic behavior is frequently seen among chronic abusers of amphetamines."

More: "Emotional responses may range from euphoria to anger and paranoia, Preliminary doses tend to produce the former, while continued use (*e.g., for three or more days*) tends to produce the latter." (emphasis added)

More: "Amphetamines are commonly abused by individuals seeking mood elevation, [but] serious mental illness including paranoia, hallucinations, and violent behavior may occur after prolonged use."

Lest anyone feel that the use of speed would somehow cripple a person from effectively carrying out a specific plan, it should be pointed out that amphetamines were originally developed, in part, as an aid to U.S. fighting men in World War Two. Surely some functioning ability must have been required in order to achieve a total victory over the Axis powers.

Another characteristic of speed that has relevance here is that it can make a person act somewhat irrationally (as anyone who has ever spent any time around a speed freak can readily tell you). As stated earlier, the copycat motive was not a good plan. But speed is a drug that is infamous for making its users think that a bad idea is a good idea. According to one Internet fact sheet, "Amphetamine use increases self-confidence, which often ignores the reality of a person's limitations. Amphetamine users may experience 'Superman Syndrome' in which they attempt to perform tasks they are incapable of performing.... Users often take unnecessary risks."30

Let's take a further look at the evidence of a possible connection of speed use to the Tate-LaBianca murders.

Much of the evidence indicating speed as being a factor in these murders comes firsthand from the mouths of two of the main participants in the crimes, Charles Watson and Susan Atkins.

In *Will You Die For Me?* Watson says that he, Susan Atkins, and Bruce Davis had a secret speed stash that they were hiding from Manson and the others at Spahn's Ranch. At his 2001 parole hearing, Watson recalled:

> There was a friend of mine across the street, that had the ranch across the street. He had obtained an ounce of it and had given me a jar of it. And Susan Atkins and myself and one other was sniffing the methamphetamine.31

Watson remembered that at around dinnertime on August 8, the night of the murders on Cielo Drive, "I didn't have a lot of pep or something, so I took some speed to get me moving...."32

He says that later in the evening, after he supposedly received murder instructions from Charles Manson, "I reeled over to the porch where [Susan Atkins] and I kept our Gerber's jar of speed hidden.... I took a couple of deep snorts of speed and went off...."33

On the next day, after the murders at the Polanski residence, Watson later recalled, "I.... spent part of the day working on dune buggies and snorting speed."34

That night, before driving off to Waverly Drive, "While people were getting things together, [Susan Atkins] and I took the opportunity to hit our speed bottle and I gave myself three good snorts in each nostril. I knew now I'd need it for what was to come."35

In *God's Prison Gang* Watson told author Chaplain Ray Hoekstra:

> It's true that there was a special feeling between Susan and me when we were members of Charlie's Family. We used to keep some drugs hidden, and when we had a chance, we'd do drugs together -- LSD and other things. In fact we did some drugs together just a few hours before the killings.36

Susan Atkins says, in *Child of Satan, Child of God*, "Tex and I had been secretly snorting, or inhaling, Methedrine -- crystal speed --*for three or four days* [before the murders]. *In violation of the unspoken family code,* we had kept our own private stash and were *using it constantly*."37 (emphasis added)

On the night of August 8, says Atkins, "We [she and Watson] were both stoned, but our senses were keen."38

The next night, while riding around in the car, "I'm not sure about the others, but I was once again quite stoned on Methedrine and was pretty much preoccupied with my own thoughts."39

At the murder trial, Linda Kasabian conceded that on the night of August 8 "Tex might have taken speed.... I don't know."40

Leslie Van Houten has never said anything about anybody being on speed, but she described Watson's behavior in the LaBianca house as "out of control, darting here and there, and.... kind of crazy acting."41

Prosecutor Stephen Kay said at Patricia Krenwinkel's 1993 parole hearing, "Watson, the second night took some speed to pep himself up."42

So, there is much evidence suggesting that Charles Watson and Susan Atkins were using speed on the nights of the murders (and for several days previous). This premise is even acknowledged and accepted by one of the prosecutors of the case.

Yet another piece of circumstantial evidence pointing to the possibility of speed being a contributing factor to the two nights of murder is the ferocity of the attacks on the victims. At the first residence one victim was stabbed seven times, one sixteen times, one twenty-eight times, and one fifty-one times! (If the reader can't fully grasp how many times that is, I would invite you to take a break from reading and "stab" the arm of the chair you're sitting in fifty-one times. Fifty-one is a lot of stab wounds.) In addition to being stabbed some of the victims were also shot and viciously kicked and bludgeoned.

At the second residence the two victims were stabbed twelve and forty-one times. The first victim was also stabbed through the neck with a knife and had the word WAR was carved into his abdomen. The number of wounds in both instances indicates a lot of ruthless energy that clearly amounted to overkill.

One of the typical symptoms of speed use is repetitive motions. "The person [on amphetamines] may exhibit anxiousness.... extreme moodiness and irritability, [and] repetitious behavior," said one drug information web site.43 *In Will You Die For Me?* Charles Watson recalled his actions in stabbing one of the victims at the Polanski house as, "I ran back to him, and once more the mechanical knife that was my arm drove down, again and again, until my wrist disappeared in the mess."44 Later in the book he remarks on this occurrence again:

> Later [during Watson's murder trial] a defense psychiatrist, Dr. Ira Frank, would explain that speed sometimes creates a phenomenon called 'preservation' -- the mechanical repetition of a manual act or series of acts. This was how it had been [during the murders], over and over, again and again, my arm like a machine, at one with the blade.45

Remarking on the sense of compulsion that can accompany speed use Watson said at his 2001 parole hearing:

> When you're on drugs, when you're on methamphetamines -- again I'm not blaming that, I chose to take those drugs, I take responsibility for that. But when you're on those drugs and when you're almost driven by those drugs and, you know, when you're driven by such a bizarre belief system that I had at that time, that I had taken on, there's just no stopping, you know.46

Still another symptom of amphetamine abuse is audio hallucinating. And Watson remembers that when they went out on August 8, "It was as though Charlie's instructions were tape recorded in my mind and being played back, step by step, as I needed them."47 And, "There in that living room on the hill, with Charlie's instructions ticking through my brain, it was as if time telescoped, until one act tripped over the next in sudden bursts of blinding color and motion."48 And, still later on, "Charlie's tape whirred...."49

I wonder, given that auditory hallucinations are repeatedly noted in chronic users of amphetamines, how much of Charles Manson's "instructions" to Charles Watson on the evening of August 8 (which Watson recalled at his own trial for murder) were actually uttered by Charles Manson and how much might have been the product of Charles Watson's own speed-affected brain -- this in addition to the possible shading of events after Manson and his three co-defendants had already been convicted and sentenced to death.

Vincent Bugliosi, though, is one person who discounts the importance of drugs to the murders (except, of course, for Manson's alleged use of LSD to gain control over his "followers") and contends that none of the killers was under the influence of any mind-altering substance when they committed their crimes. One reason for this point of view might be that the District Attorney does not want any possible drug use to mitigate his version of the murders, i.e., that Charles Manson sent his very willing (but not very high) killers out to commit murder for him. But as we have already seen, amphetamine use can actually enhance a person's performance in such a task as carrying out a military-style search and destroy mission; one of the early uses of speed was to improve the fighting capability of U.S. troops during World War Two. (And Stephen Kay disagrees with Bugliosi's belief that Charles Watson, the main killer, was not speeding.)

Another person who disputes the possible impact of speed on the murders is Charles Manson. On several occasions I brought up this speed theory with him and he always discounted it, saying that while Susan Atkins might have been involved with the "diet pills" level of speed there was no use by her or Watson of anything like crystal meth. He further told me that it would have been impossible for Watson and Atkins to have had a stash of speed hidden at Spahn's Ranch without him knowing about it. "Tex said that they had speed on the ranch and all that," he recalled. "That's bullshit. They didn't have nothing like that when I was there. Because I would have known it." But then he immediately contradicted himself in the same conversation, admitting, "Well, he *could* have been [on speed during the murders]. Maybe he was. But it wasn't on *my* ranch. It might have been on Tex's ranch, but not on my ranch -- there was none of that junk."50

The Helter Skelter version of motive is well known to even the casual student of the Tate-LaBianca murders. But although the alternative motive of "get brother out of jail" has sometimes been mentioned in books and other media about this case (usually dismissively), it has never been completely explained by considering all of the factors which have been presented so far in this book -- all of the evidence of the case, the mood of the time, the circumstances surrounding (and the dynamics of) the individual participants in the crimes, the recollections of those individuals, and possibility of the use of amphetamines by some of the killers. So, let's do that now. Let's take a complete look at the "copycat" or "get brother out of jail" scenario.

First of all, it is necessary to place the murders on Cielo and Waverly Drives into their proper context of the whole of the summer of 1969. Those murders were not primary acts ordered by Charles Manson because he was impatient with a non-starting race war. Rather, they were secondary acts committed as a result of earlier violent actions. As such they have to be considered within the totality of all of those previous actions, which began over a month earlier, on July 1, 1969, when Charles Manson shot Bernard Crowe.

One can reasonably accept the proposition that the burn of Bernard Crowe was the brainchild of Charles Watson and Charles Watson alone. He admitted in his book that it was his idea to rip off a drug dealer with little regard for any consequences. When Crowe called Spahn's Ranch after Watson's theft, Charles Manson inadvertently intercepted the phone call. Crowe told Manson that he was coming up to the ranch to burn it down and kill everybody there. To prevent this from happening Manson agreed to meet Crowe in Hollywood in order to iron out the situation away from the ranch. When this meeting occurred, however, it unfortunately deteriorated to the point where Manson was forced to shoot Crowe in self-defense. Manson thought that he had killed him, and he thought that he had killed him because of a problem created by Charles Watson. Manson thought that he had killed him because of -- and for -- Charles Watson.

Manson was understandably upset about the shooting and presumed murder. And he laid into Watson for putting him into the situation. "You *owe* me, mister," Manson told him.

As the following weeks passed, many of the people at Spahn's Ranch (and especially Charles Manson) were apprehensive about the likelihood of either Manson being arrested for the shooting or the Black Panthers coming up to the ranch to seek revenge. But nothing happened.

Then arose Bobby Beausoleil's problem of the bad mescaline deal with Gary Hinman and the Straight Satans motorcycle club. Beausoleil went to Hinman's house to straighten out the problem, and he took Bruce Davis' gun with him for backup. Soon after his arrival, however, the situation began falling apart and there was an argument and then a fight. Then Gary Hinman got possession of the weapon (this according to Beausoleil, Atkins, and Manson). Beausoleil (or someone) then called Charles Manson at Spahn's Ranch and asked for help. Manson went to the house and ended up cutting Hinman's face while taking the gun away from him.

Hinman was upset over having his face slashed, but he nevertheless promised Manson that he would not turn him in to the authorities. With that assurance, Manson left the house and went on with his life. Beausoleil, Susan Atkins, and Mary Brunner stayed at the house to help Hinman recuperate from his wound. A few days later, though, Hinman changed his mind and said that he was going to the police after all. To keep him from doing this -- and to keep him from sending his "brother" Charles Manson back to jail -- Bobby Beausoleil stabbed him to death.

Upon learning of Hinmans' death, Charles Manson had a very bad feeling: first Crowe, and now this. Manson's plan of not going back to prison by not breaking the law was being seriously undermined by him getting unintentionally and violently involved in his "brothers'" misadventures. In order to distance himself from the spiraling hassles and increasingly tense atmosphere at Spahn's Ranch he borrowed Danny DeCarlos' bread truck and left on August 3.

Of course, the prosecution maintained that Manson left Spahn's Ranch in order to go to Big Sur and recruit new "members" for "the Family," but this is not true. Manson left to get away from all of the problems in Los Angeles. He probably knew that Hinman was dead by July 28. That same day, Los Angeles County Sheriff's deputies visited the ranch on one of their periodic raids, looking for stolen cars. Life at Spahn's Ranch was becoming too busy, so Manson left for some time off.

On August 4, near Big Sur, Manson picked up a seventeen-year-old hitchhiker named Stephanie Schramm. Manson and Schramm spent the next couple of days together before arriving back at Spahn's Ranch on August 6. By then Bobby Beausoleil had been arrested for the murder of Gary Hinman, and there was much discussion among the people at the ranch about what could or should be done about the situation. Charles Manson participated in some of these discussions, then left with Schramm to go to her parents' house in San Diego, still on August 6. In San Diego they picked up Schramm's belongings and then drove back to Los Angeles and the ranch, arriving there on the afternoon of August 8.

People were still talking about Bobby Beausoleil. Manson was aware that Beausoleil had killed Hinman to keep him from turning Manson in to the police, and he felt that he owed him for that. Thus, Manson wanted Beausoleil out of jail, and he communicated this desire in no uncertain terms to the others at the ranch. But he also communicated that he was not going to involve himself in any activity that could send him back to the penitentiary. He had already shown his mettle by shooting Bernard Crowe for the people at the ranch. For that and for other episodes they owed him. And they owed him to the point of committing murder.

Manson told the people who owed him -- Charles Watson, Susan Atkins, Linda Kasabian -- to do something to get their brother out of jail. Beausoleil's situation had already been the subject of discussion for several days -- days that Charles Manson was far removed from Los Angeles. Susan Atkins later recalled that:

> Out of all the confusion and mass of words, the constant use of drugs, came a vague sort of scheme to try to convince the police that Bobby could not have done the Hinman killing. It was a plan for "copycat murders" that would make the police believe that they had the wrong man in jail since similar "revolutionary" killings were still taking place while Bobby was behind bars.51

So, having heard Charles Manson's general command to "Do something!", Charles Watson, Linda Kasabian, Susan Atkins, and Patricia Krenwinkel left Spahn's Ranch and drove to Cielo Drive.

Why Cielo Drive? Charles Watson had been there before and knew the layout.

Of course the same factors carried over into the second night when more murders were committed on Waverly Drive in order to present police with a *series* of copycat murders designed to make them think that the killer of Gary Hinman was still at large and still killing.

Consider this scenario again. It flows. It fits. It is logical. It jibes with most of the recollections and testimony of the individuals involved. It matches all of the physical evidence and accounts for every action by every participant. No aspect of it stretches the imagination or requires a leap of faith. It is reasonable.

Now consider the Helter Skelter scenario again. It is fantastic. It is bizarre. Most of the people involved in the murders refute it as the motive. It leaves many unanswered questions. It is unreasonable.

Another comparison: The "get brother out of jail" motive is not based on a presupposition of any particular individual's responsibility or guilt. But the only reason that Helter Skelter was even seriously considered as a motive was because it was the only motive that fit the prosecution's pre-conceived conclusion of Charles Manson's personal responsibility for the murders. In Charles Manson's case the prosecution took a presumed guilty defendant and molded the evidence to "prove" that defendant's guilt instead of examining all of the evidence without distortion and seeing the real motive and the real guilty parties. It was the necessity of convicting Charles Manson for the Tate-LaBianca murders that led to the necessity of the Helter Skelter motive.

What are the criticisms of the "get brother out of jail" motive?

In *Helter Skelter* Bugliosi dismissed it as "laughable." When the "brother" motive was testified to in the penalty phase of Manson's trial by his co-defendants and friends, Bugliosi countered by telling the jury that he had ten witnesses who irrevocably tied Manson to Helter Skelter. He also told the jury:

> I could give you between twenty and thirty reasons why it's obvious that this nonsensical story of the defense is fabricated out of whole cloth, but I won't take up your time with it, and I'm not going to insult your intelligence.52

This, of course, is a standard prosecutorial bluff, saying in effect, "I do have very much evidence to prove my point but I don't want to 'take up your time' (in this case in a trial where the prosecution had already spent nine months presenting its case), so I won't present any of it. But trust me; it exists."

Nevertheless, Bugliosi listed a few.

He said that Linda Kasabian never heard of the copycat motive. But Linda Kasabian didn't testify that Helter Skelter was the motive either. And besides, not hearing about something doesn't mean that it doesn't exist. (Also, she could have been lying because she might have been more involved in the copycat idea than she wanted authorities to know.)

Bugliosi pointed out that there were different types of wounds on the victims at the Hinman crime scene as opposed to the Tate and LaBianca crime scenes. But ninety-percent of the wounds inflicted at the Polanski and LaBianca residences were inflicted by Charles Watson, a person who was not present at Gary Hinman's house when he was killed. Watson had no firsthand knowledge of specifically how Hinman was killed other than that he had been stabbed. Plus, Watson's admitted use of amphetamines could easily account for the greater ferocity of the attacks on Cielo and Waverly Drives. (There is no evidence that Bobby Beausoleil ever used, much less abused, speed.)

Bugliosi said that there was different writing on the walls (and door) at each murder scene. But different people did the writing at each different location, and they might not have known exactly what the other people wrote at the other residences.

District Attorney Bugliosi had another reason at the trial for not wanting to go into the brother motive too much: He didn't want the jury to start thinking that it might be true. "My objective was to completely demolish it, yet not dwell on it so long that it would seem that I was giving it credence," he recalled.53

Stephen Kay has also scoffed at the brother motive. "It wasn't to protect Bobby Beausoleil. No, that's -- you know, an afterthought. That's what they say now because they know how bizarre the real motive was."54

I don't think that Kay's contention of the bizarreness of the "real motive" would be of any concern to the killers. I think instead that if igniting Helter Skelter really were the motive Watson, Atkins, and the others would always have been glad to say so, because it would put more of the responsibility for the murders onto Charles Manson and off of them.

Of course, the main problem with the brother motive is that it is not a personal motive for Charles Manson. We have already seen that Bugliosi would have been glad to drop Helter Skelter as a motive if he could find another motive in the evidence. There *was* another motive in the evidence -- the copycat motive -- but it was not a motive that pointed to Charles Manson as a perpetrator of the crimes.

And as has also been previously noted, not all Los Angeles prosecutors are as willing to swallow and regurgitate Helter Skelter as Vincent Bugliosi and Stephen Kay seem to be. Remember that at Bruce Davis' 1993 parole hearing Jeffrey Jonas, the representative of the Los Angeles District Attorney's office who was present to speak against Davis' release, said:

> I'm convinced that Helter Skelter was used as a means to convict Manson.... I read a lot of the things that Mr. Beausoleil said and I'm not really satisfied in my mind that Helter Skelter was the overriding thing as to why they went out and did what they did with all these other people. I think that a lot of it had to do with the original act of Gary Hinman.... And I don't think that it was a -- a specific Helter Skelter motive that caused that.... And Mr. Bugliosi did an excellent job with that and I'm sure that it was part of it and he was able to sell that to the jury.... And to this day there are several people in our office that do believe that when Beausoleil.... said that basically "the Hinman murder, I was arrested and basically it was one for all and all for one, and so they went out and tried to do copycat murders to get me out, because if I was in and they had similar murders there, that would throw, cast suspicion elsewhere...."55

The brother motive and the dynamics surrounding it also explain why the particular persons went out on the nights of murder. The prosecution has always claimed that Manson simply sent out his most trustworthy and obedient assassins on the murder forays. But there are more sensible reasons for why these particular people did what they did besides the contention that they were mind-controlled by Charles Manson.

Charles Watson went because he owed Manson for the Bernard Crowe shooting.

Linda Kasabian went because she owed Manson because he had taken care of the problems arising out of her theft of a large sum of money from her husband's friend after her husband and the friend had arrived at Spahn's Ranch demanding back the cash.

Susan Atkins went because she owed Manson for several fights and confrontations he'd had to deal with as a result of her irresponsibility.

Leslie Van Houten was eager to go because of her past relationship with Bobby Beausoleil. (And because of that relationship she might also have been more active in encouraging the murders than is generally believed.)

Patricia Krenwinkel is a different case. I could find nothing in my research that would indicate any kind of debt that she owed to Charles Manson. But by her own admission she was in love with him, so it's very possible that she went simply because of the love she felt for him and for the other members of her circle.

* * *

The Helter Skelter motive was used to convict Charles Manson of murder, but I think that this chapter has presented a reasonable case that the real motive for the Tate-LaBianca murders was to get a brother (Bobby Beausoleil) out of jail by committing copycat murders which would cause police to release him. And I also think that a good case has been presented that the reason particular individuals participated in those murders was a result of recent violent criminal occurrences and because of the dynamics of the relationships of those persons -- none of which had anything to do with starting a race war called "Helter Skelter."

The Helter Skelter motive has also been used to paint Manson and the people around him as being totally wicked and depraved. That some of those people could behave violently in a seemingly evil fashion might be apparent, but beyond that there was a considerable degree of honor and genuine love among them. The means chosen to "get brother out of jail" might not have been well thought out, but the idea itself was virtuous. And Susan Atkins' famous quote about the murders, "You have to have a real love in your heart to do this for people,"56 makes complete sense in the context of being willing to do anything -- even to the point of killing -- to gain freedom for a beloved brother.

Chapter Notes

1 The source for this quote has gotten away from me, but this officer can be seen in several video programs about the case. For more on writing at crime scenes, see the book *Clues From Killers: Serial Murder and Crime Scene Messages*, by Dirk Cameron Gibson.
2 Bill Scanlon-Murphy interview, transcript page 56.
3 Ibid., page 47.
4 Charles Manson 1992 parole hearing, transcript page 73.
5 *Helter Skelter*, page 305.
6 Interview with Vincent Bugliosi in *Penthouse* magazine, unknown month, 1976, page 101.
7 *Will You Die For Me?*, page 135.
8 *Helter Skelter*, page 577.
9 *Blood Family*, page 435.
10 *Child of Satan, Child of God*, page 134.
11 Susan Atkins 1993 parole hearing, transcript pages 74-75.
12 *Blood Family*, page 443.
13 *Helter Skelter*, page 583.
14 Leslie Van Houten at her 1996 parole hearing. I don't have the transcript of this hearing, but Van Houten's declaration is clear on the videotape of the proceeding.
15 *The Manson Women*, page 218.
16 See *Helter Skelter*, page 573.
17 Ibid, page 603.
18 Sandra Good in the 1974 documentary *Manson*.
19 From *Burning Is The End*, an unpublished memoir by Bobby Beausoleil. Sandra Good Archives.
20 This is from an undated interview in *Oui* magazine, from the Sandra Good Archives.
21 *Helter Skelter*, page 526.
22 Manson's recollection here is compiled from interviews with Ron Reagan, Jr. and Bill Scanlon-Murphy and from tape-recorded telephone conversations with the author.
23 Susan Atkins 1993 parole hearing, transcript page 64.
24 Lost source
25 Watson recalled this at his 1984 parole hearing.
26 *Will You Die For Me?*, page 123.
27 Ibid.

28 Watson's reminiscence about speed is taken from the Abounding Love Ministries web site, http://www.aboundinglove.org/.
29 *Child of Satan, Child of God*, page 145.
30 The URLS for these Internet sources on amphetamines are lost to time, but the information quoted can be verified by any number of other sources.
31 Charles Watson 2001 parole hearing, transcript page 57.
32 From Watson's testimony at his murder trial.
33 *Will You Die For Me?*, page 137.
34 Ibid.
35 Ibid.
36 *God's Prison Gang*, by Chaplain Ray and Walter Wagner, American Evangelical Association, Dallas, Texas; 1977; page 34.
37 *Child of Satan, Child of God*, page 135.
38 Ibid., page 136.
39 Ibid., page 145.
40 Recalled in *Blood Family*, page 457.
41 Leslie Van Houten at her 1996 parole hearing.
42 Patricia Krenwinkel's 1993 parole hearing, transcript page 80.
43 The Midwest HDI TA Methamphetamine FAQ
44 *Will You Die For Me?*, page 142.
45 Ibid., page 183.
46 Charles Watson 2001 parole hearing, transcript page 17.
47 *Will You Die For Me?*, page 138.
48 Ibid., page 140.
49 Ibid., page 143.
50 Charles Manson in a telephone conversation with the author.
51 *Child of Satan, Child of God*, page 133.
52 *Helter Skelter*, page 610.
53 Ibid.
54 Kay said this at Susan Atkins' 1993 parole hearing, transcript page 85.
55 Bruce Davis 1993 parole hearing, transcript pages 84-85.
56 *Helter Skelter*, page 99.

First post card from Manson

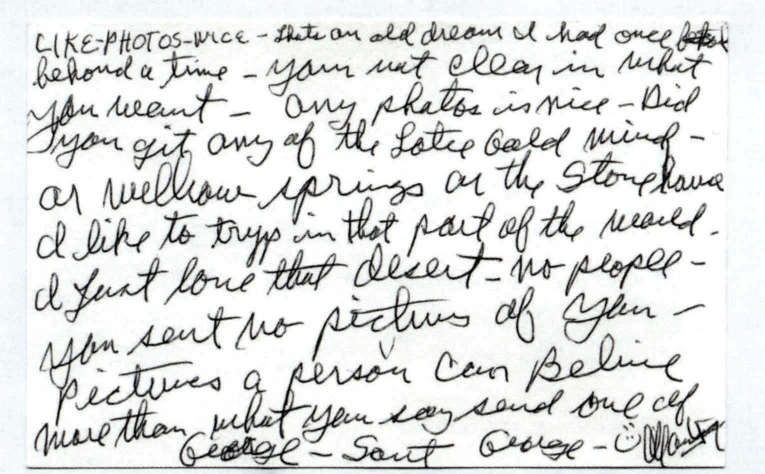

LIKE-PHOTOS-NICE - thats an old dream I had once beyond a time - you not clear in what you want - any photos is nice - Did you git any of the Lotee bald mind - or wellow springs or the Stonehave I like to trips in that part of the world. I just love that desert - no people - you sent no pictures of you - pictures a person can Belive more than what you say send one of George - Saint George - ☺ Manson

Manson and I during our second contact visit

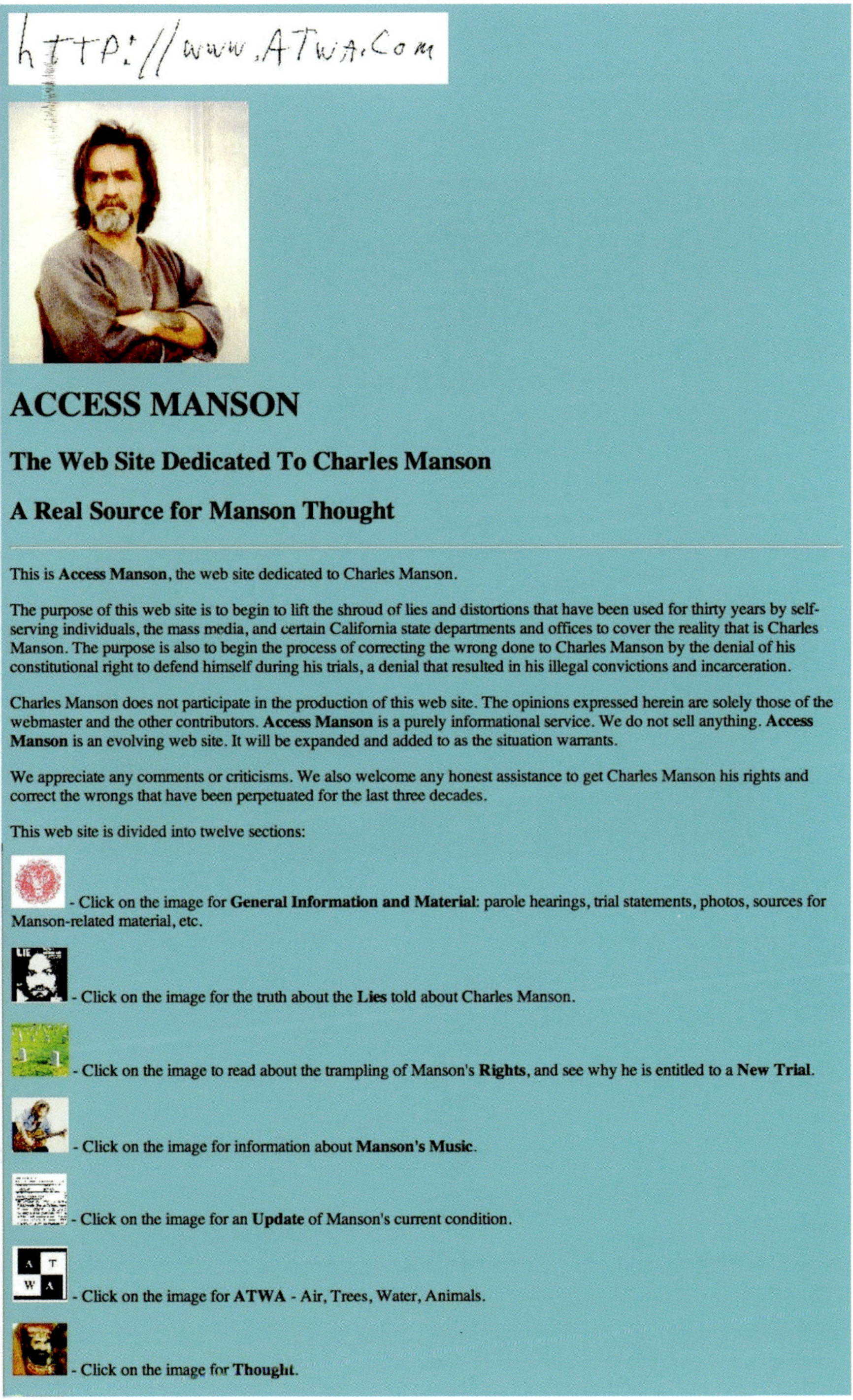

http://www.ATWA.Com

ACCESS MANSON

The Web Site Dedicated To Charles Manson

A Real Source for Manson Thought

This is **Access Manson**, the web site dedicated to Charles Manson.

The purpose of this web site is to begin to lift the shroud of lies and distortions that have been used for thirty years by self-serving individuals, the mass media, and certain California state departments and offices to cover the reality that is Charles Manson. The purpose is also to begin the process of correcting the wrong done to Charles Manson by the denial of his constitutional right to defend himself during his trials, a denial that resulted in his illegal convictions and incarceration.

Charles Manson does not participate in the production of this web site. The opinions expressed herein are solely those of the webmaster and the other contributors. **Access Manson** is a purely informational service. We do not sell anything. **Access Manson** is an evolving web site. It will be expanded and added to as the situation warrants.

We appreciate any comments or criticisms. We also welcome any honest assistance to get Charles Manson his rights and correct the wrongs that have been perpetuated for the last three decades.

This web site is divided into twelve sections:

- Click on the image for **General Information and Material**: parole hearings, trial statements, photos, sources for Manson-related material, etc.

- Click on the image for the truth about the **Lies** told about Charles Manson.

- Click on the image to read about the trampling of Manson's **Rights**, and see why he is entitled to a **New Trial**.

- Click on the image for information about **Manson's Music**.

- Click on the image for an **Update** of Manson's current condition.

A T W A - Click on the image for **ATWA** - Air, Trees, Water, Animals.

- Click on the image for **Thought**.

The home page of the *Access Manson* web site

Manson on the yard at CSP--Corcoran with artworks in progress

The finished pieces. Above: “Ghost of Fertility”

Below: “The Emperor of Japan”

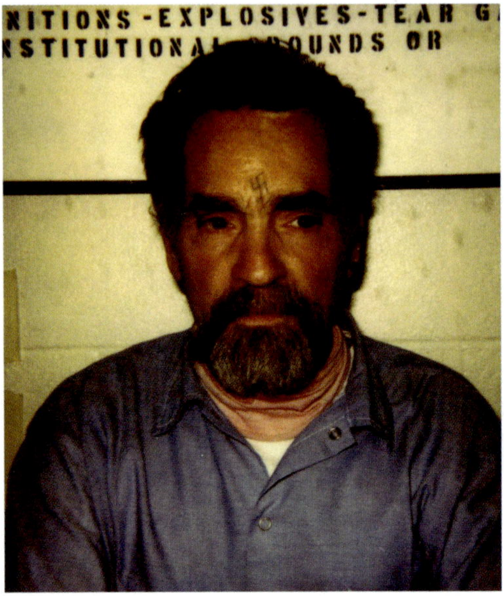
NITIONS -EXPLOSIVES-TEAR G
NSTITUTIONA ROUNDS OR

"The effect I'm trying to cause, is something different to look at. And coming to something different is difficult because everybody's always been trying to make something different. So it's hard to create something different over what everybody else has already done."

One of Charles Manson's guitars. This instrument was sent to Manson at the California State Prison at Corcoran, where he decorated it further (see next page). It was later destroyed during a prison fracas.

Manson with scorpion made from his socks

Post card art

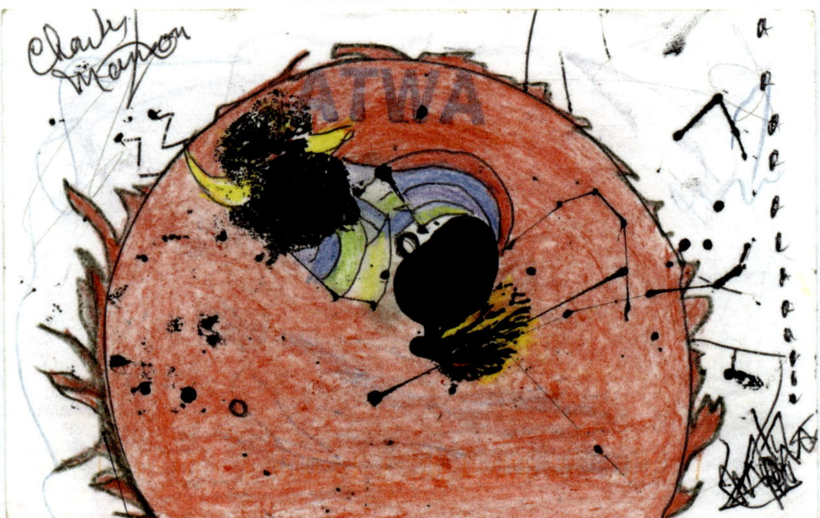

Manson with broom

"Danny made it. Just an old man named Danny. And he made it out of scraps, no less. Just little pieces of this and that. It's not a kit boat. What I was thinking about was spraying it with gold. In other words, just a little light-weight air gun, spraying it with gold flake. And just keep spraying it with gold flake until the whole thing turned gold, and then take lights and a little light over the tip of it? And then hang a little ATWA flag on it. It's already famous. It's just a bunch of little scraps. The guns came loose. A couple of the guns came loose, so you'll have to glue them two guns back on. I figured those two guns, that one is for you and one is for George. So that's the brotherhood there in the gun. There's a brotherhood in that ship. There's a brotherhood in the guns of that ship. There's six guns, and there's two machine guns in the back and the two rifles, the two long rifles, so we got a brotherhood there in that little ship, which is cool."

13
14
15
16
17
18
19
29
+
SOME
+
MUCH
1
2
3
4
5
6
7

PLOSIVES-TEAR GAS-
L GROUNDS OR

"Red and Blue"

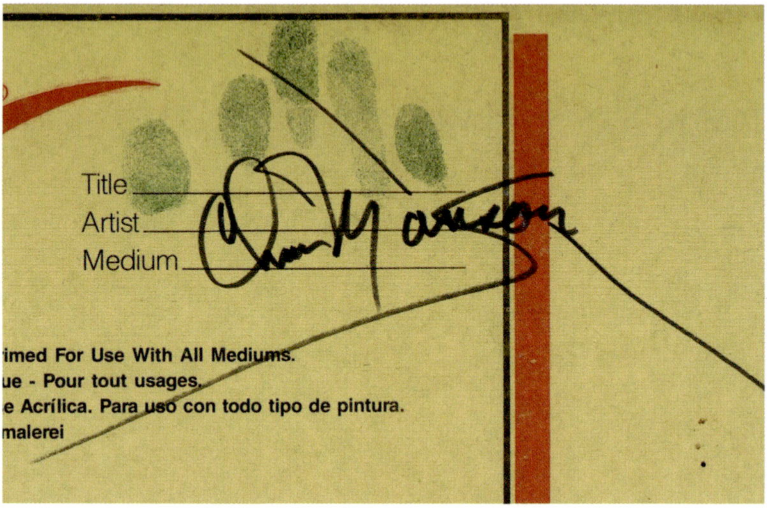

Signature and fingerprints on the back of "Red and Blue"

A pan full of prison yard rocks
painted by Manson

Manson relaxing on the yard at CSP--Corcoran

"When you see this next picture you're really gonna like it, I think. Everybody else likes it. That's what I call it, *The Purple Turkey*. It's really, it should go down in history. I've never seen anything like it in my life. And I've looked at a lot of art. It's close to a Braque. But Braque would probably laugh at this one. I don't have any talent. This is pure, pure doodle.... It's a lot of time, and a lot of little delicate things in it, just for something to do. I don't have any talent, man. Did you ever see some of the stuff that Beausoleil does? That's talent. Beausoleil has talent."

"What I do is, I paint the background in the glow-in-the-dark stuff. And then I come in with the lithographic pens, and I paint over that. Then when I put it in like a shadowy light? It jumps out at you. It don't look cheap, like a lot of that glow-in-the-dark stuff looks kind of cheap, you know. I'm trying to look into something like a different kind of perspective.... What I'm trying to do there, I'm trying to make things that are not identifiable with anything else. I don't want to make it look like something. I'm trying to make it look like nothing."

PARENTS MUST
MAINTAIN CONTROL
OF THEIR CHILDREN
AT ALL TIMES

"It's a blamer. You know what a blamer is? When everything goes wrong, the doll's name is "Egg Us." Eggus. And when things go wrong, you blame Eggus. If anything happens that's wrong, if it's an earthquake, it's Eggus' fault. Anything that happens that you don't like, you blame Eggus. Don't ever blame yourself. Don't blame me.... We blame Eggus. And then, after a while, we look at Eggus and we go hang it somewhere where our enemy is. Someone you don't like? Go hang it in [name deleted]'s yard. You know what I'm saying? In other words, after you've blamed it and you got all that negative bad on it, then you can take it over to your friend's, or someone's house that's done you wrong, and give it to them. I put a button on his knee, and I put a rock in his head. You got a rock for a head. It glows in the dark. So if I ever see the rock out behind my window, I know you're out there."

The site of Spahn's Movie Ranch

Goler Wash

The front porch of the main house at Myers Ranch

Barkcr Ranch

Goodbye Helter Skelter

Charles Manson and the Law

"I'm not saying that I wasn't involved [in the murders]. I'm saying that I did not break man's law, nor did I break God's law."

-- Charles Manson

Over the years I heard Charles Manson say some kind of variation of the above statement so many times that I began to wonder if he might be right. The resulting curiosity led to this chapter on Manson and the law, two aspects of which are deserving of special attention.

First, let's examine Manson's murder cases and convictions in an effort to determine if Manson could possibly be correct when he says that he is not guilty of breaking the law. In other words, I want to try to determine whether there is any interpretation of Manson's cases wherein he could be found not guilty of the crimes that he is universally "known" to have committed.

Second, I will look at Manson's oft-stated claim that he was not able to exercise his legal rights in the courtroom, most importantly that he was denied his constitutional right to represent and defend himself at his murder trials.

Charles Manson always claimed that with regard to the charges for which he was convicted he never violated the law. Could he possibly have been right?

The charges against Manson were, for the Tate-LaBianca murders, seven counts of first-degree murder and one count of conspiracy to commit murder. At the combined Hinman-Shea murder trial he was charged with two counts of first-degree murder. No charges were ever filed against him in connection with the shooting of Bernard Crowe.

Let's look at the circumstances of the four murder events generally attributed to Charles Manson (Hinman-Tate-LaBianca-Shea) as they have been presented in this book and see if those circumstances could have led to "not guilty" verdicts. To do this, we will accept the premises that:

Bobby Beausoleil killed Gary Hinman after Hinman went back on his word not to turn Charles Manson in to the authorities for cutting his face.

The seven persons murdered on Cielo and Waverly Drives were killed by Charles Watson, Linda Kasabian, Susan Atkins, Patricia Krenwinkel, and Leslie Van Houten in an attempt to convince the police that the killer of Gary Hinman was still at large and that Bobby Beausoleil must therefore be innocent -- in other words, to get a brother out of jail. (Helter Skelter was not the motive for these murders.)

Donald Shea was killed during a fight with about half a dozen people who thought he was a snitch.

"Murder" is generally defined as the unlawful killing of a human being, with malice aforethought.1 Beyond that there are varying degrees of the charge based on the varying circumstances under which people kill each other. In California a homicide can be either first or second-degree murder, manslaughter (voluntary or involuntary), or justifiable homicide. In Manson's cases he was charged with and convicted of first-degree murder and conspiracy to commit murder. First, let's look at the cases for murder.

"All murder which is perpetrated by means of a destructive device or explosive.... poison, lying in wait, torture, or by any other kind of willful, deliberate, and premeditated killing.... is murder in the first degree." For a person to be guilty of murder, his "criminal act must be the proximate cause of the victim's death."2

Under California law there are four essential elements that must be proven in order to obtain a conviction for first-degree murder:

premeditation, deliberation, intent, and malice. The prosecution has a burden of proof to prove all of these elements. If the prosecution does *not* prove all of these elements, a first-degree murder verdict cannot stand. Do these four elements apply to Charles Manson and the murders he was convicted of, based on his (and this book's) view of the circumstances of those murders?

The first occurrence, chronologically, where Charles Manson was eventually convicted for murder was the homicide of Gary Hinman, who was stabbed to death by Bobby Beausoleil on July 27, 1969.

Charles Manson was present at Gary Hinman's residence two days earlier, on July 25, and he did cut him badly on the side of his face on that date. But Manson left shortly after that altercation and never returned to the house. The knife wound he inflicted on Hinman was not the wound (the "proximate cause") that caused Hinman's death. So Charles Manson did not physically and personally murder Gary Hinman.

In the prosecution-presented version of the crime, Manson ordered Beausoleil to go to Hinman's residence and muscle him out of an inheritance and, in some versions, to get him to join "the Family." When Hinman balked at this proposition, Manson ordered Beausoleil (by telephone) to murder him. If this scenario were true, then Charles Manson would be guilty of murder.

But Gary Hinman's death was actually the end-result of a drug deal gone bad -- a deal that existed solely between Hinman and Bobby Beausoleil. It was not caused by any premeditated plan with homicidal intent on the part of Charles Manson.

Charles Manson did cut Gary Hinman, and he never denied this. According to Manson, he cut Hinman while disarming him. And despite Bobby Beausoleil's description of the attack as being totally unprovoked, Manson's contention is a believable explanation for the cutting. In fact, it is the *only* believable explanation that has ever been offered. Charles Manson was not a violently assaultive individual, and it is extremely unlikely that he would slash someone with a knife unless he felt that it was absolutely necessary -- such as in the case of taking a gun away from an angry and threatening person. (And obviously something was going on with the gun at some point during the incident at Hinman's house; after all, it was fired.)

When Charles Manson left Gary Hinman's residence he had an assurance from Hinman that he would not turn him in to the police for cutting him. The incident between them was over.

After Manson left, as testimony from all involved parties indicates, the people remaining at Hinman's house applied (or attempted to apply) first aid to his injury. This was not an act indicative of, or consistent with, a plan for his eventual murder. Two days later, however, Hinman had second thoughts about going to the police, and Bobby Beausoleil -- on his own -- killed him to prevent him from doing so. (Both Bobby Beausoleil and Charles Manson deny that Manson ever ordered Beausoleil to kill Hinman, therefore there is no reason to believe that he did.)

To get around the problems of Charles Manson having neither inflicted a fatal wound nor being present when Gary Hinman was killed, the prosecution has often maintained that the killing of Hinman was really a three-day torture session. This claim, however, is just an attempt to show that Manson's cutting of Gary Hinman on July 25 and Hinman's death two days later were really part of one long, murderous incident. (Helpfully for the district attorney, under California law the use of torture negates any requirement on the part of the prosecution to prove the premeditation element necessary for a first-degree murder conviction. Therefore, by labeling Hinman's death a "torture murder," the prosecution gets around the problem of there being no evidence of any premeditation on the part of Charles Manson -- or of anyone else -- regarding Hinman's death on the day that Manson cut his ear.)

What constitutes torture murder? In California, an injury can only be considered part of a torture murder if the person causing the injury *intends* that his victim die. In this case there is very strong evidence contrary to such intent, specifically that the people remaining with Hinman after Manson left applied first aid to his injury.

Charles Manson did not personally kill Gary Hinman, nor was he part of an extended torture murder. Is there some other way that Manson could be guilty of Hinman's murder? What about felony murder?

Under California law, "a killing, whether intentional or unintentional, is first degree murder if 'committed in the perpetration of, or attempt to perpetrate' certain serious felonies: *arson, rape, robbery, burglary, mayhem, or lewd act with child.*" Further, "the ordinary elements of first degree murder -- malice and premeditation -- are eliminated by the [felony murder] doctrine. The only criminal intent required is the *specific intent to commit the particular felony*.... But the elements of the *particular felony* must be proved." (emphasis in original)

None of the above examples of ancillary felonies appears to be applicable to the situation at Gary Hinman's house when Charles Manson was present. Hinman was not being burned, raped, robbed, or burgled, and nor was he a child. Besides, Charles Manson did not kill Gary Hinman at all. Bobby Beausoleil did, and he did so with no assistance or input from Charles Manson. Therefore, in the instances of those felonious examples, it would seem that Manson cannot be guilty of felony murder.

But what about mayhem? In California law, the "slitting" of a person's ear is considered to be mayhem.3 Autopsy diagrams of Gary Hinman's corpse indicate a large slash on the left side of his face and into the ear that could be interpreted as "slitting" it. If Manson's cutting of Hinman's ear is connected with the killing of Hinman by Bobby Beausoleil two days later in a scenario wherein Hinman's statements that he was going to report the cut ear to authorities "caused" Bobby Beausoleil to stab him to death, then it would appear that the mayhem trigger in California's felony law statute would mean that Manson was guilty of first-degree felony murder.

But there is an exception to the crime of mayhem if the person perpetrating the mayhem is reasonably defending himself or another person. To be precise, California criminal law will excuse an act of mayhem if the person committing it is acting in self-defense. In the case at hand, Manson has said that he was confronting an angry and armed Gary Hinman when he cut him. If that is true then clearly he was acting in the defense of himself and the others who were present and the mayhem trigger for felony murder would not apply.

Therefore, after viewing all of the circumstances surrounding the death of Gary Hinman as presented and accepted here, there could be a reasonable doubt that Charles Manson was guilty of murder. He did not premeditate or deliberate on the murder. He had no malice aforethought (he had been gone from the scene for two days before Hinman was killed) and he harbored no intent that Hinman should die. Manson's slicing of Hinman's ear does not qualify as part of a torture murder, and there was no supplementary felony committed which would trigger California's felony murder statute. (Manson's cutting of Hinman's ear would not qualify for mayhem as it was done in self-defense.) So, in the case of the Gary Hinman murder, a verdict of not guilty for Charles Manson could certainly have been reasonable and appropriate.

Moving on to the next case, the murders at the Polanski residence on Cielo Drive, Charles Manson was not within twenty-five miles of that house when the people there were killed. (Nor, as has been claimed in some accounts, did he go to the house after the murders.) Since Manson was not even present at the scene, it is not possible for him to have committed any act, criminal or otherwise, which could be considered a "proximate cause" of any of the deaths there.

Since nobody can challenge Manson's absence from Cielo Drive on August 8-9, 1969 the prosecution's case against him has depended entirely on the theory that he ordered the murders in order to ignite the race war "Helter Skelter." But since triggeringHelter Skelter was *not* the motive for the Cielo Drive murders there is no evidence of any *intent* on the part of Charles Manson that those murders should occur. Lacking this key element of intent, Manson cannot be guilty of murder.

And this is why the Helter Skelter motive is so important to the prosecution. The state does not have to demonstrate motive at a murder trial, but it does have to demonstrate intent. Intent is usually proven by evidence that indicates that the defendant did in fact commit the offense, such as physical evidence, eyewitness statements, or the defendant's own admissions. But in the case of Charles Manson and the murders on Cielo Drive there is no evidence of any intent on the part of Manson except for the fantastic Helter Skelter motive. So if we take away the Helter Skelter motive there is no evidence -- much less any proof -- of Manson's intent. And without intent there can be no conviction.

Therefore, in the case of the murders committed at Cielo Drive, Charles Manson could very conceivably have been found not guilty. (I will address Manson's conspiracy conviction for these murders in a moment.)

What about the murders of the LaBiancas? On the night that they were killed a supposed "murder search" went on throughout the whole of greater Los Angeles before and after a carload of people from Spahn's Ranch arrived at Waverly Drive. But no one was hurt or killed during this "search" and no laws were broken.

At Waverly Drive, even the prosecution agreed that Manson left the car and went up the driveway to the house next door to the LaBiancas' residence. Remember, the LaBianca house was not being lived in during the earlier period when Manson visited Harold True at 3267 Waverly. When the LaBiancas returned from Lake Isabella on August 10 they parked their car and boat on the street past the west side of their property line. (True's house was on the east side.) Rosemary LaBianca's car was parked high up in the driveway, also on the west side of the house (and also on the far side from the True house). It was out of sight from the street. Rosemary LaBianca had gone to bed in the front bedroom, so the light in that room was probably out. Leno LaBianca was in the living room reading a newspaper, with at least enough light on to do that. To a casual observer, and especially so to an observer such as Charles Manson, who was used to the house being empty, the LaBianca house could very well have looked unoccupied.

Manson's recollections of that night have already been presented earlier. He said that he and Charles Watson went to the LaBiancas' house more or less together after first going to the True residence next door. Manson also said that he was only inside 3301 Waverly for a very short time, and that he did not even see Rosemary LaBianca, before he went back to the car.

Charles Manson was not present when the LaBiancas were killed, and there is no evidence that he ordered them to be killed. To the contrary, there is much evidence of confusion over what was going to happen.

Manson could not have personally given Charles Watson any kind of instruction to kill the LaBiancas because Watson remembers saying to Patricia Krenwinkel and Leslie Van Houten (when they appeared in the house after Manson left), "Did he say to kill them?"4 Although Watson claims that the two girls nodded an affirmative answer, neither of them has recalled receiving any murderous instructions from Manson.

Since Charles Manson was not present at Waverly Drive when the deaths there occurred the prosecution also assigns the Helter Skelter motive to this crime in order to demonstrate Manson's alleged intent. But since Helter Skelter was not the motive, intent on Manson's part is not demonstrable or provable. Therefore, the same lack of intent that would acquit Manson of the murders on Cielo Drive could also acquit him of the murders on Waverly Drive.

Nor did Manson commit a serious felony that would trigger California's felony murder statute. Manson walked into the LaBianca house (a house that he thought was unoccupied) through an unlocked door. Neither of these actions, even if interpreted as trespassing or illegal entry, constitutes a serious felony.

What about taking Rosemary LaBianca's wallet? Wouldn't that be robbery? Manson does not remember taking the wallet and says that he did not even see Rosemary LaBianca in the house. Is it possible that Charles Watson took the wallet and gave it to Linda Kasabian when he returned to the car? Or could he have handed it to Manson inside the house and Manson took it thinking that it was Watson's -- or not thinking at all?

Whoever took the wallet is apparently irrelevant to the prosecution's case. At Leslie Van Houten's 1993 parole hearing L.A. County Deputy District Attorney Stephen Kay told the parole board that what happened at the LaBianca residence was not a robbery.5 (No robbery charges were filed in the case.) And if there is no robbery, then Charles Manson could not have committed a robbery-based felony murder at Waverly Drive.

In summing up, with regard to the case of the double homicide at Waverly Drive, Charles Manson had no motive (and thus no intent), he committed no act that could be considered to be a proximate cause of anyone's death, and he committed no ancillary felony that would trigger California's felony murder law. Therefore, in the case of the deaths on Waverly Drive, Charles Manson could plausibly be found innocent of first-degree murder.

But if Charles Manson is not guilty of murder in the Tate-LaBianca homicides, is he nevertheless guilty of conspiracy to commit murder for those murders? This is a very key question, because sometimes the district attorneys almost seem to concede that Manson is technically not guilty of murder since he did not personally kill anyone and was not present when anyone was killed. As Stephen Kay said at Manson's 1997 parole hearing, "[Manson] *didn't kill them himself*, so he thinks he's not responsible, but fortunately, in California, if somebody masterminds murders, they're just as guilty as the people that inflict the fatal wound."6 (emphasis added)

At first glance it might seem that Manson did conspire in these murders, especially since he admits being involved and even confesses to making certain suggestions (such as telling Charles Watson to drop the glasses or telling the girls to "leave something witchy"). Aren't such admissions evidence of a conspiratorial state of mind?

In California law "a conspiracy is an agreement between two or more persons with specific intent to agree to commit a public offense...., and with the further specific intent to commit such offense, followed by an overt act committed in this state by one or more or the parties for the purpose of accomplishing the object of the agreement." Therefore, there are five necessary elements to a conspiracy: agreement, two or more persons, specific intent, unlawful object or means (commission of a public offense), and an overt act.

The Tate-LaBianca murders were the only murders linked to the conspiracy charge. Discounting the Helter Skelter motive and accepting the "get brother out of jail" motive as the real driving force behind these homicides, do the circumstances of the murders on Cielo and Waverly Drives warrant a conviction against Charles Manson for conspiracy to commit murder?

With regard to the homicides perpetrated at the Polanski residence, the crime clearly does contain all of the five elements needed for a conspiracy conviction -- for the people who committed it, that is.

Charles Watson, Linda Kasabian, Susan Atkins, and Patricia Krenwinkel all agreed to do something to get Bobby Beausoleil out of jail.

Specific intent was demonstrated by the legal interpretation that the specific intent requirement for conspiracy is met when the accused person "had a specific intent to do an unlawful act" in furtherance of the conspiracy. It is unlikely that any of the people who drove away from Spahn's Ranch on the night of August 8 thought that they were not going out to do something that was unlawful, because all of the considered means of doing something that would result in Bobby Beausoleil's release -- whether by committing copycat murders, or by robbing people to obtain money for bail or lawyer's fees -- were clearly unlawful.

Two or more persons were involved.

All of the options considered in the effort to obtain Bobby Beausoleil's release involved some kind of illegal activity, thus meeting the "unlawful means" requirement.

And the group committed an "overt act" the minute they got into the car.

So, for the actual participants in the homicides at Cielo Drive, convictions for conspiracy to commit murder are apparently warranted. But what about for Charles Manson?

According to Manson, "The only reality I had in any of that [the murders on Cielo Drive] was, I gave Tex a pair of glasses and told him, 'Drop these somewhere.'"7 He has also said that he told the girls to go with Watson and to do whatever Watson said to do, and to "leave something witchy." Since Manson himself readily admited that he did these things, we can accept that they did happen. Indeed, most proponents of a guilty Charles Manson accept these things as being true.

But there is no evidence that Charles Manson ever agreed to participate in whatever the people leaving Spahn's Ranch were going to do. To the contrary, Manson specifically told those people that he was not entering into any agreements with them because he had already committed two seriously illegal acts (shooting

Bernard Crowe and cutting Gary Hinman) and was not going to participate in any more activity that could get him sent back to prison.

In fact, no more proof of this is needed other than the simple reality that he did not go along with the people to Cielo Drive. Manson had not hesitated to act violently when necessary, as he did in the Crowe and Hinman incidents, but if he were really inclined towards violence, as the prosecution has always maintained, he would not have hesitated to actively participate in these savage murders.

Not even the prosecution's star witness, Linda Kasabian, who was promised a grant of immunity for seven counts of first-degree murder in exchange for her complete and truthful testimony about those murders, was able to testify that Manson agreed to any murder plan. To the contrary, she testified that on the night of the murders on Cielo Drive she thought that the carload of people was leaving the ranch merely to go on a "creepy-crawly" mission.8

(Charles Watson, at his own separate trial for murder, did allege that Manson told him specifically to go to the Cielo Drive house and kill everyone there. But Watson's trial occurred after that of Manson and his co-defendants. None of his statements regarding what Manson allegedly said on the murder night were admitted as evidence at Manson's trial, nor would they have been, because accomplice testimony is inadmissible without corroboration, and there is no evidence to corroborate Watson's claim. Therefore Watson's testimony in this regard can be disregarded. His recollection of Manson's "orders" might have been totally fabricated many months after August 1969 in an attempt to mitigate his own responsibility for the murders, or he might have been "remembering" audio hallucinations caused by his own admitted overindulgence in amphetamines.)

Manson's involvement in the murders on Cielo Drive therefore amounts to a few suggestions ("Drop these glasses, leave something witchy.") that he made to people who were leaving Spahn's Ranch to go out and do something. But he had no specific foreknowledge of (nor is there any evidence that he helped plan) the events that later transpired at the Polanski residence.

In Manson's circumstance he does not meet any of the legal requirements for a conspiracy conviction for the murders at the Polanski residence. He made no agreement, he had no specific intent, he was not one of two or more persons who were parties to the crime, he did nothing unlawful, and he committed no overt action. Therefore a reasonable case might be made that Charles Manson cannot be guilty of conspiracy to commit murder for the homicides which occurred on Cielo Drive.

The second night of murder was different from the first, on several counts.

First of all, Charles Manson was present at, and even entered, the house at 3301 Waverly Drive, so even though he did not personally kill anyone inside it might appear by his presence and actions that he must have some degree of legal culpability. But is this true? Let's look at that night again.

At 3301 Waverly Drive Manson entered the house slightly ahead of Charles Watson. Manson and Watson entered through an unlocked side door, which had probably been opened and left open by Leno LaBianca when he let a dog out into the fenced-in side yard between his house and Harold True's residence after he got back from Lake Isabella. After a very brief time inside the house, Manson returned to the car, perhaps with Watson. Then Patricia Krenwinkel and Leslie Van Houten went up to the house. Manson, Linda Kasabian, Susan Atkins, and Steve Grogan drove off.

At a gas station in Sylmar, Rosemary LaBianca's wallet was dropped off, supposedly as part of the plan to try to blame the murders on blacks. Whose idea was it to drop off the wallet? Most sources say that Manson ordered Kasabian to ditch it. And Manson agrees. He told me during a prison visit that when he became aware of the wallet being in the car he wanted to get rid of it because he considered it to be "hot." He pulled into a gas station and told Kasabian to put the wallet in the toilet in the women's rest room. I asked him, "Why inside the toilet?"

"Because in prison, everything goes into the toilet," he answered.9

The contention that Manson wanted to get rid of the wallet in a black neighborhood where a black person would find it, use the credit cards, get caught, and thus be implicated in the LaBianca murders, is a prosecution fabrication that strains credibility. Sylmar, the neighborhood where the wallet was ditched, is even further out in the San Fernando Valley than Spahn's Ranch, and it is not likely that anyone could have mistakenly thought that it was a black area. (Most of the predominantly black residential areas of Los Angeles were many miles to the south.)

Charles Manson did not qualify for a conspiracy to commit murder conviction for the murders on Waverly Drive because he did not enter into any agreement, had no specific intent demonstrated by any action, had no unlawful object, and utilized no illegal means. His presence with his friends on the night of August 9 - 10 is not enough to prove his involvement in a conspiracy. As the judge instructed jurors at Manson's trial:

> Evidence that a person was in the company of or associated with one or more other persons alleged or proved to have been members of a conspiracy is not, in itself, sufficient to prove that such person was a member of the alleged conspiracy.10

In other words, Manson might have conspired to drive around greater Los Angeles with some of his acquaintances, but that's about it.

The last murder to consider is that of Donald "Shorty" Shea.

Bruce Davis' statement at his 1993 parole hearing that Manson said they were going to kill Shea could be self-serving, but it could also be disregarded for two other reasons. One, Manson has denied saying it. Secondly, that statement would be inadmissible in court because it is the uncorroborated statement of an alleged accomplice in the crime.

Although Manson was later convicted of Donald Shea's murder, there was no direct and conclusive evidence presented at the Shea murder trial that Shea had even been murdered, much less that Charles Manson had murdered him. All of the evidence was circumstantial: Shea was suddenly not around, and other people had some of his personal property, such as clothing and guns.

There was, however, some evidence against the two other persons convicted of Shea's murder. A finger or palm print belonging to Bruce Davis was found on some of Shea's disposed-of personal property, and Steve Grogan made self-incriminating (if considerably false, i.e., beheading) statements regarding his participation in the killing. But the case against Charles Manson was at least as weak as the cases against several other individuals who were never even charged with the crime.

The jury's verdict also indicated doubt. It is noteworthy that the panel did not recommend the death penalty for Manson, who was by then a previously convicted mass murderer already sentenced to Death Row and now freshly convicted of a double-murder (Hinman-Shea) wherein one victim was supposedly tortured to death and the other was supposedly beheaded and dismembered. That equivocation, and the lack of any real evidence, are enough that a reasonable doubt acquittal would not have been any less appropriate for Manson than was the total lack of indictments against other persons suspected of involvement in the crime. Therefore, in the case of the death of Donald Shea, it is possible that Charles Manson could be found not guilty of first-degree murder.

One might wonder why none of these legal points or points of view was raised by the defense at Manson's trial. If there was a reasonable possibility that Charles Manson was not guilty of murder and conspiracy to commit murder, why were none of these ideas incorporated into some kind of a defense? The short answer to that question is that at Manson' trial there was no defense.

The trial of Charles Manson and his co-defendants was the longest murder trial in California history up to that time. The vast majority of the nine-plus months of the trial, however, was taken up by the prosecution's presentation of its case. When it came time for the defense to present its side of events, it rested without presenting any evidence or calling any witnesses.

Manson's trial has been recounted in several books (*Helter Skelter*, *The Family*, *Blood Family*, *Witness to Evil*, *Reflections on the Manson Trial*), but in case the reader is unfamiliar with the proceeding here is a brief summary with some analysis.

First of all, it is important to note that the jury at Manson's first trial was only concerned with the Tate-LaBianca homicides. It was never enlightened as to the earlier crimes, i.e. the Crowe shooting and the Hinman murder, which created the atmosphere and dynamics that resulted in the murders on Cielo and Waverly

Drives. Thus, the jury was not given the full chronological story of the events that led up to the nights of August 8 and 9, 1969. (They did eventually know that Manson shot Bernard Crowe. Crowe was called briefly as a witness during the penalty phase of the trial by the prosecution to prove Manson's supposed willingness to kill.)

Charles Manson was arraigned for the Tate-LaBianca murders on December 9, 1969. On December 17 he requested that he be allowed to defend himself, or "go pro per" (from the Latin *In propria persona*, meaning "in one's own proper person"). This option is a right based on the Sixth Amendment to the United States Constitution, which guarantees defendants the right to the assistance of counsel when presenting a defense and, by implication, guarantees that an accused person can conduct his defense himself.

On December 22, Manson pleaded not guilty. Two days later Superior Court Judge William Keene granted his request that he be allowed to defend himself.

The State of California v. Charles Manson, et. al., Case # A-253156, would be prosecuted by two deputy district attorneys for Los Angeles County, Vincent Bugliosi and Aaron Stovitz.

Vincent Bugliosi was born in 1934 in Hibbing, Minnesota. At age six he began playing tennis. The sport proved to be an excellent outlet for his natural competitiveness and he excelled at it. By the time he was sixteen he was the Minnesota state champion.

It is a measure of both Bugliosi's tennis skills and their importance to his family (Bugliosi was a second generation Italian-American) that before his senior year in high school the family moved to Los Angeles solely to advance his future in tennis playing. He won the Los Angeles City High School tennis championship and then enrolled in the University of Miami on a tennis scholarship. At Miami he received a Bachelor of Arts degree and then, after deciding on a career in law, entered the University of California (Los Angeles) Law School. In 1964 he graduated as president of his class. He joined the L.A. County District Attorney's office the next year, approaching the job with the same ruthlessly competitive zeal that helped him so much on the tennis court. Out of 105 felony jury trials that he had prosecuted up to his assignment to the Manson case, Bugliosi lost only one.

Less background material is readily available on Aaron Stovitz, perhaps because he did not become a widely documented celebrity by writing a bestselling book about the Tate-LaBianca case.

In the book *Helter Skelter* Bugliosi explained his philosophy on being a prosecutor:

"The primary duty of a lawyer engaged in public prosecution is not to convict, but to see that justice is done...."

Those words are from the old Canon of Ethics of the American Bar Association.... In a very real sense they had become my personal credo. If, in a given case, a conviction is justice, then so be it. But if it is not, I want no part of it....

I've never felt that the defense attorney has a monopoly on concern for innocence, fairness, and justice.11 (emphasis in original)

Despite this declaration, however, in Charles Manson's case it never seems to have occurred to Bugliosi that Manson might possibly be anything other than what Bugliosi perceived him to be: the brainwashing absolute master of an army of slaves that he sent out to commit murder in the furtherance of his own megalomaniacal goals.

Charles Manson later remembered his prosecutor:

That guy is slick. In his world, he's slick. Like, he knows that he has to justify what he does to himself. He knows this. So what he does is, he says, "Well, these guys are no good," and then he goes off. And then he holds that "these guys are not good," so that that justifies everything else that he does. In other words, he knows that he's gonna convict somebody that's innocent, but he doesn't give a fuck because he's worried about making his record.

It doesn't matter if he destroys someone else's life. He says, "Because those guys, *they* destroyed somebody else's life." In other words, he's accusing us of what *he* does. He destroys people's lives and he destroys people's families and then he turns around and says that it's us.

And we told him the simplicity of the whole thing. "You've got yourself on trial. I'm walking with *your* children, Nixon. These ain't *my* children."

Let's look at it from his point of view. All he has is a bunch of murders and a bunch of people, and he wanted to win. And he took advantage of it completely.

Let's face it. Everybody in this world is out for Number One, and everybody uses everybody else any way they can. And don't come up like he was doing it for the better of humanity, because he doesn't give a shit about humanity no more than anybody else does.

[He said], "Let's blame it on somebody that we can get away with blaming it on. Let's blame it on some convict that ain't got no money. Let's blame it on somebody with no education."

When Bugliosi seen me, I was custom fit for his ambition.12

Manson had a statutory right to a trial within sixty days of his arraignment, which occurred on December 9, 1969. On February 6, 1970 he asked that his right be recognized and that the trial begin "tomorrow or Monday." Instead, Judge Keene set a trial date for March 30.

This delay was a Godsend for the prosecution, for while the cases against Susan Atkins, Patricia Krenwinkel, and Leslie Van Houten were strong, the case against Charles Manson was almost non-existent. Bugliosi was so worried that Manson might be set free that he called the district attorney in Inyo County and had him re-file the arson charge which been filed against Manson in connection with the burning of the Park Service's earth moving machine in case an excuse would be needed to keep him locked up. In the meantime, Bugliosi kept digging furiously for a personal motive for Charles Manson to have ordered the murders on Cielo and Waverly Drives.

And he had other problems to deal with. In mid-February Susan Atkins announced that she would not testify for the prosecution at the trial. Her testimony (a variation of which had been used at the Grand Jury proceedings in order to obtain indictments in the case) had been intended as a cornerstone of the prosecution's case.

As a result of Atkins' decision, the district attorney's office made a deal with Linda Kasabian that if she would "testify truthfully at all trail proceedings against all defendants" the DA's office would petition the trial court to grant her complete immunity after that testimony. This agreement was finalized on February 26, 1970.

On March 6 Charles Manson made several motions in court that Judge Keene deemed were "outlandish" and "nonsensical." These motions included requests that the district attorneys be "incarcerated for a period of time under the same circumstances that [Manson had] been subjected to" and that Manson be "free to travel to any place that [he] should deem fit in preparing [his] defense."13

As a result of these unorthodox motions, Judge Keene vacated Manson's status as his own lawyer and appointed a lawyer named Charles Hollopeter as his attorney of record.

Manson later recalled Hollopeter, the lawyer's defense strategy, and his own reaction to it:

> When I was going to court [the judge] came up to me and he sent a lawyer over, and this lawyer was called Hollopeter. He had a little mouse on his tie, with a diamond in its eye. And he said, "Eighteen months, diminished capacity, and I'll have you out of here."
>
> And I thought to myself, "Why should I play crazy for public opinion? I mean, why should I go and act like I'm crazy? I didn't *do* anything."
>
> And I believed in the United States of America. I believed in the Marine Corps and I believed in the Navy and the Air Force. I believed that there was such a thing as honor, truth, faith, and all those things that have substance in people. I believed in what my grandpa told me and what my father stood for, and died for. I believed in the things that we're taught in school. Like an idiot. I believed in the United States of America -- what the hell ever *that* is.
>
> And then I said, "No, I'm not gonna plead guilty to something I didn't do."
>
> And I felt that if I hadn't done anything, that I had nothing to be ashamed of, and that I had my rights and could explain to the judge -- my omnipotent father, I could explain to. My holy father. I believed in all that. I believed in the people that I had helped. I believed that I had coming back what I had gave into life.
>
> I never realized that Elvis Presley had already claimed that.14

On March 11 Susan Atkins fired her attorney, Richard Cabellero, and hired Daye Shinn in his place.

Cabellero, a former deputy district attorney, had been instrumental in having Atkins' supposedly secret Grand Jury testimony published in the *Los Angeles Times* -- and around the world -- on December 14, 1969. Four days earlier, Judge Keene had issued a gag order prohibiting just about any person associated with the case from discussing it with the news media. Atkins testified before the Grand Jury on December 5. Caballero later claimed that all arrangements to sell and distribute the secret testimony were made before the imposition of the gag order. In any case, the "testimony" printed in the *Times* (and later in the book *The Killing Of Sharon Tate*) was actually ghost written by two reporters for that newspaper, making its accuracy and reliability highly questionable. Nevertheless, this news article is what the world read and generally assumed was true about the murders. (Atkins repudiated her Grand Jury testimony soon after she gave it.)

Atkins' new attorney, Daye Shinn, had never tried a murder case before.

On March 19 Manson fired Charles Hollopeter and replaced him with Ronald Hughes. Hughes was a novice lawyer who had never tried *any* case before. He immediately moved that Manson be allowed to retain his *pro per* status. Judge Keene denied the motion.

On March 30 the scheduled date for the start of the trial came and went. By this time Manson's statutory right to have his trial begin within sixty days of his arraignment was already long gone.

On April 13 Manson filed an affidavit of prejudice against Judge Keene and had him removed from the case. Keene was replaced by Judge Charles H. Older and the trial date was rescheduled again, this time for June 15.

On June 1 Manson asked that Irving Kanarek be substituted for Ronald Hughes. The District Attorney's office objected strenuously to this request because Kanarak's reputation was that of a "legal obstructionist" and it was feared that his delaying tactics might drag the trial out for years. Bugliosi even said he was willing to allow Manson to represent himself as an alternative to Kanarak. But Judge Older denied the request, telling Manson, "It would be a miscarriage of justice to permit you to represent yourself in a case having the complications this case has."15

What did Older mean by this "miscarriage of justice" remark? Did he mean that if Manson represented himself he might be convicted and that a *conviction* would be a miscarriage of justice? Or did he consider the possibility of a Manson *acquittal* to be a miscarriage of his preconceived notion of what "justice" in the case should be? Older showed no concern that Susan Atkins was represented by a lawyer who had never tried a murder case before. Nor did he express a similar concern that Ronald Hughes, who had never tried *any* case before, could adequately represent Manson -- and later Leslie Van Houten -- in a "case having the complications this case has."16

The trial finally began on June 15, 1970. It took over a month to select a jury. The prosecution gave its opening statement on July 24. The defense made no opening statement. Then Deputy District Attorney Bugliosi began presenting the state's case.

The state opened with witnesses who gave testimony regarding the activity at the Polanski residence on the afternoon before the murders there. Other witnesses testified about the discovery of the bodies. Then, on July 27, Bugliosi introduced the state's star witness, Linda Kasabian.

Linda Kasabian has often been called the perfect prosecution witness, and there is good reason for that. She appeared forthright, sincere, precise, and honest in her testimony. At times she broke down in tears. She was a very convincing witness and the jury believed that she was being truthful.

Far and away the main witness against the defendants, Kasabian's testimony was damning. And she was, in fact, quite truthful in much of that testimony. Bugliosi reinforced this truthfulness by demonstrating that many portions of her testimony were corroborated by the physical evidence of the crimes and by other testimony regarding actions by the killers. Of course, Bugliosi had to do this, because Kasabian was still legally an accomplice of the defendants, and any incriminating evidence from an accomplice must, by law, be corroborated with other evidence.

But very little, if any, of Linda Kasabian's testimony had anything to do with any illegal activity on the part of Charles Manson.

Of course, in evaluating Linda Kasabian's testimony it is also reasonable to evaluate her character and her possible motivation for that testimony.

Before Kasabian's arrival at Spahn's Ranch in July of 1969 she had already been drifting through some of the seamier regions of the Counterculture for several years. She arrived at Spahn's Ranch on July 4. She was taken there by Catherine Share, whom she had met at the home of a mutual friend, Charles Melton. Kasabian and her two-year-old daughter Tanya had nowhere to stay and Share invited her to live at the ranch. That invitation, Kasabian recalled, was "the answer to an unspoken prayer."17

Kasabian did not meet Charles Manson the first night she was at the ranch, but she did meet Charles Watson. During that night she mentioned to Watson that Melton (who was a friend of her husband's) had recently inherited some money. Watson suggested that she steal it, and the next day she did so by sneaking into Melton's trailer and making off with $5,000. She then turned this money over to Charles Watson.

Then, during her second night at Spahn's, Kasabian met Charles Manson. She later said of this meeting, "He was kind of magnetic. There was just something about him that intrigued me."18

Soon after realizing that his $5,000 had been stolen, Charles Melton went to Spahn's Ranch and made a scene about getting it back. Charles Manson dealt with the situation and persuaded Melton to leave, once again having to stand up and face the heat for a problem created by one of the people around him -- and this time for someone who had only been around for a couple of days.

Linda Kasabian quickly proved game for anything that was going on at the ranch. She slept with all the men. She "creepy-crawled" a house. She stole.

I once asked Manson about Linda Kasabian, and he told me:

> She was doing all kinds of shit before [she got to the ranch]. She was stealing, and calling people "pigs," and disrespecting people. She was a nasty little witch. But it was none of my business, you know.
>
> Linda Kasabian was at the ranch for a week and a half, and I said maybe five words to her. And they got me telling her to do something. The whole thing is crazy.19

Sandra Good later remembered Kasabian by saying simply, "She was experienced."20

After actively participating in the murders on Cielo Drive and driving around with the killers on the second murder night, Kasabianleft Spahn's Ranch a few days later, on August 13, hoping to reestablish her relationship with her husband. She did not take her daughter with her. Tanya Kasabian was one of the children picked up in the police raid on the ranch on August 15. After the raid she was placed in a foster home. Kasabian found out about this and was eventually able to go to court and get her back.

Kasabian's husband was no longer interested in a future with her, however, so she then hitchhiked to see her father in Miami, Florida. She arrived there on the first day of November, 1969. She had only seen her father twice in the preceding fifteen years.

Later, when Kasabian's name was announced in the press as a suspect in the Tate-LaBianca murders, her father, "Rosy" Drouin, recalled her visits. "The first time she came to Miami, she stole a bunch of stuff from my apartment," he said. "I knew she was hocking it to buy dope. What can I say? She was not a bad girl. And she was not a good girl."

Drouin also remembered, "Linda seemed happy. In fact, I kept looking through her luggage to see if she was still using dope. She seemed that high.... She said she had a wonderful time in California, living off the fat of the land and all that, but I didn't want to hear about that mess."

A few weeks after Kasabian's arrival her father sent her and her daughter to stay with her mother in Boston. "I didn't like the way she was living," he said.21

Linda Kasabian was in Concord, New Hampshire when she was named as a suspect in the Tate-LaBianca murders on December 1, 1969. She immediately surrendered to authorities and was voluntarily extradited to California.

She agreed to help the prosecution in February of 1970, and by the end of the month she had her deal: The state of California would drop all charges against her (seven counts of first degree murder and one count of conspiracy to commit murder) in exchange for her truthful testimony at the trial of Manson and his co-defendants and at all other future trials against any of her former friends.

As Linda Kasabian's time on the witness stand began, she first testified about her perceptions of life at Spahn's Ranch during her five-week stay there: Manson's supposed total domination of the people around him, the idea of Helter Skelter, various individuals' interpretations of the Beatles' music, and her participation in orgies. She also testified that on the afternoon of August 8, 1969 Manson had exclaimed, "Now is the time for Helter Skelter."22

Then Kasabian related what happened later in the evening of the same day. "Charlie told me to go with Tex and do what he told me," she said. After Manson said this, she testified, she got into the car with Charles Watson, Susan Atkins, and Patricia Krenwinkel and they drove to Cielo Drive.

Linda Kasabian's testimony regarding the murders at the Polanski residence was graphic, detailed, emotional, and effective. But it had nothing to do with Charles Manson. Her testimony regarding the next night (when Manson had been along in the car) also failed to demonstrate any illegal activity or action on his part. At one point Manson interrupted her testimony. "You've already told three lies," he said.

Kasabian replied, "Oh, no, Charlie, I've spoken the truth, and you know it."23

Vincent Bugliosi later recalled in *Helter Skelter* that by the conclusion of his direct examination of Kasabian he was convinced that the jury fully believed in her truthfulness.

Of course, Linda Kasabian was not cross-examined by Charles Manson. That cross-examination was handled by the defense attorneys. For the most part, their questioning of Kasabian was fruitless, but Irving Kanarek was able to demonstrate her easy willingness to lie, as when he brought out that she had told a social worker that she had left California before the murders.

On August 10 Judge Older signed Kasabian's immunity petition. Three days later, all charges against her were dropped and she was released from custody. On August 19 she finished her testimony and walked out of the courtroom a free woman.

Ed Sanders later wrote in *The Family*, "Although the trial would heave onward for another eight months, it was obvious that it was over.... Kasabian's testimony made it obvious that the trial was going to go against the defendants."24

Chief Deputy District Attorney Joseph P. Busch agreed. "The case is in," he proclaimed.25

"The *fix* is in" was more like it.

After Linda Kasabian the prosecution called witnesses to corroborate her story of the two nights of murder. The owner of the car driven to the crimes, the maid who discovered the bodies on Cielo Drive, the L.A. County Coroner -- these witnesses did confirm much of what Linda Kasabian said. But none of them presented any evidence of any involvement of Charles Manson in the murders.

In early September the trial was delayed for several days because Susan Atkins said that she was too ill to attend the proceedings. Despite a courtroom appearance where Atkins tried to explain and demonstrate her illness, Judge Older finally concluded that she was malingering and ordered the trial to continue with her present.

Leaving the courtroom after Older's ruling, Deputy DA Aaron Stovitz commented to reporters that Atkins' effort to convince the court of her infirmity "was the best act since Sarah Bernhardt."26

On learning of Stovitz's remark, L.A. County District Attorney Evelle Younger had him removed from the case for violating Judge Keene's December 10, 1969 gag order preventing trial participants from discussing the case with the press. This was not Stovitz's first disregard of the judicial order. He had already been given a warning about talking to the press after he gave an extensive interview, in which he discussed much of the evidence in the case, to *Rolling Stone* magazine in early 1970.27

Stovitz was replaced by Deputy District Attorneys Donald Musich and Stephen Kay. While Musich has since passed into obscurity, Kay's appointment would prove to be a significant occurrence in the overall and ongoing Manson saga.

Danny DeCarlo was called as a prosecution witness on September 1. He testified to what he had seen during his time at Spahn's Ranch when, he admitted, he "was smashed ninety-nine percent of the time." DeCarlo authoritatively expounded on his understanding of Charles Manson's views on black people and on

Helter Skelter, which, Bugliosi conceded, "DeCarlo never really understood."28

Danny DeCarlo testified for the state on the condition that several criminal charges against him would be dropped in exchange for that testimony. In other words, if he had not testified for the prosecution he would have been prosecuted himself. And the district attorneys made this very clear to him. As Bugliosi later explained, "[We] eventually persuaded him that it was in his own best interests [to testify]."29

DeCarlo was also anxious to cooperate so the police would not pursue the possible implications of the fact that he possessed one of the guns of the missing and presumed murdered Donald Shea. And beyond all of these other considerations he also had a desire to share in the $25,000 reward that had been offered by several show business figures for anyone providing a solution to the murders on Cielo Drive.

DeCarlo was followed by Gregg Jakobson, whom Bugliosi called "an impressive and very important witness."30 Jakobson's important testimony is accorded one short paragraph in *Helter Skelter*. Jakobson testified about his perception of Charles Manson's belief system, but could not provide the lynchpin of the state's case against Manson: that he had ordered the Tate-LaBianca murders because he wanted to ignite a race war.

"I always took Charlie seriously," Jakobson said in court.

"You took what he said seriously, that there was going to be some kind of.... that he wanted some kind of war, if you want to put it that way, between blacks and whites?" a defense attorney asked.

"*I don't know if he wanted it*," Jakobson replied. "He believed it was going to happen." (emphasis added)

"I'm talking about Mr. Manson's intent, is what I'm talking about," the defense attorney continued. "Is it a fact that by talking to Mr. Bugliosi time after time after time, the seed was planted in your mind that Mr. Manson wanted some kind of race war?"

Bugliosi interjected, "He merely said it was imminent."

"I have no way of knowing what he wanted," Jakobson said. "He firmly believed it was going to happen. Whether he intended it to happen or wanted it to happen, I don't know."31

Former Manson associate Paul Watkins, however, did provide the lynchpin of Bugliosi's case -- the necessary link between Manson and the igniting of Helter Skelter -- during his testimony in late October. Under questioning by Bugliosi, Watkins said, "One day we was sittin' around on acid and Charlie said that the black man never did anything on his own, so somebody was going to have to show him how to start Helter Skelter."32 Watkins could not clarify who that "someone" might be. He said that Manson made this remark in the house on Gresham Street about six months before the murders.

Paul Watkins was not cross-examined by Charles Manson.

Watkins was the last of the important witnesses at the trial. On November 16, 1970, the prosecution rested its case. Three days later the defense also rested its case -- without presenting one.

Vincent Bugliosi began the state's closing arguments on December 21. The defendants were not present in the courtroom, having been expelled after a disturbance arising out of the fact that they were not allowed to present their chosen defense. Of his summation, Bugliosi later wrote, "Though the presentation took three days, it was a tight, cohesive package, and by the time I had finished I felt confident that I had established, beyond all doubt, Manson's control, his motives, his involvement, and the involvement of Watson, Atkins, Krenwinkel, and Van Houten."33

Why did Bugliosi take three whole days to present his closing argument? Because he knew that juries are made up of average citizens who frequently aren't too bright, and he needed three full days to make the complicated and fantastic Helter Skelter scenario of the murders seem understandable to the panel.

In his 1997 book *Outrage, The Five Reasons Why O.J. Simpson Got Away With Murder*, Bugliosi is frank in his condescension towards jurors. Likening them to infants or Alzheimer's disease patients, he declares that in order to convince them of your case ".... you put bibs on the jury and spoon-feed them...."34 Doubtless Bugliosi had the same realization about juries in 1970.

For the most part the defense's closing arguments were brief and ineffective. Irving Kanarek spoke for seven days, however, concentrating on the theme that Charles Watson and Linda Kasabian were responsible for the murders. Although Kanarek did raise some interesting points about the Helter Skelter motive and Linda Kasabian's credibility, they were most likely lost in the morass of his over-long presentation.

After the defense attorneys' closing remarks, Bugliosi started giving his final argument on January 13, 1971. Two days later he sat down, presumably with a well-worn spoon.

Judge Older then instructed the jury on the legal requirements for the process of its deliberations and dismissed it to begin deciding the guilt or innocence of Charles Manson and his three co-defendants. Ten days later it returned to court with its verdict: all defendants guilty on all counts.

Bugliosi's spoon-feeding had paid off. The jury eagerly and completely embraced the prosecution's versions of the crimes. The panel members had no doubts regarding the truthfulness of Linda Kasabian's testimony, basing this belief mainly on the fact that her version of the two nights of murder could not be shaken by cross-examination.35

However, some of the jury's conclusions were not necessarily logical. For example, it accepted all of Linda Kasabian's testimony as the truth simply because some of it seemed to be true. The jury also accepted eyewitness testimony that Charles Manson had once been on the grounds of the Polanski residence as a basis for the conclusion that he must have been actively involved in the later murders there.36

The jury completely bought the Helter Skelter motive, as well as the notion that Charles Manson was the unquestionable leader of his group of associates. Based on this assumption of Manson's leadership in all things, the panel reached the conclusion that he also must have ordered the murders.37

After Manson and his co-defendants were convicted the trial entered the penalty phase wherein the defense finally presented witnesses. The most important of these witnesses were the three female co-defendants and many of their friends, all of whom stated that Charles Manson had nothing to do with the Tate-LaBianca murders and that those murders were committed as part of a "copycat" plan to get Bobby Beausoleil out of jail.

Prosecutor Bugliosi argued passionately for the death penalty.

Deliberations in the penalty phase began on March 25. Four days later the jury returned with the decision that the prosecution wanted: death for all four defendants.

The trial was over.

Given the relentlessness of the prosecution and the ineptitude of the defense (not to mention all of the prejudicial pre-trial publicity) it is not surprising that the jury in Manson's case reached the decisions it reached in 1971. But if the jury had instead been given the versions of the crimes presented in this book and the legal arguments presented in this chapter, it is possible that it might have acquitted Charles Manson on all counts.

It is one of the standard procedures in any criminal trial that after both sides have presented their versions of the case the judge then reads instructions to the jury which explain how it is supposed to apply the law to the evidence that has been presented in court. In Manson's case the judge read dozens of instructions, but only three of them need concern us here. All three of them are based on the cornerstone of American law -- the premise that accused persons are presumed to be innocent until they are proven guilty beyond a reasonable doubt.

At the trial of Manson and his co-defendants, jury instruction # 2 read (in part):

> [Jurors] are not permitted to find a defendant guilty of any crime charged against him based on circumstantial evidence unless the proved circumstances are not only consistent with the theory that the defendant is guilty of the crime, *but cannot be reconciled with any other rational conclusion....*
>
> If the evidence as to any particular count is susceptible of two reasonable interpretations, one which points to a defendant's guilt and the other to his innocence, *it is your duty to adopt that interpretation which points to his innocence, and reject the other which points to his guilt.*
>
> You will notice that the second paragraph of these instructions applies only when both of the interpretations appear to be reasonable. If, on the other hand, one of the interpretations appears to you reasonable and the other unreasonable, *it would be your duty to adopt the reasonable interpretation and reject the unreasonable interpretation....*" (all emphasis added)

Instruction # 36 concerned itself with the reasonableness of various interpretations of (and conclusions based on) the circumstances that might tend to indicate the necessary legal criminal element of specific intent:

> The specific intent with which an act is done may be manifested by the circumstances surrounding its commission. But *you may not find a defendant guilty* of a willful, deliberate, premeditated murder of the first degree unless the proved circumstances not only are consistent with the hypothesis that he had the specific intent to kill a human being with malice aforethought, which was the result of deliberation and premeditation as those terms are defined elsewhere in these instructions, but are *irreconcilable with any other rational conclusion.*
>
> Also, if the evidence as to such specific intent is susceptible of two reasonable interpretations, one of which points to the existence thereof and the other to the absence thereof, *you must adopt that interpretation with points to its absence.* If, on the other hand, one interpretation of the evidence to such specific intent appears to you to be reasonable and the other interpretation to be unreasonable, *it would be your duty to accept the reasonable interpretation and to reject the unreasonable.* (all emphasis added)

Instruction # 52 was worded almost identically to instruction # 36, only it was in reference to the charge of conspiracy to commit murder:

> The specific intent in which an act is done may be manifested by the circumstances surrounding its commission. But *you may not find a defendant guilty of conspiracy* to commit murder charged in Count 8 unless the proof of circumstances are not only consistent with the hypothesis that he had the specific intent to commit murder of the first degree by means of a willful, deliberate and premeditated killing with malice aforethought, as that type of murder is defined elsewhere in these instructions, but are *irreconcilable with any other rational conclusion.*
>
> Also, if the evidence as to specific intent is susceptible of two reasonable interpretations, one of which points to the existence thereof and the other to the absence thereof, *you must adopt that interpretation which points to its absence.*
>
> If, on the other hand, one interpretation of the evidence as such specific intent appears to you to be reasonable and the other interpretation to

be unreasonable, *it would be your duty to accept the reasonable interpretation and to reject the unreasonable.* (all emphasis added)38

Any one of these three instructions is enough to sink the case against Charles Manson -- *twice.*

In Manson's case, not only can the circumstances of the Tate-LaBianca murders be reconciled in two ways, but those circumstances can be more reconciled with the "get brother out of jail" motive than with the Helter Skelter motive. There is nothing in the evidentiary circumstances of the murders that implies any kind of racial facet of the motive. But all of the circumstances of the crimes fit the "get brother out of jail" scenario. Thus, the more reasonable interpretation of the evidence points to that scenario.

It is the second part of these instructions, however, which ultimately dooms the prosecution's case: "If, on the other hand, one of the interpretations appears to you reasonable and the other to be unreasonable, it would be your duty to adopt the reasonable interpretation and reject the unreasonable interpretation...."

For a person to accept the prosecution's Helter Skelter scenario of the murders they would have to believe that the Helter Skelter motive -- with its supposed influences from the Bible and Beatles, its mind-controlling guru and abject slaves, its bottomless pit and underground cities, and its goal of world domination achieved by instigating a conflagration between the white and black races -- is a more reasonable explanation for the crimes than the "get brother out of jail/copycat crimes" motive.

The main word that the prosecutors have always used to describe Helter Skelter is "bizarre." In the book *Helter Skelter*, Vincent Bugliosi wrote, "I felt we had [a motive]. It was just that it was *unbelievably bizarre*."39 (emphasis added)

At Leslie Van Houten's 1996 parole hearing Deputy District Attorney Stephen Kay told the parole board:

> I'm sure you folks see lots of murders and cases maybe even more brutal than this one, but I doubt that you see any motives for murder that are more outrageous or bizarre than the motive that we have here, the motive of Helter Skelter.40

This is how two of the district attorneys who prosecuted Manson have characterized their version of his supposed crimes. But if the Helter Skelter motive is "unbelievably bizarre" and "outrageous," how can it be reasonable at all?

"Reasonable" is "in accordance with reason or sound thinking. *Not excessive or extreme*."41 It is "being within the bounds of reason; rational."42 It is "*logical, sane*, sensible, *plausible*."43 (all emphases added)

All of these definitions of "reasonable" are what the Helter Skelter motive is not.

The "get brother out of jail" motive, on the other hand -- even if it was ill conceived and unlikely to achieve its goal -- was a fairly simple and straightforward plan. It was not extreme or incredible. It is prima facie more reasonable than the Helter Skelter motive.

Therefore, had the entire chain of circumstances (Crowe to Hinman to Tate-Labianca) and a detailed explanation of the "get brother out of jail" motive been offered to the jury, that jury would have been required by law to accept that version of events because it was more rational and reasonable than the fantastic and bizarre Helter Skelter motive. And with the Helter Skelter motive superseded with the "brother" motive there was absolutely no evidence of any criminal intent on the part of Charles Manson that the murders on Cielo and Waverly Drives take place. And without proof of that key and necessary element of intent, a first-degree murder verdict against Charles Manson should not have been able to stand.

If all of the foregoing is correct and Manson knew about all of this at the time of his trial, why wasn't this scenario presented in court? The short answer to that question is that Charles Manson was not allowed to present it (if he had wanted to).

The convictions of Charles Manson for the Tate-LaBianca murders might have been miscarriages of justice, but they were brought on by another judicial error, the denial of Manson's constitutional right to defend himself at his trials.

It is well documented that from the very beginning of the legal proceedings against him Manson voiced his desire to represent himself.44 On December 17, just eight days after his arraignment,

Manson made a formal request to do so in the courtroom of Judge William Keene:

> Your Honor, there is no way I can give up my voice in this matter. If I can't speak, then our whole thing is done. If I can't speak in my own defense and converse freely in this courtroom, then it ties my hands behind my back, and if I have no voice, then there is no sense in having a defense. Lawyers play with people, and I am a person and I don't want to be played with in this matter. The news media has already executed and buried me.... If anyone is hypnotized, the people are being hypnotized by the lies being told them.... There is no attorney in the world who can represent me as a person. I have to do it myself.

Judge Keene ordered Manson to be examined by Joseph Ball, a former president of the California State Bar Association. Ball's assessment of Manson, presented in court on Christmas Eve, 1969, was that he was:

> .... an able, intelligent young man, quiet-spoken and mild-mannered. We went over different problems of law, and I found he had a ready understanding.... Remarkable understanding. As a matter of fact, he has a very fine brain. I complimented him on the fact. I think I told you that he had a high I.Q. [He] must have, to be able to converse as he did. And he feels that if he goes to trial and is able to permit jurors and the Court to hear him and see him, they will realize he is not the kind of man who would perpetrate horrible crimes.

Based on Ball's evaluation, Judge Keene reluctantly granted Manson his right to self-representation. "It is, in this Court's opinion, a sad and tragic mistake you are making by taking this course of action, but I can't talk you out of it.... Mr. Manson, you are your own lawyer."

This situation existed until March 6, 1970. On that date Judge Keene used supposedly "outlandish" and "nonsensical" motions filed by Manson as an excuse to vacate his status as his own attorney. Why these motions were not simply overruled was not explained, but in any case they did not really indicate that Manson was incompetent to defend himself. To the contrary, the ingenuity and novelty of his motions indicated that he was perhaps *over* competent.

Commenting on Keene's ruling, prosecutor Bugliosi told reporters:

> Judge Keene.... concluded, and I think justifiably so, that Mr. Manson is incapable of defending himself. Judge Keene held that to allow Mr. Manson to represent himself would bring about a fundamental denial of due process. [Manson is] simply incompetent in that respect. [And] I thought the handwriting was on the wall. The documents that Mr. Manson has been filing with the Court are outlandish. They make bizarre, unorthodox requests, clearly manifesting his inability to defend himself. He's almost incoherent."45

Whatever the real reasons for the denial, Judge Keene's action violated Manson's constitutional right to defend himself, and any defense presented after that ruling (and in fact there was none) could be considered invalid because it was not really Manson's chosen defense.

This issue was one of the many points of contention brought up in Manson's appeal (which would more accurately be characterized as his *lawyer's* appeal). In that appeal the California Justices denied Manson's request for a new trial claiming that a federal court ruling which absolutely affirmed the Sixth Amendment right did not apply to Manson because the decision came after his trial and "was not to be given retroactive application."

This interpretation of the law was later overruled in *Bittaker v. Enomoto*, 587 F. 2d. 400 (1978)46, wherein a United States Federal Appeals Court ruled "Although California defendant's trial occurred prior to United States Supreme Court's *Faretta*47 decision confirming to state defendants the constitutional right to self-representation, denial of the California defendants' right of self-representation was a federal constitutional defect *requiring setting aside of his conviction*." (emphasis added) Charles Manson was mentioned specifically in footnote # 2 of this decision (See below.).

The right to self-representation is as fundamental and undeniable as any other right afforded to Americans. It is every citizen's constitutional right. That is why Colin Ferguson, the seemingly deranged Long Island Railroad Gunman was allowed to defend himself at his trial. That is why accused Unabomber Ted Kaczinski, considered by some observers to be unbalanced, was going to be allowed to defend himself at his trial before he pleaded guilty in order to avoid the death penalty. It does not matter if a defendant's defense is unconventional or even outlandish -- self-representation is his constitutional right.

The denial of Charles Manson's right to defend himself during his trials could be a fatal flaw in the legitimacy of those trials. Taking it further, it could be argued that Manson's convictions, and his post-trial incarceration, were not legal.

Could the real reason that Charles Manson was not allowed to defend himself be not that he was "almost incoherent" or even because his behavior was too disruptive of the courtroom proceedings (all of the famous so-called "Manson outbursts" occurred *after* Manson's *pro per* right was taken away), but rather because there was a real fear that if he had been allowed to defend himself he might not have been convicted?

If Charles Manson had been allowed to personally cross-examine prosecution witnesses and to present and question his own witnesses, there is a good chance that he could not only have disproved that Helter Skelter was the motive for the Tate-LaBianca murders, but he also likely could have completely discredited and countered the testimony of Linda Kasabian, Paul Watkins, Danny DeCarlo, and others regarding his alleged participation in or responsibility for the crimes.

Linda Kasabian was on the witness stand for seventeen days. At the end of that time she had given very convincing testimony about what she and the others did at the Polanski residence -- but she gave no testimony about any order from Charles Manson to commit the murders there. She did testify that Manson said "Now is the time for Helter Skelter" on the afternoon of August 8, 1969, but this must have been at least five or six hours before the killers left Spahn's Ranch.48 Any linkage between that alleged statement by Manson, who is well known for speaking in quizzical non sequiturs, and any action taken by other individuals several hours later is tenuous at best. Later that night Kasabian said that Manson told her to go with Charles Watson and do what he told her to do, but she still apparently knew nothing about any murder plans, as evidenced by her testimony that she thought that the group was merely going out on a "creepy-crawly" mission.

As for the night that the LaBiancas were killed, Kasabian's testimony is conflicting and uncorroborated, at least in regard to Charles Manson. Her most incriminating claim, that Manson went into 3301 Waverly Drive alone and tied up the people inside, is contradicted by Charles Watson, who says that *he* tied up the victims. Manson could have called Watson to testify about this, and that testimony would have cast much more than a reasonable doubt on Kasabian's assertion regarding what happened at the LaBiancas' and, indeed, upon all of her testimony.

While it has often been noted that Manson and his co-defendants presented no defense at their trial, people have seldom asked why. In a phone call to me Manson explained why they didn't:

> Here's the argument on that. It comes to this play. If you take my rights to be my lawyer, then what's a defense? You've already took my rights!
>
> It's like, if I knock you down, and I knock you out, and then I say, "Well, why didn't you come out for the third round?" Well, you were knocked out in the first and second round, so how could you come out? You couldn't very well come out.
>
> How can I defend myself when I'm handcuffed in the back room? I mean, I'm handcuffed in the back room, and they've got a speaker in there with no wire on it. And then they tell the public, "Well, he's got a speaker over there and he's listening."
>
> You know, they had a speaker, but the speaker wasn't even hooked up!49

For much of the trial Manson was represented by Irving Kanarek, who was considered by many members of the Los Angeles legal community to be an obstructionist buffoon. Although Kanarek did raise some good points in Manson's defense during his cross examination of some prosecution witnesses, his performance was for the most part incompetent. Manson complained about the lawyer the court put on him numerous times during the trial. Later, Manson recalled:

> Irving Kanarek. He was representing me. He was representing my life. He was representing my words. He had no words in my world. He had no thoughts and ideas in my world. The only thing he had in my world is what they let him have in my world. And they *forced* me to accept him as a representation. I had to take that man up on my motherfucking life. Whether I wanted him or not, it didn't matter. It didn't matter at all.
>
> I got that idiot for a lawyer, because I figured I'd feed 'em that idiot -- they could take that idiot -- and that he'd be their leader.
>
> Kanarek never did anything but obstruct. He never did anything. He promised to get me my *pro per* and he lied. He didn't do it. That's the reason I hit him in the courtroom. I wanted him off of me, man.
>
> Not only did he fuck up, he sold my rights, [and] after that he sent me two or three *Playboy* magazines and fifty dollars. And then he started an appeal, without my permission. I told him, "I'm not going in that direction." He went in that direction anyway. He destroyed all my chances of getting back on purpose so he could buy and sell that. He bought and sold my life.
>
> Irving Kanarek was the focal point of man's rights. He had a chance to speak for man's rights and he didn't. Somebody put him right in that place for a particular reason....
>
> To me it's simple. The court just turns. The court turns and says, "All right, Charlie Manson has no rights. No big deal. Just one fucking poor redneck asshole down on the ground. He ain't got no rights."50

And it appears that the state of California had a great deal of apprehension over the possibility that Manson could win an acquittal for himself if he were allowed to defend himself, because it was always very resistant to any such chance. When the federal court's *Bittaker v. Enomoto* decision was announced, the news media reported on California's "boogyman Manson" fear mongering. "Court Lets Controversial Ruling Stand, Manson Could Be Affected," read the headline in the *Sacramento Bee*. The article said that "throughout the [Bittaker] pleadings.... state officials kept waving Manson as a red flag."51

California Attorney General Evelle Younger (the same Evelle Younger who was also the Los Angeles District Attorney during

Manson's murder trials) justified "waving Manson as a red flag" by saying that "the effect [of the ruling] on the administration of justice in California could potentially be catastrophic. The fact that Charles Manson and others could possibly benefit if there is retroactive application of the rule is a legitimate concern to the State of California."

In its response the federal court was firm in its condemnation of Younger's attempt to use Manson as part of a legal argument. In a footnote of its decision the court admonished:

> The state mentions several times that one of its prisoners who might benefit from the decision is Charles Manson. *We do not encourage this type of advocacy. A federal court must make its decisions in accord with the Constitution and the laws, without regard to the notoriety of parties or non-parties.* (emphasis added)

How have Manson's prosecutors addressed the self-representation issue? In *Helter Skelter* Vincent Bugliosi says that at one point in the trial he was willing to allow Manson to conduct his own defense. Judge Older still denied Manson's request. Stephen Kay, assistant prosecutor for the last weeks of Manson's trial, has brushed off this constitutional question as a mere "sticking point," without any elaboration on its possible validity.52 Both Bugliosi and Kay have claimed that Manson could have defended himself by taking the stand and testifying in front of the jury, but that option is a far cry from what Manson should have been allowed to do, such as structure the defense strategy, call and examine his own witnesses, and personally cross-examine the prosecution's witnesses.

Over the years of his incarceration Manson filed several habeas corpus petitions with the Los Angeles County Superior Court protesting his imprisonment based on the claim that he was denied the right to defend himself. All of these petitions were dismissed at the Superior Court level with no explanation other than that the petitioner (Manson) had failed to establish that the claims made in the petitions warranted the granting of the writ. This is a standard rubber-stamp denial. None of the legal arguments advanced in any of these writs was ever addressed.

But none of this should be surprising. The California courts knew that they denied Charles Manson his rights, and they were justifiably afraid of the consequences they might face if he had been given those rights. Therefore Manson never got any relief on this issue in the California court system. Only if he had appealed a new writ through any state legal system and onto the federal level would he have gotten a fair hearing. Then he could quite possibly have gotten a new trial.

If Charles Manson was so obviously guilty -- if the evidence against him was so overwhelming that his guilt and convictions were such givens -- then why was the state of California so afraid to let him back into court where he could represent himself? Because it feared that if Manson had presented his own defense, shown his innocence, and had his convictions overturned, he'd have, in his own words, "sue[d California] for Hearst Castle, probably."53

Evelle Younger was right. A Manson retrial *would* have been catastrophic for the state of California.

What kind of defense would Charles Manson have presented on his own behalf? He has said:

> I could have brought the truth out of all those children. I could have said, "Has Charlie Manson ever lied to you about *anything*?"
>
> "No."
>
> "Has he ever lied *around* you?"
>
> "No."
>
> "About anyone to anything for any reason?"
>
> "No."
>
> I could have established the truth. I could have established that I haven't lied for *years*, man. [Because] when I woke up to the truth I got up on it and I been staying with it. It's my mother. It's my way of life. It's me.
>
> I didn't break no fucking law. God knows that, I know that, and everybody at that ranch knows that. If Tex had to go down and do what Tex had to do, Tex stands responsible for what Tex had to do. If Bobby did what Bobby had to do, Bobby's responsible for what Bobby had to do. Charlie didn't do a motherfucking thing but feed the horses and sweep the floor. I didn't tell anybody to do anything other than have a good day. "Do what the fuck you think you *should* do."54

Whereas the judge at Manson's trials thought that he was not capable of representing himself, Manson actually showed a very competent understanding of legal principles and procedures, even if he did express that understanding from his own unique perspective:

What the law states is that you have to have malice aforethought. And I don't have malice aforethought about taking a piss!

I don't think ahead of nothing, man, because I live totally in Now. I've been totally in Now since I was a little kid. I don't live in the dimensions that you guys live in. I live in another dimension. I don't live in paper words. I don't live in books. I live in motions. I live in motions, music, and numbers. That's my mind, heart, and soul.

I wouldn't get involved in a conspiracy, get involved in nobody else's mind. I have my own motherfucking mind, because I burnt the school down when I was nine years old and I told 'em, "I'm keeping my own mind."

The criminal codes are set in the universal mind. I can quote you the scriptures, if you want scriptures from the Bible, that say the same thing. If you and I set down and we enter into an agreement to do something, [if] you say, "I'm gonna rob a bank."

And I say, "Okay."

You say, "You want to come with me?"

If I say, "Yeah, I'll come with you," and I give you my word that I'll be with you, and enter into that agreement with you, I'm honor bound to stand by you. I'm honor bound to have the getaway car there at 8:05 when I say 8:05 and my word has to be my bond and my bond has to be my life.

But if you say, "I'm gonna rob a bank," and I say, "Well, I don't think I want to enter in to that," and I *don't* make any agreements, I'm not obligated by the laws of God in any Bible or any religious book in the world, I'm not obligated to run and tell on you.

And if I say, "No, I'm not going to have anything to do with that," then that's none of my affair. I have no business in that. That's not my business.

Now, if you come and ask me, "How do you get past the Ace and Ace burglar alarm?" and I tell you, that *still* doesn't put me in no agreement. In other words, if I don't enter into no agreement with you to go do what you're gonna do, then I'm not obligated in any perspective towards that act. I'm responsible for my own business and I mind my own business, just like the Bible says. If I'm minding my own business and you go up and you do bobby dooba doop boop, you have to be responsible for those actions, according to the law.

When I was in reform school I used to say, "Why can't I have no rights?"

And they said, "Because you're not twenty-one." They'd say, "You get rights when you're twenty-one, and ignorance of the law is no excuse."

Well, now the whole thing turns around. I know the law and they *don't*. So that's on them. It's not on me. Why should I suffer because they don't know the law? God's law. God's law is the number one law. Man's law is a game played over God's law....

God's law is not man's law. God's law is God's law. Man's law is shabby, shaky, and it's full of games and shams and fakes and phonies. I can get a judge's robe and go in business for myself and probably do a better job than they're doing. In other words, what saves me from being a policeman? I was the policeman on that ranch. Anybody that told a lie, I had to deal with that.... If someone steals my cows, and I let 'em get away with it, then that's on me. You know, like, I got to look out for my perspective. I gotta watch out for me and I gotta look out for mine. First of all, nobody's gonna look out for me but me. No one's ever looked out for me but me. No one's ever helped me but me.

I didn't want the job of holding anyone to the truth. When I told Bobby, "You know what to do, you got a mind of your own, do what you think is right," they convicted me for saying, "You know what to do." Well, I would tell anyone that.

The big point in my whole defense would have been, I never broke nobody's will. I agreed with everybody, I got along with everybody, and I did everything that everybody asked me -- up to a point. And that point was when I cut Hinman's ear off. And then I started to pulling back, saying, "Whoa, man. This is all going into insanity." And I *told* everybody there, "You're all putting me back in the penitentiary. I'm getting out of here."

And everybody said, "Oh, don't leave. If we have any trouble we'll deal with it."

So I said, "All right," you know. And I hung around. And I *knew* better. I *knew* better. I knew better than let people hang around me, I knew better than [to] get too many people. I *knew* better.

I wasn't out to get people [recruit "followers"]. I really wasn't. I wasn't incorporating nothing. I wasn't running nothing. George [Spahn] was running it. George is still running it. George and the horses are running it.... It's got nothing to do with me as a personality, because I lost that personality in 1952 in Petersburg, Virginia.55

Despite Charles Manson's loss of personality he still had lucid opinions, not only of what a judicial system should do, but of what he felt that California did to him:

> When you've got someone in society that did wrong, you take 'em to the courtroom, you give 'em a trial, you try 'em and convict 'em, and you send 'em to prison.
>
> But when you don't have a case on somebody, and you see that the media is screaming for this guy -- you don't have a case in the courtroom so you take your case to the media. And that's what the DA did. The district attorney moved the *L.A. Times* into the district attorney's office. They were getting around-the-world headlines every day from the district attorney's office.
>
> Then the judge came back and said, "Well, somebody violated a gag order," that they was getting all them newspaper stories from, and all those zillions of dollars being made, they came back and got the newspaper reporter [William Farr] and said, "You tell us who gave you the information or we're gonna put you in jail."
>
> So they made a big thing by acting like they're putting this guy in jail. And they put him in a soft cell with color TV and room service, and he gets to do anything he wants for a few days, and they make a big thing like they're trying to find out who gave him the information and broke the gag order. Well, it was the damned district attorney and judge was in cahoots with all that shit to start with!
>
> I used to ask the lawyer, "Why are you saying all this stuff? You're prejudicing the jury. You're saying stuff that don't need to be said."
>
> He said, "Well, I got to say that or I can't get it in the book."
>
> I said, "What do you mean?"
>
> He said, "Well, anything that's put into public record, you can use for books. Legally."
>
> So they put all kinds of shit in the trial that didn't have a *fucking* thing to do with the trial. They'd have special sessions and lock me up in the back and just talk a whole bunch of shit about all kinds of stuff. They brought computer analysis in, psychiatrists. They brought twelve psychiatrists in going in twelve different directions, and each one of 'em had something different to say. They'd just say a bunch of Goddamn words that don't say nothing, man. Just go through a lot of circles. And then the public don't know what they're saying, and they *think* that they're saying something. And all the time they're winking at each other.

This is what I believed in when I went to court. I believed that I had rights. I believed I had a country. I believed I had a constitution. I didn't know that all that was bought and sold, that the politicians had sold that out. I didn't know that.

That's the reason I didn't plead guilty and get diminished capacity. Had I pled guilty, I'd have been out in eighteen months.56

Chapter Notes

1 In this case, the definition is from *Barron's Law Dictionary*, Third Edition,
Barron's Educational Services, Inc.; New York; 1991.
2 The summaries of California law used in this book are taken from the *Witkin's California Criminal Law* encyclopedia, third edition.
3 California Penal Code, Section 203.
4 *Will You Die For Me?*, page 148.
5 Leslie Van Houten 1993 parole hearing, transcript page 73.
6 Charles Manson, 1997 parole hearing, transcript page 39.
7 From a Charles Manson telephone conversation with Sandra Good, 1996. Sandra Good Archives.
8 *Blood Family*, page 91.
9 Author conversation with Charles Manson at the California State Prison-Corcoran.
10 *Blood Family*, page 381.
11 *Helter Skelter*, page 158.
12 Manson's reflections on his prosecutor are from a tape-recorded telephone conversation with Sandra Good, 1998 (Sandra Good Archives) and from Bill Scanlon-Murphy's 1993 interview with Manson.
13 *Helter Skelter*, page 358.
14 This reminiscence is from a telephone call between Charles Manson and Sandra Good, 1996. Sandra Good Archives.
15 *Helter Skelter*, page 402.
16 Van Houten would also be represented by Maxwell Keith. Patricia Krenwinkel's attorney was Paul Fitzgerald.
17 *Helter Skelter*, page 347.
18 Interview on *A Current Affair*, undated but nineteen years after the murders. Sandra Good Archives.
19 From a tape-recorded telephone conversation between Charles Manson and Sandra Good.
20 To the author, July 1999.

21 Rosy Drouin's recollections of his reunions with his daughter are presented in *Five To Die*, pages 234-235 and in *The Killing Of Sharon Tate*, page 57.
22 *Helter Skelter*, page 433.
23 Ibid., page 437.
24 *The Family*, updated 1989 edition, page 410.
25 *Witness To Evil*, page 322.
26 *The Family*, page 419. Vincent Bugliosi says Stovitz said, "It was a performance worthy of Sarah Bernhardt." (*Helter Skelter*, page 464.)
27 *Rolling Stone* magazine, No. 61, published June 25, 1970.
28 *Helter Skelter*, page 479.
29 Ibid., page 338. DeCarlo previously had a motorcycle theft charge dropped in exchange for his testimony at Bobby Beausoleil's re-trial for the murder of Gary Hinman.
30 *Helter Skelter*, page 506.
31 This exchange is taken from an undated page of trial transcript, Sandra Good Archives.
32 *Witness To Evil*, page 356.
33 *Helter Skelter*, page 537.
34 *Outrage, The Five Reasons Why O. J. Simpson Got Away With Murder*, page 19.
35 This in not particularly surprising, since much of what Linda Kasabian said was true. But she said little which directly implicated Charles Manson in the crimes, and she was not cross examined by Manson.
36 *Blood Family*, page 396.
37 Ibid., page 404.
38 These jury instructions are taken from *Blood Family*, pages 366, 378, and 387.
39 *Helter Skelter*, page 292.
40 Kay at Leslie Van Houten's 1998 parole hearing. The quote is taken from a videotape of that hearing.
41 According to *The American Heritage Dictionary of the English Language.*
42 According to *The Merriam-Webster Dictionary.*
43 According to *Roget's Thesaurus.*
44 This summary of Manson's efforts to defend himself is taken from the trial record as recorded in *Helter Skelter*.
45 This is on the Channel 2 KCBS (then KNXT) tape.
46 See 61 C. A. 3d 102 (1976).
47 *Faretta* is at 422 U. S. 806.
48 Manson told me that he very well could have made such a statement.

49 From a tape-recorded telephone conversation in the Sandra Good Archives.
50 Ibid.
51 *Sacramento Bee*, April 17, 1979, page A 7.
52 This in an October 21, 1997 article "Manson Family Website, History Rewritten By Losers" on the *New York Cybertimes* web site wherein Kay responded to arguments about the violation of Manson's sixth amendment rights on the *Access Manson* web site.
53 Charles Manson, 1992 parole hearing, transcript page 68.
54 From a tape-recorded telephone conversation in the Sandra Good Archives.
55 Ibid.
56 Ibid.

50
50
50

Aftermath

"If you're a revolutionary and you lose, you get the blame and you're called a criminal. If you win, then you get the glory and you're called a hero. In other words, it's just a matter of -- inside yourself -- did you win for what you believed in, or did you lose? I think we won. Even though we were too little, too late. We didn't make it, but we still won. We won within our own dreams. We won within our own selves."

-- Charles Manson

Charles Manson and his co-defendants were originally sentenced to death, but in 1972 a combination of decisions by the California and United States Supreme Courts temporarily abolished capital punishment and those sentences were changed to life in prison with the possibility of parole. Although some of Manson's co-defendants entertain hopes of winning paroles (or did at one time), Manson didn't see getting a parole himself, and he spoke about the release procedure derisively to say the least:

All that Mickey Mouse motherfucking horse shit ain't about nothing. That's a face play you play for them Goddamn parole boards, man. When you're trying to play act for some old silly motherfucking woman laying in behind some motherfuckin couch potato punk watching that motherfucking football game....

I've been outside. There's nothing out there but insanity, man. I mean, it's hard enough to learn to live with people in here, but you get out there, man, it's almost impossible. I can't live with them people out there. There's no way in hell I could live with them people out there. They're all crazy. They lie, they cheat, they do all the things that they say that the crooks do, only they do it all the time. They're automatically doing it, you know?

[And] killing is just getting to be the thing [outside of prison] nowadays, because it's a lot easier just to go ahead and do whatever you have to do rather than pay your bills, you know. Or pay rent. It's a lot easier just to go shoot the landlord.

You know, that's what the DA wanted. And that's what the movies want, and maybe that's what Polanski's bringing back into play....

[But] this is what makes me me and you you. I don't really care if I ever get out....

If all the people that I came in with -- if I can't be with them, who would I want to be with? I don't want to be with anybody that ain't with me.1

As for any hopes for a new trial, Manson was philosophical:

It's not important that I get a new trial. It's not important to me. The time is already done. The wound is already perpetrated on my life. All my friends, and everything I was doing is just totally, completely destroyed.

My only reason for wanting a trial is to reestablish rights in the United States of America through the Constitution of the United States of America and George Washington. Because it's my honor, it's my soul, it's my life, it's my children, it's my love, it's all the people that I still hold in my mind as being my friends.

It's not for me personally, it's for me as a being, as a human. It's me for the trees, and the animals, and the wildlife. It's me for life on earth.

I'm not in my little personal trip that I want to *be* somebody in particular, because I've already transcended all that horse shit. I had that before. I could of been a Beach Boy and a heech boy and a geech geech. I had all that. You know that. I walked off from that world. I didn't want none of that. That's a worse prison than the one I'm in now.

All I wanted was to be, *there*, man. To be alive. To experience *my* life. But that was taken away.

In the ensuing decades since the Tate-LaBianca murders the lives and relationships of the people at Spahn's Ranch have changed drastically. None of the free people from the old days whom I met during my research for this book expressed any regret for their past experiences or harbored any ill will towards anyone. But all of Manson's convicted and incarcerated co-defendants have repudiated him and said that they were truly sorry for the crimes they committed.

The main killer at the Polanski and LaBianca residences, Charles Watson, was one of the earliest to break away. In *Will You Die For Me?* he recalled his decision to leave, which occurred in October of 1969 when he was in Goler Wash. He had fled to the desert with the rest of the ranch people after the murders. While secreted in a recess in the ceiling over the bathroom at the Barker Ranch he had the realization that he was done with killing:

> Suddenly I didn't believe we were ever going to find the secret hole into the Pit; suddenly I knew the world was not going to end; suddenly I was hungry; suddenly I didn't care what Charlie had told me to do -- all I knew was that I would not kill anyone. Not again.2

As a partial explanation for his sudden change of heart and decision to flee the desert and his life in California, he offered, "I think it had something to do with being without drugs for two or three weeks."3

Whatever the reason, Watson fled the desert at the beginning of October.

Charles Manson remembers Watson's sudden exit somewhat differently:

> You know that little hideaway in Barker's place? Well, I used to sleep up in there, and all the mice used to have to crawl over me to get out to go to the water, right? And I'd have these buckskin pants on, and they would start chewing on my pants.
>
> So, one night, when it was Tex's turn -- because what we'd do is like keep a point up there, and anybody would come, we'd listen to what they was saying. So, it was Tex's turn to see if the cops was gonna come up, you dig, so he was gonna be stashed there, you know, to see what the

cops was gonna say. And we'd always leave a coffee pot there, and we'd leave a couple pounds of coffee and all that kind of stuff....

So [Tex] was over that night, and them rats came out and started chewing on them pants. He freaked out and he couldn't deal with it. He run home to his mother, man. He left the pants there, man, and the rats ate a fucking hole in the pants and shit. Fucking rats ate my pants up. That's cold, huh?

After he was arrested in Texas Watson fought extradition to California with such success that his trial for murder occurred after that of Manson and his three female co-defendants. At his trial Watson admitted to all of his homicidal activities, but he blamed his behavior on the overwhelming influence of Manson. After his conviction (for example in his book and at all of his parole hearings) Watson has still readily admitted to his actions, albeit while continuing to put the ultimate responsibility on Manson as an evil mastermind. At his 2001 parole hearing Watson said of his killing:

[I did it] to please Charlie Manson. That's the way I went through it. And to please the family. I was a people pleaser. And I, you know, that's all I can say. I didn't have a good identity. I was more concerned about pleasing Charles Manson, pleasing the family, than I was anything else. I completely turned my back on my [own] family, I felt I was unpleasing to them, and I was so prideful and not willing to say I had failed my family. And think I was striking out a lot of anger that -- because of my fear of failure.4

Despite Watson's defection and blame, Charles Manson harbored no ill will towards the man whose actions precipitated the violent events of July and August of 1969:

[Tex] kept his word. He did what he was supposed to do. And they come up and ask me things about him and I say, "Man, I ain't got nothing bad about the man. What the man said was cool with me," you know."

It's like, people say, "Why ain't you mad at Tex? He's got all them babies and you got nothing?"

And I say, "Well, cool. That's cool. If he got it, he must have had it coming, because if he didn't, he wouldn't have it."

(Charles Watson is currently incarcerated at the Richard J. Donovan Correctional Facility in San Diego, California. He has been denied parole seventeen times. His next hearing is scheduled for 2021.)

The second most infamous murderous "Manson Family member" was Susan Atkins. Her break with Manson and the others also occurred fairly early on. Because of the fact that statements Atkins made to authorities (including her grand jury testimony) were responsible for everyone's legal predicaments, she began to be estranged from the group as early as during the murder trial. As the years passed she became even further removed from her past life with the Spahn's Ranch people. She became a born again Christian in 1974 and did her best to put Sadie Mae Glutz behind her. At her 1993 parole hearing she expressed her then current attitude towards herself and her crimes:

> I sit before you a convicted murderess. I understand that. I was convicted of a jury of my peers in participating in horrible and gruesome crimes. Nothing will ever change that. Nothing will ever bring back the victims. But I am asking that you believe me when I tell you, I did not kill anybody. I did not by my own hand kill any human being. I was there. I participated. I did nothing to stop what was going on. It is inexcusable behavior.5

Atkins also sympathized with the families of the victims of her crimes:

> I feel their pain every single day. And I am determined that whether I do if for the rest of my life.... incarcerated, or whether I'm given an opportunity to be a free citizen in this country, then I will do everything in my power to raise the awareness of people in the community to let them know: crime hurts.6

As for her attitude towards Charles Manson, in a 1994 letter in reference to the contemporary uproar over the rock group Guns 'n' Roses recording a version of Manson's song "Look At Your Game, Girl" Atkins wondered:

How can anyone endorse this profiting on the infamy of such a hideous criminal? ....To make a novelty out of person like Charles Manson, whose self-serving wickedness (I can attest) is beyond any of your comprehension, is truly unconscionable.... While, to a younger generation who was not alive at the time, Charles Manson must seem like a cartoon character, I can assure you.... that his depravity and depth of cruelty make him a truly base human being, deserving of no one's attention, let alone admiration.7

Charles Manson later remembered Atkins as well:

Sadie had a nice body when she was young jumping around up there in Frisco. But as soon as she had that baby, she let her body go.... [and] she wasn't gonna get no action. Now, when a broad don't get no action, she's gonna turn around and act like she don't want no action, and stick her nose up in the air and talk about she's somebody else, and then she found Jesus. She had to find Jesus to try to get one man that she could hold up in her so she could get a little action going, because without Jesus, and without one husband tricked off into one hole she wasn't ever gonna get no play anyway.

[But] it doesn't matter or make no difference if I'm mad at Susie. What Susie has already gave to the world -- how could I take away from that? Susie's already a giant. she's a saint. She's already all those things -- to other people, to herself, to her children, to whoever's with her. And that's cool. And I'm with her. And I'm glad that she's got whatever she can get.

(Susan Atkins was denied parole seventeen times and remained incarcerated until she died of brain cancer on September 24, 2009.)

For years after her conviction for murder Patricia Krenwinkel remained a somewhat enigmatic character, and rumors circulated of her continued loyalty towards her former associates and their way of life together. But in reality she soon sized up her prison predicament and came to the terms that would help her survive. As she told a parole board in 1978:

Now you got twenty-three hours a day that you sit in a confined area. You either start dealing with your mind or you go mad. I don't think you have a choice. Because when you're completely isolated for periods of time, when you constantly sit from day to day, you eventually have to deal with your own head.8

In dealing with her own head Krenwinkel put much of the onus for her crimes on drugs and on Charles Manson:

There are many factors involved, such as my own view of myself which was very poor which allowed, between the drugs and someone like Charlie Manson to be able to manipulate those factors within myself that were at work, which were not able to stand up against such kind of manipulation.9

In prison Krenwinkel studied English history and Shakespeare. For a time she worked on the prison newspaper with Leslie Van Houten. She took courses in Earth Sciences and took up oil and acrylic painting and learned to play the guitar.

Asked about her relationship with her female co-defendants, in 1989 Krenwinkel said:

Well, we speak, I mean we're not very close. I think each of us has found our own niche and are involved in our own things, but we all, you know, speak when we see each other. You know, it's an okay relationship. But like I said I think most of us are involved in, have basically developed our own lives. I guess most of us, we've grown apart.10

Four years later, at her 1993 parole hearing, Krenwinkel said of her past:

It's grotesque. It's absolutely horrible. It's very difficult for me to live with the fact that I could do anything so horrible and horrendous. Because that is not who I am. That is not what I believe in.

I always felt that things should be treated with gentleness, tenderness, and love, because that's the most lacking thing that I have found in my life and in most people's lives. I never tried to create something that was ugly, and that's what came out of me. So, I try every day, the best I can, to deal with that. Every day of my life, I try to define to myself that I have a little bit of self-worth, because it is terribly difficult to live with this.... Because I feel terrible about it, but I cannot change it. No matter what they do I cannot change one minute of my life, and as I have said before, I don't expect the board to say that I can go home. I am paying for this as best as I can.... There is nothing more I can do, outside of being dead, to pay for this, and I know that is what you wish. But I cannot take my own life. I'm sorry.11

In an interview broadcast on the 1994 ABC-TV news program *A Turning Point* Krenwinkel recalled Charles Manson as "a man who, I think, felt that society had totally dumped him. I think he felt a rage and hatred for society." Regarding life and events for the people at Spahn's Ranch in the summer of 1969 she said, "There was not one thing done, that was even *allowed* to be done, without [Manson's] express permission."

"Every day, I wake up and know that I'm a destroyer of the most precious things, which is life. And living with that is the most difficult thing of all, and I do that because that's what I deserve, is to wake up every morning and know that."

As far as the continued interest in Manson and the public image of his "Family," Krenwinkel said:

If there's anything I could say to any of those children, is that he is not the man to follow. And I think maybe that's one of the reasons I'm talking, because every once in a while I get letters from children, and they seem to think that what we did was all right. There is nothing -- nothing! -- that we did that is all right. Nothing!

Charles Manson said:

The only thing that holds people like Leslie, Patty, and all those other people, is somebody else. They don't have no center. They're gonna be with whoever has got the banana. And Patty never, never shaved me in any direction. She never lied, she never cheated. I never seen a more perfect person in my life -- until she got on TV.

She must be doing it [turning] because she's afraid of somebody, or somebody's got her mind, or she's trying to do something else for some other reason. I don't know. I guess she's got her reasons for what she's doing.

She's done told two or three lies on TV that I seen. She's lying. So am I gonna get her to admit she's lying on TV when I can't put my hands on her? If I can put my hands on her, then, "Oh, I'm sorry, I didn't mean anything."

Lulu [Leslie Van Houten] and Patty's over there and they probably got four or five of them bull daggin' fucking witches over there in their ass. They got to say not only what they say for them, but they got to say it for the people that they're talking to, and the way they're gonna cut up the interview to suit them, you dig? And they're not gonna put the good foot forward.

Maybe they said some good things that they didn't put on the [program]. Like, we said some good things that they didn't put on the [program]. So it's like there's all kinds of things. And I can't judge Patty.

(Patricia Krenwinkel currently serves her multiple life sentences at the California Institution for Women in Chino, California. She has been denied parole fourteen times, the latest being in 2017. Her next hearing is scheduled for 2022. Krenwinkel has been incarcerated longer than any other woman in the California prison system.)

In 1977 Leslie Van Houten was granted a new trial on the grounds that she had not been represented sufficiently at her original trial because her defense attorney disappeared near the end of those proceedings. The new trial began in January 1977 and lasted for eight months before ending with a deadlocked jury. While awaiting a third trial she was released on bail and enjoyed six months of freedom before being convicted a second time in 1978. Once considered to be the likeliest of Manson's Tate-LaBianca co-defendants to win a parole, her fortunes changed in the 1990s due in large part to the efforts of crime victims' advocacy groups. She has been denied parole ever since. In 2004 she said of her crimes:

> I can't justify them in any way to you. That all I can say is that I have done everything in my power to live a life as a person that doesn't hurt others. I can't -- I can't begin to try to explain them or place the blame on someone else. It was me.

Recalling later how things began to fall apart and become violent at Spahn's Ranch, Van Houten told a parole board:

> It didn't start out that way [violently]. It started out like a commune. And then the more [Manson] would measure how much we believed in him, then the violence would become more acute until at the end when it was very, very prevalent.... He would slap people more for questioning him and become more abusive verbally. And my role there was that I was the dumb one that didn't know anything.... He poked fun of [my parents] and over a process and a period of time where he defined our values so that they became his, by making fun of the ones I had been raised with.
>
> [Once] I wanted to leave and I told him I was going to leave. And he took me to the edge of a cliff and he told me that I may as well just jump because if I left, I would die. And I -- Now you know, when you say something like that years and years and years and years later, and it seems so small. But at the time, I believed him. I believed that if I left him, that I would be -- Well that if I left him, the very same thing that happened to Leno and Rosemary LaBianca would happen to me.12

When asked about Manson at her 1991 parole hearing, Van Houten responded:

> I feel that he's a very pitiful and pathetic human being and that I'm very sorry that people still continue to give him attention, that his only danger is in the attention he's given. If he were ignored and left alone he would probably just fade away.13

In 1996 she said, "I resent his dishonesty in [not] assuming his responsibility for his part in the crime. I have no relationship with him. He's just a creep."

And, "[Charles Manson is] an opportunist of the cruelest, most vicious kind, [for] his own [ag]grandizement.... At the time he seemed like a big deal. And I feel very responsible for creating a monster."14

Manson to Van Houten:

> You're only talking to yourself. You're only lying to yourself, because we *know* what happened. You can't bullshit *us*. Leslie - turncoat

-- she done us wrong, so now she's turning around and trying to put it back off on me.

She's the one that went back for the new trial. When we was supposed to get a new trial, they wouldn't give us a new trial. Then she sold out and took the new trial. So when she sold out and took our new trial, she dumped us all down the shitter for her own ambition.

Figure that Green [Van Houten] is mean because she's got some reason for what she's saying. See, I don't judge the girl. I know her, you dig? I know she's got a reason, if she's doing that she's up on what she's doing. That's the reason I say, "Praise Yellow [Patricia Krenwinkel] all the way." I love her, no matter what. That is word, see. Maybe she's playing for a local establishment, and she wants to get in the prison union and air her grievances about the treatment that her children are receiving.

At the ranch, sure, Leslie and Patty were right there.... [But Leslie] didn't know three things I was thinking. She was just an airhead broad that was just hanging around the ranch that Bobby left.... I started to make it with her, man, but like, uh, sexually she just wasn't there, man. Not to me. I didn't have time. I didn't have time to get to know everybody.

I got to know Pat a little bit. And Pat never did lie. But when she was on TV, she lied about two or three things, you know.

Green is telling me where she's at and what her perspective is in Green. She's not wrong in what she's saying. She's *perfect* in what she's saying. What she's saying is perfect in the mind that she's perfect in. We can't look down at her like she's wrong, because we can't see what she's looking at. She may be surrounded by something we don't understand. So we accept what she's saying as being the reality and the life in what she's saying, because the truth is, when Green and I go behind the barn, Green belongs to me. I'll do anything I want. And she'll agree and say anything I want her to say, if that's the game we want to play. But that's not the game I want to play. I want her to be herself and say and do what's best for her survival. Because if she can survive, I'll be the baby in that. I'll be a little baby [on] the floor in that, because if I can survive in my air, and my water, and my bugs, and my trees, and my zoo -- that's what I'm looking out for. I'm not looking out for the personalities of people who need to go on TV.

You know, LuLu's got a whole bunch of shit in her head. And I think she believes half that trash. And she wants to believe it because it's good for her position to believe that. And if someone was paying her five dollars a day to believe it, she would believe it more. But.... if I'm standing there looking at her, she'd start melting. And then she'd just start going through all of her changes.... I wouldn't have to say anything.

(Leslie Van Houten is currently serving her sentence at the California Institution for Women in Chino, California. After over twenty denials, on April 14, 2016 a California Parole Board finally granted Van Houten's request for parole. Any celebration on her part was short lived, however, as then California Governor Jerry Brown overruled the Board's decision because, "both her role in these extraordinarily brutal crimes and her inability to explain her willing participation in such horrific violence cannot be overlooked and lead me to believe she remains an unacceptable risk to society if released."15 She was recommended for parole again in 2017 but Governor Brown again vetoed her release. Her legal team then appealed Brown's decision in court but the judge ruled against her, stating, "Unless the inmate can demonstrate that there is no evidence to support the governor's conclusion that the inmate is a current danger to public safety, the petition fails to state a prima facie case for relief and may be summarily denied."16 Apparently Van Houten's forty-plus years of cooperative and nonviolent behavior during her incarceration was not considered to be suitable evidence that she was not a danger to public safety. In 2019 Van Houten was recommended for parole yet again, but yet again the recommendation was overruled, this time by Governor Gavin Newsom, who stated that she was still a danger to society and had a potential for future violence.)

In a trial separate from the Tate-LaBianca proceedings Bruce Davis was convicted for the murders of Gary Hinman and Donald "Shorty" Shea. Like the other persons convicted along with Charles Manson, Davis has long since seen the error of his earlier ways. At his 1993 parole hearing, the man who once told reporters that he was turning himself in to face a murder charge to help Charles Manson because "he would do it for me"17 remembered when he decided it was time to distance himself from his former friend:

> In 1973, I was in Folsom, we went down to L.A. for somebody's trial, and somebody called us as witnesses. Something happened in the county jail, or -- I don't remember exactly. But anyway, we were on the

same bus -- on the CDC bus together. They picked up Manson in San Quentin, I suppose, came by Folsom and got me. I think Steve Grogan was there....

And so we had a bus trip. And I was sitting next to Manson. And I was talking to him about whatever, and he still acted like everything was okay and that, that us being in prison was just, it was nothing. It was like, "Well, let's see now, what are we going to do?" I mean, he was just carrying on as if nothing had happened.

And I began to think, you know, "You don't, you don't care what's going on with anybody. And you don't.... seem to realize or care that, man, there's people in prison for the rest of their lives, as far as they know. And people are dead and it didn't work out anything like it was put up it was going to work out like. And you're still wanting us to go for the same old thing? Something's terribly wrong here."

And I began to really question at that point.... And I began to look at this and go, "Wait a minute, something is really -- I mean, this sure is crazy."18

In 2000 Davis recalled his life at the ranch and why he stayed, even after things got violent:

You know, in a sense I wasn't opposed to what other people did, to what they did. I mean, I wouldn't have suggested it but they did it and I certainly wasn't going to tell them I was opposed to it.... And I knew -- Hey, when Gary Hinman got killed I wasn't sure that -- I wasn't sure that was going to happen but when it did happen then I -- I knew.... Well, anyway after Gary got killed I knew I should have left. I didn't. I had adopted Charlie as my dad, my father figure. Now, I didn't tell him that and we didn't have any ceremony but it was something that was in me. So I -- I was -- I just was not equipped to leave in my head.19

Charles Manson remembered:

I helped Bruce. Bruce would have been over there on the same job, doing the same thing, had he not met me. He would have never played the guitar. He would have never done anything but go over there and work on a pipeline until he retired. The same thing with Bobby. Bobby would have married that girl and went on down the road, and maybe he would have been happy. Instead, I altered the course of everybody's life at that ranch.

I get disgusted with, and I'm mad at someone, and I say, "Well, I'm not gonna never talk to Bruce again. Bruce said bad things, so I'm never gonna talk to Bruce again." You know, I'm not judging Bruce. If Bruce was here, Bruce could go through his changes and air his grievances to the mirror on the wall. It doesn't matter to me. Or, he don't have to say anything. It doesn't matter to me.

But if Bruce is gonna be at the ranch, if he's gonna survive, and he's gonna work at the ranch, and I'm paying the bills, and I'm paying the rent, then Bruce will do what the hell ever Bruce is told to do. Just like it works in the military. If Bruce is a sergeant and I'm a lieutenant, and I tell him, "Stand to attention, mister!" Mr. Bruce will stand to attention. There's nothing wrong with that. There's a certain chain of command. If George [Spahn] said, "Get off the ranch," what did I do? I never had to get off the ranch. I could have told George, "Fuck you. You can't see. I can do what I want." But I never did that. I said, "Yes, sir." I respected him.

(Bruce Davis was sentenced to two life terms for his convictions in the murders of Gary Hinman and Donald "Shorty" Shea. In 1973 he was saved by Jesus Christ. He is currently imprisoned at the California Men's Colony in San Luis Obispo. A regular parole hearing attendee, he was first recommended for parole by the Board of Prison Terms in 2010 but that decision was vetoed by California's governor, Arnold Schwarzenegger. Two years later he was recommended again, but Governor Jerry Brown also refused to go along with the Parole Board's decision, saying, "Until Davis can acknowledge and explain why he actively championed the family's interests and shed more light on the nature of his involvement, I am not prepared to release him. After forty-two years of incarceration, it is encouraging that Davis is beginning to reveal the actual details of what happened. But it is clear that he continues to withhold information about these events."20 Davis was again approved for parole in 2014, 2015, and 2017 but all decisions were subsequently rescinded by the governor. On June 28, 2019, at his thirty-second parole hearing, Davis was approved for parole for the sixth time. As of this writing the board's decision is awaiting review by Governor Gavin Newsom. Bruce Davis is seventy-six years old.)

Although he has never overtly denounced Charles Manson, Bobby Beausoleil told a parole board in 1992, "there is no love lost between me and that individual." Beausoleil has always denied the pre-arrests existence of anything called a "Manson Family," that he was ever a "member " of said "family," or that he was aware of any Helter Skelter plan to take over the world. He has always supported the idea that the murders on Cielo and Waverly Drives were committed as reactions to his arrest for the murder of Gary Hinman.

In May of 1994 Beausoleil was granted a request to be transferred to the Oregon State Penitentiary. He has maintained his interest in music while incarcerated and has been involved with many musical projects both inside and outside of the prison. He is also an accomplished artist. Beausoleil remained in the Oregon prison system until 2015, when he was returned to California.

In 2000 he told a parole board:

> I'm very sorry for what had happened in my relationship with Mr. Hinman. He was a friend. I feel that I have come a long way in the past thirty years in understanding the dynamics of the choices that I -- surrounding the choices that I had made. I've sought every way available to me to make amends to the community, to both the outside community and the community in which I live, in the human community. I believe that I have a great deal to offer, and I'm certainly not a danger to anyone.21

Manson:

> Bobby wants to be me. He's wanted to be me since the day he seen me. Everything he does has been trying to be me. Now he's me, but he's better than me. He's been better than me. But he's such a damn fool that he don't see himself as being what he is. He wants to be something that he thinks is an illusion that's me and that's not me.
>
> After all the shit we went through, to get Bobby out of jail, when Bobby was going to trial his lawyers wrote and told me, "This guy's gonna testify against you."
>
> So I wrote Bobby a note and I said, "Go ahead and tell 'em anything they want to hear, 'cause one of us out is better than two of us in." So I saved his ass again. I've been saving him all the way down the line. He

didn't have to do what he did. I backed him, whatever he did, because I thought he was a brother, you know.

When [Beausoleil] stabbed Hinman in the heart? It's like, when you got a veteran that puts his life on the line for you and fights another battle for you, he goes into war for you, and he gives you his life in the battlefield, he gets [stood] up to attention, he eats shit, he does KP duty, he does pushups. He wears funny clothes. He's gotta go through all that degradation shit. And he goes through all that shit for you, and your country and your God, I mean, you're supposed to have some gratitude for that man. You're supposed to have some compassion for someone that would do that for you.

But then he won't even answer your letters. What kind of brother is that? We went through twenty-five years of hell for that asshole. And he hasn't done a Goddamn thing but run off down the road and change his name to "Lucifer." I heard he's calling himself "Lucifer" now. [But] whatever he calls himself, he still owes that ranch.

(Bobby Beausoleil is currently serving his sentence at the California Medical Facility at Vacaville. He is seventy-one years old. On January 3, 2019, after eighteen previous failed suitability hearings, Beausoleil was approved for parole by the California Board of Prison Terms. But like Van Houten and Davis before him, any optimism about future freedom was dashed when Governor Gavin Newsom reversed the board's decision. In his reversal, in which he "carefully examined the record" Newsom said that the Hinman murder was the first in a series of homicides that were committed in "an attempt to start a civilization-ending race war." He also made the heretofore unheard of -- and false -- claim that "Mr. Manson sliced Mr. Hinman's throat."22)

Like Davis and Van Houten before him, Bobby Beausoleil is not a prisoner of his past. Instead, he continues to be imprisoned because of a false narrative that, as part of the official court record, is unfortunately accepted by the powers that be as true. In almost a dozen instances California Parole Boards have found Bruce Davis, Leslie Van Houten, and Bobby Beausoleil to be suitable candidates for release. In just as many instances California governors have overruled the boards' decisions.

In California the governor cannot reverse a Parole Board's decision to release an inmate "unless there is firm evidence indicating they are still a threat," according to a spokesperson for Governor Brown in 2014.23 But in the cases of Van Houten, Davis, and Beausoleil there is no evidence that any one of them is currently a threat. Indeed, none of them has engaged in any kind of violent or dangerous behavior since their commitment offenses over half a century ago.

By any reasonable observation none of the three "Manson Family members" who have earned their parole can seriously be considered to be a danger to public safety. They are elderly, tired, and worn. They have submitted one hundred percent to the system that imprisons them -- only to discover too late that the same beast they warred against in 1969 is still warring against them today.

How different things were for Steve Grogan! Grogan was convicted of the murder of Donald Shea in 1971, but by 1977 he had a change of heart and cooperated with authorities in locating Shea's missing body. As he explained to a parole board in 1981:

> It was, I think, [a] culmination of my growing and maturing and coming to grips with myself about the crime and what I did, the acknowledgment, the fact that I was tired of lying, having to tell everybody I didn't do it, [the] lie that I perpetrated, the fact that I wouldn't own to the responsibility. There were a lot of facets that, you know, they add to my coming forth for this disclosure of where the body was.24

Another factor in Grogan's turnaround was the empathy he developed for Shea after his own stabbing by members of a prison gang in 1977:

> Plus [an] incident happened in '77 which really made me cognizant in a way that put me in my victim's shoes, the attack that was led on me. You know, I -- that made me cognizant of the act that I did to the other person, what he must have felt, the terror and fear when I was being stabbed.25

In apologizing for his crime, Grogan said:

I'm not trying to make excuses for what I did. There's no excuse for what I did. There's no justifiable motivation for my crime regardless of what they told me on the ranch and my fear. I'm not trying to make, you know, blame it on anybody and, you know, excuse myself or any actions I did. What I did was totally wrong, against all the morals I have ever been brought up with in society. I'm not excusing that at all.26

Grogan's age at the time of his crime was a major factor in his being granted a release. At one parole hearing Grogan commented on his age and how it contributed to his perception of his manipulation by Charles Manson:

I was young, sixteen years old, you know. I was vulnerable to any hustler what would want to hustle me, really, because of my lack of street experience, my lack of just being out in the world, period. I probably would have gone for anything, hook, line, and sinker, any salesman or hustler that wanted to hustle me, because they caught me at that age, that point of vulnerability. I was manipulated very easily. My defenses for what [Manson] had for me were, you know, almost non-existent. It was two years after I was already incarcerated that I realized the games that he had run on me, psychological games. I was over my head, out of my awareness.

In looking back, I had a child's mind. I was thinking like a child. I was being led around and influenced like a child.27

He also recalled how he split from his former friends:

Well, after couple of years being in prison, after reflecting clear in my head, all the cobwebs, what I call the drug residue, I just started thinking. I came to myself. Man, I started thinking, well, what am I doing with these people? Man, why am I still even letting them write to me?

So I cut them loose….

To them there's no getting out. Because it's -- it's kind of difficult to explain, I guess, the attachment they had to each person that was involved with them over the years and they didn't want to let go of it…. It's like we're supposed to be bonded together for life, you know, for eternity. Almost to a, like a vow, you know, to that. That was their viewpoint of my involvement with them and I didn't see it that way. And they was highly upset that I would leave them and just told them to get the heck away.28

And, like his former cohorts from 1969, Grogan conveyed his sense of remorse for his former life:

I want to express the feeling that it was a terrible thing that I did and there's nothing I can do to change what already happened. I can't undo it. It's already done. The only thing that I can do is what I've been doing in changing myself as a person and making my own safeguards that something like that will never happen again.29

Manson:

When I pulled Steve up to where he was at, he was in the garbage can. I pulled him out of the garbage can. He didn't have any *shoes* on. He was running with dogs. I pulled him up, man, I said, "Come here, go woo woo." So I bring him up, show him the lifestyle, show him what we're doing. He takes my motions -- he moves just like me now. You know, he can move. He's a sharp young man, now. He plays music better than I play. He took what I was playing and then improved on all that. He took the game I was playing and took it and improved on it.

He's not turned his back on me. I never told him, I never put any, any membership on him. I mean, you know, he's always did what he wanted to do. I never told him what he could do or couldn't do.

[On giving up Donald Shea's body], here's what he did. He went and said [name deleted] if it was alright if he told 'em where the body was so he could make parole. And she said, "Yeah," and everybody said, "Yeah," you know. I don't say he did, I don't say he didn't.

Everybody that was there is still there, in my mind. There's no difference.

Clem is, like, one hundred percent for Clem. He's taken everything we've taught him and applied it to him. Which is cool, you know.... I don't think he wants to see anybody but Clem. He's pretty much into what he's doing and he doesn't want to do anything to drag him back from what he wants to do. But now, whenever I'm around Clem, Clem will do whatever I tell him, just like always. Which practically everybody does anyway. But see, I never realized that.

See, there's a lot of things I never realized. I wasn't trying to be nobody's leader. I wasn't trying to be nobody's boss. It's just automatically that I start looking out for everything around me. I look out for my own life, and then in doing that I look out for everybody's life that's involved with my life. It's like, we were on the mainline at the ranch.

And I ran the ranch just like I did the mainline. And that was for my survival. I wasn't trying to be nobody's anything.

But I've learned a lot since then. I didn't want to be a leader [and] I still don't want to be a leader. But I still have certain obligations to keep going with this ATWA. I don't have no choice.

(Steve Grogan was sentenced to death for his role in the murder of Donald "Shorty" Shea, but the judge in his case reduced the sentence to life imprisonment based on the contention that Grogan was too much under the influence of Charles Manson to make his own decisions. Grogan programed well in prison, learning a trade in aircraft mechanics and perfecting his musical and artistic talents. He was released on September 18, 1985 and has remained clean ever since. He is currently a musician in California.)

While the attitude changes of Charles Manson's convicted crime partners might well have been due to genuine remorse, Manson himself had his own insights into why his former associates seemingly turned against him:

A big part of the reason that people started denying one another is because if they went to the parole board and said that they had any contact -- like that's why nobody would write me and Red [Lynette Fromme]. They were made to believe or know that if they had any contact with us they would never get out. So then their minds started turning and believing that everything was negative about, everything.

They have kept us apart for twenty-five years. And everything that they have offered to those people has been "You go against Charlie and we'll let you do this. If you don't go against Charlie we're gonna keep you locked up over here." So it's pretty much "go against Charlie" to go anywhere or do anything, they've had to compromise their own original position, and justify it in their own minds to where they've had to go against me all the way down the line or they'd still be in solitary confinement.

All of them people that don't want to talk to me? That's because they're afraid to listen to what they're thinking about themselves. They don't want that no more. They want to go off into that illusion. That's cool. [But] they'll come back around whenever they see that it's best for them that they do.

I'm the worst fucking animal in the zoo. But the people at the ranch, they showed me kindness, I tried to reflect that, and I tried to be right with that....

I did a lot of bad, mean things to people who misused somebody that was with me. If you're with me, if somebody misuses you, that's misusing me. Then I get nasty. I get very, very mean. I'm very protective towards me, my own circle.... I got along good with you guys [ranch people] because we was all in a mission, we was all going for something, for the earth.

Everything I've ever done in my life has been wrong. I've always been wrong. And everything I've done's been a mistake. I've never done anything right in my whole life, according to *anyone*. That's the reason I was by myself, doing what I do. Because *I* don't even think I ever *made* a mistake. I didn't know what the hell a mistake is. If I make a mistake, I'm gone. I live in a world, if I make a mistake, that's it. I make a mistake, somebody steps in and takes it. I haven't dropped it. I haven't dropped one step. I haven't dropped one stitch. I'm still on everything that we was on before, but the only thing that I fell down was, I fell down when I was standing on other people's words. When I was standing on what other people told me, then I started falling down when they started falling down.... then everybody started sluffing a little bit, and falling back a little bit, and not doing this a little bit, and then pretty soon it just fell apart.

Everybody wanted to see what Manson was doing. Now, the only thing they have seen in the last twenty-five years is the cover-up over Manson. They had never seen Manson. Because they don't want to look at Manson. But that's cool with Manson, because Manson don't give a fuck about none of 'em anyway. He only cares about the ones that was with him. Now, even if you dump me, like Patty did, what about all the times, the good, the wonder of what she did to start with? I can't divorce myself from all the giving that she's already gave. In other words, you bake me a loaf of bread that's good, and you feed me for ten years, and then you bring me a stone to eat, I can get mad at you, but look at all the good you've done, you know. I see your misunderstandings, and I see how you fell down in your own mind, because you've let your mind be influenced by all those who are expert at influencing other minds. She fell back underneath that same old brainwash that she was locked into in school. That's all that is.

You know, each person is a world. Do you see that? Everybody's world that was on that ranch gave their world to one thought. They can't take it back. They can try to take it back, but they can't take it back because it's locked in eternity. You don't go sacrifice nine or ten people and make a circle and then say that you're sorry.

I didn't plot none of this. I wasn't out to be a hippie cult leader. I wasn't out to be nobody's leader or boss, I wasn't headed in this direction. I got pushed into this episode, whether I liked it or not. I sometimes look at other people and I think I failed, because I wasn't aware of things. I just didn't think about stuff like that, you know. I wasn't aware of cults or what a leader was. I was an ignorant hillbilly. I still am a stupid hillbilly. I don't have any idea about all those things. I'm not the guy that everybody's made me into be. I got stuck in the position of, uh, whatever this Manson character is, you know. I appreciate you not turning against me, like Patty and all them guys. But in the end, all those people will turn back around to that ranch, because that ranch was only a mirror. Because believe me, I'm not very smart, but I do know how to reflect people back. And that's what I did. I reflected.

Everybody at that ranch has developed their own point of view towards everything. And everybody's got me doing all the things that they need me to do, whether that's what I did or not. And I think that I'm guilty of doing the same thing. It's like, Bobby's got me as doing whatever was best for whatever his position was. And Steve has got me in the position of being, doing, and saying everything for what's best for what he's doing. And so has Tex. Tex has got me over here with the devil because he wants to go church and do what he's doing, you dig? And everybody's got me in a different place, and I'm thinking to myself, "Well, where in the hell am I, really? And, really, where *are* we going?"

Whatever you do is your own fucking business. I don't care what you do. That's your mind, that's your life. I don't get in your life telling you nothing. But if you come over in my life, and you're in my life, and you're doing what I'm doing, then you got to do it my way.

If I'm in your life, and you're gonna climb a mountain, and I say, "Hey, can I come over and climb that mountain?"

And you say, "Yeah."

I say, "Okay. Then we'll do it the way you say to do it. And I'll be totally and completely in submission and in harmony with however you want to do it. If you want to do it backwards, we'll do it backwards."

But if you come into me and say, "What are you doing? Can I come?"

And I say, "Yeah, come on."

And then you tell me, "Let's go around the other side."

I say, "No, no, no. I'm doing it. I'm doing it my way. Now, if you want to come with me and do this, okay."

So you say, "Okay, I'm coming with you to do this." So, we're all in this ranch thing together.

And we're doing this thing together. And then, all these people are gonna do doo doo doo doo doo, and it all matches up, everybody puts their little two cents in, I put my little two cents in -- everybody's got a little bit into this investment, okay? Gypsy's got her little thing in, Mary's got her little thing in, T.J. goes as far as he can, everybody's got a quarter, somebody's got a dollar, somebody's got fifty cent, everybody's got a different little investment in this particular venture. And I'm obligated to everybody because everybody's got me in the middle, because I'm so stupid that I really don't know what's going on outside. If I did I'd have got out of there the first chance I got. But I didn't know.

So I was the clown in that outfit and I got caught up in everybody else's problems.

So then everybody else left the coats and hats and put the blame on me and ran down the road and said it was all my fault. I could have easily said it was all *you* guys' fault. You got me involved in that. You got me trapped up in that. You got me fighting your fights and your wars and helping you with your problems, and then when you got your problems straightened around, and I got in over my head and I couldn't help you no more, then you just turned around and dumped me and went back to your mother.

You only used me when your mother didn't want you, when your boyfriend didn't write you. You only wanted me when your father kicked you out of the house and you didn't have no place else to go. And then, as soon as you got another place to go, you went back to your father....

So, everybody went off and left me holding the bag....

I know there's nine dead bodies, and somebody's gonna be responsible for those nine dead bodies. And I'm tired of holding up the Goddamn fucking heat on it. You can accuse me of being responsible for that, and I'll take my share of responsibility, just like everybody else. But there's one thing I'm not responsible [for]. Would you hear me well on this? I'm not responsible to society to tell them any of my business. And anybody past that ranch and past George [Spahn], I don't owe no explanations to *anything*.

So then, when Patty thinks that I'm supposed to get up and tell the world my part in this cosmic drama of mayhem and madness, you know, my part in this play -- God knows it. And that's the only guy I got to live with.

Chapter Notes

1 All Manson speech in this chapter is compiled from tape-recorded telephone conversations between Charles Manson and Sandra Good or the author.
2 *Will You Die For Me?*, page 29.
3 Ibid.
4 Charles Watson 2001 parole hearing transcript page 21.
5 Susan Atkins 1993 parole hearing transcript page 13.
6 Ibid., page 104.
7 Lost source.
8 Patricia Krenwinkel 1978 parole hearing transcript page 27.
9 Patricia Krenwinkel 1988 parole hearing transcript page 31.
10 Patricia Krenwinkel 1989 parole hearing transcript page 40.
11 Patricia Krenwinkel 1993 parole hearing transcript pages 74-75.
12 Leslie Van Houten 2004 parole hearing transcript, pages 25, 60-61.
13 Transcribed from a video of Van Houten's 1991 parole hearing.
14 Transcribed from a video of Van Houten's 1996 parole hearing.
15 As reported by the Associated Press on 22 July 2016.
16 *Los Angeles Times*, 29 June 2018.
17 This is on the Channel 2 KCBS (then KNXT) tape.
18 Bruce Davis 1993 parole hearing transcript pages 77-78.
19 Bruce Davis 2000 parole hearing transcript page 27.
20 See http://bigstory.ap.org/article/calif-governor-rule-ex-manson-follower
21 Bobby Beausoleil 2000 parole hearing transcript page 23.
22 From California Governor Gavin Newsom's ruling on Bobby Beausoleils' parole recommendation, April 26th, 2019
23 See: www.cbsnews.com/news/1400-lifers-released-from-california-prisons-in-last-3-years/
24 Steve Grogan 1981 parole hearing transcript page 28.
25 Steve Grogan 1982 parole hearing transcript, page 29.
26 Ibid., page 27.
27 Steve Grogan 1979 parole hearing transcript pages 30 & 61.
28 Steve Grogan 1981 parole hearing transcript pages 35 & 37.
29 Steve Grogan 1980 parole hearing transcript page 23.

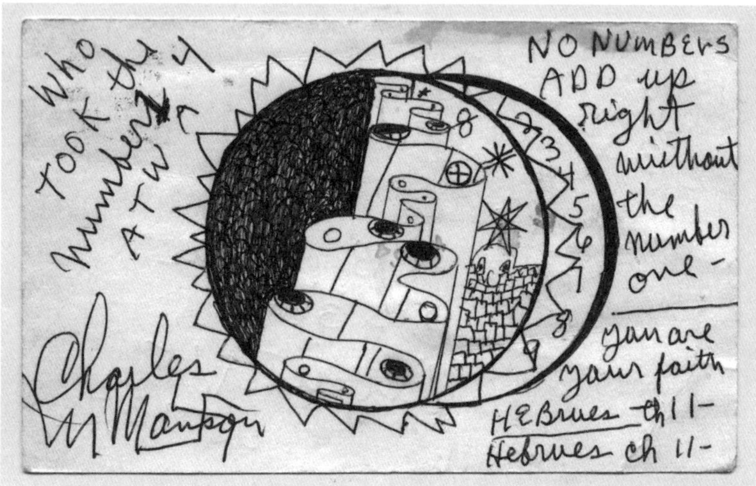
Who TOOK the number 1 AWAY
NO NUMBERS ADD up right without the number one -
you are your faith
HEBrues ch11-
Hebrues ch 11-
Charles M Manson

Charles Manson

"All my life I've lived in total paranoia."

-- Charles Manson

The central character in the entire Tate-LaBianca murders experience has always been Charles Manson. And today, fifty years after those murders, Manson is still the subject of much public interest and interpretation.

Whenever someone finds out that I knew Charles Manson the first question is always, "What was he like?"

Well, even though I might be better positioned to answer that question than most people, before trying to give an answer I have to qualify my relationship with Manson by saying that I have only been with him in the singular and heavily restricted conditions of the Security Housing Unit (SHU) or the Protective Housing Unit (PHU) visiting rooms at the California State Prison at Corcoran (and once in the maximum security, non-contact visiting room at the Pelican Bay State Prison in Crescent City). Therefore, I can only comment on how I perceived him in those situations.

Between 1991 and 2001 I visited Charles Manson almost two hundred times. Sixty or so of those visits took place while Manson was confined in SHU. The rest -- well over a hundred -- occurred when he was in PHU. My first visit with Manson occurred in the Corcoran SHU visiting room on May 31, 1991.

Goodbye Helter Skelter

When I first meet people I try not to jump to conclusions about them, and Charles Manson was no exception. But I couldn't say that I had nothing in my mind when I initially met him.

To begin with, I had the residue of countless books, newspaper and magazine articles, television programs, and other media that, for the most part, described him as "the most dangerous man alive."

Then I also had input from people like Sandra Good, who assured me that Manson's seldom surpassed reputation for evil was overstated.

Finally, there was my own impression -- which came across through all that I had read and seen about him -- that he seemed to be a person I could get along with.

That was in the beginning. Almost two hundred visits and hundreds of phone calls later, I managed to gain some insights into Charles Manson based on my personal, firsthand experiences with him. And the main insight I gained was that when it comes to Manson it's best to let him speak for himself.

But before trying to find out what Charles Manson was like it would perhaps be a good idea to determine what he was *not* like.

When a reader consults *Helter Skelter*, "the true story of the Manson murders," for insights into Charles Manson's thinking, he is given four pages of text which basically reduce the influences on Manson's philosophy to two sources: The Process Church of the Final Judgement and Adolf Hitler. (Sometimes other sources of Manson's alleged philosophy are also claimed. The July 1999 issue of *Us* magazine, for example, also listed Buddhism, Friedrich Nietzsche, Scientology, and Satanism.)

The first supposed influence listed in *Helter Skelter* is based, in part, by the fact that recruiters for the alternative "religions" of Scientology and Dianetics were active in some of the prisons where Manson was incarcerated prior to his release in 1967. But while such recruiters did exist, they made little impression on Charles Manson. Decades later he remembered:

> A lot of the guys [in prison] were interested in studying the way to process the mind and how to clear your mind from past confusion, how to resurrect the soul and be reborn within yourself. So that's where Sci-

entology started. And then they started selling it, and then it got to be the Process, and then the Church of the Last Day, the Last Judgment.

Although Manson was exposed to such teachings, he was not really impressed by them. "They'd come to me with that old ancient- ass shit that I had already been through, and it wasn't nothing but kicking the dirt around as far as I was concerned. It never really touched me."

Branching off from this basic misinformation about the influences of the Process Church and Scientology on Manson is another well publicized, but false, facet of the man: his supposed connection with Satanic groups. This idea has been around since shortly after the arrests for the murders in 1969 and sprang partly from the early media reports that the murders on Cielo Drive appeared to be devilishly ritualistic.

The concept of a Satanic Manson got an early boost with the release of the 1970 book *The Family*. This book, which is unfortunately considered to be one of the primary sources of information on Charles Manson and some of the people around him, is full of anonymously attributed Satanic adventures and anecdotes. None of these tales can be verified, and with good reason: they are not true. (The author Ed Sanders wrote these unsubstantiated horror stories with such a reckless abandonment of accuracy that after the initial release of the book the Process Church of the Final Judgment successfully sued him and his publisher to have all mention of it removed from future editions.)

The "Manson-Satan" connection got an even greater boost during the national Satanism scare of the late 1980s with the Geraldo Rivera *Satanism* special that was broadcast on syndicated television channels in 1988. This special included scenes of satanic ritual sites, interviews with experts on the subject, a woman who claimed to have sacrificed her own baby on an alter to the devil, and sections of an interview that Manson granted to a then-member of Anton LaVey's Church of Satan. One quote from Manson that got much airplay, "I guess you could call me Satan," was played to the public as proof of Manson's "self-professed role" as the devil incarnate.

But in my opinion the Manson-Satan connection is really just another example of the media sensationalism inherent in the "Manson is the devil" explanation for the circumstances surrounding the Tate-LaBianca murders. In conversations with me Manson rarely discussed Satanism in any manner. In fact I can't remember any specific conversation about it at all. But I do remember Manson's reply to a reporter who asked him about his supposed connections to the Church of Satan. "I'm too stupid for any of that," he said.

While it is true that Charles Manson was exposed to many alternative (i.e., non-Christian) philosophies, and that he was knowledgeable of them, their effect on him was minimal.

But if Manson wasn't a devil worshipper (or the devil himself), what was his religion? What did he think of God? Manson said:

> God is everywhere. God is nobody. God is no one. God isn't anyone. He's *all* of us. God is eighty horses in a corral, thirty-five dogs. God is my crow, my birds. God is George [Spahn]. God is everybody at that ranch, as far as I was concerned. That ranch was God.
>
> The sun is God. We don't need no dead man on a stick for God. Good God, man! An idiot would worship a dead man on a stick! What kind of crazy shit is that? You know what I'm saying? The whole fucking world has been doing that for two thousand years because they won't admit they want to execute their children.
>
> Jesus Christ was not God. He was just a prophet. A prophet is just simply somebody that's aware of something. If you can read the signs on the road and somebody else can't, you're a prophet, because you know when the road's gonna turn and they don't. So they would have a tendency to call you a prophet, because they're stupid.

Did Manson consider himself to be a prophet?

> It's not that I'm smarter than anyone else; I'm not. It's just that I've been in prison longer than anyone else. So when I got out I seen a more pure picture of what was going on....
>
> Then I began to wake up. And as I began to wake up I influenced everybody at that ranch. I brought everybody into my mind, everybody into the thought of one world, of one mind, of one peace on earth. And I tried to bring everybody into the thought of that One....

I was a servant, to God.... whatever God is. It's just a word.... Someone'll say, "Well, you're God." – [No], I'm just a witness to God.

It has often been said, usually with incredulity and disdain, that Charles Manson subscribes to a philosophy wherein God and the devil are the same, and/or that all people have God and the devil in them. Usually, this idea is advanced as another example of Manson's supposedly schizophrenic thinking. In reality, it is just an articulation of the concept of duality and the idea that people have within them both "good" and "bad." Manson:

In China, and in Japan, and in the Orient, Abraxas ia a reality. It's similar to [Ying and Yang]. It's Christ and the devil in one. They believe that Abraxas is the axis that everything turns on. There's two of them. There's one with God and there's one with the devil.

But an intelligent man knows that God and the devil are his own interpretation. Omar Kayam said that "I myself am heaven and hell. I am God, and I am the devil, within my own existence and my understanding of both. I must balance and dance with my own eternity." That's what we are. That's what we're about. That's what the "Manson Family" was about. We're trying to balance all the worlds and all the religions of all the worlds and all the people of all the worlds. We're trying to balance everybody's mind into one mind so that we can have one government long enough to fix the air and get up off the ocean. Because the ocean is dying because we're dumping too much stuff in the ocean. And without an international court, without an international police force, we're not gonna have any fish left in the ocean, because everybody's overdoing it. They're destroying the whole planet because we won't submit ourselves to one thought. One God. We're all fighting each other for some stupid thing that was leftover from some dead people.

That's what our music is about. That what our sacrifices were about. That's what our lives were about. They've lied about us, they've cheated us, they've sold us, they've dumped all their confusion on us, they've done everything they could do to us.... because our efforts were for a holy war, the same holy war that's been going on since the first man woke up to what the will of God really is.

When you wake up that you're God, you're always in the nut ward. When you wake up that everybody's God, and that God's in control of everything, then you've got to be crazy because you believe in God. Because anybody that believes in God has gotta be crazy. Because nobody believes in God. The church is the biggest cover-up over God in the world. That's all they do is cover up God.

[So] it's all one God to me. I'm looking at one God. I'm not looking at two Gods. I'm looking at all Gods in one God, man.

Returning to the second of the influences listed by Vincent Bugliosi as being the major molders of Charles Manson's mind, it has often been written and stated that Manson regarded Adolf Hitler as his hero. But what did Manson himself say about it?

I think Hitler was a concerned citizen who tried to put some order into the world. People didn't see the reality of what he was saying. They still don't.

He was a good man. They told so many lies about that guy....

Can you imagine how powerful he must have been to have all that love stand up for him like that? Look at all the people standing up, raising their hands for him.

When I was kid, the way they portrayed that guy, man, I always thought he was a tyrant, [that] he was just a terrible person. But in the perspective [of Hitler's reality], you've got to be a terrible person. In other words, you can't be a "good" dictator. Benevolence only goes so far. If you're gonna survive, if your horses are gonna survive, you've got to be whatever it takes to survive. You ain't go no choice.

But what about the swastika that Manson had on his forehead for over forty-five years? Isn't that an indication of some sort of sympathy or support for the ideas of Hitler and National Socialism? To the contrary, Manson viewed the swastika in an overall context as a symbol that has occurred in countless cultures for thousands of years as a universally regarded symbol of good fortune -- and of life itself:

We all worship the sun god, [and] the swastika is the sun god symbol. It's the symbol of the sun as being God. It's the coming of Christ. It's Christ's witness to what really is God. And God is the sun. It's not a man. It's not a dead man on a stick. It's not a woman. It's not anything but the energy that we live in. And beyond the energy that we live in, we submit ourselves to these little marks. And we put these marks on our heads.

As for Adolf Hitler's would-be heirs, the so-called "white power movement" in the United States, Manson mostly viewed it with contempt. Certainly its members did nothing to help the most politically abused white man since Rudolf Hess. When it came to "the movement," Manson perhaps summed up his attitude best when he said:

> The American Nazi Party is the worst thing that ever happened to the Nazi Party. The American Nazi Party made the Nazi Party look terrible. A bunch of fat, sloppy, fucking assholes. A bunch of fruitcakes is what it was.

But despite this assessment of his purported peer group, was Charles Manson a racist? Manson was certainly conscious of his race (as are most people in this racially obsessed United States), and he did think that the white race was the most highly developed race in terms of ingenuity. As he once said:

> Technology, the space shuttles, and the 747s, were put there by the highest minds on this planet. Those minds are the highest minds on the planet. They may not be the *best* minds, but they're the most creative minds....
>
> If the Pharaoh was setting here, and Montezuma was setting here, and Buddha was setting here, and they was talking about the great pyramids they created and all the things that they've done on earth, and they seen a 747 fly by in the sky, they would all change their perspectives. They'd bow down to it.

So, by dictionary definition ("Racism -- a belief that some races are by nature superior to others.") that might have made Manson a racist. But he did not hate other people based on their races. I never witnessed any hostility between him and inmates or correctional officers of other races. To the contrary, he got along very well with them. And I received many letters from black and Hispanic inmates and outside people who wrote to me and expressed their high regard for Charles Manson. (I did hear Manson say "nigger" on perhaps three or four occasions over a period of over ten years, but usually when referring to black people he called them "negroes.")

But Manson did believe that the white race is the one that leads the way in many aspects of human development and endeavor:

There ain't no difference [between races]. The only difference is capacity. The taller people can do taller things. The shorter people do short things. There's no real judgement. Its like the guy said, he said the German's preach superiority. I said, "That's bullshit." Any man knows that if you got a superior you have to have an inferior. So the only game of preaching superior is that you're trying to overcome the inferior. You're already stuck in the inferior, so you're trying to raise the levels of consciousness to a superior. But in reality, those in the know know there's no such thing as superior because there's no such thing as inferior. That's just two games that you play on a fucking checkerboard. Life is not a game. You don't win or lose. You just survive.

When you're hungry and there's one loaf of bread, I'm going to get it and I'm going to eat it. And if you starve, then I'm a racist or anything else you want to call me. But I'm going to survive. That's the way it's always been, and that's the way it'll be. The strong survive. If you fold up underneath that bullshit game of knuckling down to somebody else's fear -- wearing white hats and playing games with other people's games -- that's not going to work.

The same you that's me that's in you that's in me, that's the same one that's in all of us. It's in the tiger in the zoo. When it's chow time, the tiger's gonna growl for himself. Everybody's looking out for Number One. That's a natural thing, man. You can't blame someone for looking out for Number One.

You can't blame any one people. They're not any better than anyone else. If they [black people] was on the top spot, we [white people] probably wouldn't even be here.

Of course, Manson's supposed racism was a big buttress for the prosecutorial concept of Helter Skelter:

They said, "You predicted a race war."

I said, "There's always been a race war." There's been a race war since two people came out of caves. As long as the hairy guys and the smooth guys don't like the hairy guys, and the tall guys don't like the little guys, and anything they can find as an excuse to have a race war, they're gonna have it. That's always been going on. If I show weakness and I fall down, everybody eats me up. I have to keep my own balance. I have to stand up for mine, and walk with my own, as much as I can.

So I have to look at me first, get me straightened around.
And the guys says, "Well, you're prejudiced against us."
I said, "I'm not against anyone. I'm for me. If I can get me in order, then I'll deal with you."

There's only one mind, and it ain't got no color. That's why I told you, you gotta be reborn. You only got people, man. I mean, there are differences in ethnic nature -- a cocker spaniel's not a sheep dog and a sheep dog's not a pit bull -- but you can't rightly judge one thing against another.

I think we make up what they [blacks] are, anyway. Because they generally watch what we do, 'cause you got the creative mind.... But beyond that they don't know what to do unless we show 'em, or tell 'em, or lead 'em to water, because they wouldn't know where to find it.

As Manson recognized the white race's leadership position in terms of human "civilization," he also recognized its responsibility for what has gone wrong with the human species:

I hate all white people. White people are rotten. And black people are just like 'em. Because you've made 'em just exactly like you. They walk like you, they talk like you -- everything they do is like you. They want to be you so much, they love your woman more than you do. They know your mind better than you do, they wear your clothes -- they've even learned to wear your shoes.

You take them out of the jungle, and you want to make them into "man." Why couldn't they be left to God? Why did you want them to be a man? In the jungle, they were God.

But if the supposed influences of the Process Church and Nazism on Charles Manson's thinking are inaccurate and incomplete, what *did* influence his mind and shape his life? In my many hours of conversations with him I noticed one thing about Manson that is also true about most other people I have known: He talked about things that were important to him. Often he repeated stories over and over as he recalled the big events in his life and how they impacted him. I concluded, after my own conversations with him as well as listening to tape recordings of hundreds of hours of more conversations with other persons, that the things that really affected Charles Manson -- just like the things that importantly affect most people in their lives -- come much more from his early years as a child and his years in prison prior to 1967. And while it is indisputable that Manson did brush up against many organizations and/or movements such as Scientology and the Church of Satan before and after his 1967 prison release, I am convinced that these contacts had very little impact on his core being.

So, what were the big influences that made Charles Manson into the person that he is? The answer to this question might sound surprising at first, but on closer thought it reflects clear and common sense: The biggest influences on the personality of Charles Manson were the people and experiences which were a part of his life when he was growing up.

One of those biggest influences on young Charles Manson was, not surprisingly, the relationship that he had with his mother.

Manson's mother has frequently been described as a prostitute. While this is not exactly true, she certainly was not a prude; she was pregnant at age fourteen. Manson later recalled the impact that this pregnancy and his birth had on her:

> My mother was a fourteen-year-old runaway child. Alone. She had no past. She just started a new world. She started without a man, without a father. She was the rebirth of World War One.
>
> My mother? The biggest disappointment in her life was getting pregnant when she was fourteen years old. When she got pregnant, she said, "Wow, man!" And I came. And there wasn't no abortion clinics, you dig. And I ruined her life. I destroyed her whole life. I was the biggest disappointment in her life.
>
> And all her life, she queered everything I ever tried to do. She would tell me she was coming to get me, and leave me standing there dressed in a little suit waiting to go home on Monday morning, and she wouldn't show. And then they'd take me back and then tell me "Next week," and then she wouldn't show. And then she would just tear my heart out and throw it on the ground and stomp on it. She tortured me and tormented me and destroyed me a thousand times. She kept me locked up for over twenty-two years.
>
> There's one thing I learned, see, from my mother. My mother was my best teacher. She was a runaway little fourteen-year-old girl, and she went to the penitentiary when she was sixteen, and she always lied about everything. She never told the truth about nothing. She would lie when there was no reasons to lie. She just constantly lied all the time. She never smiled, and she lied all the time. And she didn't like people....

[And so] all my life I've never trusted anyone. My mother set me to do that.... She taught me not to trust anyone. She taught me not to believe anyone.

So, [it's like] I always tell [Lyn Fromme], "You can believe me, but I'm not gonna believe nobody." If you want to believe me, that's up to you. But as far as me believing anybody -- I never have. I never have believed in anyone, because I've never had anyone that I could ever believe in. So I had to believe in myself.

You know, all my mother's life, I never seen her smile. And I treated her like shit. I beat the shit out of her two or three times. She tried to throw me out of the window. She fucked me around two or three times. She lied on me, cheated me -- she did me a lot of bad, man....

My real mother, the one I knew.... I remember when I was a kid she worked at the Blue Moon Cafe, and she lived in one room up over the bar. And I remember they used to play the music. There was a one-legged saxophone player who played music.

But she used to come up and get me out of bed. And I used to have to go down and walk around on the street corner while she would lay with this guy. And then she would come and get me and I would go back to bed and then she would come and get me out of bed and send me back down on the corner again. So, later on I figured that out, what she was doing.

And they was all my "Uncle Johns." Different uncles and a lot of booze and a lot of drinking. And she lived a fast life, man.

I never knew her that much. She was just another broad. [She went with] whoever had enough whiskey to get her drunk. Yeah, she liked whiskey. She liked to drink. She drank a lot.

She was a barmaid, a waitress, you dig? She wasn't a prostitute like a flat-back prostitute in a whore house. She hustled the bars. She got a guy that had some money, you dig?

I remember this one time she had a guy with a big, fat wallet. I took his wallet out and I took a whole lot of money out and I put the wallet back in his pocket. And she come and she says, "Where's my money?"

"What money?"

"The money you took out of his wallet."

I said, "I don't know what the hell you're talking about."

She said, "Well, I worked this fucking trick for fucking three hours to get that wallet. And now you got the money." She said, "You give me the money."

And I told her, "No."

And she hit me in the nose with a sugar bowl. She hit me in the nose, and I punched her and knocked her down underneath the table and kicked her. In other words, Mother was a tough little girl.

Mother didn't play no shit. She carried a fingernail file and she'd sharpen it on the floor, on the cement. And she had a real sharp fingernail file and everybody in the bar -- when she tended bar -- nobody'd fuck with her, 'cause they knew she'd bust 'em upside the head with a fifth of whiskey. She's been known for that. And everybody respected that.

When I whipped her once, she said, "You're the only man in the world can get away with that." She said, "If it was anyone else, I'd kill you ten times." She didn't let nobody misuse her. She was a very, very treacherous little girl. She was tough. She'd been in prison. She knew what prison was. But she didn't graduate prison like a mouse. She came out of there like a lion, you know.

And I had a lot of respect for her, and I liked her, even though she lied to me. She cheated me a lot, man. She fucked me over something terrible, in a lot of different ways. But, I mean, that was the way of the life that we lived and the way it rolled.

[Once] she hit this Beanie Brother in the head with a fifth of Jim Beam whiskey. And she came up and got me on the run because this Beanie Brother was on trial [for] killing a woman. He cut her head off and put her head on a pole and threw her body in the river. So Mom run off with a Holland Furnace salesman, and took me to Indianapolis, Indiana.

Then she took me over to boys school in Terre Haute, in a catholic reform school, and told to stay with those dudes and do what they said do, that she would be back to get me. And she was supposed to pay thirty dollars a month room and board for me until she came back to get me. She never did come back. So, that cost me eleven years of my life.

And I would write my aunt, and ask my aunt for help, and she wouldn't even send me a dollar. She wouldn't send me five dollars for canteen. She'd just tell me, "Have faith in Jesus."

So I did the first eleven years of my life -- when you was going to high school, and you was doing all the little things that you was doing -- I was crying. I was in the hole. I was fighting. I had to hold up my prison gang, and I had to hold up my own. I held up all the people, that for all the things that we talk about now, I held that up for twenty-two years.

My mother was the worst whore in the world. My mother hurt me more than you can dream about. You think your mother was bad? Your mother was a saint. Your mother bought you shoes and sent you to school. My mother gave me a handful of comic books and sold me for a pitcher of beer. She ran off and left me, and went to the penitentiary, you dig? And what do you think that did to my brain?

What *did* these experiences do to Charles Manson's brain? Despite all of these unconventional anecdotes and the seeming bitterness, he was philosophical about the overall effect that his mother had on his life:

> Sometimes the bad turns out to be the best, man. It's like, my mother was the worst mother in the world, but I learned more from that. If she'd of been a good mother and taught me a lot of shit and made me weak.... She wasn't a good mother. I had to find it out for myself. The best thing she ever did was just leave me alone [and] let me go, man.
>
> So sometimes the worst mothers are the best mothers. Sometimes a mother that treats you bad makes you strong, you know? It either kills you, or you get strong.
>
> The only thing that puts me aside from most is my mother. My mother let me go. The best thing my mother ever gave me, she gave me myself.

Another major influence on Charles Manson's life was another woman, his first wife Rosalie Jean Willis. Manson married her in McMechen, West Virginia in 1955:

> When I was kid -- I never even met a woman till I was twenty. The first girl I ever met, man, before she'd let me fuck her, she made me marry her. I didn't know what the hell all that [sex] was. In my days, when I was a kid, they didn't have *Playboy* magazines to tell you what was going on. You had to find out on your own. You had to ask everybody, and they didn't know....
>
> I meet a girl, she says, "Let's go to California." We steal a car and we come to California. We come to California with a shotgun. We come to California burglarizing people, and robbing and stealing. We come to California like Dirty Harry, Mary, Larry, and all them things they make them movies with, you dig?
>
> So when we get to California [I was arrested for auto theft]. She goes for divorce, and she takes the child away and she takes the guitar away, you dig? She takes my life away. And she gives it to her boyfriend, who she married, that she can control. He's not a criminal. He's not a car thief. He's a square guy that goes to work and gives her his money. So she gives my guitar to a guy from Tennessee....
>
> The fucking broad -- I was pushing her with my incompetence, accusing her of cheating when she wasn't. Then she was cheating when I

wasn't accusing her. We were both screwed up. Because we didn't have no raising up. No one told us anything. We were just kids, bumping into each other.

I had hang-ups, too. Like, I got married. I tried to do right by this woman, and she would run around with other people, man. And she would do things behind my back. And when I got busted, man, she's running and jumping in bed with all my friends, and they're all laughing at me. And how do you think that makes me feel? I had to go through all the incompetent feelings, and I've laid up in solitary confinement and cried like a baby.

I ran off. I tried to climb the damn walls. Over there in TI [Terminal Island Federal Prison], when you see that screen on the right-hand side going into D Block, I busted all the windows up getting on top of the wall, jumping up there on top of the tower, taking a chance on getting my brains blown out. They had to wrassle me down in the parking lot behind a woman, behind the feelings and emotions that that broad had hurt me with. Now that shows you how much I was married. I had to get five years probation for that.

I wasn't gonna give my wife up. I didn't believe in that. I believed if you got married to somebody and you swore to do, that person, be real with that person and not lie or cheat on that person, I believed that with my life. And I still believe it.

We stood in front of God, so to say, and we swore that we would be with each other and that we wouldn't cheat on each other, and that we would, uh, till death do us part, and all that. And I held my way. I held my loyalness. And she went off down the road and started fucking other people and I just went crazy.... I guess that's what we call "jealousy."

I didn't run off and leave her, she ran off and left me. She left me in the penitentiary and started writing them "Heartbreak Hotel" songs, and talking about "Hound Dog" and "Jailhouse Rocks," and all that shit. And I'm in solitary confinement for that.

But, I mean, what the fuck, man? I can't beat the whole Goddamn world. 'Cause they gave her my fucking balls and then screwed my head on backwards and throw me back in the fucking pit and everything they can do to get me killed so they can put me over in the graveyard. I mean, what the fuck can I do? I'm an idiot. I'm a fucking class-action fucking snake-dumb clown idiot, [because] I went back to this shit [prison] again, man.

My nature was broken down by a girl named Rose. Because she just destroyed me. She tore my heart out and threw it on the floor. She destroyed me, [and] gave my guitar to Elvis Presley. She gave my fucking asshole to the world. She destroyed me. She did me dirt. She used me poorly, and there was nothing I could do about it, because I was stupid. I didn't know anything about women.

So I go around from everybody and I try to find out, what is this thing, "woman"? And I go from guy to guy trying to figure our what this "woman" was.

And then I learned what the woman was. Then I found myself. *I* was the woman. *I* was my mother. I was as much my mother and my sister as my brother and my father. And I was as much my father as my uncle and my cousin. And then I found I was as much God as I was the devil. And then I was nothing. And then I just went in a circle. I just went around and around and around. Then I said, "I'm gonna start all over. I'm gonna come from nowhere, going to nowhere, and start over and start living a little bit of my own life."

If she hadn't divorced me and ran off with somebody from Nashville, Tennessee to be a rock and roll star, I would have been a married man and doing a job and staying out of jail.

Manson's bad experiences with some of the women in his life have been the basis for claims that he hated women. This was not true, but he was what could be considered to be old-fashioned when it came to his views on the relationship between woman and man:

Look here, you know, I'm not into a superior/inferior type of thought patterns. I don't think someone is better than someone or worse than no one. I'm not really into this 'man-woman' thing that you guys are into, you know.

But I know the nature, and the ways of nature. Like, you refer to the lion in your mind. Can you do that? Now the mama lion is really the baddest one. She takes care of business. She looks out for the kids. In other words, mama lion is really cool. She'd kick daddy in the ass. But it's only because daddy lets her. Because really, when the chips come to the end of the play, the jackal can beat a female lion. But the jackal cannot beat a male lion.

You must admit, whatever life form, the male is the creator. Woman receives the creation from man. The creation comes through the man.... whether it be in the invention of a bowl, or a cup, or a match, or a 747, or a baby.

As soon as we accept the truth in our lives, then we can see this.... Woman is the earth. Woman is everything that is. She's a receptacle, a

receiver. She's the water, she's the planet, she's the sun, the moon, stars. She's everything that *is*. Man is everything that is *not*. He's everything that is not: the universe, the darkness,
the completion, the total, the Now.

In order for man to exist, he must have woman. In order for woman to exist, she must accept man.

Manson had other relatives besides his mother and wife, and they too made their impressions on him. Manson's family (his real, biological one) has had its roots traced back to the late eighteenth century. His forbears were among the first settlers of what is now eastern Kentucky. Here Manson remembers his grandparents, starting with his mother's mother, Nancy Maddox, a real Kentucky mountain woman:

Grandma wouldn't let us go to movies. She said that movies were sinful and they were run by the devil and they were the downfall of humanity.

She knew, when she came out of the mountains, that everybody on the flatland was all sinners. They were all bad. That the people in the mountains were the only good people because them other people had lost sight of God.

Grandma was a hell of a woman. She never lied, she never wore makeup, she never cheated, she had one man -- that was it. She was a cook in the Salvation Army when she died. And, like, she didn't watch movies, she didn't read any book except the Bible. And her husband went to war and came home with all the heroes and honors and all that.

In other words, like, I didn't just happen there. I earned all of that.

Manson particularly remembered a story about his grandfather, Charlie Maddox, in the First World War:

My grandfather told my grandmother that in World War One he was standing on a dead body and seen a Bible in the guy's pocket. And he reached down and got the Bible, and he opened it up, and there was the man's picture with his wife and his two, three, children, you dig? And he had a chain with a cross on it. And he looked at the Bible, and he looked at the man's children, and he looked at the cross, and he looked down and he seen himself. He said, "What am I doing fighting my brother?"

So why did my grandfather kill himself? He came back and told my grandmother, "I was fighting my brothers and I don't even know why."

Another influential relative was Manson's Uncle Jess. The exact genealogical linkage between the two men is not clear, but the effect that the older man had on young Charles Manson certainly is:

I believed my Uncle Jess and I did pretty much what my Uncle Jess raised me up to do. My Uncle Jess was God in the holler. He ran the moonshine, he ran the Mason jars, and he lived in Morehead, Kentucky. And there was no bullshit in Uncle Jess. Uncle Jess was a bad motherfucker. He had a long gun and he'd shoot people if necessary. He died in the nut ward in Louisville, Kentucky.

My Uncle Jess told me, "Boy, keep your own mind." He said, "The mountains here are dying. You gotta go down there and get it."

[I said], "But I"m just one little kid."

"Well, there's only one little world. Get on about it. You ain't got no choice."

So, it's the same thing I say to you, you know. You got to stand it up and do right with it. Get it in line or you ain't got nothing left.

I'm a hillbilly. I live up in the mountains. I make moonshine. I got a long gun, and I shoot a long ways, and I'm God in the holler. I let the woman to to church – gives her something to do, you know -- but I know who God is and I know who Jesus is and I know who the devil is, and I really don't need anything on the flatland because the mountain holds the light. But when the mountains are dying, then I got to come down into the flatland and I got to put the balance in it -- keep them from strip-mining and taking down the trees to where there's nothing left. So that's what I'm paying for the last forty years, where my Uncle Jess sent me.

Beyond his personal experiences with his mother, grandmother, wife, and other relatives, Charles Manson was also formed by experiences and the people he met during his years of incarceration in various penal institutions throughout the country. Manson's experiences with prison began at an early age, even before he was old enough to commit any kind of act that might have resulted in him being jailed:

I started visiting my mother in jail when I was barely walking. When she got out she come and got me from a foster home and took me and put me in a boys school. So I been military raised....

My body started in 1944 in Father Gibault's School for Boys, then it went to White's Institute School for Boys, then it went to juvenile hall, and then it went to Boys Town Father Flannigan's Nebraska, then it went to Danville, Illinois, then it went to Plainfield, Indiana, then it went to Salt Lake City, went to court, went to federal joints, went to Natural Bridge School for Boys in Washington, DC, Natural Bridge Camp, Petersburg, Virginia Correctional Institution, sixteen, seventeen, Lewisburg, Pennsylvania Prison. In other words, like Goddamn man, I got forty-seven years in these places.

When I was nine years old I was put in the reform school for setting the school on fire. I set the school on fire and I haven't been back since. Now, they said to me that everybody goes to school until they're sixteen. And I told them, at ten years old, "Fuck you." I have been contrary, and a rebel, and backwards to everybody since I was ten years old. I haven't went to school. When all the monks in the catholic school said I will stand in the confirmation line and be confirmed, I told 'em, "Suck my dick. You're not confirming me. Fuck you in your fucking Irish assholes."

[So] I don't have no education. I've never checked into a hotel, I've never rented an automobile, I've never had a job -- [No] I had a job once. I've never filled out an application for a driver's license. I don't have enough sense to do that. Mary used to have to do that. I used to sneak in. She used to fill it out and [we'd] switch papers. That was the only way I could get a driver's license. In other words, I don't fit in that educated criteria of booby boop.

There's a whole lot of things I wasn't in on. I never got to play football, I never went to high school, I didn't go to the prom, I didn't have any parents, I never lived in a house, I never had three meals a day like you, I never had a bicycle, I never had a teddy bear, I never got a Easter basket, I never went to Christmas parties, I never had a birthday party, I never did all that. I didn't get to play with other kids. I was thrown in the fucking county jail with winos. I was sleeping on the floor underneath the motherfucking bunk, people spitting and puking all over me. At age thirteen, 1946-'47, I was in county jail.

You know how I got unlocked? In reform school they used to beat us. They used to hold us down on these little sleds and whup us with big leather straps. And I used to remember when I would get up from there I would feel like -- I would be relieved. I'd feel stronger and better. When

I was going through it, it was hurting, and it was a bad experience. But when I would get over it and get through it, it would be like I was starting all over again. I was being relieved of all my guilt, and I wasn't afraid. I was afraid going in. I'd be shaking. But then afterwards, I'd no longer be afraid. In fact, it was some of the better experiences for existence have been the worst experiences.

Prisons are often called universities of crime, and they are. Charles Manson didn't waste his educational experience:

All the old Italians that came to prison, I was a young boy working in the hospital. I cleaned their bedpans, I swept the floor, I listened to them. I ran and got their newspapers. And I heard everything they had to say. They told me everything they knew. I picked their brains, and I watched them all die. And I got the truth of what was happening in the underworld, from the horseshoe pits, to Frank Costello, Lucky Luciano, Arthur Rocco, all the way down -- Capollo Brothers -- all the way to the underworld.

So they all died and I grew up and the ones that snitched lost their underworld. I didn't snitch. [So I hold the underworld.]

Manson remembered one incident with an old Italian that made a profound impression on him:

When I was a little kid I whipped the lieutenant in a correctional institution in Petersburg, Virginia. So the lieutenant and the captain sent me to the prison, the first prison I was ever in. They said, "This is not a little kid. This is the devil." Because I had whipped everything. After they taught me how to fight in Gibault -- I never learned to read and write, but I learned how to fight. So I was fighting everybody and I didn't know what I was fighting for. I was just fighting against everything that fought against me.

So then when they put me in Lewisburg they had this big Italian guy. And everybody in the joint would look at that guy like, whoa, he was really something. And we'd go out and we'd pitch horseshoes, and he talked down the side of his mouth, and I didn't know who the fuck he was. He was just somebody that everybody looked up to, right?

So we went in the mess hall and [there were] all these fucking tin plates and tin cups and everything was quiet and you wasn't allowed to talk, you know. And you had to march into the mess hall. It was like an old *Gangbusters* movie, you know? And all these guys were around the gun rail with these shotguns and they had sticks and axe handles, you dig? And everything was real quiet. And mess hall's real dangerous, man.

And so we all walked in, and this old man has got a newspaper. And he pulls the newspaper out, and he folds it in a little fold, and he holds it in his hand, and he sets at the table and he's reading this newspaper.

Cops come over and says, "Mr. Costello, there'll be no reading of the newspaper at the breakfast table," you dig?

And the old man said, "Look here, Sonny. I buy this newspaper with my money. It's my money, it's my newspaper. I'll read it wherever my eyes can get to it. I read the paper at the breakfast table at home, and I read the paper here," you dig?

And the cops says, "Mr. Costello, you're not at home now."

So the old man stood up. And when he stood up, the whole God-damn mess hall turned quiet. Not one fucking spoon was hitting on one tray. Everything was just bone quiet, man. And he said, "Look here, son. You're settin' in *my* neighborhood. This is *my* neighborhood here. *I* run this underworld here."

And the cop looked at him, and he looked at all them convicts, and everybody was getting ready to jump up, man. So that cop turned around and got the hell out of there.

And every morning [after that], when that breakfast table went, that old man would pull that newspaper out of his pocket and set there and read it.

That was the high point of my life. I never seen anybody get over on a cop like that!

Manson learned to survive in prison:

I've been fighting for my life since I was ten years old. In prison, you can't miss one move. If you miss one move, someone gets you. You know how prison is. If you're not up on the water, if you're not up on the air, if you're not up on everything that moves -- if anything moves that you don't know about, it could get you. I've been raised in the eye of that all my life.

If you're in jail, and you don't have any friends, then you are a scapegoat. If you're a scapegoat, then people can use you until you're gone. Unless you're very tough. You've got to be tougher than everybody else. Because if one person can beat you, they'll beat you to death. It's like the chickens. If one chicken can peck you, and get some blood, the rest of 'em will peck you to death.

Always on the yard I can never let anyone know what I'm thinking, because I'm too small. When you're a big guy you can afford to get hit two or three times, before you get mad. When you're a little guy you cannot afford to get hit once. Because one time's enough. So, I'm like a scorpion. I'm little, but I'm very deadly. And I'm dangerous. And everybody knows it. So therefore, they stand off of me and they give me respect.

Much of Manson's personality, and thus much of his behavior, is the result of the lessons and the values that he learned in prison. One of the main lessons he learned was to mind his own business and to keep his mouth shut:

You know where you come out of the bakery [at Terminal Island]? I was sweeping the floor down that hallway and I looked over in the butcher shop, man, and they got these big old butcher knives and they're stabbing this guy. And they stabbed him and they put him in a garbage can. They broke his back. They didn't want the cops to know they killed him in the kitchen, because that's paranoid on that level. So.... they put him in the garbage can and take him out the back door because we couldn't get in the storeroom in them days....

What they did was, like, they stabbed this guy to death and they couldn't get him bent over in the garbage can, his arms and legs was sticking out of the garbage can, so they laid him up on the block and took them meat cleavers and when I seen 'em they seen me looking at them, they said, "Get over on the point, Manson."

So I got over on the point down there over by the office where they got the pots and pans, and I'm looking, and I'm sweeping in one spot, looking, and they chopped this guy in half. They put half of him in one garbage can and they put half of him in the other garbage can. [They cut him up with a] meat cleaver. They had him up on the block, chopping his spine, just like you'd chop up a pig or something. Then they put him in one can and pushed his arms down, put his legs in another can.... so his legs went one way and his arms went the other way.

And the guys that did it, when they come out, man, they looked at me and I just, you know, and they moved on.

And the [officer] come up and says, "What's this blood all around here?"

I said, "Well, I think they -- I don't know. I'm not sure. I didn't see. I think they, uh, chopped up some meat or something."

And I just swept on through it. Because I've always, I've *always* carried that broom. That broom has been my broom since 1944.

All my life I've been on that line.... I know nothing. I know nothing. I'm zero. I don't get involved. I don't run and tell them cops, "Protect me." I protect myself. And whatever happens, happens, man. People getting killed around me is no new thing. You come to prison, man there's people getting killed in prison all the time.... In other words, you got all kinds of violence and fear that runs in these places. When you live a life like that, it becomes a natural thing.

That's where I learned to walk a line. That's the reason I could have proved that I never entered into the minds of anyone on that ranch. I just accepted their minds and walked in the world they lived in. I didn't really let no one in my world. I never opened up my world, except a couple times.

Manson also mastered the underworld quid pro quos:

It's like, somebody kills somebody for you, because [for example] they raped your daughter. So they go kill 'em. Okay? So then when [they] kill them, then you owe 'em one. You owe them a favor. I other words, in the Mafia everything runs on favors. It don't run on money. You keep those favors and you wait for the right time and then you drop that favor on 'em. They got to pay that favor or their whole family's in blood.

If you owe me a favor, and you're in the underworld, and your word is good and you're an honorable person, and you owe me a favor, and I come and want that favor, I don't give a fuck if you like the favor or if you don't like the favor. It's got nothing to do with the favor. The favor belongs to me. And anything that's mine belongs to me. I can do anything I want to do with it.

It has often been said that Charles Manson was institutionalized and that he was very accustomed to the regimented life of a person in prison. This contention is not only true but it is also very understandable. After all, Manson spent nearly all of his life *in* institutions.

Part of any institutional existence is the hierarchy inherent in systems that rely on the enforcement of rules. Prison is no exception. Thus, Charles Manson knew very well about rules and procedures. And he knew how to follow them. (In fact, he might have known how to follow them too well.) Adding to the circumstance of Manson being raised mostly in structured systems of ranks was the fact that many of those ranks were filled by ex-servicemen who took employment in correctional facilities upon their release from the armed forces. These men not only understood rank, procedures, and orders, but they also knew about the realities of war. Manson absorbed their knowledge and understanding of war, just as he learned from everyone and everything else around him:

War is just flat out the green bugs are destroying the blue ones. And there ain't no in-between. They'll eat every blue bug on the board, if they can. And then you come and you say, "Well, now all of us blue bugs have got to get together," and if one blue bug says, "Well, I'm a conscientious objector" -- there ain't no such thing. You know, you all get together or you all die. You live together, and you stand together, or you fall together. There ain't no in-between, you dig? That's what this country is based on....

When you're in a war action, there's no slack. There is not one little bit of slack. It's razor sharp. You all stand to attention, and when the sergeant says, "Left face!" everybody turns left face. If you don't turn left face, they'll take you over and kneel you down and put a gun to your head and blow your brains out. There's ain't no bullshit to it.

"War" is a word that you use when someone is coming to kill you. There's no talk about it; they're just coming to kill you. Period. There's no way you can talk 'em out of it. There's no way you can give 'em any pussy. There's no way you can pay 'em. There's no way you can do *anything*. They're coming to take your life. Period.

If one king is coming to kill another king, the king goes to the count and he tells the count, "We're going to war." Now the count knows that he will do what the king tells him, or the king will torture him to *death*. The king will murder his parents, he'll kill his children, they'll butcher his dogs, they'll dig up his grandmother and beat her bones. They'll torture him. They'll do everything that's conceivable to do against the count if the count don't do what the king tells him to do. And when the count knows this, he knows that the king will not give him no slack, there's no act, it's not a movie. This is reality.

He goes to the duke. And he tells the duke, "The king said...." you dig? Now, the count can use the king for all the king has got. Because the count knows he is the king. He's got a point on the crown. And he can use the king. He can tell the king, "I want your soldiers to go over and do so and so," and king's soldiers will do whatever the count tells 'em. In other words, he's in the will of the king. And the king and the count is in the same will, they're in the same chamber.

A military is, simply, you do what you have to do. You've got the lines and the guidelines of authority. In other words, if the authority says, "You shit," then you squat and shit. If your pants is still on, that's tough shit. You've just got to do what you're told to do, man. That's the truth. That's the only way you can survive....

In the military, when the order is given, you've got to do it. It's not a question of whether you *want* to do it. You're fighting for God, man. You're in a holy war. When God says something's got to be done, it's got to be done. It has nothing to do with personal conflict or what you think is right or wrong.

Right or wrong ain't got nothing to do with it. If you've got something that's coming to take your life, you've got to run. And if they say, "Run," you run. You don't stop and say, "Why am I running?".... That's the only way it'll work.

I'll explain to you why. All right, you got a ranch, okay? You're running the ranch. You say, "Clean the barn out."

And I say, "Well, uh, we cleaned the barn out yesterday. And I really don't think it needs a cleaning out."

And then somebody else says, "Well I don't feel like cleaning it out either, I would rather clean the chicken coop out."

And then somebody says, "Ah, fuck the chicken coop, man, just let the chickens go. We don't need to keep the chickens locked up." You dig?

So then we let the chickens go and we think it's cool to let the chickens go, and we see the little chickens running around trying to stay out from underneath the horses, and the horses are stomping on the little baby chickens. And we're too busy thinking about the horses stomping on the baby chickens, so we say, "Well, you didn't exercise authority and make 'em clean out the barn, and all the baby chickens got killed.

And then pretty soon you find out that you don't have any adult chickens because all the adult chickens got old and there was no baby chickens left, so we lost two or three generations of baby chickens because you didn't make them clean out the barn when you knew the barn had to be cleaned out. You got to stand out on the front porch and say, "I want the barn cleaned out. If you're not gonna clean the barn out when I tell you to clean the barn out, then get off this ranch. The barn needs cleaning out. Go down there and clean the damn thing out. I don't want to hear what you think about it, whether you think it should be, whether you think it shouldn't be -- we're not taking a vote on it. The vote was already taken when you put me in this office."

Without doubt one of the most important concepts to develop in Charles Manson's philosophy from his life's experience was his idea of "the brotherhood."

Since getting a brother out of jail was the real motive for the Tate-LaBianca murders, the idea of "brother" must have been pretty important. And to Charles Manson, it was. Despite anything said by the prosecutor during Manson's murder trial (and in the decades since), Manson was not obsessed with the idea of Helter Skelter. But his owns statements suggest that he was defintiely obsessed with his brother:

> I'm down, I'm mean, and I'm an outlaw, and I'm a rebel, and I haven't surrendered, but I respect truth. I respect honesty and honor. And I hold my word. I hold my word for my brother.
>
> In my world there is a circle of men that are called "brother." And these brothers, they don't lie. They don't misuse their circle. They're very precise in what they do. They're very dangerous. Do you understand dangerous?
>
> Let me explain my brotherhood to you. When I was a kid, I never had anyone. I was alone, all my life. And when I went to Gibault Boys School the monks used to have ropes tied around their stomachs, and they wore these robes. And they made you call them "brother." They would paddle you if you didn't call them "brother."
>
> And so, I got the sense of this thing called "brother." And all my life I've lived at that, because I didn't have any other thing. I didn't have a mother. I didn't have a father. I didn't have friends. I just had that brotherhood of all the men I met -- not as one individual or person, but all people in the thought of one.
>
> Any man that was a wino or a bum, that was down and out, I'd help him. Any brother that had nobody and needed change for a phone call or something, you know, I was always there. I wouldn't let nobody beat nobody up or play bully games on the smaller, weaker people. In other words, I've always looked out for the Christian brother.
>
> [The monks] taught me by example. They didn't teach me as much by telling me something, they taught me by *doing* it. And I would see them doing it. Well, all I did was continue what they were doing. Becuase I was them and they were me. All they did was, they gave themselves a guy called "brother."
>
> I believed that I had a brother in jail. I really did. When the monks started me out, they used to beat us if we didn't call them "brother." And

we never lied to them, because if we lied they used to beat us. So, that kind of set me as a child that there was such a thing as the truth, and that there was such a thing as a brother.

And I believed that. And then when I learned to fight, I went to reform school and then I fought and I beat everybody. I always ended up beating everybody, because I had a lot of fear and I felt that if I couldn't beat everybody then maybe somebody would want to get me. So I always had to be on top of everybody. And I run everything I've ever done. Whatever I had to do, I would stay on top of whatever I was doing, because I thought that was the only way I could survive.

So, when I got out, and I would tell you guys all these things I learned -- well, I did. I learned it from guys in jail. But I thought these guys in jail were my brothers. I thought they were cool. I didn't realize that they were afraid of me. Because I didn't know what "afraid of me" was.

Manson lived up to his standard of "brother." In the summer of 1969 he gave himself to his brother, Charles Watson, by shooting Bernard Crowe in order to resolve the problems created by Watson's marijuana rip off. A few weeks later, Bobby Beausoleil gave himself to *his* brother, Charles Manson, when he stabbed Gary Hinman to death to keep him from turning Manson in to the police. Manson later explained the debt he felt he owed Beausoleil for that act:

It's almost impossible to help someone. Jesus Christ helped the Good Samaritan 2,000 years ago, and they crucified him for it. Ain't nobody helps anyone.... The only reason I was helping someone, is because I thought there *was* someone. I thought I had a brother.

I like the people on the ranch first. I like Bobby because he could [play] music and he's young and he's healthy and he's cool, you dig? So, then he brings some girls over and I tolerate those girls because of him. For him. Because I believe in a guy called "brother." I believe my brother is Jesus Christ. I believe my brother, in spirit, gave his life for me. I believe my brother's a veteran, he fought for me, that he gave me his life, and I think the graveyard is full of my brothers.

Manson took the debts that brothers owe each other very seriously:

If I've got a brother that went off into the war, put a uniform on, picked up a gun and went off and died, for God and country, man, I can't deny that man his will back. When he comes from the grave and says, "Hey man, I died for you in Gettysburg, I died for you again at Bull Run, I died for you in Scotland, I was thrown off the castle walls in Ireland, I died for you all the way down the line -- now stand up, Goddamn you! Stand up to attention!"

If you don't stand up to attention, what kind of honor would you have? There would be nothing there. You got to do it. It's not a question of whether you want to. You got to do it.

This is what happened to me, with twenty-five years of my life thrown down the shitter, because I thought I had a brother. The value of having a brother is having someone you can count on, someone that'll help you, and that's almost impossible in the world today, unless you're paying for it.

It comes down to the simple fact that, I gotta be brother to me. I can't be brother to no one else. Everybody's got to be brother to themselves. I thought I had brothers that I didn't have. And I misrepresented to some of you people that I had all these beautiful, wonderful brothers, you dig? And I really thought I did. Because a lot of the guys I had been with, to me, they were super. But it was because they were afraid. I never realized they were afraid.

Although Charles Manson spent the vast majority of his life in prison, there were times when he was not locked up, and he tried various lifestyles during these periods of freedom:

The first time I got out of prison I burglarized everybody's pad, I ripped people off, I did anything I wanted, I knocked people down, I would trick 'em, I would do all kinds of terrible things. And then I would have to go back to jail and I didn't have no friends. I didn't have no money. And I felt bad and I'd suffer like hell. So the next time I got out I tried a little different thing. And each time I got out I tried a different trip.

Before I met you, I was that kind of guy [in the book *Manson In His Own Words*]. The Manson that [Nuel Emmons] knew in the old days, I rode around in a Cadillac, I had a silver pistol, I run a poker game out of the Hollywood Roosevelt Hotel, and I run the Boulevard. And I put my bullets in people's kneecaps. I controlled just about anything I wanted. I was a terrible fucking pimp. That's exactly what I was. I was a fucking jailhouse shyster, a fucking sleazy white slaver, I was the worst motherfucking scumbag that fell out of the fucking penitentiary. That's the truth.

Well, when I got out last time, I tried not hurting anybody or not beating nobody up or not getting nasty with nobody. I tried being good with everybody. And I tried not breaking other people's will. I never forced people to do *anything* that they didn't want to do. The thing I held over them women was this: If you don't get in line and tell the truth, get up on the highway and go on down the road.

Of course, Manson's efforts to keep from returning to prison after his release in 1967 were ultimately unsuccessful. But he believed that nothing -- no amount of good behavior on his part -- could have kept him out:

I knew I was going back to the joint. As long as there's a joint, they got to have me in it. They ain't never gonna let me stay out of prison, because I hold their fucking heads, man. I hold their minds up. They ain't got no fucking brain without me. I've been the emperor of this Goddamn fucking crime since I was fucking nine years old. [Prison] is my mind. It's my mind. It's *my* prison. My mind is my prison. It's my whole world.

Manson's world was one of institutions. And institutions, and especially prisons, frequently tend to stifle individuality. Although Charles Manson was definitely an individual, he was also not without the effects of his decades of incarceration. These effects, as should be expected, have to some extent molded the way his mind worked -- or how it didn't:

I was raised in a collective mind. I was not raised in a family like your family. I was raised in a collective mind. I've been raised in boys schools that had maybe sixty or seventy young kids running together. So half the time, I'm not doing the thinking in what you would call my mind.

In other words, I'll be at the ranch and I'll come up with the opinion, and I'll carry around the decision, but the opinion and the decision is not mine. George may have said, Well, I don't want the horses rented out today."

And somebody else said, "Well, it's gonna rain, so we gotta get the hay in."

And someone else says, "Somebody's coming up with a gun and there's gonna be a fight behind the barn."

And then somebody else says something else and then I'm out front saying, "Well, we're closed today."

And the guy says, "Well, who are you to close it? Are you making the decision to close this place?"

I said, "Well, I'm standing on no one's coming in this parking lot. This place is closed. So get the hell out of here." You dig?

Then they say, "Charlie's making all the decisions here."

See, it wasn't *my* decision. I'm just running on the decisions that were made by everybody else. I'm running in a collective thought.

Charles Manson was "running in a collective thought" when he was with the people he was with from 1967 to 1969. He was *in* the thought and he was *part of* the thought but, contrary to the popular perception, he wasn't the *mastermind* of the thought.

One thing that can make Manson difficult to understand is the way he communicated. Often he could be coherent, eloquent, and even poetic. At other times he seemed to lapse into gibberish. Sometimes he responded to what appeared to be a perfectly simple question with an answer that seemingly didn't follow. Cryptic references abounded. But Manson said that there is a method to his apparent madness:

I've got an abstract mind. I'm not educated in my ways. And sometimes I have to go through all kinds of different things to communicate, because I can't communicate to the book. It's difficult for me to communicate to a book.

I do go in circles. I have a lot of ironies and paradoxes in my mind. And I do go in a circle sometimes on purpose to let you make up the mind about it and see which way you want to go. I tell you all the things that I'm going through, and what I'm doing with, and who I'm dealing with, and what I'm doing....

I have so much in my mind that I can't remember it all. I mean, it just floats around like in a big vacuum, you know, all these disoriented facts that just kind of trip around in there, you know.

[Do] you see where my mind is in relation to a lot of the things that I talk in letters that don't make no sense, then when I say it, it don't really make no sense either? But there's a bigger picture to it.

If I don't give people answers in the dimension they live in, then I'm considered crazy. If I say I come from nowhere and I'm going nowhere and I'm no one, they don't understand that. I have to be coming from somewhere and going somewhere and I have to be somebody, or I don't register in their computer. And when I don't register in their computer, then something's wrong, and they won't accept *themselves* as being wrong, so it's got to be *me* being wrong.

You know, and I've been wrong all my life. I've never done anything right. I was born wrong. And I've been wrong all of my days. You were the only people that seen any right in me. And the right you seen in me was your own. I told you over and over, "What you see in me is in you."

Manson was well aware that media interviewers never intended to present him to the public with any kind of impartiality. Therefore he typically adapted to that situation:

I know they're gonna take anything I say and if it's negative, they're gonna pounce on that. They're gonna pounce on the craziness and they're gonna pounce on the worst part. So I give 'em that little bit of crazy. I give 'em that Geraldo Rivera-type thing, because that's what a lot of those people want. They want some kind of screaming maniac, so I give 'em the old ding-dong maniac so they're gonna come back for more. Then when they come back for more -- boom. I drop a little intelligence on 'em. Then I drop a little ding-dong on 'em, and then I bounce 'em back and forwards, and I play 'em like a game. I got them on a video game. I'm playing the media. And I've played it right on down the line.

Did he care that the media misrepresented him?

That's [just] another part of them destroying themselves. It doesn't matter. If they cut me up [edit interviews unfavorably] it's okay. They have to deal with it. I don't. I don't. You know, I mean they can twist me and say I said anything, and then what ever they say I said, that's only real to them. It's got nothing to do with me personally.

But If Manson was running things, the media wouldn't be allowed to misrepresent:

If I was the leader, and somebody printed something bad to me, I'd burn their press down. I'd kill everybody on their staff. And then I'd hang 'em out on the fucking poles, and then tell the rest of the press,

"Why don't you take a picture of *that*, and print it, and if I catch you printing it and telling on somebody else about it, I'll kill you too."

I wouldn't tolerate no badding the realm. Nobody could talk bad about the realm. Because if you do, you're downing yourself. All those people that destroyed the United States -- they're destroying themselves. They're destroying the United States that *they* live in. I'm not destroying the United States *I* live in.

Of course, the reader shouldn't take Manson's revelations of what he would have done if he were running things as an indicator that he *wanted* to run things. But like most people he had opinions and ideas and thought about the world that he would have liked to have lived in:

We could stand a small chance to survive on the planet earth, but only with the one-world. Only with the one-world consideration, with everybody in the same mind for the same problems and the same reality to deal with those problems. Then [after that] we could be back into the individual trips and stuff.

We've got to have an international law. If we don't have an international law -- one law for all the world -- then we don't have no law at all. Because the world's moving fast now. We're not riding wagons. We're flying six, seven thousand miles in the sky. We've got satellites going off to the moon. It don't make sense that we're still laboring under a primitive system that's not really covering the needs of the people.

Everything is one. That's the reason that the Germans woke up that you had to take the world, because you can't just take part of the world. You can't say, "Well, stop cutting the trees down in Minnesota and New Mexico and Arizona, and go ahead and cut the trees down in Alabama and Brazil." That won't work that way. You got to quit cutting the trees down, period. All over the world. That's *all* the trees.

And then people say, "Well, there's gonna be a lot of people die if you do that." Well, there's gonna be a lot of people die if you *don't*. So how many people are gonna die if you don't? There's gonna be more people die if you don't than there are if you do.

So, if I had the power to own that, then I would say I'll take the side of that thought that less people die

With regards to the issue of Manson and leadership, the idea of an organized, structured "Manson Family" led by Charles Manson is the second most major misrepresentation of the entire Tate-

LaBianca affair. (The first is the prosecution's version of the motive for the murders.) But as for Manson being the leader of an *unstructured* group of people, it would be accurate to say that he often unwittingly and unwillingly found himself to be in a leadership position among the people around him. However there are several perfectly logical reasons for this that do not have to do with anything sinister.

First of all, Charles Manson was ten to fifteen years older than many of the persons he associated with, so he was already in a leadership position by virtue of his age alone. It is natural and right for people to look to their elders for guidance.

Second, Manson took a genuine interest in people and their problems, and he often helped people with some of their difficulties (for example, by finding them a place to live). Thus it was natural that some people would look to him as a person who could perhaps solve their other problems as well.

Third, Manson had an instinct for survival that many people recognized. And many people are happy to be led by others who appear confident and in control of their own lives.

Finally, Charles Manson *was* a natural leader. He was charismatic. He was enthusiastic. He had a self-assured contentment that others admired, envied, and wanted to emulate. He had real authority. And -- most importantly -- he led by example.

But here we get to a crucial question regarding this case. For even if Charles Manson was a leader to some of the people around him, does that mean that he intended to be one? Manson himself was emphatic that any leadership role he might have assumed was reluctant:

> Even though I walk around with people, I'm not really personally involved in their minds. I just reflect them to them.
>
> Like you, for example. I've never put any demands on you in any way whatsoever. And I've never judged you. I've just accepted you and walked along with you. Well, that's pretty much the way I do with everybody that I come into contact with.
>
> I'm not nobody's leader, or follower, or anything. I'm just a mirror, walking around reflecting it.... [And] I try to do what Christ said. I try to treat people the way I want to be treated. I want to be respected, so I give

respect. I feel respect should respect respect back, and when it doesn't respect itself, then it's not in what I would call God.

But that's only my interpretation of it. I'm not pushing that. I'm not preaching it, and I'm not teaching it.

My shadow is really a terrible beast. [But] it's really got nothing to do with me personally. It really doesn't. My shadow ran through the lines of those people in the ranch. But it wasn't *me*.

I do what I do, people see that and hear that. And they jump up and start following that. They say, "Hey, man, look at the way that guy moves." So they end up and they start following the way I move. They start following.

Always at the ranch, I never really told anyone what to do. I told them what they *could* do, from my point of view. And I would give 'em, like, a circle, like I would help them hold their mind on their problem by asking them questions about the problem, by using my attention span to hold their attention span on a particular problem long enough so they could come up with their own solution.

And many times you can offer a solution, like if someone says, "I got a problem. I drink too much."

And you can tell 'em, "Well, stop drinking." Or, you can tell 'em, "Well, why don't you drink some more? Go ahead. Get drunk."

And he says, "Well, hell, everybody else is telling me to stop."

I said, "Well, that don't seem to be working, so I'll tell you to go ahead. Just drink, drink, drink. Drink yourself 'til you're dead. Then maybe you'll stop."

In other words, I'm not really telling him to drink. I'm just showing him the other side of that wheel.

I wasn't a leader. I wasn't even thinking leader. You know, in other words, all that "Family" shit they put on me after I got busted. If I'd have known I was supposed to be that, I'd have had everybody ready for it. Believe me, I would have. But I didn't know that.

I never put myself up to be a leader. I got stuck in this position and I'm reflecting it. I reflect this position that I'm in. I got to. I ain't got no choice. I got to be this "Manson" character.

If Charles Manson was disdainful of "this 'Manson' character," what did he think he was really like?

If anyone knows me, I would be disappointed. Because I don't really want anyone to know me. I want people to know themselves. Nobody can know me. I have to know myself. Like, I can't know you. You have to know yourself.

If you want to look at Charlie Manson? Charlie Manson is mediocre, he's small, he's short, he's ugly, he doesn't do anything well. Everything he does is just about half-way. He doesn't belong anywhere. He doesn't fit anyplace. He's never believed in nobody. He doesn't have no education. He can barely read and write. He's incompetent, he's inadequate, he's really -- at that ranch, Charlie Manson was pretty close to being the last guy in line. That's the truth. I'm incompetent. If I was not incompetent, I would have been a millionaire and I would have been out of here a long time ago....

I'm not a tough guy. I don't want no trouble. I want to promote harmony, and if I have to put my life out front, that's what I *been* doing. My life is so far out front now, they owe me so much that they can't come back with my own Goddamn fucking rights. They can't even give me my own rights, so their rights ain't no good.... It ain't got nothing to do with me, it's gonna come to 'em anyway, you know. I told the dude, I says, "You know what, man?" I says, "We helped you oppressed people -- all these oppressed people games that you guys play -- we struggled with you for fucking twenty-nine years of hell to get you in a position where you could bring some change and do some good for the planet earth and all the people that are oppressed, you dig? And then you come back and you won't do right. You won't do right. You're just like the fucking pig that we offed.

I'm an honorable human being, in spite of what the world calls me. I'm a person. I am a man. If no one wants to let me be a man, if they want to strip me from my clothes and look up my rectum and degrade me and make me feel less than a bug, I'm still a man. It doesn't matter what they do to me. They can beat me, they can do anything they want. They can burn me, they can crucify me, but it doesn't change the fact that I still am a man and I'm an honorable man and a truthful man and I'm a loving man and I'm a man with concern, compassion, and kindness. I'm a man with soul. I'm a man of God.

I've got to hold everybody's mind and go through all this fucking madness -- why? Because of you, woman.... You woman as Red, Blue, Green, Gold, Yellow, Mary, Susie, Betty, uh, "let's stop the war, let's don't blow the world up, let's save the water. The sky is dying, we've gotta stop the automobiles, we've gotta help ATWA." All I want to do is fuck and ride my motorcycle and play a little music. I'm not the world's savior. I didn't want to save nobody. You all seen Jesus in me. I didn't see Jesus in me. I seen a hobo in me. I seen a tramp on the road. I would have been out there, running free, for the next twenty-five years of my life had it not been for woman. Now, I'm not blaming woman, I'm blaming myself for letting woman close to me. I should have never let that many women around me. I should have got me one woman, if anything, put her on the back of that motorcycle, and then just jacked off looking at magazines or something. Or went to the whorehouse for an extra piece of pussy now and then. But I didn't, because it wasn't that time. That time was the sexual revolution. I'd hitchhike and I'd pick up somebody and they'd want to suck my dick, I'd get compromised by every little young broad coming by that wanted to give me half a joint, and ask me if they wanted to fuck me. You don't realize what it's like being a guy on the edge of society where you got all these women and no dudes. All the dudes are either in school or in the army, and then all these young girls are hitting on you and you've been in jail for twenty-five years, jacking off, and you got all this pussy around you? Man, you go crazy! I was out of my fucking gourd! All I was doing was jumping from hole to hole, fucking from everything I could do. I fucked everybody I could think of, everybody I could get into. I know [now] damn well it was a mistake. Fucking right, it was a twenty-five year mistake. It's not my fault. It's not my fault it was a mistake. That was what was happening at the time. I couldn't have done that had society not let me do it.... The truth about the thing, if I went with one woman I would have married the first girl I got to and I'd have never met you. If I hadn't have trusted anyone I would have never met you. There wouldn't have been ten or fifteen people at Summit Drive if I hadn't of trusted them. I trusted Bruce; I let him in my house.... I trusted all these different people, and for every person that I've helped, I've had to suffer for that help.

I like people. That's my problem. That's where I get fucked up. I let too many people in on me. I try to do too much, and I don't even know why.

I should never anticipate that somebody is going to do what they say. I always try to do what I say, so I anticipate that other people will do the same, and then when they don't, then, well it breaks my heart is what it does, because I don't have that much left. Everything that I tried to do in relation to what was thrown on me, I tried to utilize all the perspectives as best I know how, but I'm a miserable failure is what it boils down to. I just failed in every perspective. All I've done is been the whipping boy for everybody that can get away with doing anything they want to do to Charlie Manson like it's okay. And, like, there don't seem to be any particular end to it. I don't see no end to it, so I don't know why I keep continuing on with it. It don't make no sense. Like, I'm doing it for the very same people that are doing me. That's why I'm so upset with so many people that have set me in motion and then ran off doing something else. I wasn't standing up for what *I* was thinking. I was standing up for what *they* were thinking. So here I'm fighting their battles and they're off making fun of me, like I'm some kind of idiot. And I think basically that's pretty much what I am.

I'm like a little child in a lot of ways. You know, everything is really simple to me. It's not complicated, it's simple. But these people have complicated my dreams and they've complicated my time. It's *my* time. I've done all the time in the world three times. Everybody in prison has left but me. And I'll stay here because this is my home. I got nowhere to go. If I go outside I'm lost. I just walk around with the kids. The kids pick me up and say, "Hello."

I say, "Hello."

They say, "Where you goin'?"

I say, "Uh, nowhere."

They say, "Where you coming from?"

I say, "Well, I'm not really coming from anywhere."

"What are you doing?"

"Well I'm not really doing anything."

"Well, what are you doing there?"

"I don't know. I'm just *here*."

I live in the world all by myself. Completely. I'm the Emperor of China. I'm the Emperor of Japan. I'm everything in the world. I'm nothing. I'm a bug out by Myers Ranch. I'm a scorpion over there in that old wooden shack. I don't care about people. All I'm caring about is that water, that atmosphere, those trees, and those animals. And that's all I care about. I don't care about no people. The only people I care about's the ones that's got the marks on their heads. That's the only ones I care about. The other ones are dead as far as I'm concerned. All of 'em. I don't care how many books they read or what they're talking.

There's no stupid son of a bitch as dumb as I am. I'm the dumbest asshole in the world, because I *earned* my freedom. I did twenty-two years in the same fucking hallway that you did ten years in. Since I was ten years old. I know all the suffering that you went through in that ten years. But consider. Ten years before that, if you were ten years younger, how much more it would have been. When you're in juvenile hall in boys school, children don't have no mercy on each other. Children are very vicious. They're born predators. The shit that I went through before I met you, when I met you guys, I knew that no one was no fucking good. They treated me bad because they could get away with it. They just look for someone they can get off on. They get off on anybody they can. They get you on four-point restraint and no one's looking, you dig? Then they do all kinds of things that you ain't even ever dreamed -- you ain't seen the bottom of this pit, sweetheart. You've only seen the little part.

There's an image and a person that the District Attorney created called "Manson Helter Skelter." And there's an image that's in the press that you've been reading and watching and looking at for years. And that's built up in your mind. That's not me. That's an image that somebody else made up. It's got nothing, really, to do with me personally. That's not me. I am not that guy. But yet that guy is built up in your mind and you think that that guy is me. You think that I'm that fire-breathing, seven-foot-tall, no good hippie cult leader bullshit bunkum punk shit that they put on me, you know. And then sometimes I think you guys get to believing that shit. Like Leslie. That's not me. I might be *worse* than that, in some ways.

[People] ask me, "What do you think about that [his image]?"

I say, "Well, they're always trying to make me look good."

And they always say, "What?"

I say, "Yeah, all this fucking media's trying to butter me up and make me look cool....They're making me look good compared to what I really am."

Just because I didn't have anything to do with killing those people don't mean that I'm not worse than that. I mean, you guys were angels, and that's what *you* did. I was about fifty times worse than that.

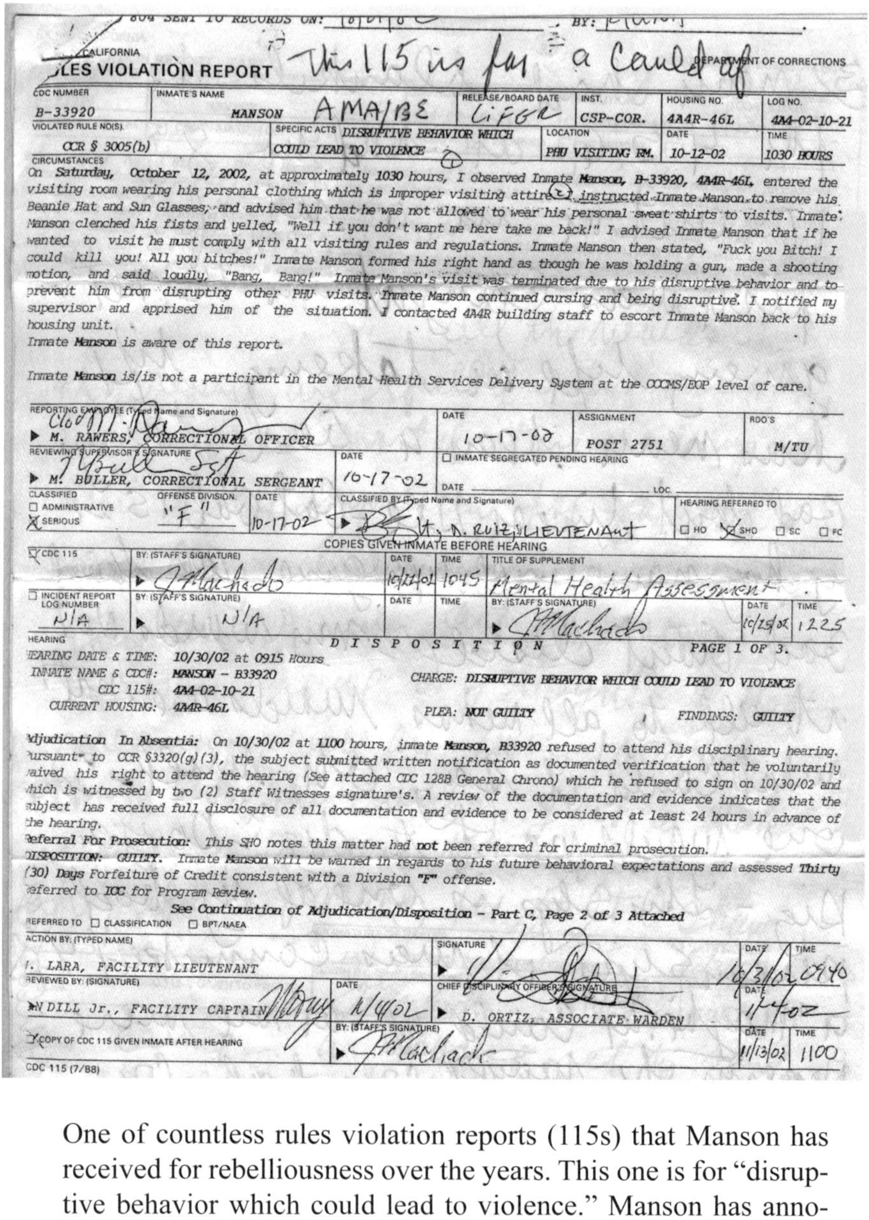

804 SENT TO RECORDS ON: [illegible] BY: [illegible]

STATE OF CALIFORNIA
RULES VIOLATION REPORT — This 115 is for a could of — DEPARTMENT OF CORRECTIONS

CDC NUMBER	INMATE'S NAME	RELEASE/BOARD DATE	INST.	HOUSING NO.	LOG NO.
B-33920	MANSON AMA/BE	LIFER	CSP-COR.	4A4R-46L	4A4-02-10-21

VIOLATED RULE NO(S).	SPECIFIC ACTS	LOCATION	DATE	TIME
CCR § 3005(b)	DISRUPTIVE BEHAVIOR WHICH COULD LEAD TO VIOLENCE	PHU VISITING RM.	10-12-02	1030 HOURS

CIRCUMSTANCES
On Saturday, October 12, 2002, at approximately 1030 hours, I observed Inmate Manson, B-33920, 4A4R-46L, entered the visiting room wearing his personal clothing which is improper visiting attire. I instructed Inmate Manson to remove his Beanie Hat and Sun Glasses, and advised him that he was not allowed to wear his personal sweat shirts to visits. Inmate Manson clenched his fists and yelled, "Well if you don't want me here take me back!" I advised Inmate Manson that if he wanted to visit he must comply with all visiting rules and regulations. Inmate Manson then stated, "Fuck you Bitch! I could kill you! All you bitches!" Inmate Manson formed his right hand as though he was holding a gun, made a shooting motion, and said loudly, "Bang, Bang!" Inmate Manson's visit was terminated due to his disruptive behavior and to prevent him from disrupting other PHU visits. Inmate Manson continued cursing and being disruptive. I notified my supervisor and apprised him of the situation. I contacted 4A4R building staff to escort Inmate Manson back to his housing unit.
Inmate Manson is aware of this report.

Inmate Manson is/is not a participant in the Mental Health Services Delivery System at the CCCMS/EOP level of care.

REPORTING EMPLOYEE (Typed Name and Signature)	DATE	ASSIGNMENT	RDO'S
▶ M. RAWERS, CORRECTIONAL OFFICER	10-17-02	POST 2751	M/TU

REVIEWING SUPERVISOR'S SIGNATURE	DATE	☐ INMATE SEGREGATED PENDING HEARING
▶ M. BULLER, CORRECTIONAL SERGEANT	10-17-02	DATE ____ LOC. ____

CLASSIFIED	OFFENSE DIVISION:	DATE	CLASSIFIED BY (Typed Name and Signature)	HEARING REFERRED TO
☐ ADMINISTRATIVE ☒ SERIOUS	"F"	10-17-02	▶ D. RUIZ, LIEUTENANT	☐ HO ☒ SHO ☐ SC ☐ FC

COPIES GIVEN INMATE BEFORE HEARING

☒ CDC 115	BY: (STAFF'S SIGNATURE)	DATE	TIME	TITLE OF SUPPLEMENT
	▶ J. Machado	10/21/02	1045	Mental Health Assessment

☐ INCIDENT REPORT LOG NUMBER	BY: (STAFF'S SIGNATURE)	DATE	TIME	BY: (STAFF'S SIGNATURE)	DATE	TIME
N/A	▶ N/A			▶ J. Machado	10/25/02	1225

HEARING
DISPOSITION — PAGE 1 OF 3.

HEARING DATE & TIME: 10/30/02 at 0915 Hours
INMATE NAME & CDC#: MANSON - B33920 — CHARGE: DISRUPTIVE BEHAVIOR WHICH COULD LEAD TO VIOLENCE
CDC 115#: 4A4-02-10-21
CURRENT HOUSING: 4A4R-46L — PLEA: NOT GUILTY — FINDINGS: GUILTY

Adjudication In Absentia: On 10/30/02 at 1100 hours, inmate Manson, B33920 refused to attend his disciplinary hearing. Pursuant to CCR §3320(g)(3), the subject submitted written notification as documented verification that he voluntarily waived his right to attend the hearing (See attached CDC 128B General Chrono) which he refused to sign on 10/30/02 and which is witnessed by two (2) Staff Witnesses signature's. A review of the documentation and evidence indicates that the subject has received full disclosure of all documentation and evidence to be considered at least 24 hours in advance of the hearing.
Referral For Prosecution: This SHO notes this matter had not been referred for criminal prosecution.
DISPOSITION: GUILTY. Inmate Manson will be warned in regards to his future behavioral expectations and assessed Thirty (30) Days Forfeiture of Credit consistent with a Division "F" offense.
Referred to ICC for Program Review.
See Continuation of Adjudication/Disposition - Part C, Page 2 of 3 Attached
REFERRED TO ☐ CLASSIFICATION ☐ BPT/NAEA

ACTION BY: (TYPED NAME)	SIGNATURE	DATE	TIME
I. LARA, FACILITY LIEUTENANT	▶	10/31/02	0940

REVIEWED BY: (SIGNATURE)	DATE	CHIEF DISCIPLINARY OFFICER'S SIGNATURE	DATE
▶ N DILL Jr., FACILITY CAPTAIN	11/4/02	▶ D. ORTIZ, ASSOCIATE WARDEN	11-4-02

☒ COPY OF CDC 115 GIVEN INMATE AFTER HEARING	BY: (STAFF'S SIGNATURE)	DATE	TIME
	▶ J. Machado	11/13/02	1100

CDC 115 (7/88)

One of countless rules violation reports (115s) that Manson has received for rebelliousness over the years. This one is for "disruptive behavior which could lead to violence." Manson has annotated, "This 115 is for a could-of, a maybe."

Afterword

For many people Charles Manson ranks alongside his supposed hero Adolf Hitler as one of the most evil men ever to have lived. To some people he is even the devil himself. But beyond those fearsome and simplistic characterizations is a more complicated reality.

The Charles Manson that I knew was a man, and in my hundreds of contacts with him I got to experience him under many different circumstances. And one major aspect of him that stood out after years of interaction was the consistency in the way he described the events of the summer of 1969. It was a consistency compatible with someone who is telling the truth. Manson remained so steadfast in his contentions of why things happened fifty years ago that it is practically impossible to think that he was not being honest about it -- unless one simply assumes that he was a sociopathic liar.

But an assumption that Manson is a sociopathic liar is just that: an assumption. Still, I would be willing to concede that he might have been a sociopathic liar if the proponents of and believers in the Helter Skelter scenario of the Tate-LaBianca murders would be willing to concede that he might have been telling the truth.

I don't know what you think of when you think of Charles Manson, but I think of the man I knew. He was a man who had spent the vast majority of his life in penal institutions, and he had been totally shaped by that experience. If I had to describe him in one word the word would be "prison." I was fairly close to him for almost a dozen years. I saw a man of late middle age, small, with occasional physical ailments, brilliant in some regards but deficient in others. Sometimes I wondered about his intelligence, because he often seemed quite naïve about things. But then he could turn around and come across like the wisest sage on earth. Believe it or not there was a childlike innocence to him in the way he occasionally conducted himself. I used to get aggravated with him because he was so often trying to help other people when I thought he should have been looking out more for himself. He was sometimes ill tempered and negative, and he was frequently preoccupied with things that he wouldn't confide in me about. But many other times he was good humored and full of enthusiasm. He was fun. I only saw him in visiting room situations, so I can't gauge his life within the various units he inhabited when I knew him, or his relationships with all of the other inmates around him, but I do know that some inmates genuinely thought the world of him and cared about him very much. Some correctional officers liked him, and some seemed to hate him.

The physical world Manson lived in was not a pleasant place. Not only was he physically confined and kept down for decades under conditions that are unimaginable for outside people but he has also had to deal with the unparalleled infamy that was heaped upon him. Nevertheless he dealt with it and did what he had to do in order to survive. And that he survived for as long as he did is a testament to his integrity.

Charles Manson was a small-time criminal with a limited formal education and an equally light amount of worldly experience who got caught up in a horrific crime and the ensuing media circus. I often found his media reactions to this, although at times superficially entertaining, to be unfortunate and somewhat sad, a misdirection of his energy and potential. I thought that he had more to offer the world than a series of performances. But he often said that he had no choice but to respond the way he did to his image, given that "that's the hand I was dealt."

"How would you play it?" he once asked me.

"Why do you have to play it at all?" I answered. He looked at me like he didn't understand me.

In reality, though, he understood the chasm between his image and his real self very well. As he once told a friend from the Spahn's Ranch days:

> I have all those human frailties that everyone else has. But I'm expected to be something different. I'm supposed to be something supernatural. I don't get sick, or I'm not supposed to fall down, or get old. I'm supposed to be all the things that I'm convicted for being, which is just totally insane. They convicted me for being Jesus in one courtroom and the devil in the other courtroom, you know. And the reality of that is, I was only putting faces on for you guys.

* * *

There is one final point that I would like to make here. In *Helter Skelter* and other media Charles Manson is depicted as a heartless sociopath who sacrificed the lives of the people around him in the furtherance of his own homicidal goals. That his co-defendants were sentenced to death is said to have had little significance for him. But in reality the opposite is true. The events of the summer of 1969 were not part of a planned program aimed towards a criminally insane goal. Instead, they were a series of disastrous events that sprung from the varied activities of separate occurrences and individuals. Like everyone else involved, Charles Manson got caught up in circumstances that were spiraling out of control. His responsibility for the ultimate outcome of those circumstances can be subject to debate, but as I see it Manson's involvement in the Tate-LaBianca murders was tenuous enough that he could have severed his case from that of his co-defendants and possibly won a lighter sentence at their expense. Instead, he chose to stand by his friends, even if it meant the possibility of dying in California's gas chamber with them. I don't know how one would characterize such a decision, but the quote from the New Testament Bible verse John 15:13 comes to mind: "Greater love hath no man than this, that a man lay down his life for his friends."

By my experience Charles Manson was not an extraordinarily (or even an inherently) evil person. If people want to think that he was, that's their privilege. And given his general reputation, that's the easy thing to do. But while condemnation is easy, it is difficult -- but far more interesting and fulfilling -- to understand. Or at least to try to.

In my case, trying to understand Charles Manson made me a better person. My spending time with him allowed me to glimpse parts of human and worldly experiences that I otherwise never would have known. He was really remarkable. And I think that anyone who ever spent any time with him would say the same thing.

So my personal conclusion is that, yes, Charles Manson could be a pretty bad guy. But I would also have to conclude that he could be a pretty good guy. And as such I can't consider him to be anything like an icon of evil. Instead, I consider him to be an icon of humanity.

Appendix - The Bugliosi Letter

The Bugliosi Letter was sent to me by a person who had received it from a literary agent after he had asked the agent for examples of pitch letters for a book. Amazingly, among the pitch letter examples sent by the agent was the one that Vincent Bugliosi wrote when he was trying to sell the concept of what would later become the bestselling true-crime book of all time -- *Helter Skelter*.

Bugliosi early on recognized the financial possibilities of the case he had been assigned to prosecute, and already *during the trial* he made arrangements with the literary establishment to position himself as *the* authority who could write the definitive book about the Charles Manson case.

In his book *The D.A.: A True Story*, retired Los Angeles Deputy District Attorney Lawrence Taylor recalled that during the trial of Manson and his co-defendants, "Unknown to anyone at the time, Bugliosi had already arranged to write a book about the trial -- with himself as the hero; his ghostwriter, Curt Gentry, was given a valued press pass and sat in the courtroom audience. The book, *Helter Skelter*, eventually became a bestseller."1

The Bugliosi letter confirms this. Clearly the letter was written while the trial was still in progress. Note the references "*After the trial,* many more books will be written...." (page 2, emphasis added) and "*I'm the one* who is engaging in a veritable life and death struggle with Manson and *who will ultimately ask the jury* to return a verdict of death against Manson and his 3 female co-defendants." (page 3, emphasis added). The defendants were not even convicted and yet Bugliosi was very eager to go.

"It's a big case," Bugliosi wrote to the literary agent. "The book we're contemplating will likewise have to be 'big' in every sense of the word....

"I feel there should be one definitive, authoritative book on this case. I believe that I'm the one to write this book.... Other than Charles Manson himself, I don't think that there's any other person who knows as much about these murders and the madness that led to them as I."

Among the most base selling points, Bugliosi recognized, would be the inclusion of the death photos from the murder scenes on Cielo and Waverly Drives. "The book will have official photos of the murder scene that no other book on the market could possibly have since only the Los Angeles Police Department and the District Attorney's office have said photos," he explained to the agent.

Compare this photo pitch to the reason Bugliosi gave in *Helter Skelter* for not providing the defense with evidentiary copies of the death scene photos before the trial: "I also strongly opposed providing the defense with copies of the death photos. We had heard that a German magazine had a standing offer of $100,000 for them. I did not want the families of the victims to open a magazine and see the terrible butchery inflicted on their loved ones."2

Perhaps sensing the unseemliness of people finding out that he was shopping around a book about a trial while he was in the process of prosecuting it Bugliosi later presented a different version of why and when he decided to write *Helter Skelter*. In a 1997 interview with *Playboy* magazine, when asked about the circumstances that led him to write the book, he replied (and lied), "When the trial was over I kept expecting someone of Truman Capote's stature to write a book about the case. But there was no one, and *that's when I decided to do it.*" (emphasis added)

Notes

1 *The D.A.: A True Story*, pages 33-34.
2 *Helter Skelter*, page 286.

Dear

The Tate - La Bianca murders have been the "story on page one" not only here in Los Angeles, but throughout the world. It is generally agreed that this case has received more publicity than any other case in history. (President Kennedy's assasination, of course, never resulted in a trial) These seven, incredible murders were perhaps the most bizarre, savage, nightmarish murders in the recorded annals of crime. Sharon Tate's husband, director Roman Polanski, who has a penchant for horror films, could not himself have conceived of a more monstrous, macabre scene of human terror and massacre than that which took place at his own home in the early morning hours of August 9, 1969. Many people have called these murders "the crime of the century." At first blush, this sounds rather extravagant, but when you compare the other leading murder cases in American history with this one, they pale into comparative insignificance. It's a big case, Mike. The book we're contemplating will likewise have to be a "big" book in every sense of the word.

Several books have already been written on the Manson family and these murders. All have been embarrasingly superficial.

After the trial, many more books will be written. The likelihood is that they too will be superficial. I feel there should be one definitive, authoritative book on this case. I believe that I'm the one to write this book. Other than Charles Manson himself, I don't think there's any other person who knows as much about these murders and the madness that led to them, as I.

As I envision the book, it should tentatively be broken down into six basic areas.

(1.) The book will have to capture my total immersion in the case. I was assigned by District Attorney Evelle Younger on 11-18-69 to work exclusively on the case. Although the role of a prosecutor is not to be an investigator, but rather, to present evidence in court gathered by law enforcement agencies, because of some shocking and thought-provoking realities, I became, out of pure necessity, the chief investigator in the case. Ever since being assigned to the case, I have virtually lived with it, working 12 - 14 hours a day, 7 days a week. Other then quickly scanning the sports page over breakfast in the morning, I have almost insulated myself from the outside world. I have personally interviewed over 100 witnesses in great depth. The book will have to detail my struggle in discovering the motive for these ghastly murders, my exhaustive preparation for trial in making an anemic case more robust, the day to day courtroom battles I engaged in while presenting the evidence in court. The book should take the reader into the very mind of the prosecutor as I wrestle with countless problems and obstacles in my quest for 1st degree murder convictions and death penalty verdicts against Manson and his three "girls," Susan Atkins, Patricia Krenwinkel and Leslie Van Houten. The book should also examine the disruption of my home life, and the fears my wife and I have. After all, it's not going to be the judge who sends these people to the gas chamber. I'm the one who is engaging in a veritable life and death struggle with Manson and who will ultimately ask the jury to return a verdict of death against Manson and his 3 female co-defendants. Though I've never owned a gun before, I have one now. There are new locks on the doors of my home. The police come by my house every hour, 24 hours a day. 3 months ago, I sent my wife and two children to Miami to stay with her parents lest Manson decided to shock society again by having his zombie come after me and my family, but my wife has since returned, feeling that if anything happened, she wants to be with me.

(2.) The writer you get to work with me on this book, Mike, has to be top drawer. And he has to be a writer who has his fingertips on the pulse of the fringe elements in our socie He has to be incisive and be willing to work hard at learning just who Charles Manson really is. In my opening statement to the jury, I described Manson as being a vagrant wanderer, a frustrated singer-guitarist, a pseudo-philosopher, but most of all, a killer who cleverly masqueraded behind the common image of a hippy, that of being peace-loving. I also described him as being a megalomaniac who coupled his delusions of greatness with a thirst for power and intense obsession for violent death. A man who has had the infinite humility, if you will, to refer to himself as Jesus Christ.

But obviously, Charles Manson is unfortunately much more than all of these things. Charles Manson took girls from average American homes and in a diabolical, satanic fashion, stripped away their layers of civility until they were sub-human robots who would gladly murder for him without question. The sight of these young girls dressed in black, armed with sharp bayonets, entering the homes of total strangers in the depth of night and mercilessly stabbing their helpless victims to death, is too ghastly a thought for the average mind to contemplate for more than a moment. How did Manson literally transplant his mind into their minds and make them so subservient that even to this day they would consider it an honor to die for him? True, to accomplish this, Manson effectively used LSD, sex, fear, the father and Christ image, some cheap mysticism and an unmistakable charisma and magnetism he possessess in his slight and graceful body. But the amalgam of all these things still doesn't explain how Manson was able to do what he did, just as Hitler's exploitation of Germany's dissatisfaction with the Treaty of Versailles doesn't explain why Hitler was able to rise to power. (Manson believed Hitler to be a "tuned in guy who leveled the Karma of the Jews." Manson wanted to level the Karma of the white man)

Manson, like Hitler, has some other aspect to his personality, an intangible, frightening quality and power that no one has yet discovered. Sometimes people have traits with which they themselves are unaquainted. I don't think that this is the case with Charles Manson. I believe he has full knowledge of the formula he used. This book has to tell the reader what that formula is so that society can take certain prophylactic measures to immunize itself from the cancerous growth of other Charles Mansons. Charles Manson epitomizes anti-establishment hatred. To understand Charles Manson isn't just advisable, it is probably imperative. What happened on the hot summer nights of August 9 and 10, 1969 could very well be a sick barometer of the direction in which the hippy movement is going in this country. Manson may merely be a foreboding extrapolation of what could be a common occurrence in the years to come. Law enforcement looked at these murders and when they opened up their dusty, pedestrian books on police science, the murders appeared to be motiveless and senseless. They weren't. As Manson has said, "No sense makes sense." In point of fact, Manson had multiple motives for these murders, the most important of which was to ignite a black-white civil war, a war in which he foresaw he would be the ultimate beneficiary. The fact that the means he chose to ignite such a holocaust were obviously ineffectual is actually irrelevant.

The book has to place Charles Manson under a high-powered microscope and almost clinically dissect and analyze this Mephistophilian and messianic guru who raped and bastardized the minds of those who so willingly gave themselves so totally to him. The virulent infection that ran through Charles Manson was an unquenchable lust for death, blood and murder. Because the infection was contagious to other members of his "Family," seven people were savagely butchered to death. By way of an horrendous footnote, Manson credits himself with a total of 35 murders.

The writer who looks through that microscope, Mike, has to have a nimble and perceptive mind and be willing to join with me in endless hours of just plain hard work.

(3.) The book should of course trace the origin of Manson's family at Haight Ashbury in March of 1967 to its virtual demise with their arrest in October of 1969 at Barker Ranch, a secluded, rock-strewn hideout from civilization on the shadowy perimeters of Death Valley in Inyo County, California. It should also include an examination of the remaining remnants of the Family who still live at Spahn Ranch, still believing that Manson is God and who are still irrevocably bound to him by an invisible umbilical cord that transcends Manson's jail cell and defies description.

(4.) The book should explore the societal impact of these murders, e.g., the fear that pervaded Los Angeles for months after the murders and still continues with diminishing intensity; societies new look at the hippy, previously thought to be peaceful by definition; the examination by sociologists on whether the life style of Manson and the structure of his family unit was of such a chemistry that it inevitably had to culminate in these two nights of horror.

The book should explore the Manson idolatry that exists among many peripheral elements in our society, and the new Mansonesque culture that is so appetizing to twisted, warped minds and which is threatening to take wild root here and there in our land. Perhaps the book should frighten the reader into the realization that their own daughters -- who may be in another room watching television or doing their homework as the reader is turning the pages of the book -- if subjected to the likes of Charles Manson, could someday be knife-wielding, cold-blooded murderers.

In other words, Mike, I want this book not only to be an addition to already glutted bookstands across the country, but a timely contribution to our society.

(5.) Although the book should primarily examine the killers, the victims should not be ignored. Other than Stephen Parent, each of the other six Tate - La Bianca victims were surprisingly interesting persons with widely diverse backgrounds and history. The fate that made them the victims of Charles Manson's madness should be closely examined.

(6.) I want the writer to attend the trial so that he will be able to capture, on the pages of the book, the sights, smells and sounds of perhaps the most sensational, complex murder trial ever to evolve in an American courtroom. The cold, bare transcript doesn't reveal the taste of the courtroom drama; for example, the child-like smile Charles Manson had on his face as he displayed to the jury the Los Angeles Times banner headline "Manson guilty, Nixon declares."

The book should contain the highlights of the trial. As opposed to other books, most or all of which will only have the notes of the trial proceedings the author took himself, this book will have the official trial transcript as prepared by the court reporter. It will even contain secret discussions in chambers among the judge, attorneys and defendants which the press does not have access to, even by purchasing the transcript, inasmuch as these proceedings are sealed to the public. The book will contain personal discussions I've had with the 3 female defendants and Manson himself in which he and I shadow-boxed with each other, each knowing that although the other is keeping time to a different drummer, we're colliding head-on in the courtroom drama.

The book will have official photos of the murder scene that no other book on the market could possibly have since only the Los Angeles Police Department and the District Attorney's office have said photos.

The book will take the reader behind the scenes to facts and events that will never come out at the trial, such as the "Family's" involvement in other murders.

The book should, in part, re-examine our judicial system. For instance, the manner in which the trial has sometimes descended into a carnival-like atmosphere. Also, the right of defendants to a fair trial, that is, twelve people who have not been exposed to prejudicial pre-trial publicity, viz a viz the public's right to be fully informed by the media of all aspects of crimes that they, as citizens, have a vested right in knowing.

I am very eager to get started on writing the book, Mike. Because of the magnitude and complexity of the story and the profound, in-depth manner in which we've agreed the book should be written, the more quickly we find a co-author and publisher the better. Hoping you and your wife are enjoying your new island. I enjoyed the two meetings we had together very much.

Sincerely,

Vince Bugliosi

Vince Bugliosi

Sources

Newspaper and magazine, parole hearing, and television interview sources are cited in the Chapter Notes

Books

(Note: Page numbers may vary depending on the particular edition used.)

Andrews, Frank Earl, Editor; *Prose and Cons*; Pyramid Books; New York; 1976

Atkins, Susan, with Slosser, Bob; *Child of Satan, Child of God*; Logos International; Plainfield New Jersey; 1977

Bishop, George; *Witness to Evil: The Inside Story of the Tate/Labianca Murder Trial*; Nash Publishing; Los Angeles; 1971

Bugliosi, Vincent, with Gentry, Curt; *Helter Skelter: The True Story of the Manson Murders*; W.W. Norton & Company, Inc.; New York; 1974

Bugliosi, Vincent; Outrage: *The Five Reasons Why O.J. Simpson Got Away With Murder*; W.W. Norton & Company; New York; 1996

Fromme, Lynette; *Reflexion*; The Peasenhall Press, Cobb, California; 2018

George, Ed, with Matera, Dary; *Taming The Beast: Charles Manson's Life Behind Bars*: St Martin's Press: New York; 1996

Harder, Emmett C.; *These Canyons are Full of Ghosts: The Last of the Death Valley Prospectors*; Real Adventure Publishing; San Bernardino, California; 2001

LeBlanc, Jerry, and Davis, Ivor; *5 To Die*; Holloway House Publishing Company, Los Angeles; 1970

Livsey, Clara; *The Manson Women: A "Family" Portrait*; Richard Marek Publishers; New York; 1980

Markman, Ronald, and Bosco, Dominick; *Alone With The Devil: Famous Cases of a Courtroom Psychiatrist*; Doubleday; New York; 1989

Moss, Jason, with Kottler, Jeffrey; *The Last Victim: A True Life Journey into the Mind of the Serial Killer*; Warner Books, Inc.; New York; 1999

Murphy, Bob; *Desert Shadows: The Bizarre and Frightening True Story of Charles Manson*; Falcon Press; Billings, Montana; 1986

Noguchi, Thomas, with Dimona, Joseph; *Coroner*; Simon & Shuster; New York; 1983

Sanders, Ed; *The Family: The Story of Charles Manson's Dune Buggy Attack Battalion*; E.P. Dutton and Company, Inc.; New York; 1971

Sanders, Ed; *The Family: The Manson Group and its Aftermath*; Penguin Books USA; New York; 1989

Schiller, Lawrence; *The Killing of Sharon Tate*; The New American Library, Inc., New York; 1969

Schreck, Nikolas; *The Manson File*; Amok Press; New York; 1988

Taylor, Lawrence; *The D.A, -- A True Story*; William Morrow and Company; New York; 1996

Terry, Maury; *The Ultimate Evil: An Investigation into America's Most Dangerous Satanic Cult*; Doubleday & Company; Garden City, New York; 1987

Watkins, Paul, with Soledad, Guillermo; *My Life With Charles Manson*; Bantam Books, New York; 1979

Watson, Charles "Tex" (as told to Chaplain Ray); *Will You Die For Me?*; Fleming H. Revell Company, Old Tappan, New Jersey; 1978

Zamora, William; *Trial By Your Peers* (AKA *Blood Family*); Maurice Girodias Associates, Inc. New York; 1973

About the Author

George Stimson lives in northern California.

Also from The Peasenhall Press

Reflexion

by Lynette Fromme

"You likely heard of the murders. This book is what happened before and after them along California's beaches and bluffs, San Francisco's Haight-Ashbury, the redwoods, Topanga Canyon, Beverly Hills, the Santa Susana Mountains, and the outback of the Mojave Desert. It's about the Charles Manson I perceived and a gathering of people like me preparing to survive either a revolution or the static institutions that were systematically trading all of our vital necessities for money."

-- L. F., 2018

Available in bookstores or at:

www.goodbyehelterskelter.com